Radical Economics

General Editor: Sam Aaronovitch

Debates between economists are not just technical arguments amongst practitioners but often reflect philosophical and ideological positions which are not always made explicit.

Discontent grew with the prevailing economic orthodoxy as the long period of economic expansion in the advanced capitalist economies came to an end in the 1970s; disenchantment was expressed in open discussion about the 'crisis' in economics and in the rise of various kinds of radical economic theory, often using the general title of 'political economy'.

Many economists have looked for a more fruitful point of departure in the ideas of Marx and the classical economists and also in such contemporary economists as Kalecki and Sraffa. Although it is possible to identify a broad radical stream, it does not mean that there are no significant controversies within this radical approach and, indeed, it would be unhealthy if this were not the case.

Can radical economic theory interpret the world better than the current orthodoxy which it challenges? And can it show also how to change it? This is a challenge which this series proposes to take up, adding to work already being done.

Each book will be a useful contribution to its particular field and should become a text around which the study of economics takes place.

Radical Economics

Published

Amit Bhaduri, *Macroeconomics*
Michael Bleaney, *The Rise and Fall of Keynesian Economics*
Keith Cowling, *Monopoly Capitalism*
Paul Hare, *Planning the British Economy*
Michael Howard, *Profits in Economic Theory*
M. C. Howard and J. E. King, *A History of Marxian Economics: Volume 1, 1883–1929*
Antal Matyas, *History of Modern Non-Marxian Economics*
David Purdy, *Social Power and the Labour Market*
Malcolm C. Sawyer, *The Economics of Michał Kalecki*
J. E. Woods, *The Production of Commodities: An Introduction to Sraffa*

Forthcoming

Terry Byres, *The Political Economy of Poor Nations*
Matthew Edel, *Urban Economics*
M. C. Howard and J. E. King, *A History of Marxian Economics: Volume 2, 1929–1990*

The Production of Commodities

An Introduction to Sraffa

J. E. WOODS

M
MACMILLAN

First published 1990

Published by
MACMILLAN EDUCATION LTD
Houndmills, Basingstoke, Hampshire RG21 2XS
and London
Companies and representatives
throughout the world

British Library Cataloguing in Publication Data
Woods, J. E.
The Production of Commodities: an Introduction
to Sraffa.—(radical economics).
1. Economics. Theories of Sraffa, Piero,
1898–1983
I. Title II. Series
330.15′5
ISBN 978-0-333-43629-5 ISBN 978-1-349-20483-0 (eBook)
DOI 10.1007/978-1-349-20483-0

To Anne, Patrick Daniel and Andrew

Contents

Preface

It became evident to me over a number of years that the general level of awareness of Sraffa's work among economists was lamentable. There was, I perceived, a clear need for a book which explained in the simplest terms possible the line of argument in Sraffa's *Production of Commodities by Means of Commodities*, chapter by chapter, even section by section.

In the Preface to his book, Sraffa wrote:

> It is, however, a peculiar feature of the set of propositions now published that, although they do not enter into any discussion of the marginal theory of value and distribution, they have nevertheless been designed to serve as a basis for a critique of that theory. If the foundation holds, the critique may be attempted later, either by the writer or someone younger and better equipped for the task. (p. vi)

My purpose is not to attempt the critique: It is to disseminate knowledge of the basis laid by Sraffa.

J. E. Woods

Acknowledgements

I began work on this book in spring 1986 while visiting the Department of Economics, Queen Mary College, University of London. Let me, first of all, thank the Department, especially Richard Allard, for the generous provision of facilities.

The first draft of Chapters 2–11, written between April and June that year, was read by Professor Christian Bidard of the University of Paris. To leave it at that would be a gross misrepresentation because, in an intensely stimulating correspondence (for me at least), he provided me with detailed comments. I consider myself extremely fortunate that Christian was willing to devote so much of his time to my efforts. I would also like to thank Dr Antonio D'Agata, of the Universities of Catania and Manchester, for his constructive criticisms of successive drafts of Chapter 10, Dr Morgan Kelly of Yale University for comments on Chapters 1–11, Professor Neri Salvadori, of the Universities of Catania and Denver, for comments on the third draft of Chapter 10 and Mr Sam Aaronovitch, the series editor, for his advice. The usual disclaimer applies: I alone am responsible for any errors in this book.

It will be clear to the reader that I have accumulated substantial intellectual debts. Acknowledgement here is, I recognise, an unsatisfactory means of repayment. Nevertheless, let me record the names of those whose work has influenced me the most. Apart from Piero Sraffa, who occupies pride of place, I mention Professors Pasinetti, Garegnani, Champernowne, Steedman, Bidard and Salvadori.

I am grateful to Professor Garegnani, Piero Sraffa's literary executor, for permission to quote at length from *Production of Commodities by Means of Commodities* and the 1926, 1930 and 1962 *Economic Journal* articles, and to the editors of the *Scottish Journal of Political Economy* for permission to use in section 6.4

material from my article (Woods, 1988). I also wish to thank the Master and Fellows of Trinity College, Cambridge, for allowing me to use an engraving of the Wren Library as a cover illustration: Dr. T. Hobbs of the College Library kindly advised on selection.

I am pleased to acknowledge the work of the Macmillan editorial and production staff: given the complexity of the manuscript, particular mention should be made of the copy-editors and typesetters. I would also like to thank the commissioning editor, Stephen Rutt, for his advice and efforts on my behalf.

Though the final revisions were made after joining Bacon & Woodrow, readers should note that I write in a personal capacity, not as a corporate representative.

Let me end on a personal note. I would not have been able to write this book without the support and encouragement of my wife, Anne. It gives me great pleasure to dedicate it to her and our two children, Patrick Daniel and Andrew.

J. E. Woods

1 Introduction

1.1 A Brief Outline

Piero Sraffa is best known for his edition of *The Works and Correspondence of David Ricardo* (1951 onwards) and his book, *Production of Commodities by Means of Commodities* (1960).[1] Less well known perhaps are his critique of Marshallian value theory, embodied in three articles on the laws of returns (1925, 1926, 1930) and his review of Hayek's *Prices and Production* (1932), where he introduced the concept of the own-rate of interest.[2] Though my purpose is to evaluate all Sraffa's work, I shall concentrate on PCMC because it represents his major positive contribution to economic theory.[3] Furthermore, it is a book which continues to generate intense academic debate some twenty-five years after publication: see, for example, Hahn (1982) and Burmeister (1980, 1984), on the one hand, and Eatwell and Milgate (1983) and Kurz and Salvadori (1987), on the other. Given this state of affairs, my priority is to offer an elementary, dispassionate account of PCMC. Accordingly, most of this book, Chapters 2–11, is devoted to this end: in these chapters, I deal mainly with the technicalities of Sraffa's analysis, which is essential in a work of this nature. In the final chapter, I take a broader view, discussing the connection between PCMC and the rest of Sraffa's output and contrasting his approach with that of the prevailing neo-classical methodology: in addition, I illustrate some areas of economic theory where new insights have been obtained by taking the neo-Ricardian standpoint.

The arrangement of material in Chapters 2–11 follows PCMC quite closely. In Chapters 2–7, I deal with single-product industries, circulating capital models having only produced means of production – as in Part I of PCMC. That is, each industry produces one final, or marketable, commodity for sale either to other industries (as replacement and/or net investment) or to consumers. The inputs in a typical process are homogeneous labour and heterogeneous capital (or produced means of production), the latter being entirely used up in the production period: all capital is thus circulating capital. This assumption on capital cannot be defended as an approximation to reality, but then that is not its purpose. By assuming that each process requires some circulating capital, I insist that means of production must be advanced. It will be demonstrated later that this is crucial in two respects: first, in the specification of the price equations corresponding to the processes of production;[4] second, with regard to the proper treatment of durable means of production, whether produced, such as fixed capital, or non-produced, such as land.[5] On this second point, it will be seen that, once understood for the simpler cases in Chapters 2–7, the analytical principles can be extended to more complex models. Note that, in Chapters 2–7, I abstract from the use of natural resources in production.[6] Once again, this is not intended as a realistic assumption: it is made solely to enable me to concentrate on a proper treatment of (circulating) capital. Having suggested the similarities between my analysis in Chapters 2–7 and that in Part I of PCMC, I now indicate two differences. First, Sraffa assumes that each industry has only one process available to it. I follow Sraffa in Chapters 2–5 but, in Chapters 6 and 7, allow industries to have alternative processes. This necessarily gives rise to the question of choice of process of production, which is considered by Sraffa in Part III of PCMC. I give an account of the theory of choice of process in Chapter 6. This leads naturally to the second difference: in Chapters 6 and 7, I discuss some (micro and macroeconomic) implications of this theory.

In Chapters 8–11, I consider multiple-product industries models, as in Part II of Sraffa. In general, each industry can now produce more than one final commodity (e.g. wheat and straw) using labour and commodity inputs. With such an assumption, I begin to adopt a more realistic assumption of production processes – see Steedman (1984a). However, multiple-product industries models are analysed not only to accommodate intrinsic, or pure, joint production but also to provide the framework for the proper treatment of durable means of production, be they fixed capital

(Chapter 9) or land (Chapter 10). It will be seen that the question of choice of process is implicit in the specification of any multiple-product industries model, whether for fixed capital, land or intrinsic joint production: this question is addressed as it arises in each case.

There is one respect in which my analysis differs noticeably from that in PCMC. Sraffa considers general multisector models with n industries and n commodities. In this book, I deal with only two-sector models. While the restriction to two sectors precludes the derivation of some results, the loss is of the second order of importance: the essential theory can be presented in terms of two-sector models.

The choice of names for the commodities is, with one proviso, immaterial. In Chapters 2–7, where there are single-product industries, I assume that the first sector produces wheat, the second iron. When I treat fixed capital in Chapter 9, it will be necessary to have (if only for the sake of appearance) a machine sector. In the analysis of pure joint production in Chapter 11, the association between a commodity and an industry is lost – which provides further reason for the arbitrary choice of names for commodities.

Of more importance than the naming of commodities and industries is the description of production processes. Throughout this book, it will be assumed that both (produced) commodities can be used as capital goods, or means of production, in each industry. A process of production in the wheat industry is thus described by commodity inputs of wheat and iron, a direct input of homogeneous labour (and in Chapter 10 an input of land) and an output of wheat; similarly, a process in the iron industry is described by inputs of the two commodities and labour and an output of iron. The outputs of each industry in any period can be used as inputs into both processes in the following period.[7] The essential point being made here is the interdependence between industries arising from their input requirements.

Such interdependence is absent from the more familiar two-sector model, where one industry produces a consumption good, the other a capital good; the consumption good is not used as means of production in either industry, while the capital good is used as means of production in both.[8] In a sense, the capital good plays a more important role in this model than the consumption good, for the simple reason that it is required to produce both commodities and can itself be produced without the consumption good. Such a situation cannot arise in the model analysed in Chapters 2–7, where both wheat and iron are required to produce each commodity. Given the role of both commodities as means of production in my model, it is natural to ask if either can be consumed. The restriction to two sectors and two commodities implies that it is impossible to satisfy the following requirements simultaneously: first, that the model is realistic in the sense that there is an identifiable consumption good; second, there are at least two commodities that can be used as means of production. The obvious way of avoiding this impasse is to assume that wheat can play a dual role – as consumption good and capital good.[9]

Given the interpretative problems that have arisen, why should I restrict myself to a two-sector model? I offer two answers. First, from the viewpoint of economics, a two-sector model is the simplest in which the capital employed in each sector can be heterogeneous. Thus, if I desire to study a proper capital model, I must have at least two industries. Why not more than two? This leads to the second answer, which arises from the viewpoint of mathematics. By restricting myself to a two-sector model, I place only the following requirements on the reader: an ability to solve first a pair of simultaneous linear equations and second a quadratic equation. For a three-sector model, I would have to solve first a system of three linear equations and second a cubic equation. Economic considerations dictate that there should be at least two sectors, mathematical considerations that there should be at most two.

At least two reasons can be advanced in justification of the mathematical approach adopted here. First, it is an aid in the presentation of formal arguments. Precise definitions can be stated and specific propositions or theorems derived. In a work such as this, where clear exposition is essential, the advantage of a mathematical method cannot be overestimated. Second, it enables a common structure to be perceived in the analysis of ostensibly different questions. For example, it will become clear that the price system of a single-product industries, circulating capital model is structurally similar to the quantity system: both can be analysed using the same mathematical tools. A less trivial example concerns the relation between circulating capital and fixed capital models. From an economic point of view, the latter can be regarded as a generalisation of the former. Having recognised this structural similarity, it is natural to suppose that the mathematical analysis constructed for the circulating capital case can be modified to the fixed capital case. Such an intuition is justified, as will be made clear in Chapter 9. I claim not only that circulating and fixed capital models can be treated in essentially the same terms, but also that there is one mathematical theorem (*Result 3* in Chapter 3) underlying the analysis of all single-product industries models.

1.2 A Historical Perspective

Sraffa's book deals with production of commodities by means of commodities. It is, therefore, explicitly multisectoral. Is this its distinguishing feature? In the Preface to PCMC, Sraffa stated that his 'standpoint . . . is that of the old classical economists from Adam Smith to Ricardo' (p. v). Given that there are no other references to classical theory in the text of PCMC, apart from Appendix D, some introductory remarks on this topic are in order.

An immediate feature of classical economics is its emphasis on production. This is evident from the Introduction to Smith's *The Wealth of Nations* (1970), where he argued that the level of income per head must 'be regulated by two different circumstances: first, by the skill, dexterity and judgement with which its labour is generally applied; and, secondly, by the proportion between the number of those who are employed in useful labour, and that of those who are not so employed' (p. 104). The role of natural resources was secondary. 'Whatever may be the soil, climate or extent of territory of any particular nation, the abundance or scantiness of its annual supply must, in that particular situation, depend upon those two circumstances' (ibid.). Further evidence to support this view comes from Books One and Two of *The Wealth of Nations* which deal respectively with 'The Causes of Improvement in the Productive Powers of Labour', beginning in chapters I–III with the division of labour, and 'The Nature, Accumulation and Employment of Stock'. Smith's approach was adopted by Ricardo. In chapter I of *The Principles of Political Economy and Taxation*, he distinguished two types of commodities according to the sources of their exchangeable value – scarcity or the quantity of labour required to produce them. Those in the first category – for example, 'some rare statues and pictures, scarce books and coins, wines of a peculiar quality' (p. 12) – constituted 'a very small part of the mass of commodities daily exchanged in the market. By far the greatest part of those goods which are the objects of desire, are procured by labour; and they may be multiplied, not in any one country alone, but in many, almost without any assignable limit, if we are disposed to bestow the labour necessary to obtain them' (ibid.). The commodities in the second category preponderate; consequently, Ricardo devoted his attention to them. 'In speaking then of commodities, of their exchangeable value, and of the laws which regulate their relative prices, we mean always such commodities only as can be increased in quantity by the exertion of human industry, and on the production of which competition operates without restraint' (ibid.). This leads naturally to a discussion of Ricardo's theory of value.

Ricardo adopted Smith's distinction between the market and the natural price of a commodity, the latter being the subject of analysis.

> Having fully acknowledged the temporary effects which, in particular employments of capital, may be produced on the prices of commodities, as well as on the wages of labour, and the profits of stock, by accidental causes, without influencing the general price of commodities, wages or profits, since these effects are equally operative in all stages of society, we will leave them entirely out of our consideration, whilst we are treating of the laws which regulate natural prices, natural wages and natural profits, effects totally independent of these accidental causes. In speaking then of the exchangeable value of commodities, or the power of purchasing possessed by any one commodity, I mean always that power which it would possess, if not disturbed by any temporary or accidental cause, and which is its natural price. (Ricardo, 1951, pp. 91–2)[10]

What determined the natural price? In chapter I of *The Principles*, Ricardo isolated two causes: the amount of labour embodied in a commodity and the distribution of income. The first determinant was clearly explained in section II by reference to the mundane example of stockings – Ricardo detailed the various stages of their production, in each of which labour was required. The second determinant was dealt with in sections IV and V. For example, two industries 'may employ the same amount of capital; but it may be very differently divided with respect to the portion which is fixed and that which is circulating' (p. 32). Consequently, the natural prices of their respective outputs will in general differ under the assumption of a uniform rate of profit. For, though both industries will have the same profit payments, the one with the higher proportion of circulating to fixed capital will have the higher depreciation charges and so must have the higher price.[11] Clearly, the assumption of a uniform rate of profit plays a crucial role. How can it be justified?

Two closely connected reasons can be advanced. The first follows from the *raison d'être* of the capitalist class. Quite simply, the capitalist seeks to maximise his rate of profit. 'Whilst every man is free to employ his capital where he pleases, he will naturally seek for it that employment which is most advantageous; he will naturally be dissatisfied with a profit of 10 per cent, if by removing his capital he can obtain a profit of 15 per cent' (p. 88). The second is essentially a corollary to the first. 'This restless desire on the part of all the employers of stock, to quit a less profitable for a more advantageous business, has a strong tendency to equalize the rate of profits of all' (ibid.). It is competition between capitalists which brings about a uniform rate of profit. Ricardo illustrated this in chapter IV of *The Principles* with an example in which the demand for silks increased, while that for cloth decreased. The first industry grew, the second declined. 'Capital is transferred from one employment to another, without the necessity of a manufacturer discontinuing his usual occupation' (p. 89). Furthermore, this process was efficient: 'the principle which apportions capital to each trade in the precise amount that is required is more active than is generally supposed' (p. 90).

The classical notion of competition, which is not defined in terms of the number of producers, is crucial to the establishment of natural prices.

> It is then the desire, which every capitalist has, of diverting his funds from a less to a more profitable employment, that prevents the market price of commodities continuing for any length of time either much above, or much below their natural price. It is this competition which so adjusts the exchangeable value of commodities, that after paying the wages of labour necessary to their production, and all other expenses required to put the

> capital employed in its original state of efficiency, the remaining value or overplus will in each trade be in proportion to the value of the capital employed. (p. 91)

This provides a clear statement that relative prices depend on the distribution of the surplus. A change in the distribution of income will in general affect all natural prices.[12]

So, according to Ricardo, relative prices depended on the conditions of production and income distribution.[13] This contrasts with the neo-classical view that prices depend on supply and demand.

> It is the cost of production which must ultimately regulate the price of commodities, and not, as has often been said, the proportion between the supply and demand: the proportion between supply and demand may, indeed, for a time, affect the market value of a commodity, until it is supplied in greater or less abundance, according as the demand may have increased or diminished; but this effect will be only of temporary duration, (p. 382)

Smith had provided a similar argument in chapter VII of *The Wealth of Nations*, advancing the idea that natural prices were centres of gravitation for market prices.

> The natural price . . . is, as it were, the central price, to which the prices of all commodities are continually gravitating. Different accidents may sometimes keep them suspended a good deal above it, and sometimes force them down even somewhat below it. But whatever may be the obstacles which hinder them from settling in this centre of repose and continuance, they are constantly tending towards it. (pp. 160–1)

Natural prices are the result of permanent forces at work, whereas market prices are influenced by temporary phenomena. It is natural prices that are the subject of Sraffa's (and Ricardo's) analysis.

1.3 Some Preliminaries

I conclude this opening chapter by referring to Newman's perceptive review (1962) of PCMC, where he made the following points, among others. First, with respect to the nature of Sraffa's book, he argued that 'It is essentially and explicitly mathematical, yet gives few adequate proofs and no mathematical references' (p. 58). Later, he provided an 'example of the inadequacy of several of Sraffa's proofs' (p. 72). Newman's assertion is unexceptionable. Indeed, one of the purposes of this book is to subject Sraffa's analysis to rigorous examination and to fill the lacunae indicated by Newman. As stated in section 1.2, this will be achieved within the context of two-sector models to minimise the mathematical demands on the reader.[14] While the mathematical difficulties could be overcome (in Newman's opinion), problems might arise from the nature of the economic theory being propounded – this is Newman's second point.

> Compressed and mathematically incomplete as it is, the main trouble lies not there, but in wrenching oneself out of the more usual Walrasian approach to general equilibrium, and in substituting a Ricardian approach . . . [PCMC] is clearly tangential at several points to much modern work on general equilibrium models, but no guide is given to the similarities or differences: (p. 58)

Again, Newman's assertions are unexceptionable. In section 1.2, I have provided an introduction to Ricardian theory: and in Chapter 12, I shall relate Sraffa's approach to general equilibrium theory. Newman's third point relates to Sraffa's method of analysis. 'An added potential source of difficulty stems from Sraffa's elegant but formal method of presentation. Quite detailed propositions are derived from a model that apparently has almost no assumptions about reality at all, a methodological procedure that is uncommon in modern economic theory (though not necessarily the worse for that)' (p. 58).

As with almost all the other reviews, Newman concentrated on Part I of PCMC. 'Once the first half has been mastered, then the rest of the book – which contains some brilliant pieces of analysis – is relatively easy territory and may be left to the reader to explore' (p. 59). For once, exception can be taken to Newman's views – not that Parts II and III do not contain brilliant pieces of analysis, but that they are relatively easy territory. The reader can decide on this after reading Parts II and III of PCMC and Chapters 8–11 below. After completing his study of Part I of PCMC, Newman considered that 'It is a reasonable presumption that the more extended analysis of Part II rests on secure foundations' (p. 75). It will be seen in Chapters 9 and 10 that Newman's presumption is justified for fixed capital and land and in Chapter 11 that it is not justified for intrinsic joint production.

Commentary

Introductions to Sraffa's life and work can be found in Pasinetti (1979), Roncaglia (1983), Kaldor (1984, 1985) and Eatwell (1987).

Two fundamental contributions to classical economic theory are Smith's *The Wealth of Nations* and Ricardo's *Principles of Political Economy and Taxation*. Sraffa's edition of the latter (Ricardo, 1951) is recommended. The theories of value and distribution in the classical scheme are discussed by Garegnani (1984, 1987). *The New Palgrave* (1987) contains numerous articles on classical and neo-Ricardian economic theory and economists.

Notes to Chapter 1

1. Hereafter referred to as PCMC.
2. This concept was taken up by Keynes and employed in chapter 17 of *The General Theory*.
3. Notwithstanding its subtitle, 'Prelude to a *Critique* of Economic Theory' (emphasis added).
4. See Chapter 3 onwards.
5. See Chapters 9 and 10.
6. Alternatively, I assume that they are free.
7. For ease of exposition, I assume that the processes in both industries take the same amount of time – that is, there is a uniform period of production.
8. See the Appendix to Chapter 6 for the analysis of the more familiar model. Also, see Chapters 2 and 3 for examples of a model where a consumption good can serve as a means of production.
9. This assumption is reasonable as wheat is required to produce wheat.
10. Compare:

    > When the price of any commodity is neither more nor less than what is sufficient to pay the rent of the land, the wages of the labour, and the profits of stock employed in raising, preparing and bringing it to market, according to their natural rates, the commodity is then sold for what may be called its natural price. (Smith, 1970, p. 158)

11. See Ricardo (1951), p. 39. Assume, for the sake of simplicity, that both industries have the same direct labour requirements and thus the

same wage payments. '[A] rise in the wages of labour would not equally affect commodities produced with machinery quickly consumed, and commodities produced with machinery slowly consumed' (ibid.).

12. 'This difference in the degree of durability of fixed capital, and this variety in the proportions in which the two sorts of capital may be combined introduce another cause, besides the greater or less quantity of labour necessary to produce commodities, for the variations in their relative value – this cause is the rise or fall in the value of labour.' (p. 30)
13. Conditions of production subsume embodied labour and other factors, such as different ratios of fixed to circulating capital, which are explained in sections IV and V, chapter I of the *The Principles*.
14. I employ more elementary and less powerful mathematical artillery than Newman who was one of the first to demonstrate the application of Perron–Frobenius theory (on semi-positive matrices) to the analysis of natural prices: see also Schwartz (1961) in this context.

2
A Subsistence Economy

2.1 Introduction

In section 1.2, I argued that, in the Ricardian approach, relative prices depended on the conditions of production and the distribution of income – a statement that will be substantiated in this chapter and the next two. Here, I wish to illustrate the dependence of prices on the conditions of production, which can be achieved by examining a model with gross outputs just sufficient for reproduction. As the economy does not produce a surplus, the influence of the distribution of income cannot arise. Consideration of this simple model will also provide a useful opportunity to introduce the method of analysis to be employed in this book.

There are two single-product industries, wheat and iron, each having only one process of production. The operation of each process, which takes a year say, requires inputs of both commodities and labour at the beginning of the production period for the single final, or marketable, commodity to emerge at the end of the period. I assume, in this chapter and the next, that labour is paid a subsistence wage which is advanced and specified in terms of the commodities produced; the wages paid to labourers can thus be incorporated into the commodities advanced as means of production, for there is no essential difference here between the use of a commodity as a component of the wage basket and as a physical input into a production process. Let $\bar{X}_{ij}$ denote the quantity of commodity i advanced as means of production in industry j, $i,j = 1,2$;[1] it consists of a purely technical component and a wage component.[2] I shall assume that all four inter-industry flows are non-zero. To describe a production process, I need to know not only the commodity inputs but also the commodity output. Let $\bar{X}_j$ denote the quantity of commodity j which emerges at the end of the production period, $j = 1{,}2$; $\bar{X}_j$ is the gross output of industry j. So, the two processes of production are completely described by the expressions:

$$\bar{X}_{11} \text{ qr wheat} \oplus \bar{X}_{21} \text{ t iron} \ominus \bar{X}_1 \text{ qr wheat} \tag{2.1a}$$

$$\bar{X}_{12} \text{ qr wheat} \oplus \bar{X}_{22} \text{ t iron} \ominus \bar{X}_2 \text{ t wheat} \tag{2.1b}$$

where $\oplus$ means 'combined with' and $\ominus$ 'to produce'. To complete the specification of the model, I require two further assumptions. First, all capital is circulating capital: this means that $\bar{X}_{ij}$ of commodity i is used up in the j-th production process, for all i,j. Second, the gross output of each commodity is just sufficient to meet total inter-industry requirements.[3] So, I can now write down these equations:

$$\bar{X}_{11} + \bar{X}_{12} = \bar{X}_1 \tag{2.2a}$$

$$\bar{X}_{21} + \bar{X}_{22} = \bar{X}_2 \tag{2.2b}$$

Equation (2.2a) states that the quantity of wheat used up as means of production in both wheat and iron industries is equal to the gross output of wheat: that is, the *net* output of wheat, which is just the gross output minus the total amount used up as means of production, is zero. Similarly for the iron industry, from (2.2b). I now have a model resembling that in chapter I of PCMC in all essential respects.

Before proceeding with the analysis of this model, I introduce one final assumption: namely, that there are constant returns to scale in each production process.[4] This means that, in the wheat industry for example, there are fixed relations between $\bar{X}_{11}$ and $\bar{X}_1$, and also between $\bar{X}_{21}$ and $\bar{X}_1$; similarly, for the iron industry. Instead of requiring three numbers to describe a process, I can now proceed with two, the input–output coefficients. Define the typical input–output coefficient by:

$$\bar{a}_{ij} = \bar{X}_{ij}/\bar{X}_j \qquad i, j = 1{,}2 \tag{2.3}$$

$\bar{a}_{ij}$ is the quantity of commodity i required as means of production and used up per unit of gross output of commodity j. Substituting for $\bar{X}_{ij}$ from (2.3) into (2.1), I obtain as the expressions describing production processes:

$$\bar{a}_{11}\bar{X}_1 \text{ qr wheat} \oplus \bar{a}_{21}\bar{X}_1 \text{ t iron} \ominus \bar{X}_1 \text{ qr wheat} \qquad (2.4a)$$

$$\bar{a}_{12}\bar{X}_2 \text{ qr wheat} \oplus \bar{a}_{22}\bar{X}_2 \text{ t iron} \ominus \bar{X}_2 \text{ t iron} \qquad (2.4b)$$

Dividing (2.4a) by $\bar{X}_1$, (2.4b) by $\bar{X}_2$, I have these expressions:

$$\bar{a}_{11} \text{ qr wheat} \oplus \bar{a}_{21} \text{ t iron} \ominus 1 \text{ qr wheat} \qquad (2.5a)$$

$$\bar{a}_{12} \text{ qr wheat} \oplus \bar{a}_{22} \text{ t iron} \ominus 1 \text{ t iron} \qquad (2.5b)$$

The essential information for this model is carried by the quadruple $\{\bar{a}_{11}, \bar{a}_{21}; \bar{a}_{12}, \bar{a}_{22}\}$, which succinctly describes technical possibilities. A point made in section 1.1 is that both commodities can be used as means of production in each industry. To capture this interdependence between industries, I assume that:

$$\bar{a}_{ij} > 0 \qquad i \neq j \qquad (2.6)$$

Wheat is used to produce iron and vice versa.

2.2 The Quantity System

Using (2.3), the quantity equations (2.2) can be rewritten as:

$$\bar{a}_{11}\bar{X}_1 + \bar{a}_{12}\bar{X}_2 = \bar{X}_1 \qquad (2.7a)$$

$$\bar{a}_{21}\bar{X}_1 + \bar{a}_{22}\bar{X}_2 = \bar{X}_2 \qquad (2.7b)$$

I now characterise a subsistence economy in terms of the input–output coefficients. Suppose that (2.7) has a positive solution, $\bar{X}_1$, $\bar{X}_2$.[5] Rewrite (2.7) as:

$$(1 - \bar{a}_{11})\bar{X}_1 = \bar{a}_{12}\bar{X}_2 \qquad (2.8a)$$

$$\bar{a}_{21}\bar{X}_1 = (1 - \bar{a}_{22})\bar{X}_2 \qquad (2.8b)$$

As $\bar{X}_1 > 0$, $\bar{X}_2 > 0$, by hypothesis, and $\bar{a}_{12} > 0$, $\bar{a}_{21} > 0$ from (2.6), it follows from (2.8) that:

$$1 - \bar{a}_{11} > 0, \; 1 - \bar{a}_{22} > 0 \tag{2.9}$$

Using (2.9) in (2.8), I obtain:

$$\bar{X}_2/\bar{X}_1 = (1 - \bar{a}_{11})/\bar{a}_{12} = \bar{a}_{21}/(1 - \bar{a}_{22}) \tag{2.10}$$

From (2.6) and (2.9), the denominators in (2.10) are positive; so, the last equation in (2.10) can be rewritten as:

$$(1 - \bar{a}_{11})(1 - \bar{a}_{22}) - \bar{a}_{12}\bar{a}_{21} = 0 \tag{2.11}$$

I have established that, if both industries operate at a positive level in a subsistence economy, inequalities (2.9) and equation (2.11) must hold: that is, (2.9) and (2.11) are necessary conditions for the positive solution of (2.7).[6]

Now suppose that (2.9) and (2.11) hold. Does it follow that (2.7) has a positive solution? From (2.9) and (2.11), the last equation in (2.10) holds. By assigning to $\bar{X}_2/\bar{X}_1$ the positive value indicated in (2.10), it follows that (2.8) holds with both $\bar{X}_1$ and $\bar{X}_2$ positive. That is, (2.7) does have a positive solution. So, I have established that, if (2.9) and (2.11) hold, the subsistence economy described in (2.7) has a positive solution: that is, (2.9) and (2.11) are sufficient conditions for the positive solution of (2.7).

Summarising this discussion, I have:

> *Result 1*: There is a positive solution to (2.7), which is unique up to scalar multiplication, if and only if (2.9) and (2.11) hold.

Above, I have proved first of all the 'only if' part (that is, the positive solution implies that (2.9) and (2.11) hold) and then the 'if' part. Uniqueness up to scalar multiplication means that the ratio $\bar{X}_2/\bar{X}_1$ is uniquely determined and not the absolute values of $\bar{X}_1$ and $\bar{X}_2$.

I have derived *Result 1* in detail because it is an example of the type of proposition that will be considered in later chapters.

2.3 The Price System

By the subsistence hypothesis, the quantities of wheat and iron emerging from their respective processes at the end of the production period are equal to the total amounts required at the beginning of the period: the economy can just reproduce itself. As the system does not produce a physical surplus, or positive net output, there is no surplus value to be distributed. The value of wheat output is therefore equal to the value of inputs into the wheat industry; similarly, for the iron industry. With $\bar{P}_1$ denoting the price of wheat, $\bar{P}_2$ the price of iron. I have as the price equations corresponding to (2.5):

$$\bar{P}_1\bar{a}_{11} + \bar{P}_2\bar{a}_{21} = \bar{P}_1 \tag{2.12a}$$

$$\bar{P}_1\bar{a}_{12} + \bar{P}_2\bar{a}_{22} = \bar{P}_2 \tag{2.12b}$$

Equation (2.12) is structurally similar to (2.7), once $\bar{P}_i$ is associated with $\bar{X}_i$, $i = 1,2$, $\bar{a}_{21}$ in (2.12a) with $\bar{a}_{12}$ in (2.7a) and $\bar{a}_{12}$ in (2.12b) with $\bar{a}_{21}$ in (2.7b). *Result 1* applies *mutatis mutandis* to the price system. The necessary and sufficient conditions for a positive solution to (2.12), unique up to scalar multiplication, are given by the inequalities (2.9) and:

$$(1 - \bar{a}_{11})(1 - \bar{a}_{22}) - \bar{a}_{21}\bar{a}_{12} = 0 \tag{2.13}$$

(2.3) differs from (2.11) only in the order of the product of the coefficients $\bar{a}_{12}$ and $\bar{a}_{21}$. Obviously, (2.13) is equivalent to (2.11), so that I can state:

> *Result 2*: There is a unique set of relative prices solving (2.12) if and only if (2.9) and (2.11) hold.

This justifies Sraffa's assertion that 'There is a unique set of exchange-values which if adopted by the market restores the original distribution of the products and makes it possible for the process to be repeated; such values spring from the methods of production' (PCMC, section 1, p. 3). In other words, relative prices depend on the conditions of production.

Results 1 and *2* are dual to each other in the sense that the same underlying set of conditions applies to both price and quantity systems. Other duality results will be derived in Chapters 3,4,7 and 11. There is one final comment: I have derived the result on the quantity system first which was then applied to the price system; equivalently, I could have analysed the price system before the quantity system.

2.4 Other Cases

In this section, I consider briefly the implications of relaxing (2.6): that is, I permit at least one of $\bar{a}_{12}$ and $\bar{a}_{21}$ to be zero. Suppose first that $\bar{a}_{12} = 0$, $\bar{a}_{21} > 0$. Then, from (2.8a), $\bar{X}_1 = 0$ unless $\bar{a}_{11} = 1$. So, let $\bar{a}_{11} = 1$. It then follows from (2.12a) that $\bar{P}_2 = 0$. A similar conclusion can be drawn if $\bar{a}_{12} > 0$, $\bar{a}_{21} = 0$. The existence of a positive solution to both price and quantity systems seems to require interdependence in production in the sense that (2.6) must be satisfied – each commodity must be used in the production of the other.[7]

2.5 Conclusion

The main purpose of this chapter has been achieved for I have shown that the relative price depends on the conditions of production. There is a limited amount that can be done with a pure subsistence economy because (2.2) holds and the wage is fixed in advance. Hereafter, I relax the assumption that the economy is at subsistence level.

Commentary

This chapter is based on chapter I of PCMC. See Harrod's review of PCMC, Harrod (1961), and Sraffa's reply, Sraffa (1962).

Exercises

1. Find the prices for each of the following economies:

   (i) 280 qr wheat ⊕ 12 t iron ⊖ 400 qr wheat
   120 qr wheat ⊕ 8 t iron ⊖ 20 t iron
   (See section 1, PCMC.)

   (ii) 280 qr wheat ⊕ 10 t iron ⊖ 400 qr wheat
   120 qr wheat ⊕ 10 t iron ⊖ 20 t iron

   (iii) 250 qr wheat ⊕ 12 t iron ⊖ 400 qr wheat
   150 qr wheat ⊕ 8 t iron ⊖ 20 t iron

   (iv) 250 qr wheat ⊕ 10 t iron ⊖ 400 qr wheat
   150 qr wheat ⊕ 10 t iron ⊖ 20 t iron

2. Find the prices for this economy:

240 qr wheat $\oplus$ 12 t iron $\oplus$ 18 pigs $\ominus$ 450 qr wheat
90 qr wheat $\oplus$ 6 t iron $\oplus$ 12 pigs $\ominus$ 21 t iron
120 qr wheat $\oplus$ 3 t iron $\oplus$ 30 pigs $\ominus$ 60 pigs

(Note that this is a subsistence economy, as the gross output of each commodity is equal to the sum of inter-industry requirements.)

3. Find the prices for this economy:

240 qr wheat $\oplus$ 12 t iron $\oplus$ 18 pigs $\ominus$ 450 qr wheat
60 qr wheat $\oplus$ 3 t iron $\oplus$ 6 pigs $\ominus$ 21 t iron
150 qr wheat $\oplus$ 6 t iron $\oplus$ 36 pigs $\ominus$ 60 pigs

(Comparing exercises 2 and 3, note that the wheat sector has the process of production.)

4. Starting with two industries and two commodities, industry (one) may produce an excess of its commodity over the amount of it that is used in its own production, and similarly with industry (two). The rate of exchange of one for two is determined quite simply by the ratio of the excess production of one to the excess production of two. (Harrod, 1961, p. 783)

Is this true? Consider a three-sector model as in exercises 2 and 3. 'If we proceed to a greater number of industries and commodities we have a system of simultaneous equations, in which the exchange values of the commodities in terms of one another are determined by the same principle' (ibid.). Contrast this with Sraffa's argument in PCMC section 2.

5. Consider the economy in exercise 1(i). Suppose that the price system is $P_1 = 1$, $P_2 = 5$ instead of $\bar{P}_1 = 1$, $\bar{P}_2 = 10$. Trace the implications, period by period, of these prices for the economy; in particular, can the economy reproduce itself?

6. (Decomposition of the input–output coefficients.) Introduce labour into the specification of production processes in the following way: replace (2.1) by:

$$\underline{X}_{11} \text{ qr wheat} \oplus \underline{X}_{21} \text{ t iron} \oplus \underline{L}_1 \text{ labour} \ominus \underline{X}_1 \text{ qr wheat} \qquad \text{(i)}$$

$$\underline{X}_{12} \text{ qr wheat} \oplus \underline{X}_{22} \text{ t iron} \oplus \underline{L}_2 \text{ labour} \ominus \underline{X}_2 \text{ t iron} \qquad \text{(ii)}$$

$\underline{L}_1$ is the direct labour required in the wheat industry, $\underline{L}_2$ that in the iron industry. Suppose that labourers are paid in units of a subsistence wage basket defined as $\underline{\omega}_1$ qr wheat and $\underline{\omega}_2$ t iron. $\underline{L}_1$ in (i) can then be replaced by $\underline{L}_1\underline{\omega}_1$ qr wheat $\oplus$ $\underline{L}_1\underline{\omega}_2$ t iron; similarly, for $\underline{L}_2$ in (ii). So, (i) and (ii) can be rewritten as:

$$\underline{X}_{11} \text{ qr wheat} \oplus \underline{X}_{21} \text{ t iron} + \underline{L}_1\underline{\omega}_1 \text{ qr wheat} \oplus \underline{L}_1\underline{\omega}_2 \text{ t iron} \ominus \underline{X}_1 \text{ qr wheat} \quad \text{(iii)}$$

$$\underline{X}_{12} \text{ qr wheat} \oplus \underline{X}_{22} \text{ t iron} \oplus \underline{L}_2\underline{\omega}_1 \text{ qr wheat} \oplus \underline{L}_2\underline{\omega}_2 \text{ t iron} \ominus \underline{X}_2 \text{ t iron} \quad \text{(iv)}$$

Simplify (ii) and (iv) so that they resemble (2.1a) and (2.1b) respectively. Define:

$$\underline{a}_{ij} = \underline{X}_{ij}/\underline{X}_j \;,\; i \;,\; j, = 1{,}2$$

$$\underline{l}_j = \underline{L}_j/\underline{X}_j \;,\; j = 1{,}2$$

Hence express $\bar{a}_{ij}$ in terms of $\underline{a}_{ij}$, $\underline{\omega}_i$ and $\underline{l}_j$, $i, j = 1{,}2$.

7. Reconsider the specification of processes in exercise 6. Let $\underline{v}_i$ denote the amount of labour required directly and indirectly to produce one unit of commodity i. ($\underline{v}_i$ is thus the labour embodied in commodity i.) Then from (i) and (ii) of 6:

$$\underline{v}_1\,\underline{a}_{11} + \underline{v}_2\,\underline{a}_{21} + \underline{l}_1 = \underline{v}_1 \quad \text{(i)}$$

$$\underline{v}_1\,\underline{a}_{12} + \underline{v}_2\,\underline{a}_{22} + \underline{l}_2 = \underline{v}_2 \quad \text{(ii)}$$

$\underline{a}_{ij}$ and $\underline{l}_j$ are given, $i,j = 1{,}2$. Solve (i) and (ii) for $\underline{v}_1$ and $\underline{v}_2$.

8. (Continuation of exercise 7.)
Investigate the conditions under which $\underline{v}_1 = c\underline{l}_1$, $\underline{v}_2 = c\underline{l}_2$, where c is a positive constant. (That is, the embodied labour in a commodity is a multiple of the direct labour required to produce that commodity, the multiple being the same for both commodities.)

Exercises 6–8 should be re-examined if necessary after studying Chapter 4, where a similar model is expounded.

Notes to Chapter 2

1. Three points about notation: (i) in Chapters 2–7, capital letters denote absolute quantities; (ii) in a single-product industries model, the ordering of subscripts indicates the direction of flow of commodities (i.e. from industry i to industry j; (iii) the 'bar' above X indicates that I am dealing with a subsistence economy and is thus specific to this chapter.
2. This decomposition will be explicitly demonstrated in the Exercises.
3. If the gross output of each commodity were less than the total inter-industry requirements of that commodity, the economy would be consuming more than it was producing. Also, the assumption of only circulating capital is reasonable for a subsistence economy: the presence of fixed capital implies that not only has accumulation taken

place in the past but also that it can occur in the future, both of which contradict the subsistence hypothesis.

4. Though he explicitly states in the Preface to PCMC that he does not employ this assumption, Sraffa does not preclude its use 'as a temporary working hypothesis'. I return to this point in Chapter 12.
5. I do not assert that the solution is unique, for if $\bar{X}_1$ and $\bar{X}_2$ solve (2.7), it is clear that $c\bar{X}_1$ and $c\bar{X}_2$ also solve (2.7), where c is any non-zero number.
6. It is clear from (2.10) that the ratio of gross outputs is unique even though, as shown in note 5, the gross outputs themselves need not be unique.
7. This point was made by Newman (1962).

3

Production with a Surplus – Subsistence Wage

3.1 Introduction

It is now time to relax at least one of the assumptions of Chapter 2 – that the gross outputs of the economy are just enough to ensure reproduction and that the wage is at subsistence level. Clearly, the latter cannot be modified first. For, if the wage were raised above subsistence level but the technical coefficients were initially such that reproduction was just possible, the economy would be unable to produce enough to meet requirements: that is, more of both commodities would be used up than produced. So, it is necessary to relax, first of all, the assumption that the economy produces levels of gross output just sufficient to meet inter-industry requirements. Retaining the assumption that the wage is fixed (at subsistence level), advanced and incorporated into the input–output coefficients, I have as the two production processes:

$$\widetilde{X}_{11} \text{ qr wheat} \oplus \widetilde{X}_{21} \text{ t iron} \ominus \widetilde{X}_1 \text{ qr wheat} \quad (3.1a)$$

$$\widetilde{X}_{12} \text{ qr wheat} \oplus \widetilde{X}_{22} \text{ t iron} \ominus \widetilde{X}_2 \text{ t iron} \quad (3.1b)$$

where now:

$$\widetilde{X}_1 \geqslant \widetilde{X}_{11} + \widetilde{X}_{12} \quad (3.2a)$$

$$\widetilde{X}_2 \geqslant \widetilde{X}_{21} + \widetilde{X}_{22} \quad (3.2b)$$

with at least one strict inequality.[1] Contrast these expressions with (2.1) and (2.2) respectively of Chapter 2. In the previous chapter, gross output levels were necessarily fixed from period to period. Now, if the economy is capable of producing a surplus, the possibility of accumulation arises. As I shall discuss growth in Chapter 7, I assume now that any surplus product is consumed. The system to be analysed in this chapter resembles that in the previous chapter, in the sense that gross output levels are fixed from period to period: the circulating capital used in production is replaced but there is no net investment. To ensure the absence of all dynamic elements from the economy, I also assume that the labour force is constant through time.

I am interested in characterising an economy capable of producing a physical surplus (over and above inter-industry requirements), or positive net output, of both commodities. This does not mean that the economy has to produce a net output of both commodities, only that it can do so. To analyse this particular question, I define, first of all, the net output of commodity i by:

$$\widetilde{F}_i = \widetilde{X}_i - \widetilde{X}_{i1} - \widetilde{X}_{i2} \quad i = 1,2 \tag{3.3}$$

$\widetilde{F}_i$ is also referred to as the final demand for commodity i. The input–output coefficients are defined analogously to (2.3) of Chapter 2:

$$\widetilde{a}_{ij} = \widetilde{X}_{ij}/\widetilde{X}_j \quad i,j = 1,2 \tag{3.4}$$

Using (3.3), the inequalities (3.2) can be rewritten as equations; after substituting from (3.4), I obtain:

$$\widetilde{X}_1 = \widetilde{a}_{11}\widetilde{X}_1 + \widetilde{a}_{12}\widetilde{X}_2 + \widetilde{F}_1 \tag{3.5a}$$

$$\widetilde{X}_2 = \widetilde{a}_{21}\widetilde{X}_1 + \widetilde{a}_{22}\widetilde{X}_2 + \widetilde{F}_2 \tag{3.5b}$$

Equation (3.5a) states that the gross output of wheat, $\widetilde{X}_1$, is divided between replacement of means of production in both wheat and iron industries ($\widetilde{a}_{11}\widetilde{X}_1 + \widetilde{a}_{12}\widetilde{X}_2$) and consumption ($\widetilde{F}_1$); similarly for the gross output of iron in (3.5b).

3.2 The Quantity System

I wish to find conditions under which (3.5) has solution $\widetilde{X}_1 > 0$, $\widetilde{X}_2 > 0$, given *any* $\widetilde{F}_1 > 0$, $\widetilde{F}_2 > 0$. An economy capable of producing net outputs in any proportion is called productive. The absolute values of $\widetilde{F}_1$ and $\widetilde{F}_2$ are less important than the ratio between them; clearly, very large values of $\widetilde{F}_1$ and $\widetilde{F}_2$ could not be met in reality because the labour constraint would be violated. To provide motivation for the problem under discussion, consider the following three numerical examples in each of which $\widetilde{F}_1 = 2$, $\widetilde{F}_2 = 3$.[2]

1. $\widetilde{a}_{11} = 1/2, \widetilde{a}_{21} = 1/3; \widetilde{a}_{12} = 1/4, \widetilde{a}_{22} = 1/5$ (3.6)

Substituting these values into (3.5), it is a straightforward matter to show that $\widetilde{X}_1 = 141/19$, $\widetilde{X}_2 = 130/19$. This appears to be an example of a productive economy.

2. $\widetilde{a}_{11} = 1/2, \widetilde{a}_{21} = 1/3; \widetilde{a}_{12} = 3/8, \widetilde{a}_{22} = 3/4$ (3.7)

This example differs from the first only with respect to the second process. Substituting from (3.7) into (3.5), I find that (3.5) does not have a solution. In fact, this is a subsistence economy, as it satisfies (2.9) and (2.11) of Chapter 2. Clearly, this economy cannot meet any semi-positive final demands, $\widetilde{F}_1$ and $\widetilde{F}_2$.

3. $\widetilde{a}_{11} = 1/2, \widetilde{a}_{21} = 1/3; \widetilde{a}_{12} = 1/2, \widetilde{a}_{22} = 3/4$ (3.8)

This example differs from the previous two only with respect to the second process. Substituting from (3.8) into (3.5), I obtain $\widetilde{X}_1 = -48$, $\widetilde{X}_2 = -52$. The presence of negative gross outputs in the formal solution appears to suggest that this is an example of an unproductive economy.

While they cannot be used to prove results, numerical examples can be employed to provide counter-examples to assertions. The third example is definitely an unproductive economy because it cannot produce net outputs of the two commodities in the ratio of 2 to 3. Whether the first example is of a productive economy remains to be seen. Rather than deal with a particular example, I derive a general result below for the class of models under consideration. First, there is an inference that can be drawn from the numerical examples above – the notion of productiveness cannot be immediately applied to an individual process. As each process produces only one commodity, requiring an input from the other process, a given set of final demands cannot be met by operating only one process. It is necessary to operate both even if there is a final demand for only one commodity. Thus, productiveness is a concept that is applicable to a pair of processes such as (3.1), that is, a technique. Productiveness could be applied to an individual process if there was some way of evaluating inputs and outputs: as inputs are heterogeneous, the price system suggests itself as a candidate. So, a process could be described as productive at a given price system if it produced a positive net value.[3] There are two reasons for rejecting this suggestion. First, as the price system will be seen to depend on technical coefficients, it is clear that such a definition is not primitive. The second reason can perhaps be best appreciated by comparing the following example with the third one above:

$$4.\quad \tilde{a}_{11} = 1/5, \tilde{a}_{21} = 1/10; \tilde{a}_{12} = 1/2, \tilde{a}_{22} = 3/4 \qquad (3.9)$$

Given $\tilde{F}_1 = 2$, $\tilde{F}_2 = 3$, the corresponding gross outputs are $\tilde{X}_1 = 40/3$, $\tilde{X}_2 = 52/3$.
It might have been thought that, by comparison with the first two, the third example was of an unproductive economy because of the second process. Yet this fourth example appears to be a productive economy, with the same second process as the third example. So, by comparing 3 and 4, it could be argued that the first process is the cause of unproductiveness in the former, the opposite of the original tentative conclusion.

On the basis of these considerations, I restrict the notion of productiveness to techniques, not processes, of production. Accordingly, the question of productiveness resolves itself into the conditions for the positive solution of (3.5), given $\tilde{F}_1 \geqslant 0, \tilde{F}_2 \geqslant 0$. I state this formally as:

Definition 1: The system (3.5) is productive if it has a positive solution $\tilde{X}_1, \tilde{X}_2$ for any $\tilde{F}_1 \geqslant 0, \tilde{F}_2 \geqslant 0$, walosi.

I shall now derive a result on productiveness which is fundamental to the analysis of single-product industries models in this book.

Assume that the given technique is productive: that is, (3.5) has a positive solution $\tilde{X}_1 > 0, \tilde{X}_2 > 0$, given $\tilde{F}_1 > 0, \tilde{F}_2 > 0$. (For ease of exposition, I take both final demands as positive: see the Exercises.) From (3.5a), I have:

$$(1 - \tilde{a}_{11})\tilde{X}_1 = \tilde{a}_{12}\tilde{X}_2 + \tilde{F}_1 \tag{3.10}$$

As the right-hand side is positive by hypothesis and $\tilde{X}_1 > 0$, I obtain:

$$1 + \tilde{a}_{11} > 0 \tag{3.11a}$$

Similarly, from (3.5b), I obtain:

$$1 + \tilde{a}_{22} > 0 \tag{3.11b}$$

(3.10) and (3.11a) yield:

$$\tilde{X}_1 = (\tilde{a}_{12}\tilde{X}_2 + \tilde{F}_1)/(1 - \tilde{a}_{11}) \tag{3.12}$$

Substituting from (3.12) into (3.5b), I have:

$$(1 - \tilde{a}_{22})\tilde{X}_2 = \tilde{a}_{21}(\tilde{a}_{12}\tilde{X}_2 + \tilde{F}_1)/(1 - \tilde{a}_{11}) + \tilde{F}_2$$

or

$$((1 - \tilde{a}_{11})\ (1 - \tilde{a}_{22}) - \tilde{a}_{12}\tilde{a}_{21})\tilde{X}_2 = \tilde{a}_{21}\tilde{F}_1 + (1 - \tilde{a}_{11})\tilde{F}_2 \tag{3.13}$$

The right-hand side of (3.13) is positive by hypothesis and (3.11a); then as $\tilde{X}_2 > 0$, I obtain:

$$(1 - \tilde{a}_{11})(1 - \tilde{a}_{22}) - \tilde{a}_{12}\tilde{a}_{21} > 0 \tag{3.14}$$

So, I have just shown that, if the system is productive, (3.11a), (3.11b) and (3.14) must hold; that is, these three sets of inequalities are necessary conditions for productiveness.

Now assume that the inequalities (3.11a), (3.11b) and (3.14) hold and consider the solution of (3.5). From (3.5a), I can obtain (3.12) because (3.11a) is satisfied. Substituting (3.12) into (3.5b) yields (3.13). As the right-hand side of (3.13) is positive and the bracketed term on the left-hand side is positive, by the hypothesis, I conclude that:

$$\tilde{X}_2 > 0$$

Using this inequality in (3.10), I obtain:

$$\widetilde{X}_1 > 0$$

I do not appear to have used (3.11b), which might therefore appear to be superfluous. This is not so, as can be seen by eliminating $\widetilde{X}_2$, rather than $\widetilde{X}_1$, in the procedure for obtaining the solution. I have established that the three inequalities are also sufficient for productiveness.

I summarise this discussion in:

Result 3: A technique is productive if and only if (3.11a), (3.11b) and (3.14) are satisfied.

Contrast this with *Result 1*. Equations (3.11a) and (3.11b) are identical to (2.9) in Chapter 2. Equation (2.11) of section 2.2 is replaced by inequality (3.14) above.

Having derived the fundamental result on the quantity system, I can now attend to the solution of the price equations.

3.3 The Price System

As the economy produces a physical surplus, the value of this positive net output must be distributed. As wages are restricted to subsistence level and are advanced, the surplus value is equal to profits which, in a capitalist economy, are paid in proportion to the value of capital advanced. The uniform rate of profit cannot be determined before or after prices are known: 'The result is that the distribution must be determined through the same mechanism and at the same time as the prices of commodities' (PCMC, section 4, p. 6). With $\widetilde{r}$ denoting the rate of profit, $\widetilde{P}_1$ and $\widetilde{P}_2$ the prices of wheat and iron respectively, I have as the price equations corresponding to (3.1):

$$\widetilde{P}_1 = (1 + \widetilde{r})(\widetilde{P}_1\widetilde{a}_{11} + \widetilde{P}_2\widetilde{a}_{21}) \tag{3.15a}$$

$$\widetilde{P}_2 = (1 + \widetilde{r})(\widetilde{P}_1\widetilde{a}_{12} + \widetilde{P}_2\widetilde{a}_{22}) \tag{3.15b}$$

In (3.15a), $\widetilde{P}_1\widetilde{a}_{11} + \widetilde{P}_2\widetilde{a}_{21})$ is the value of capital advanced and used up in the wheat industry at prices $\widetilde{P}_1$, $\widetilde{P}_2$. $\widetilde{P}_1$ must be set to cover the cost of capital used up in production and to pay profits at the uniform rate $\tilde{r}$. Similarly, in the second industry. My purpose here is to ask the fundamental question: do there exist natural prices and a uniform rate of profit so that (3.15) is satisfied?

(3.15) is a system of two equations in three unknowns – $\tilde{r}$, $\tilde{P}_1$ and $\tilde{P}_2$. As the system is homogeneous, I can solve only for the relative price $\tilde{P}_2/\tilde{P}_1$, by analogy with the solution of the price system for the subsistence economy in Chapter 2. In fact, if I identify $(1 + \tilde{r})\tilde{a}_{ij}$ in (3.15) with $\bar{a}_{ij}$ in (2.12) of section 2.3, I can apply *Result 2*. (3.15) has a positive solution if and only if:

$$1 - \bar{a}_{11} > 0 \tag{3.16a}$$

$$1 - \bar{a}_{22} > 0 \tag{3.16b}$$

$$(1 - \bar{a}_{11})(1 - \bar{a}_{22}) - \bar{a}_{12}\bar{a}_{21} = 0 \tag{3.16c}$$

or

$$1 - (1 + \tilde{r})\tilde{a}_{11} > 0 \tag{3.17a}$$

$$1 - (1 + \tilde{r})\tilde{a}_{22} > 0 \tag{3.17b}$$

$$(1 - (1 + \tilde{r})\tilde{a}_{11})(1 - (1 + \tilde{r})\tilde{a}_{22}) - (1 + \tilde{r})^2 \tilde{a}_{12} \tilde{a}_{21} = 0 \tag{3.17c}$$

The rate of profit, $\tilde{r}$, is calculated from (3.17c); this value can then be substituted in (3.15) to obtain the relative price $\tilde{P}_2/\tilde{P}_1$. The immediate question is thus the solution of (3.17c). $\tilde{r}$ is determined as that value of r for which:

$$\tilde{f}(r) \equiv (1 - (1 + r)\tilde{a}_{11})(1 - (1 + r)\tilde{a}_{22}) - (1 + r)^2\tilde{a}_{12}\tilde{a}_{21} = 0 \tag{3.18}$$

As $\tilde{f}(r)$ is a quadratic in r, there are two solutions to (3.18). As is well known, a quadratic equation can have real or complex roots, the former being positive or negative, the latter occurring in conjugate pairs. I am interested only in positive real solutions to (3.18).

As a first step in obtaining a solution, rewrite the quadratic in (3.18) as:

$$\tilde{f}(r) = (1 + r)^2((s - \tilde{a}_{11})(s - \tilde{a}_{22}) - \tilde{a}_{12}\tilde{a}_{21}) \tag{3.19}$$

where $s \equiv (1 + r)$. Given r $\geqslant 0$, $\tilde{f}(r) = 0$ if and only if:

$$\tilde{\theta}(s) \equiv (s - \tilde{a}_{11})(s - \tilde{a}_{22}) - \tilde{a}_{12}\tilde{a}_{21} = 0 \tag{3.20a}$$

or

$$s^2 - s(\tilde{a}_{11} + \tilde{a}_{22}) + \tilde{a}_{11}\tilde{a}_{22} - \tilde{a}_{12}\tilde{a}_{21} = 0 \tag{3.20b}$$

The formula for the roots of a quadratic equation can be applied more easily to (3.20b) than (3.18). I have as the roots of (3.20):

$$\tilde{s}_1, \tilde{s}_2 = (\tilde{a}_{11} + \tilde{a}_{22} + \sqrt{(\tilde{a}_{11} + \tilde{a}_{22})^2 - 4(\tilde{a}_{11}\tilde{a}_{22} - \tilde{a}_{12}\tilde{a}_{21})})/2 \tag{3.21}$$

Note, first of all, that these two roots are real because the terms under the square root sign can be simplified to:

$$(\tilde{a}_{11} - \tilde{a}_{22})^2 + 4\tilde{a}_{12}\tilde{a}_{21}$$

which is always positive. Let $\tilde{s}_1$ be the larger root in (3.21):

$$\tilde{s}_1 = (\tilde{a}_{11} + \tilde{a}_{22} + \sqrt{(\tilde{a}_{11} + \tilde{a}_{22})^2 - 4(\tilde{a}_{11}\tilde{a}_{22} - \tilde{a}_{12}\tilde{a}_{21})})/2 \tag{3.22}$$

Clearly, $\tilde{s}_1 > 0$. Consider the other root. $\tilde{s}_2$ can be negative – for example, if $\tilde{a}_{11} = \tilde{a}_{22} = 0$; in such a case, the corresponding value of r, $\tilde{r}_2$, must also be negative from the definition:

$$\tilde{s}_2 = 1/(1 + \tilde{r}_2)$$

(Note that $r \neq -1$, otherwise the procedure described above is not defined.) $\tilde{s}_2 < 0$, together with the corresponding value, $\tilde{r}_2$, is not a candidate for the solution of (3.15). Having examined the case where $\tilde{s}_2 < 0$, now suppose that $\tilde{s}_2 > 0$. It is obvious from (3.21) that:

$$\tilde{s}_1 > \tilde{s}_2$$

From the definition of s, this is equivalent to:

$$1/(1+\tilde{r}_1) > 1/(1+\tilde{r}_2)$$

or

$$\tilde{r}_2 > \tilde{r}_1 \tag{3.23}$$

(3.23) directs attention to $\tilde{r}_1$ which is the smallest positive value of r at which $\tilde{f}(r) = 0$. I now put aside the study of $\tilde{s}_2$ and $\tilde{r}_2$ for the moment to investigate the properties of the other root.

The first question to arise concerns the sign of $\tilde{r}_1$. Though $\tilde{s}_1 > 0$, it does not automatically follow that $\tilde{r}_1 > 0$; $\tilde{s}_1 > 0$ implies that $1/(1+\tilde{r}_1) > 0$, which is consistent with $\tilde{r}_1 < 0$. I am looking for $\tilde{r}_1 > 0$, which is equivalent to $\tilde{0} < \tilde{s}_1 < 1$. Having already established that $\tilde{s}_1 > 0$, I assume that $\tilde{s}_1 \geqslant 1$ with the intention of deriving a contradiction. Using (3.22), I have:

$$(\tilde{a}_{11} + \tilde{a}_{22} + \sqrt{(\tilde{a}_{11} + \tilde{a}_{22})^2 - 4(\tilde{a}_{11}\tilde{a}_{22} - \tilde{a}_{12}\tilde{a}_{21})})/2 \geqslant 1$$

or

$$\sqrt{(\tilde{a}_{11} + \tilde{a}_{22})^2 - 4(\tilde{a}_{11}\tilde{a}_{22} - \tilde{a}_{12}\tilde{a}_{21})} \geqslant 2-(\tilde{a}_{11} + \tilde{a}_{22}) \tag{3.24}$$

Squaring both sides, I obtain:

$$(\tilde{a}_{11} + \tilde{a}_{22})^2 - 4(\tilde{a}_{11}\tilde{a}_{22} - \tilde{a}_{12}\tilde{a}_{21}) \geqslant 4 - 4(\tilde{a}_{11} + \tilde{a}_{22}) + (\tilde{a}_{11} + \tilde{a}_{22})^2$$

or

$$\begin{aligned} 0 &\geqslant 1 - (\tilde{a}_{11} + \tilde{a}_{22}) + (\tilde{a}_{11}\tilde{a}_{22} - \tilde{a}_{12}\tilde{a}_{21}) \\ &= (1 - \tilde{a}_{11})(1 - \tilde{a}_{22}) - \tilde{a}_{12}\tilde{a}_{21} \end{aligned} \tag{3.25}$$

(3.25) contradicts (3.14). So, $\tilde{s}_1 < 1$. As $\tilde{s}_1 > 0$, I conclude that $0 < \tilde{s}_1 < 1$, which implies that the corresponding value of r, $\tilde{r}_1$, is positive, as desired.

This completes the first part of the analysis of (3.15), concerned with the rate of profit. I must now demonstrate that the corresponding prices are positive. Rewrite (3.15) with $s = \tilde{s}_1$ as:

$$\tilde{s}_1\tilde{P}_1 = \tilde{P}_1\tilde{a}_{11} + \tilde{P}_2\tilde{a}_{21} \tag{3.26a}$$
$$\tilde{s}_1\tilde{P}_2 = \tilde{P}_1\tilde{a}_{12} + \tilde{P}_2\tilde{a}_{22} \tag{3.26b}$$

or

$$\tilde{P}_1(\tilde{s}_1 - \tilde{a}_{11}) = \tilde{P}_2\tilde{a}_{21} \tag{3.27a}$$
$$\tilde{P}_1\tilde{a}_{12} = \tilde{P}_2(\tilde{s}_1 - \tilde{a}_{22}) \tag{3.27b}$$

Suppose that $\tilde{s}_1 \leqslant \tilde{a}_{11}$. Using (3.22), I then obtain:

$$(\tilde{a}_{11} - \tilde{a}_{22} - \sqrt{(\tilde{a}_{11} + \tilde{a}_{22})^2 - 4(\tilde{a}_{11}\tilde{a}_{22} - \tilde{a}_{12}\tilde{a}_{21})})/2 \geqslant 0 \tag{3.28}$$

Straightforward manipulations on (3.28), similar to those above, yield:

$$0 \geqslant 4\tilde{a}_{12}\tilde{a}_{21} \tag{3.29}$$

As this is obviously a contradiction, it follows that:

$$\tilde{s}_1 > \tilde{a}_{11} \tag{3.30a}$$

An analogous argument establishes:

$$\tilde{s}_1 > \tilde{a}_{22} \tag{3.30b}$$

It now follows from (3.27) and (3.30) that:

$$\tilde{P}_2/\tilde{P}_1 = (\tilde{s}_1 - \tilde{a}_{11})/\tilde{a}_{21} = \tilde{a}_{12}/(\tilde{s}_1 - \tilde{a}_{22}) > 0 \tag{3.31}$$

So, (3.15) has a positive solution, $r = \tilde{r}_1 = 1/\tilde{s}_1 - 1$, with $\tilde{s}_1$ given by (3.22) and the relative price given by (3.31).

It remains to establish that there is not another positive price system: in the discussion of $\tilde{s}_2$, it was observed that $\tilde{r}_2$ may be positive. Consider (3.15) with $s = \tilde{s}_2$:

$$\tilde{P}_1(\tilde{s}_2 - \tilde{a}_{11}) = \tilde{P}_2\tilde{a}_{21} \tag{3.32a}$$
$$\tilde{P}_1\tilde{a}_{12} = \tilde{P}_2(\tilde{s}_2 - \tilde{a}_{22}) \tag{3.32b}$$

Suppose that $\tilde{s}_2 \geqslant \tilde{a}_{11}$ which from (3.21) and (3.22) can be rewritten as:

$$(\widetilde{a}_{22} - \widetilde{a}_{11} - \sqrt{(\widetilde{a}_{11}+\widetilde{a}_{22})^2 - 4(\widetilde{a}_{11}\widetilde{a}_{22}-\widetilde{a}_{12}\widetilde{a}_{21})})/2 \geqslant 0 \qquad (3.33)$$

Further straightforward manipulations, similar to those performed above, yield (3.29). As this is a contradiction, it follows that:

$$\widetilde{s}_2 < \widetilde{a}_{11} \qquad (3.34a)$$

Similarly:

$$\widetilde{s}_2 < \widetilde{a}_{22} \qquad (3.34b)$$

Applying (3.34) to (3.32), it follows that:

$$\widetilde{P}_2/\widetilde{P}_1 < 0$$

So if $r = \widetilde{r}_2$, the price equations have a formal solution with one of the prices negative: this is true whether $\widetilde{s}_2$ is positive or negative.

So, I have proved that the solution corresponding to $r = \widetilde{r}_1$ is the only reasonable one for (3.15). I summarise this in:

> *Result 4:* If the system is productive, there is a unique positive solution to the price equations, (3.15).

This result justifies Sraffa's assertions on the solution of the price equations for this model (see sections 4 and 5 of PCMC).

It was suggested above, and will be illustrated in the Exercises, that there can be two positive values of $\widetilde{r}$ satisfying (3.15). I have proved above that the smaller of the two values always has positive prices corresponding to it, while the larger has one positive and one negative price. On the basis of this result, it is unnecessary to calculate prices to determine the relevant solution of (3.15): it is the smaller of the two positive values of $\widetilde{r}$ at which $\widetilde{f}(r) = 0$; and in the case where there is one positive and one negative value of r solving (3.15), it is the positive value that is relevant.

In Chapter 2, it was shown that the relative price depended on the conditions of production. Now, with a surplus being produced, prices also depend on the distribution of income, as demonstrated in (3.31). Apparently, in this model, income distribution plays a secondary role because the total value of net output is distributed as profits. This follows from the assumption that the wage is restricted to a given subsistence level. In the next section, I examine the implications of relaxing this assumption, so that income distribution has a direct role to play in price determination.

3.4 Changes in the Wage Rate

Though he took the wage rate to be given, Ricardo did not assume that it was immutable. 'It is not to be understood that the natural price of labour, estimated even in food and necessaries, is absolutely fixed and constant. It varies at different times in the same country, and very materially in different countries. It essentially depends on the habits and customs of the people' (Ricardo, 1951, pp. 96–7). I can examine the effects of increasing the real wage by contrasting two economies, denoted 'a' and 'b', which have the same purely technical coefficients of production.[4] As shown in exercise 6, Chapter 2, each input–output coefficient can be divided into technical and wage components. Given identical technical components in the two economies, it follows that if the real wage is higher in the *b*- than in the *a*-economy:

$$\tilde{b}_{ij} \geqslant \tilde{a}_{ij} \qquad \text{walosi, } i, j = 1, 2 \tag{3.35}$$

I assume that the *b*-economy is productive so that the question of comparison is not vacuous. From *Result 3*, I have:

$$1 - \tilde{b}_{11} > 0 \tag{3.36a}$$

$$1 - \tilde{b}_{22} > 0 \tag{3.36b}$$

$$(1 - \tilde{b}_{11})(1 - \tilde{b}_{22}) - \tilde{b}_{12}\tilde{b}_{21} > 0 \tag{3.36c}$$

The analysis of section 3.3 applies *mutatis mutandis* to the *b*-economy to yield a positive rate of profit:

$$\tilde{r}_1^b = 1/\tilde{s}_1^b - 1 \tag{3.37a}$$

where

$$\tilde{s}_1^b = (\tilde{b}_{11} + \tilde{b}_{22} + \sqrt{(\tilde{b}_{11} + \tilde{b}_{22})^2 - 4(\tilde{b}_{11}\tilde{b}_{22} - \tilde{b}_{12}\tilde{b}_{21})})/2 \tag{3.37b}$$

and the corresponding prices are given by:

$$\widetilde{P}_2^b/\widetilde{P}_1^b = (\widetilde{s}_1^b - \widetilde{b}_{11})/\widetilde{b}_{21} = \widetilde{b}_{12}/(\widetilde{s}_1^b - \widetilde{b}_{22}) > 0 \tag{3.37c}$$

The increase in the wage between the *a*- and *b*-economies results in a different rate of profit and different prices. So, even for this restricted model, prices depend on the distribution of income. Can any definite conclusion be drawn on the relation between $\widetilde{r}_1^a$ and $\widetilde{r}_1^b$?

From section 3.3, $\widetilde{r}_1^b$ is determined as the first positive value of r at which:

$$\widetilde{f}^b(r) \equiv (1 - (1+r)\widetilde{b}_{11})(1 - (1+r)\widetilde{b}_{22}) - (1+r)^2\widetilde{b}_{12}\widetilde{b}_{21} = 0 \tag{3.38}$$

From (3.36c) and (3.38), it follows that:

$$\widetilde{f}^b(0) > 0 \tag{3.39}$$

$\widetilde{r}_1^a$ is the first positive value of r at which:

$$\widetilde{f}^a(r) \equiv (1 - (1+r)\widetilde{a}_{11})(1 - (1+r)\widetilde{a}_{22}) - (1+r)^2\widetilde{a}_{12}\widetilde{a}_{21} = 0 \tag{3.40}$$

Now consider

$$\widetilde{f}^b(\widetilde{r}_1^a) = (1 - (1+\widetilde{r}_1^a)\widetilde{b}_{11})(1 - (1+\widetilde{r}_1^a)\widetilde{b}_{22}) - (1+\widetilde{r}_1^a)^2\, \widetilde{b}_{12}\widetilde{b}_{21} \tag{3.41}$$

As $\widetilde{b}_{ij} \geqslant \widetilde{a}_{ij}$ walosi from (3.35), it follows that:

$$1 - (1+\widetilde{r}_1^a)\widetilde{b}_{ii} \leqslant 1 - (1+\widetilde{r}_1^a)\widetilde{a}_{ii} \quad i = 1,2 \tag{3.42a}$$

$$- (1+\widetilde{r}_1^a)\widetilde{b}_{ij} \leqslant \quad - (1+\widetilde{r}_1^a)\widetilde{a}_{ij} \quad i \neq j \tag{3.42b}$$

walosi. (3.40)–(3.42) imply that:

$$\widetilde{f}^b(\widetilde{r}_1^a) < 0 \tag{3.43}$$

As $\widetilde{f}^b(r)$ is a continuous function of r, it follows from (3.39) and (3.43) that $\widetilde{r}_1^b$ must lie between 0 and $\widetilde{r}_1^a$. That is, the effect of (3.35) is to reduce the uniform rate of profit from $\tilde{r}_1^a$ to $\tilde{r}_1^b$. This is reasonable because (3.35) implies that, given gross output levels feasible for both *a*- and *b*-economies, the physical surplus is smaller and physical capital (that must be advanced) is larger in *b* than in *a*. Regardless of the change in prices, the uniform rate of profit is lower in *b* than in *a*. So, I have:

Corollary 4.1: If (3.35) and (3.6) hold, $\tilde{r}_1^b < \tilde{r}_1^a$.

(3.35) can arise in three ways:

(i) an increase in the subsistence wage, the purely technical coefficients constant;
(ii) an increase in the purely technical coefficients, the subsistence wage constant;
(iii) changes in both technical coefficients and the subsistence wage, the net effect being that (3.35) holds.

(i) is the interpretation adopted above. As an example of this, consider the special case where only wheat enters the wage basket. Then:

$$\tilde{b}_{11} > \tilde{a}_{11}, \tilde{b}_{12} > \tilde{a}_{12}, \tilde{b}_{21} = \tilde{a}_{21}, \tilde{b}_{22} = \tilde{a}_{22} \tag{3.44}$$

Increases in $\tilde{b}_{11}$ and $\tilde{b}_{12}$, attributable to a rising real wage, make $(1-\tilde{b}_{11})$ smaller and $-\tilde{b}_{12}\tilde{b}_{21}$ larger. Hence, continuous increases in the subsistence wage will eventually reach the point where:

$$(1 - \tilde{b}_{11})(1 - \tilde{b}_{22}) - \tilde{b}_{12}\tilde{b}_{21} = 0 \tag{3.45}$$

That is, the economy becomes of the subsistence type, as analysed in Chapter 2. This brief discussion suggests that there is an inverse monotonic relation between the level of the subsistence wage and the rate of profit, which, as will be shown in Chapter 4, is a general feature of single-product industries models.[5]

3.5 Basic Commodities

It was seen in section 2.4 that inequality (2.6) was necessary for positive prices in a subsistence economy. Is the same condition also necessary for the surplus economy considered in this chapter?

Suppose that $\tilde{a}_{12} > 0$ and $\tilde{a}_{21} = 0$: that is, wheat is used to produce iron but not vice versa. The price equations become:

$$\tilde{P}_1 = (1 + \tilde{r})\tilde{P}_1\tilde{a}_{11} \tag{3.46a}$$

$$\tilde{P}_2 = (1 + \tilde{r})(\tilde{P}_1\tilde{a}_{12} + \tilde{P}_2\tilde{a}_{22}) \tag{3.46b}$$

This system becomes decomposable for the rate of profit is determined solely in the wheat industry: from (3.46a), I have:

$$\tilde{r} = \tilde{r}_1 = 1/\tilde{a}_{11} - 1 \tag{3.47}$$

This contrasts with the system (3.15), for which the rate of profit depends on the conditions of production in both industries, as is clear from (3.22). When (3.47) is substituted into (3.46b), I obtain:

$$\tilde{P}_2/\tilde{P}_1 = \tilde{a}_{12}/(\tilde{a}_{11} - \tilde{a}_{22}) \tag{3.48}$$

The sole purpose of the second price equation is to determine the price of iron relative to wheat. As long as $\tilde{a}_{11} > \tilde{a}_{22}$,[6] the relative price is positive.

In contrast to the subsistence model of the previous chapter, the surplus model can support a positive price system even when one commodity is not used as means of production in the other industry; however, the rate of profit is then determined by the conditions of production in only one industry. In (3.46), wheat is an example of a basic commodity because it is used in the production of wheat and iron; iron is non-basic because it is used only in the production of itself. To appreciate the distinction between basic and non-basic commodities, consider the following technique:

$$\tilde{a}_{11} = \tilde{a}_{22} = 0, \tilde{a}_{12} > 0, \tilde{a}_{21} > 0 \tag{3.49}$$

the corresponding price equations being:

$$\tilde{P}_1 = (1 + \tilde{r})\tilde{P}_2\tilde{a}_{21} \tag{3.50a}$$

$$\tilde{P}_2 = (1 + \tilde{r})\tilde{P}_1\tilde{a}_{12} \tag{3.50b}$$

Wheat is used directly to produce only iron and iron is used directly to produce only wheat. Wheat enters the production of itself indirectly through its input into iron; similarly, for iron. So, in this case, both wheat and iron are basic commodities because they 'enter (no matter whether directly or indirectly) into the production of all commodities' (§ 6, p. 8).

Equivalently, it can be seen that, in the example described in (3.45), both commodities are basic by examining the quantity equations (3.5). Even if there is a final demand for only one commodity, both commodities must be produced.

I summarise this discussion in the following Definition, Result and Corollary:

> *Definition 2:* A commodity is basic if it is used directly or indirectly in the production of all commodities. Any commodity not satisfying this condition is non-basic.
>
> *Result 5:* Both commodities are basic if and only if $\tilde{a}_{12}\tilde{a}_{21} > 0$.
>
> *Corollary 5.1:* Commodity i is non-basic if and only if $\tilde{a}_{ij} = 0$, $j \neq i$.

Under the reasonable assumption that labour is required directly in each process, it follows that each commodity entering the (subsistence) wage basket is basic.

3.6 Conclusion

The purpose of this chapter has been to derive and solve the price equations for a productive economy with a subsistence wage. I have shown first that there is a unique positive solution to the price system, and second, that the relative price depends on the conditions of production and the distribution of income. I have also demonstrated that, in progressing from the subsistence model of Chapter 2 to the productive model of this chapter, it is sensible to draw a distinction between basic and non-basic commodities.

Commentary

This chapter is based on sections 4–7 of PCMC. See the review of PCMC by Reder (1961).

Exercises

1. Confirm the results of the numerical examples (1)–(4) in section 3.2.

2. (i) Establish *Result 3* for the case $\widetilde{F}_1 \geqslant 0$, $\widetilde{F}_2 \geqslant 0$, walosi.
(ii) *Definition 1* was based on the assumption that $\widetilde{a}_{ij} > 0$ if $i \neq j$. How do *Definition 1* and *Result 3* need to be modified if this assumption is relaxed? (i.e. $\widetilde{a}_{ij} = 0$ for at least one $i \neq j$)

3. Prove that the following economy is productive:

   280 qr wheat ⊕ 12 t iron ⊖ 575 qr wheat
   120 qr wheat ⊕ 8 t iron ⊖ 20 t iron

   Calculate prices and the rate of profit. (See section 5, PCMC.) Contrast this with exercise 1(i) of Chapter 2.

4. Analyse each of the following models:

   (i) 4 qr wheat ⊕ 1 t iron ⊖ 8 qr wheat
   1 qr wheat ⊕ 4 t iron ⊖ 6 t iron

   (ii) 16 qr wheat ⊕ 4 t iron ⊖ 32 qr wheat
   2 qr wheat ⊕ 8 t iron ⊖ 12 t iron

   (iii) 80 qr wheat ⊕ 40 t iron ⊖ 640 qr wheat
   21 qr wheat ⊕ 8 t iron ⊖ 48 t iron

   (iv) 6 qr wheat ⊕ 3 t iron ⊖ 48 qr wheat
   42 qr wheat ⊕ 16 t iron ⊖ 96 t iron

5. 'The rate of profit is defined as the value of output less value of inputs divided by value of output' (Reder, 1961, p. 689). Do you agree?

6. Derive (3.29).

7. Derive (3.30b).

8. Derive (3.33), (3.34a) and (3.34b)

9. Following the approach in exercise 6, Chapter 2, let:

$$\underline{a}_{11} = 1/2,\ \underline{a}_{12} = 1/4,\ \underline{a}_{21} = 1/3,\ \underline{a}_{22} = 1/2,$$
$$\underline{l}_1 = 1/3,\ \underline{l}_2 = 1/4,\ \underline{\omega}_1 = 1/2,\ \underline{\omega}_2 = 0.$$

   (i) Express $\widetilde{a}_{ij}$ in terms of $\underline{a}_{ij}$, $\underline{\omega}_i$ and $\underline{l}_j$, $i,j = 1,2$.
   (ii) Examine the effect of increasing $\underline{\omega}_1$ to 2/3, other things remaining constant.
   (iii) Examine the effect of increasing $\underline{\omega}_2$ to 1/5 other things remaining constant.

10. Consider the technique given in (3.49). Prove that both commodities must be produced even if there is a final demand for only one commodity.

11. Consider a technique with $\tilde{a}_{12} = 0$. Express gross outputs in terms of final demands, considering in particular the cases:

    (i) $\tilde{F}_1 = 0, \tilde{F}_2 > 0$; (ii) $\tilde{F}_1 > 0, \tilde{F}_2 = 0$.
    From this example, would you say that commodity 1 is basic? Is commodity 2 basic?

12. Prove *Result 5.*

13. Derive *Corollary 5.1.*

14. (Two positive values of r satisfying (3.15).) Find $\tilde{r}_1$, $\tilde{r}_2$ and the corresponding prices for this technique:

$$\tilde{a}_{11} = \tilde{a}_{22} = 1/2, \tilde{a}_{12} = 1/4, \tilde{a}_{21} = 1/3.$$

15. Find the rate of profit and prices for the technique in (3.49).

Notes to Chapter 3

1. The use of a tilde denotes the fact that I am dealing with a surplus economy where the wage is at subsistence level. I use the acronym 'walosi' instead of '*w*ith *a*t *l*east *o*ne *s*trict *i*nequality'.
2. Given the statements above, the conclusions drawn from the examples above would be unaffected if, say, $\tilde{F}_1 = 200$, $\tilde{F}_2 = 300$.
3. That is, the value of output is greater than the value of inputs, evaluation being performed at the given price system.
4. 'a' and 'b' can refer to the same economy at different times or to different economies at the same time. The *a*-economy is described by the quadruple $\{\tilde{a}_{11}, \tilde{a}_{21}; \tilde{a}_{12}, \tilde{a}_{22}\}$ and the b-economy by $\{\tilde{b}_{11}, \tilde{b}_{21}; \tilde{b}_{12}, \tilde{b}_{22}\}$.
5. Compare Ricardo (1951): 'There can be no rise in the value of labour without a fall of profits' (p. 35). 'Every rise of wages . . . is the same thing (as a) fall of profits' (p. 39).
6. See Appendix B of PCMC and the correspondence between Newman and Sraffa, published as an Appendix to Bharadwaj (1970).

4

Production with a Surplus – Wage Above Subsistence

4.1 Introduction

By no longer restricting the wage to a given subsistence level, but permitting it to share in the surplus, I am immediately faced with the following question: does the wage contain a subsistence component? If so, it is necessary to divide the wage into subsistence and surplus components. For ease of exposition, I adopt Sraffa's expedients of treating the whole of the wage as variable and paid at the end of the production period.[1] In so doing, it is possible that commodities entering the wage basket, hitherto basic, can become non-basic simply because they no longer appear as means of production. I avoid this problem by assuming that wheat plays a dual role, as means of production and consumption, though now it is basic simply because of the former.

In the previous chapter, where the wage was restricted to subsistence level, the value of net output was necessarily equal to the amount of profits. In this chapter, the value of net output is distributed between wages and profits. It thus becomes necessary to have direct labour explicitly mentioned in each production process. I now have as the expressions for the wheat and iron industries:[2]

$$X_{11} \text{ qr wheat} \oplus X_{21} \text{ t iron} \oplus L_1 \text{ labour} \ominus X_1 \text{ qr wheat} \qquad (4.1a)$$

$$X_{12} \text{ qr wheat} \oplus X_{22} \text{ t iron} \oplus L_2 \text{ labour} \ominus X_2 \text{ t iron} \qquad (4.1b)$$

where X_{ij} is the amount of commodity i advanced as means of production in industry j and L_j is the amount of direct labour required in industry j, $i,j = 1,2$. I assume that both commodities are basic and that this system is productive, so that these familiar inequalities hold:

$$X_1 \geqslant X_{11} + X_{12} \tag{4.2a}$$

walosi

$$X_2 \geqslant X_{21} + X_{22} \tag{4.2b}$$

Following the procedure in the two previous chapters, I now introduce these input–output coefficients:

$$\text{commodities:} \quad a_{ij} = X_{ij}/X_j \quad i,j = 1,2 \tag{4.3a}$$

$$\text{labour:} \quad l_j = L_j/X_j \quad j = 1,2 \tag{4.3b}$$

Result 3 applies so that these inequalities hold:

$$1 - a_{11} > 0 \tag{4.4a}$$

$$1 - a_{22} > 0 \tag{4.4b}$$

$$(1 - a_{11})(1 - a_{22}) - a_{12}a_{21} > 0 \tag{4.4c}$$

4.2 The Price System

With m denoting the money wage and p_i the money price of commodity i, $i = 1,2$, the price equations for the two processes in (4.1) are given by:

$$p_1 = ml_1 + (1+r)(p_1a_{11} + p_2a_{21}) \tag{4.5a}$$

$$p_2 = ml_2 + (1+r)(p_1a_{12} + p_2a_{22}) \tag{4.5b}$$

At prices p_1 and p_2, $(p_1a_{11} + p_2a_{21})$ is the value of means of production advanced and used up per unit of output of wheat. p_1 must therefore cover wage costs, ml_1, the cost of capital used up (or depreciation), $(p_1a_{11} + p_2a_{21})$, and pay profits at the uniform rate r on the value of capital advanced, $r(p_1a_{11} + p_2a_{21})$; similarly, for (4.5b). The first question concerns the existence of a positive solution to (4.5).

To answer this, associate ml_i with $\widetilde{F}_i$ in (3.5) of Chapter 3, $(1+r)a_{ii}$ with $\widetilde{a}_{ii}$ and $(1+r)a_{ij}$ with $\widetilde{a}_{ji}$, $j \neq i$. Then, from *Result 3*, I know that (3.5) has a positive solution if and only if the following inequalities hold:

$$(1 - \tilde{a}_{11} =)\, 1 - (1+r)a_{11} > 0 \tag{4.6a}$$

$$(1 - \tilde{a}_{22} =)\, 1 - (1+r)a_{22} > 0 \tag{4.6b}$$

$$((1 - \tilde{a}_{11})(1 - \tilde{a}_{22}) - \tilde{a}_{12}\tilde{a}_{21} =)$$

$$(1 - (1+r)a_{11})(1 - (1+r)a_{22}) - (1+r)^2 a_{12}a_{21} > 0 \tag{4.6c}$$

That is, given $ml_1 > 0$, $ml_2 > 0$, there is a positive solution p_1, p_2 to (4.5) if and only if (4.6) holds. Whether these inequalities are satisfied depends on the value of r, as the a_{ij} are constant; obviously, for sufficiently large values of r, neither (4.6a) nor (4.6b) will be true. The quadratic in (4.6c) is of the same form as that in (3.17c) and (3.18) of Chapter 3; hence, properties of the latter can be applied to the former. First of all, define:

$$f(r) \equiv (1 - (1+r)a_{11})(1 - (1+r)a_{22}) - (1+r)^2 a_{12}a_{21} \tag{4.7}$$

By the productiveness conditions, (4.4c), it follows that:

$$\mathrm{f}(0) > 0 \qquad (4.8))$$

From *Result 4* of section 3.3, there is a positive value of r, denoted by R,[3] such that:

$$f(R) = 0 \tag{4.9a}$$

At this value of r:

$$1 - (1+R)a_{11} > 0 \tag{4.9b}$$

$$1 - (1+R)a_{22} > 0 \tag{4.9c}$$

To see that (4.9b) and (4.9c) are true, consider first the case where $a_{11} \neq a_{22}$, say $a_{11} > a_{22}$. Suppose that:

$$1 - (1+R)a_{11} < 0 \tag{4.10a}$$

$$1 - (1+R)a_{22} \geqslant 0 \tag{4.10b}$$

Then $f(R) < 0$, as $a_{12} \neq 0 \neq a_{21}$. So, (4.10a) and (4.10b) cannot hold. Similarly:

$$1 - (1+R)a_{11} \geqslant 0 \tag{4.11a}$$

$$1 - (1+R)a_{22} < 0 \tag{4.11b}$$

cannot hold. Suppose next that:

$$1 - (1+R)a_{11} \leqslant 0 \tag{4.12a}$$

$$1 - (1+R)a_{22} \leqslant 0 \tag{4.12b}$$

Let $a_{11} > a_{22}$. Then there exists a positive value of r, $r_1 < R$, such that:

$$1 - (1+r_1)a_{11} = 0 \tag{4.13a}$$

$$1 - (1+r_1)a_{22} \geqslant 0 \tag{4.13b}$$

It follows from (4.7), (4.13a) and (4.13b) that, at this value of r:

$$f(r_1) < 0 \tag{4.14}$$

As $f(r)$ is a continuous function of r, I conclude from (4.8) and (4.14) that there is a positive value of r, $r_2 < r_1$ such that:

$$f(r_2) = 0 \tag{4.15}$$

This contradicts the definition of R as the smallest positive value of r at which $f(r) = 0$.[4]

I have proved that (4.1), (4.11) and (4.12) cannot hold. The only other possibility is (4.9). So, (4.9) holds under the assumption that $a_{11} > a_{22}$. Exactly the same line of argument establishes (4.9) if $a_{22} > a_{11}$. This leaves $a_{11} = a_{22}$. So, suppose first that:

$$1 - (1+R)a_{11} = 1 - (1+R)a_{22} = 0 \tag{4.16}$$

Then $f(R) < 0$ as $a_{12} \neq 0 \neq a_{21}$. This contradicts the definition of R and so cannot occur. Next suppose that:

$$1 - (1+R)a_{11} = 1 - (1+R)a_{22} < 0 \tag{4.17}$$

It follows from (4.17) that there is a positive value of r, $r_3 < R$, such that:

$$1 - (1+r_3)a_{11} = 1 - (1+r_3)a_{22} = 0 \qquad (4.18)$$

Then:

$$f(r_3) < 0 \qquad (4.19)$$

So, from (4.8), (4.19) and the continuity of $f(r)$, there is a positive value of r, $r_4 < r_3$, such that:

$$f(r_4) = 0 \qquad (4.20)$$

This contradicts the definition of R. As neither (4.16) nor (4.17) can be true, it follows that (4.9b) and (4.9c) hold when $a_{11} = a_{22}$.

The conclusion to be drawn from (4.10)–(4.20) is that (4.9b) and (4.9c) are valid regardless of the relation between a_{11} and a_{22}. Hence, (4.6c) is the first inequality of the three in (4.6) which fails to be satisfied as r is increased from zero. For $0 \leqslant r \leqslant R$, (4.6a)–(4.6c) hold, where R is calculated as the smallest positive solution of $f(r) = 0$, in the same way as $\tilde{r}_1$ was calculated in section 3.3, i.e. as the solution of:

$$f(r) \equiv (1+r)^2(s^2 - s(a_{11}+a_{22}) + a_{11}a_{22}-a_{12}a_{21}) = 0 \qquad (4.21a)$$

where $s = 1/(1+r)$, or

$$\theta\,(s) = s^2 - s(a_{11}+a_{22}) + a_{11}a_{22} - a_{12}a_{21} = 0 \qquad (4.21b)$$

$\theta\,(s) = 0$ has two roots s_1, s_2, where $s_1 = 1/(1+R)$.

From section 3.3, I have:

$$s_1 = (a_{11}+a_{22}+\sqrt{(a_{11}+a_{22})^2-4(a_{11}a_{22}-a_{12}a_{21})})/2 \qquad (4.22a)$$

where

$$s_1 < 1, s_1 > a_{ii}, i = 1,2 \qquad (4.22b)$$

So, for $0 \leqslant r < R$, (4.5) has a positive solution p_1, p_2, m.[5]

Next consider (4.5) when $r = R$. Using (4.9b) in (4.5a), I obtain:

$$p_1 = (ml_1 + (1+R)p_2a_{21})/(1 - (1+R)a_{11}) \tag{4.23}$$

Substituting for p_1 in (4.5b), I have:

$$p_2((1 - (1+R)a_{11})(1 - (1+R)a_{22}) - (1+R)^2a_{12}a_{21})$$
$$= m(l_1a_{12}(1+R) + l_2(1 - (1+R)a_{11})) \tag{4.24}$$

As the bracketed term on the left-hand side of (4.24) is zero and that on the right-hand side is positive, it follows that $m = 0$. Then (4.5) becomes:

$$p_1 = (1+R)(p_1a_{11} + p_2a_{21}) \tag{4.25a}$$
$$p_2 = (1+R)(p_1a_{12} + p_2a_{22}) \tag{4.25b}$$

which has a unique positive solution p_2/p_1 by *Result 4*.

To summarise so far: (4.5) has solution for each value of r lying between 0 and R:

(i) if $0 \leqslant r < R$, m, p_1 and p_2 are all positive;

(ii) if $r = R$, $m = 0$, p_1 and p_2 are both positive.

The purpose of this extended discussion has been to establish that there is a range of feasible values of the rate of profit over which both prices are positive. Then either commodity or a basket containing both in any proportions can be chosen as numeraire or standard of value. For ease of exposition, I select the first commodity as numeraire, i.e. $p_1 \equiv 1$.[6] The price equations can now be rewritten as:

$$1 = w_{(1)}l_1 + (1+r)(a_{11} + p_{(1)}a_{21}) \tag{4.26a}$$
$$p_{(1)} = w_{(1)}l_2 + (1+r)(a_{12} + p_{(1)}a_{22}) \tag{4.26b}$$

where $w_{(1)} \equiv m/p_1$ is the real wage measured in terms of the first commodity and $p_{(1)} \equiv p_2/p_1$ is the relative price. (4.26) is a system of two equations in three unknowns. I can solve for $p_{(1)}$ and $w_{(1)}$ as functions of r in the following way. Eliminating $p_{(1)}$ from (4.26):

$$w_{(1)} = \frac{(1 - (1+r)a_{11})(1 - (1+r)a_{22}) - (1+r)^2 a_{12}a_{21}}{l_1(1 - (1+r)a_{22}) + (1+r)l_2a_{21}}$$

$$\equiv f(r)/g(r) \tag{4.27}$$

Eliminating $w_{(1)}$ from (4.26):

$$p_{(1)} = \frac{l_2(1 - (1+r)a_{11}) + (1+r)l_1a_{12}}{l_1(1 - (1+r)a_{22}) + (1+r)l_2a_{21}} \equiv \frac{h(r)}{g(r)} \tag{4.28}$$

It follows from (4.9b) and (4.9c) that:

$$\left.\begin{array}{l} h(r) > 0 \\ g(r) > 0 \end{array}\right\} \quad \text{for } 0 \leqslant r \leqslant R \tag{4.29a}$$

and from (4.6c), (4.8) and (4.9a) that:

$$\left.\begin{array}{ll} f(r) > 0 & \text{for } 0 \leqslant r < R \\ f(r) = 0 & \text{for } r = R \end{array}\right\} \tag{4.29b}$$

Hence from (4.29a):

$$p_{(1)} > 0 \qquad \text{for } 0 \leqslant r \leqslant R \tag{4.30a}$$

and from (4.29a) and (4.29b):

$$\left.\begin{array}{ll} w_{(1)} > 0 & \text{for } 0 \leqslant r < R \\ w_{(1)} = 0 & \text{for } r = R \end{array}\right\} \tag{4.30b}$$

So, I have established:

> *Result 6:* The price equations (4.5), or (4.26), for a productive economy have a positive solution if $0 \leqslant r < R$; when $r = R$, the real wage is zero and the relative price is positive.

It follows from *Result 3* that the price equations cannot have a positive solution if $r > R$. Note also that the essence of *Result 6* is unaltered by a change of numeraire. Suppose that the second commodity is chosen as standard of value. Then:

$$w_{(2)} = \frac{m}{p_2} = \frac{f(r)}{h(r)} = \frac{f(r)}{g(r)} \cdot \frac{g(r)}{h(r)} = w_{(1)}p_{(2)} \tag{4.31a}$$

$$p_{(2)} = \frac{g(r)}{h(r)} = \frac{1}{p_{(1)}} \tag{4.31b}$$

the bracketed subscript indicating the choice of numeraire. As $p_{(2)} > 0$ if and only if $p_{(1)} > 0$, it follows from (4.31) that $w_{(2)} > 0$ if and only if $w_{(1)} > 0$.

In *Result 6*, I have obtained not only the solution to the price equations but also the range of values over which it exists. Furthermore, I have shown in (4.28) the dependence of the relative price on both technical coefficients and the distribution of income, the latter operating through variation in the rate of profit.[7] A constituent of the solution is the real wage rate–rate of profit curve, (4.27), which is the locus of combinations of $w_{(1)}$ and r that can be supported by the given technique of production. In the next section, I shall analyse the variation of the relative price and the real wage with changes in the rate of profit.[8]

4.3 Relative Price Variation

Having derived (4.28), it is a relatively simple matter to examine the dependence of the relative price on income distribution. Hereafter, the first commodity is chosen as numeraire, unless stated to the contrary: so, I drop the bracketed subscript on p and w in (4.27) and (4.28).

Differentiating (4.28) with respect to r, I obtain:

$$\begin{aligned} dp/dr &= \{[l_1(1 - (1+r)a_{22}) + (1+r)l_2a_{21}]\,(l_1a_{12} - l_2a_{11}) \\ &\quad - [l_2(1 - (1+r)a_{11}) + (1+r)l_1a_{12}]\,(l_2a_{21} - l_1a_{22})\}/(g(r))^2 \\ &= (-l_1l_2a_{11} + l_1^2a_{12} + l_1l_2a_{22} - l_2^2a_{21})/(g(r))^2 \\ &= (l_1(l_1a_{12} + l_2a_{22}) - l_2(l_1a_{11} + l_2a_{21}))/(g(r))^2 \end{aligned} \tag{4.32}$$

So:

$$dp/dr \gtreqless 0 \text{ as } l_1(l_1a_{12} + l_2a_{22}) \gtreqless l_2(l_1a_{11} + l_2a_{21})$$

$$\text{i.e. as } (l_1a_{12} + l_2a_{22})/l_2 \gtreqless (l_1a_{11} + l_2a_{21})/l_1 \qquad (4.33)$$

As it depends only on the given technical coefficients, dp/dr is always one-signed; either $dp/dr > 0$ or < 0 or $= 0$, but never a combination of them.[9] If it is possible to characterise $dp/dr = 0$, it should also be possible to characterise the other two possibilities. To this, I now turn.

Put $dp/dr = 0$, with λ the common ratio in (4.33). Then:

$$l_1a_{11} + l_2a_{21} = \lambda l_1 \qquad (4.34a)$$

$$l_1a_{12} + l_2a_{22} = \lambda l_2 \qquad (4.34b)$$

Eliminating l_1 from (4.34). I obtain:

$$l_2((\lambda - a_{11})(\lambda - a_{22}) - a_{12}a_{21}) = 0$$

or, as $l_2 \neq 0$:

$$(\lambda - a_{11})(\lambda - a_{22}) - a_{12}a_{21} = 0 \qquad (4.35a)$$

In fact, I have obtained:

$$f(\lambda) \equiv \lambda^2 - \lambda(a_{11}+a_{22}) + a_{11}a_{22} - a_{12}a_{21} = 0 \qquad (4.35b)$$

the quadratic in λ which is identical to that in s considered above, namely (4.7) in section 4.2 and (3.20) in Chapter 3. Applying the theory developed above:

$$\lambda = s_1 = 1/(1+R) \qquad (4.36)$$

where s_1 is given in (4.22). It was shown in section 3.3 that $\tilde{s}_1$, the analogue of s_1, was that root which had an associated positive solution. Summarising this discussion, I have:

> *Result 7: dp/dr* is given by (4.33). The relative price is invariant to changes in r if and only if (4.34) holds, with $\lambda = 1/(1+R)$.

Interpretations of the case dp/dr are provided in the Exercises.

4.4 Real Wage Rate Variation

Having considered relative price variation above, I now examine the dependence of the real wage rate on the rate of profit. If $w = 0$ in (4.25), $r = R$; if $r = 0$, $w = f(0)/g(0) > 0$ from (4.29). How does w behave as r varies between 0 and R? Rather than differentiate (4.27) directly, I adopt an indirect procedure using (4.26). Differentiating this pair of equations, I obtain respectively:

$$0 = dw/dr \cdot l_1 + (a_{11}+pa_{21}) + (1+r)a_{21} \cdot dp/dr \tag{4.37a}$$

$$dp/dr = dw/dr \cdot l_2 + (a_{12}+pa_{22}) + (1+r)a_{22} \cdot dp/dr \tag{4.37b}$$

which can be manipulated to yield:

$$dw/dr = (-(a_{11}+pa_{21}) - (1+r)a_{21}dp/dr))/l_1 \tag{4.38a}$$

$$dw/dr = ((1 - (1+r)a_{22})dp/dr - (a_{12}+pa_{22}))/l_2 \tag{4.38b}$$

dw/dr can be of any sign.

If $dp/dr > 0$, $dw/dr < 0$ from (4.38a).

If $dp/dr < 0$, $dw/dr < 0$ from (4.38b).

If $dp/dr = 0$, $dw/dr < 0$ from either (4.38a) or (4.38b).

The w–r trade-off is thus unambiguously downward sloping. To determine its curvature, differentiate (4.37) to obtain:

$$0 = d^2w/dr^2 \cdot l_1 + 2a_{21}dp/dr + (1+r)a_{21}d^2p/dr^2 \tag{4.39a}$$

$$d^2p/dr^2 = d^2w/dr^2 \cdot l_2 + 2a_{22}dp/dr + (1+r)a_{22}d^2p/dr^2 \tag{4.39b}$$

Eliminating d^2p/dr^2 from (4.39), I obtain:

$$\begin{aligned} dp/dr &= -d^2w/dr^2 \cdot (l_1(1 - (1+r)a_{22}) + (1+r)l_2a_{21})/2a_{21} \\ &= -d^2w/dr^2 \cdot g(r)/2a_{21} \end{aligned} \tag{4.40}$$

As $g(r) > 0$ for $0 \leqslant r \leqslant R$, it follows from (4.40) that:

$$\text{sign } d^2w/dr^2 = (-1)\text{sign } dp/dr \tag{4.41}$$

I summarise the discussion in sections 4.3 and 4.4 in

Result 8: Let the first commodity be numeraire.

1. There is a real wage rate–rate of profit trade-off, $w = w(r)$, such that:
   1.1 When $r = 0$, $w = W = \max w > 0$;
   When $w = 0$, $r = R = \max r > 0$;
   1.2 $dw/dr < 0$ for $0 \leqslant r \leqslant R$;
   1.3 If the second (respectively first) industry has the higher ratio of value of capital to labour, w is concave (respectively convex).
2. The relative price satisfies these conditions:
   2.1 $p > 0$ for $0 \leqslant r \leqslant R$;
   2.2 $dp/dr \gtreqless 0$ as $(a_{12}+pa_{22})/l_2 \gtreqless (a_{11}+pa_{21})/l_1$ (4.42)

As I have established 1.1, 1.2 and 2.1 above, it remains to prove 1.3 and 2.2, both of which involve value capital–labour ratios. From (4.28), I obtain instead of (4.32):

$$\begin{aligned} dp/dr &= (g(r)(l_1a_{12} - l_2a_{11}) - h(r)(l_2a_{21} - l_1a_{22}))/(g(r))^2 \\ &= (l_1a_{12} - l_2a_{11})/g(r) - (h(r)/g(r))\cdot(l_2a_{21} - l_1a_{22})/g(r) \\ &= (l_1a_{12} - l_2a_{11} - p(l_2a_{21} - l_1a_{22}))/g(r) \qquad (4.43) \end{aligned}$$

using the definition of p. So:

$$\begin{aligned} dp/dr \gtreqless 0 &\text{ as } l_1a_{12} - l_2a_{11} \gtreqless p(l_2a_{21} - l_1a_{22}) \\ &\text{i.e. as } l_1(a_{12} + pa_{22}) \gtreqless l_2(a_{11} + pa_{21}) \\ &\text{i.e. as } (a_{12} + pa_{22})/l_2 \gtreqless (a_{11} + pa_{21})/l_1 \qquad (4.44) \end{aligned}$$

This establishes 2.2. 1.3 follows by application of (4.41) and (4.44). I summarise the possibilities in Figure 4.1 overleaf.

1.2 in *Result 8* is a generalisation of *Corollary 4.1*. In section 3.4, I demonstrated that an increase in the subsistence wage resulted in a decrease in the rate of profit for a given technique: the statement of 1.2 above is essentially similar. This proposition is self-evident for a one-sector, or wheat, model. Wages, profits, capital, gross and net output can all be measured in physical terms, say qrs of wheat: there is no need to introduce prices to evaluate these homogeneous variables. The net output is distributed be-

Figure 4.1

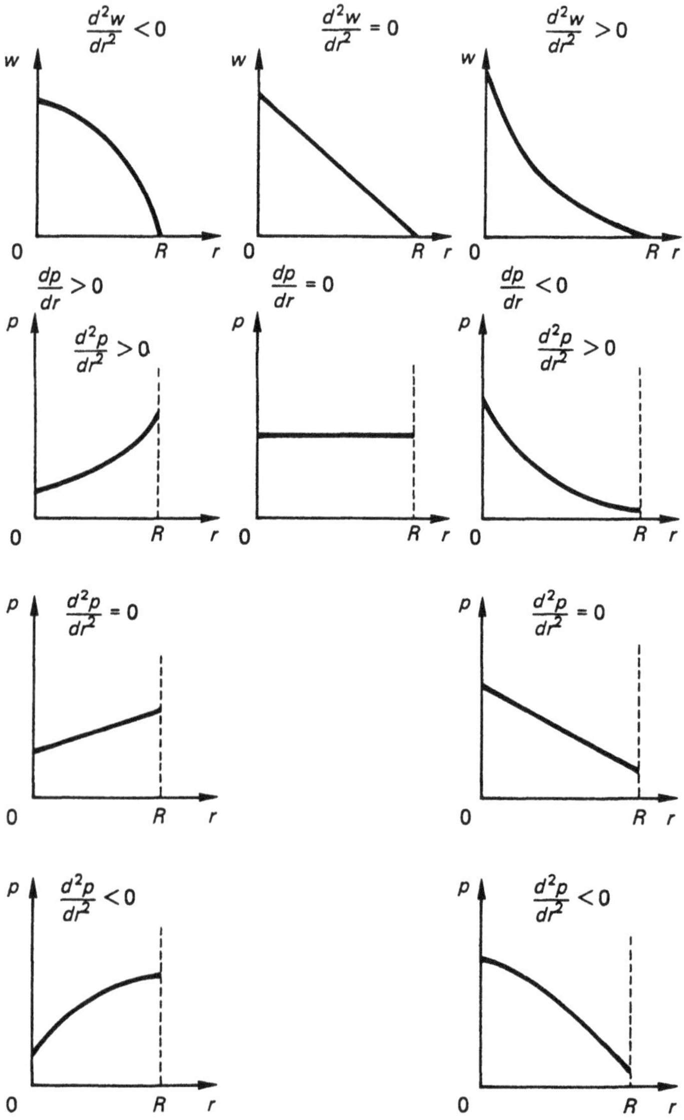

$\frac{d^2w}{dr^2} < 0$
$\frac{d^2w}{dr^2} = 0$
$\frac{d^2w}{dr^2} > 0$
w
0
R
r
$\frac{dp}{dr} > 0$
$\frac{dp}{dr} = 0$
$\frac{dp}{dr} < 0$
p
$\frac{d^2p}{dr^2} > 0$
$\frac{d^2p}{dr^2} = 0$
$\frac{d^2p}{dr^2} < 0$

tween wages and profits: an increase in the real wage necessarily causes a fall in the rate of profit. It might be thought that this result is equally self-evident for a multisector model, say the two-sector version employed here. It is self-evident when the relative price is invariant to changes in the rate of profit. However, this intuitively plausible result needs to be derived in a multisector model because a change in one of the parameters, say the rate of profit, affects relative prices. Might it not therefore be possible for an increase in the rate of profit to so affect the relative price that the value of net output increases to such an extent as to accommodate an increase in the real wage? *Result 8* states that such a possibility cannot arise for a single-product industries model.

4.5 Subsistence Component to the Wage

In this section, I take up the two questions about the wage raised at the beginning of section 4.1. There is no issue of principle over dividing the wage into subsistence and surplus parts. The approaches adopted in Chapters 2 and 3, on the one hand, and this chapter, on the other, can be synthesised. That they are not is largely a matter of convenience and tradition. 'The drawback of this course is that it involves relegating the necessaries of consumption to the limbo of non-basic products' (PCMC, section 8, p. 10). This criticism cannot be properly answered, as Sraffa recognised: 'Necessaries are essentially basic and if they are prevented from exercising their influence on prices and profits under that label, they must do so in devious ways (e.g. by setting a limit below which the wage cannot fall; a limit which would itself fall with any improvement in the methods of production of necessaries, carrying with it a rise in the rate of profits and a change in the prices of other products)' (ibid.).

Consider next the question of whether the wage is advanced. A wage paid *post factum* is certainly easier to reconcile with the treatment of profit as an independent variable. For, if the wage is advanced, the rate of profit emerges from the analysis as a residual. A consequence of assuming that the wage is paid at the end of the production period is that 'the classical economists' idea of a wage "advanced" from capital' has to be abandoned (ibid., section 9, p. 10).

4.6 Conclusions

This chapter has been devoted to establishing for a productive economy with a surplus wage the principle advanced in Chapter 3 that prices depend on technical conditions and income distribution. In the earlier chapter, it was shown that, if the economy was productive with a given advanced subsistence wage, a unique positive rate of profit was determined. Once the assumption of a given subsistence wage is dropped, a locus of feasible real wage rate–rate of profit combinations is obtained: this *w–r* curve is a generalisation of the relation between subsistence wage and the rate of profit discussed in Chapter 3.

Commentary

The material in this chapter is based on chapters II and III of PCMC. My approach differs from Sraffa's with regard to the analysis of price changes (see, sections 13–20). See section 42 for Sraffa's discussion of the properties of *R*.

It is clear from section 4.3 that the case of relative price invariance is a watershed. The question of relative price invariance has been addressed on a number of occasions in the literature, including, for example, Pasinetti (1977a) and Woods (1980, 1985).

Exercises

1. Consider the proof of *Result 6*.
   (i) Prove that (4.9) holds if $a_{22} > a_{11}$.
   (ii) Derive (4.22).
   (iii) Derive (4.27) from (4.26).
   (iv) Derive (4.28) from (4.26).
   (v) Establish (4.29a).

2. What is the effect on *Result 6* of changing the numeraire to the second commodity? In particular, how are the maximum wage rate and the rate of profit affected?

3. Analyse the following model:

   1 qr wheat ⊕ 1 t iron ⊕ 1 labour ⊖ 2 qr wheat
   1 qr wheat ⊕ 4 t iron ⊕ 4 labour ⊖ 8 t iron

   i.e. Express the relative price and the real wage in terms of the rate of profit (with the first commodity as numeraire). What is the effect of switching to the second commodity as numeraire?

4. Repeat exercise 3 for this model:

   3 qr wheat ⊕ 8 t iron ⊕ 3 labour ⊖ 12 qr wheat
   6 qr wheat ⊕ 4 t iron ⊕ 8 labour ⊖ 16 t iron

5. Repeat exercise 3 for this model:

   2 qr wheat ⊕ 1 t iron ⊕ 1 labour ⊖ 4 qr wheat
   1 qr wheat ⊕ 2 t iron ⊕ 1 labour ⊖ 3 t iron

6. What is the effect on *Result 7* of changing the numeraire to the second commodity?

7. Can the same relative price occur at two distinct feasible values of r? Under what conditions (necessary and/or sufficient)?

8. What is the effect on *Result 8* of changing the numeraire to the second commodity?

9. Refer to exercises 7 and 8 of Chapter 2. State the equations satisfied by the embodied labours, v_1 and v_2. Prove that prices, embodied labours and direct labours are all proportional if and only if $(l_1a_{11} + l_2a_{21})/l_1 = (l_1a_{12} + l_2a_{22})/l_2 = \alpha$, a constant.

10. Derive the w–r curve if the condition in exercise 9 is satisfied.

11. (i) From the price equations (4.5) or (4.26), define the labour share in the value of gross output in each industry.
    (ii) Prove that the relative price is constant if and only if there are equal labour shares in gross output at any feasible value of r.

12. (i) Define the labour share in the value of net output in each industry.
    (ii) Prove that the relative price is constant if and only if there are equal labour shares in net output at any feasible value of r.

13. Prove that the relative price is constant if and only if the ratio of direct to indirect labour is the same for both commodities. (Indirect labour is equal to embodied labour minus direct labour.)

14. Prove that the relative price is constant if and only if the ratio of value of net output to means of production is identical for both industries at any feasible value of r.

15. Is the relative price constant if the ratio of value of gross output to value of means of production is identical for both industries at any feasible value of r?

16. Prove that the relative price is constant if and only if there is a uniform value–capital/labour ratio at each feasible value of r.

17. Derive the wage rate–rate of profits curve if the wage is advanced.

18. Derive the w–r curve if any of the conditions in exercises 11–16 is satisfied. Does your conclusion depend either on choice of numeraire or whether the wage is advanced?.

19. Prove that the relative price is constant if $a_{ij}/l_j = \alpha_j$, a constant. Interpret this condition. Show, by means of an example, that (4.33) can be satisfied even if the condition above is not.

20. Consider the following economy:
a_{11} qr wheat ⊕ l_1 labour ⊖ 1 qr wheat
a_{12} qr wheat ⊕ a_{22} t iron ⊕ l_2 labour ⊖ 1 t iron
    (i) Are both commodities basic?
    (ii) Write down the productiveness conditions.
    (iii) State the price equations, solving them in terms of wheat.
    (iv) Repeat (iii), but use iron as numeraire.
    (v) Does *Result 6* need to be modified for this model? (See 2 above.)
    (vi) How does *Result 7* need to be modified for this model? (See 6 above.)
    (vii) How does *Result 8* need to be modified for this model? (See 8 above.)

21. If the first commodity is numeraire, labour-commanded prices are defined as:

$$P_1 = 1/w_{(1)},\ P_2 = p_{(1)}/w_{(1)}.$$

How do P_1 and P_2 vary with r?

22. Analyse the following techniques:
    (i) 14/9 qr wheat ⊕ 20/9 t iron ⊕ 4/5 labour ⊖ 10/3 qr wheat
    7/9 qr wheat ⊕ 10/9 t iron ⊕ 1/5 labour ⊖ 10/3 t iron
    (ii) 1 qr wheat ⊕ 14/5 t iron ⊕ 3/5 labour ⊖ 3 qr wheat
    1 qr wheat ⊕ 6/5 t iron ⊕ 2/5 labour ⊖ 4 t iron
    (iii) 3/4 qr wheat ⊕ 3/8 t iron ⊕ 1/3 labour ⊖ 5/2 qr wheat
    3/4 qr wheat ⊕ 3/8 t iron ⊕ 2/3 labour ⊖ 3/4 t iron

    This exercise is due to Robinson and Naqvi (1967).

23. 'For this technique (i.e. (ii) of exercise 22), the w–r curve is a straight line, because at zero rate of profit the ratio of the value of means of production to labour in the wheat and (iron) industries is the same. As a necessary consequence it follows that the relative price of the two commodities is constant at different rates of profit' (Robinson and Naqvi, 1967, p. 586). Prove this statement.

24. Analyse the effects of changing commodity and labour input coefficients on the curvature of the w–r trade-off.

Notes to Chapter 4

1. In section 4.5, I discuss the advisability of adopting such an approach.
2. Note the absence of such distinguishing marks as tildes and bars.
3. In the event of there being two positive values of r at which $f(r) = 0$, choose the smaller value.
4. The same conclusion can be drawn by putting $a_{11} < a_{22}$.
5. Alternatively, given any positive money wage, m, there are positive prices solving (4.5) if and only if r is non-negative and less than R. Note that this conclusion has been obtained without actually finding the explicit solution to (4.5).
6. Sraffa chooses a different numeraire: this choice is discussed in Chapter 5.
7. See section 1.2. In this respect, Sraffa's theory of value is neo-Ricardian.
8. In chapter III of PCMC, Sraffa initially analyses the effect on the rate of profit and the relative price of changes in the real wage rate (see PCMC, section 13, p. 12); but at the end of chapter V, he is led to reverse this practice. 'The rate of profits will therefore be treated as the independent variable' (section 44, p. 33). For purposes of exposition, I treat r as the independent variable from the outset.
9. In a general multisector model, a relative price can increase over one interval of values of r and decrease over another.

5

Price Variations and the Standard Commodity

5.1 Introduction

Though a feature of Sraffa's (neo-Ricardian) theory of value, the dependence of relative prices in general on income distribution[1] caused Ricardo insuperable analytical difficulties. To appreciate this, it is necessary to reconsider briefly the classical approach. The wealth of nations increased through production and the accumulation of capital. In his 'Essay on Profits', Ricardo (1952b) argued that the implementation of the Corn Laws would reduce the domestic rate of profit, thereby affecting the incentive for accumulation and growth adversely. The distribution of income between rent, profits and wages thus occupied a central role in Ricardo's scheme: 'To determine the laws which regulate this distribution is the principal problem in Political Economy' (Ricardo, 1951, p. 5). In the course of developing his theory of value, Ricardo came across the disconcerting fact that a rise in the real wage rate could cause not a rise in the value of all commodities, as argued by Smith, but a fall in the value of some commodities (produced with large amounts of capital relative to labour). Consequently, even if the quantity side of the economy were unaffected (i.e. the amounts of commodity outputs and means of production were constant), a change in the distribution of income would alter the size of such aggregates as net output, value of capital and profits: this follows from the fact that, as they consisted of heterogeneous commodities, these aggregates could be constructed only by evaluating their commodity components at a given set of prices. However, the price system varies with income distribution, as demonstrated in Chapters 3 and 4. In particular, a change in the real wage could so alter the value of net output that the effect on profits was indeterminate. In an attempt to overcome this problem, Ricardo sought an invariable measure of value.[2] It will be recalled from section 1.2 that Ricardo isolated two causes of changes in value: the conditions of production and the distribution of income. Accordingly, Ricardo's standard measure of value would have to be invariant to both types of change. 'Of such a measure it is impossible to be possessed' (Ricardo, 1951, p. 43). Ostensibly, the Ricardian problem was taken up by Sraffa who, assuming a constant technique, eliminated one of the two causes of variation at a stroke. The desired measure of value had to be invariant with respect to changes only in income distribution.

The purpose of this chapter is to discuss whether Sraffa's Standard Commodity, as analysed in chapters IV and V of PCMC, does solve even the restricted Ricardian problem. In section 5.2, I consider a one-sector model: as it is occasionally claimed that Sraffa's Standard System represents a multisector analogue of a one-sector model, the essential results on the simpler model should be stated at the outset. In section 5.3, I follow Sraffa's construction of the Standard Commodity, deriving its properties in section 5.4. Finally, in section 5.5, I discuss whether the Standard Commodity is an invariable measure of value.

5.2 A One-sector Model

Consider a very simple one-sector wheat model, where both the total labour force and the net output of wheat are equal to one (by choice of units). With the wheat input–output coefficient denoted by a, the price (or distribution) equation is:

$$(1+a) = w + (1+r)a \qquad (5.1)$$

where the left-hand side is the gross output of wheat (note that a is defined so that net, not gross, output of wheat is equal to one). (5.1) can obviously be rewritten as:

$$1 - w = ra \qquad (5.2)$$

When $w = 0$, $r = R = 1/a$, the maximum rate of profit. So, (5.2) is:

$$r = R(1 - w) \tag{5.3}$$

(5.1) is not really a price equation, as there are no relative prices in this model: there is only one commodity, wheat, which is output, capital, wages and profits. This makes the analysis of distribution particularly simple: an increase in one parameter is necessarily accompanied by a decrease in the other, obeying (5.3).

The purpose of Sraffa's Standard System is to extend these notions to a multisector model. The Standard Commodity is a particular basket of goods produced by means of itself and labour: in this respect, it resembles wheat in the one-sector model. Also, the Standard Commodity does not vary in value relative to its own means of production, again a property trivially satisfied by wheat in the one-sector model, but not satisfied in general either by an individual commodity or by a basket of commodities in a multisector model. This property, in Sraffa's view, gives the Standard Commodity some claim to be viewed as a good choice of numeraire.

> The necessity of having to express the price of one commodity in terms of another which is arbitrarily chosen as standard, complicates the study of the price-movements which accompany a change in distribution. It is impossible to tell of any particular price-fluctuation whether it arises from the peculiarities of the commodity which is being measured or from those of the measuring standard. (PCMC, section 23, p. 18)

Sraffa's contention is that the Standard Commodity does not possess such peculiarities.

5.3 Construction of the Standard Commodity

'The key to the movement of relative prices consequent upon a change (in distribution) lies in the inequality of the proportions in which labour and means of production are employed in the various industries' (ibid, section 15, p. 12) This has been demonstrated in 2.2 of *Result 8*. 'It is clear that if the proportion were the same in all industries no price changes could ensue, however great was the diversity of the commodity composition of the means of production in different industries' (ibid.). Take account here of Sraffa's footnote on p. 13 regarding the interpretation of the word 'proportions': in PCMC, Sraffa is referring to the value-capital/labour ratio in each industry and not the physical-capital/labour ratios.[3] As an illustration of this point, consider the following example:

1/4 qr wheat ⊕ 3/4 t iron ⊕ 3/4 labour ⊖ 1 qr wheat	(5.4a)
1/6 qr wheat ⊕ 1/4 labour ⊖ 1 t iron	(5.4b)

From (4.4) and (4.28) of Chapter 4, it follows that $p = 1/3$.[4] So the ratios of means of production to labour are:

$$\text{wheat industry: } \left(\frac{1}{4} + \frac{1}{3} \cdot \frac{3}{4}\right) / \frac{3}{4} = \frac{2}{3}$$

$$\text{iron industry: } \frac{1}{6} \Big/ \frac{1}{4} = \frac{2}{3}$$

For this example, equality holds in (4.33) or (4.42) of Chapter 4. 'For the same reason, it is impossible for prices to remain unchanged when there is inequality of "proportions"' (ibid., section 16, p. 13).

Sraffa's price equations differ from those used in earlier chapters only in the choice of numeraire. Instead of a particular commodity, he selected the actual net output of the economy as standard of value. The appropriate price equations for a two-sector model are:

$$p_1 = w_y l_1 + (1+r)(p_1 a_{11} + p_2 a_{21}) \tag{5.5a}$$

$$p_2 = w_y l_2 + (1+r)(p_1 a_{12} + p_2 a_{22}) \tag{5.5b}$$

$$1 = p_1((1 - a_{11})X_1 - a_{12}X_2) + p((1 - a_{22})X_2 - a_{21}X_1) \tag{5.5c}$$

From (4.1) and (4.3) of Chapter 4, (5.5c) is clearly equivalent to:

$$1 = p_1 F_1 + p_2 F_2 \tag{5.5d}$$

F_i being the net output of commodity i. The subscript 'y' on w refers to the fact that net output is numeraire: w_y is thus the share of wages in the value of net output. p_1 and p_2 are the relative prices of wheat and iron respectively in terms of net output.

Assume that equality does not hold in (4.42) of Chapter 4 and that all income is initially paid as wages. With $w_y = 1$ and $r = 0$, the corresponding values of p_1 and p_2 can be found from (5.5). Suppose that w_y is reduced from one and r is increased from zero. Then, by hypothesis, there is one industry with the lower proportion of labour to means of production for which the reduction in wage payments is insufficient to meet profit payments: such an industry is a deficit industry. However, there is another industry, with the higher proportion of labour to means of production, for which the proceeds of the wage reduction exceed the required profit payments: such an industry is a surplus industry. This is another way of saying that the initial prices corresponding to $w_y = 1$ and $r = 0$ are inappropriate for $w_y < 1$ and $r > 0$: relative prices must change to bring about uniform rates of wages and profits (see PCMC, section 18). More importantly, Sraffa argued:

> There must be a 'critical proportion' of labour to means of production which marked the watershed between deficit and surplus industries. An industry which employed that particular 'proportion' would show an even balance – the proceeds of the wage-reduction would provide exactly what was required for the payment of profits at the general rate. (ibid., section 17, p. 13)

A composite industry characterised by that 'proportion' would also exhibit it in its own means of production, and in its means of production of means of production, etc. To see that this must be so, assume that an industry exists with the desired 'proportion' and examine its means of production. If the 'proportion' did not apply to the aggregate means of production, *a fortiori* it could not apply to the industry. Hence, the 'proportion' must be exhibited in the successive 'layers' of means of production of the industry. The output of such an industry 'would consist of the same commodities (combined in the same proportions) as does the aggregate of its own means of production – in other words, such that both product and means of production are quantities of the self-same composite commodity' (ibid., section 24, p. 19). The last statement gives us the clue to the construction of the Standard Commodity.

Let $(X_1{}^*, X_2{}^*)$ be the basket describing the Standard Commodity, X_i^* being the gross output of commodity i, $i = 1,2$. To produce gross outputs of X_1^* and X_2^*, the means of production required are:

$$a_{11}X_1^* + a_{12}X_2^* \text{ of commodity 1}$$

$$a_{21}X_1^* + a_{22}X_2^* \text{ of commodity 2}$$

Then the Standard Commodity satisfies:

$$a_{11}X_1^* + a_{12}X_2^* = \varphi^* X_1^* \tag{5.6a}$$

$$a_{21}X_1^* + a_{22}X_2^* = \varphi^* X_2^* \tag{5.6b}$$

By *Result 4*, (5.6) has a positive solution if and only if:

$$(\varphi^* - a_{11})(\varphi^* - a_{22}) - a_{12}\, a_{21} = 0 \tag{5.7}$$

This is the same quadratic equation in φ^* as that in s encountered in section 4.2. Hence:

$$\varphi^* = s_1 = 1/(1+R) \tag{5.8}$$

(5.6) determines the unique positive ratio X_2^*/X_1^*. To fix the size of the Standard System, an appropriate normalisation can be used. Following Sraffa, I determine the absolute values of X_1^* and X_2^* by:

$$l_1X_1^* + l_2X_2^* = 1 \tag{5.9}$$

The Standard System is fixed at that level which employs the available labour force, assumed equal to one. So, X_1^*, X_2^* and φ^* solve (5.6) and (5.9). As an example, consider the following economy:

280 qr wheat ⊕ 12 t iron ⊕ 1/2 labour ⊖ 575 qr wheat (5.10a)

120 qr wheat ⊕ 8 t iron ⊕ 1/2 labour ⊖ 20 t iron (5.10b)

$$a_{11} = 280/575,\ a_{21} = 12/575,\ l_1 = 1/2.1/575;$$
$$a_{12} = 120/20,\ a_{22} = 8/20,\ l_2 = 1/2\cdot 1/20. \tag{5.11}$$

As (4.4) of Chapter 4 are satisfied, this system is productive. Then:

$$\varphi^* = s_1 = (a_{11}+a_{22} + \sqrt{(a_{11}+a_{22})^2-4(a_{11}a_{22}-a_{12}a_{21})}\ /2$$
$$= (510 + 410)/575\cdot 2 = 4/5 \qquad (5.12a)$$

So:

$$R = 1/\varphi^* - 1 = 1/4 \qquad (5.12b)$$

Now solve (5.6) with the values of the coefficients given in (5.11) and φ^* from (5.12a):

$$280X_1^*/575 + 120X_2^*/20 = 4X_1^*/5 \qquad (5.13a)$$
$$12X_1^*/575 + 8X_2^*/20 = 4X_2^*/5 \qquad (5.13b)$$

Both equations in (5.13) imply that:

$$X_1^* = 115X_2^*/6 \qquad (5.14)$$

Using (5.14) in (5.9), I obtain:

$$X_2^*/60 + X_2^*/40 = 1$$

or

$$X_2^* = 24$$

Then from (5.13):

$$X_1^* = 460 \qquad (5.15b)$$

So, multiplying (5.10a) by 460/575 = 4/5 and (5.10b) by 24/20 = 6/5, I obtain:

224 qr wheat ⊕ 48/5 t iron ⊕ 2/5 labour ⊖ 460 qr wheat (5.16a)
144 qr wheat ⊕ 48/5 t iron ⊕ 3/5 labour ⊖ 24 t iron (5.16b)

The actual net output is 175 qr wheat, as can be seen from (5.10). In the Standard System, (5.16), the net output consists of 92 qr wheat and 24/5 t iron. It is easily seen that in the Standard System:

Net output of wheat = 92 qr wheat
= 1/4.(368 qr wheat)
= *R*.(total wheat used as means of production)

Net output of iron = 24/5 t iron
= 1/4.(96/5 t iron)
= *R*.(total iron used as means of production)

5.4 Properties of the Standard System and the Standard Commodity

Suppose that the economy is actually in the proportions of the Standard System, with the Standard Net Output corresponding with the actual net output, which is the numeraire. As shown in section 5.3, the ratio of Standard Net Product to means of production is equal to R (= 1/4 in the example) for both commodities. This implies that the value ratio of net output to means of production in the Standard System is equal to R, regardless of prices. As profits are given by the rate of profits times the value of means of production, it follows that the ratio of profits to net income is given by:

$$\frac{r.\text{(value of means of production)}}{\text{value of net output}} = \frac{r}{R} \tag{5.17}$$

The value of Standard Net Output is one, by choice of numeraire. Standard Net Output is distributed as either wages or profits, the former denoted by w^*. So, I have:

$$1 = w^* + r/R$$

or

$$r = R(1 - w^*) \tag{5.18}$$

which is analogous to (5.3) above, the distribution equation for the one-sector model.

Sraffa demonstrated that (5.18) was not restricted in application solely to the Standard System, but could be derived for the actual economy as long as the Standard Net Product was chosen as numeraire. By the assumption of constant returns to scale, a change in activity levels, from the Standard to the actual system, does not affect prices and the real wage rate at a given value of r. So (5.17) is also valid for the actual economy. This establishes:

> *Result 9:* If the Standard Net Product is used as numeraire, the real wage rate–rate of profits curve is given by (5.18).

A virtue of (5.18) is its simplicity. 'Particular proportions, such as the Standard ones, may give transparency to a system and render visible what was hidden, but they cannot alter its mathematical properties' (PCMC, section 31, p. 23). Qualitatively, the w–r curve (5.18) has the same properties as that in section 4.2 where wheat is the numeraire. When applied to the same technology, both yield the same maximum rate of profit, R, and both are downward sloping. Sraffa's point is that these features can be more easily appreciated when the Standard Commodity is employed. Though he explicitly derived the w–r curve given by (5.18), Sraffa was aware of the implications of choosing another numeraire.

> It follows that if the wage is cut in terms of any commodity . . . the rate of profits will rise; and vice versa for an increase of the wage. It also follows that if the wage is cut in terms of any one commodity, it is thereby cut in terms of all; and similarly for an increase. The direction is the same in relation to all commodities, however different may be the extent. (ibid., section 49, p. 40).

In other words, $dw_{(i)}/dr < 0$ for any choice of numeraire i; $w_{(i)} = 0$ when $r = R$.

5.5 Is the Standard Commodity an Invariable Measure of Value?

In what sense can the Standard Commodity be described as an invariable measure of value? Trivially, if chosen as numeraire, it would be invariable – an observation that applies to any numeraire. At this stage, reconsider Sraffa's intuitive argument in chapter III of PCMC:

> We now revert to the 'critical' proportion which has been mentioned above as constituting the borderline between 'deficit' and 'surplus' industries. Suppose that there was an industry which employed labour and means of production in that precise proportion, so that with a wage-reduction, and *on the basis of the initial prices*, it would show an even balance of wages and profits. (PCMC, section 21, pp. 16–17, emphasis added)

It is clear from the discussion in section 5.3 that the Standard System, producing the 'balanced' commodity, was intended to be such an industry.

I now follow Sraffa's instructions in evaluating the Standard Commodity at two distinct rates of profit. Before performing these calculations, note that the price equations are given by (5.5) of section 5.3, i.e. the actual net income is numeraire. Let the initial rate of profit be r^1, with corresponding prices $p_1{}^1$, $p_2{}^1$ and real wage $w_y{}^1$. After the reduction in the wage rate, let $r = r^2 > r^1$, $w_y = w_y{}^2 < w_y{}^1$. Then, Sraffa's hypothesis is that the Standard Commodity breaks even at the price system r^2, $w_y{}^2$, $p_1{}^1$, $p_2{}^1$ as well as at the initial price system. This means that when evaluated at the former, the Standard Commodity has the same total costs of production, inclusive of profits at the prevailing rate, as when it is evaluated at the latter. To see the implications of this hypothesis, first of all evaluate the Standard Commodity at the initial price system. Multiply (5.5a) of section 5.3 by $X_1{}^*$, (5.5b) by $X_2{}^*$, add and calculate at r^1, to obtain:

$$p_1{}^1X_1{}^* + p_2{}^1X_2{}^* = w_y{}^1(l_1X_1{}^* + l_2X_2{}^*) + (1+r^1)[p_1{}^1(a_{11}X_1{}^*$$
$$+ a_{12}X_2{}^*) + p_2{}^1(a_{21}X_1{}^* + a_{22}X_2{}^*)] \tag{5.19a}$$
$$\equiv w_y{}^1 L^* + (1+r^1)K^* \tag{5.19b}$$

where L^* and K^* are defined as the bracketed terms multiplying $w_y{}^1$ and $(1+r^1)$ respectively in (5.19a). Now evaluate the Standard Commodity at the price system r^2, $w_y{}^2$, $p_1{}^1$, $p_2{}^1$. By hypothesis, the Standard Commodity breaks even so that:

$$p_1{}^1X_1{}^* + p_2{}^1X_2{}^* = w_y{}^1L^* + (1+r^1)K^*$$

$$= w_y^2 L^* + (1+r^2)K^* \qquad (5.20)$$

Subtracting (5.19) from (5.20):

$$0 = (w_y^2 - w_y^1)L^* + (r^2 - r^1)K^*$$

or

$$-K^*/L^* = (w_y^2 - w_y^1)/(r^2 - r^1) \qquad (5.21)$$

Now from the price equations, (5.5), and the quantity equations, (5.6) and (5.9) of section 5.3, it can be shown that:

$$K^*/L^* = w_y^1/(R - r^1) \qquad (5.22)$$

(5.21) and (5.22) imply that:

$$w_y^1(R - r^1) = w_y^2/(R - r^2)$$

for all feasible choices of r^1 and r^2, i.e.

$$w_y/(R - r) = b, \text{ a constant} \qquad (5.23)$$

for all feasible values of r. Put $r = 0$ in (5.23): then $w_y = 1$ and $b = 1/R$. So (5.23) becomes:

$$w_y = 1 - r/R$$

or

$$r = R(1 - w_y) \qquad (5.24)$$

Now (5.24) is of the same form as (5.18), where the Standard Net Product is numeraire. However, I have been operating with the actual national income as numeraire. So I have proved that, if the Standard Commodity satisfies Sraffa's hypothesis, namely that (5.20) holds, the *w–r* curve, in terms of actual national income, is of the form (5.24).

Suppose, on the other hand, that the *w–r* curve obtained from the price equations (5.5) is given by (5.24). Then:

$$w_y^i + r^i/R = 1 \quad i = 1,2 \qquad (5.25a)$$

or

$$w_y^i/(R - r^i) = 1/R \quad i = 1,2 \tag{5.25b}$$

Now from (5.22):

$$K^*/L^* = w_y^1/(R - r^1) = 1/R \tag{5.26}$$

using (5.25b). Equation (5.19) obviously holds. I now wish to see whether the Standard Commodity breaks even at the price system r^2, w_y^2, p_1^1, p_2^1. So evaluate:

$$\begin{aligned} w_y^2L^* + (1+r^2)K^* &= L^*(w_y^2 + (1+r^2)K^*/L^*) \\ &= L^*(w_y^2 + (1+r^2)/R) && \text{using (5.26)} \\ &= L^*(w_y^2 + r^2/R + 1/R) \\ &= L^*(w_y^1 + r^1/R + 1/R) && \text{using (5.25a)} \\ &= L^*(w_y^1 + (1+r^1)K^*/L^*) && \text{using (5.26)} \\ &= w_y^1L^* + (1+r^1)K^* \\ &= p_1^1X_1^* + p_2^1X_2^* && (5.25) \end{aligned}$$

using (5.19). Hence, (5.20) holds: that is, the Standard Commodity breaks even at the price system r^2, w_y^2, p_1^1, p_2^1.

So, I have proved that the Standard Commodity satisfies Sraffa's hypothesis if and only if the *w–r* curve is of the form (5.24). Obviously, there is no difficulty with this line of argument if the Standard Net Product is chosen as numeraire. However, the purpose of Sraffa's analysis is to derive the Standard Commodity from the price equations (5.5), not from these price equations:

$$p_1 = w^*l_1 + (1+r)(p_1a_{11} + p_2a_{21}) \tag{5.28a}$$

$$p_2 = w^*l_2 + (1+r)(p_1a_{12} + p_2a_{22}) \tag{5.28b}$$

$$1 = p_1[(1-a_{11})X_1^* - a_{12}X_2^*] + p_2\,[(1-a_{22})X_2^* - a_{21}X_1^*] \tag{5.28c}$$

(The asterisk denoting that the Standard Net Product is numeraire.) I summarise this discussion in

Result 10: The Standard Commodity satisfies Sraffa's hypothesis – that is, it breaks even at r^1, $w_y^{\ 1}$, $p_1^{\ 1}$, $p_2^{\ 1}$ and at r^2, $w_y^{\ 2}$, $p_1^{\ 1}$, $p_2^{\ 1}$ – if and only if the w–r curve, in terms of actual national income, is of the form:
$r = R(1 - w_y)$.

As an illustration, consider the following numerical example:

$$1 \text{ t iron} \oplus 1/2 \text{ labour} \ominus 1 \text{ qr wheat} \qquad (5.29a)$$

$$1/4 \text{ qr wheat} \oplus 1/2 \text{ labour} \ominus 1 \text{ t iron} \qquad (5.29b)$$

From (5.29), I have these coefficients:

$$a_{11} = 0 = a_{22},\ a_{12} = 1/4,\ a_{21} = 1,\ l_1 = 1/2 = l_2 \qquad (5.30)$$

Net output consists of 3/4 qr wheat, which is the numeraire:

$$3p_1/4 = 1 \qquad (5.31)$$

The price equations corresponding to (5.29) and (5.31) are:

$$(1+r)p_2 + w_y/2 = p_1 \qquad (5.32a)$$

$$(1+r)p_1/4 + w_y/2 = p_2 \qquad (5.32b)$$

Solving (5.31) and (5.32), I obtain:

$$w_y = (1 - (1+r)^2/4)/(3(r+2)/8) \qquad (5.33a)$$

$$p_2 = (r+5)/(3r+6) \qquad (5.33b)$$

Applying the data in (5.30) to (5.6) and (5.9), I obtain:

$$\varphi^* = 1/2,\ R = 1,\ X_1^* = 2/3,\ X_2^* = 4/3 \qquad (5.34)$$

Multiplying (5.29a) by 2/3, (5.29b) by 4/3, I obtain as the Standard System:

$$2/3 \text{ t iron} \oplus 1/3 \text{ labour} \ominus 2/3 \text{ qr wheat} \qquad (5.35a)$$

$$1/3 \text{ qr wheat} \oplus 2/3 \text{ labour} \ominus 4/3 \text{ t iron} \qquad (5.35b)$$

Suppose that, initially, $r^1 = 0$ with $w_y^{\ 1} = 1$, $p_1^{\ 1} = 4/3$, $p_2^{\ 1} = 5/6$ from (5.32). Now assume that $r^2 = 1/10$, $w_y^{\ 2} = 275/315$ and evaluate the wheat and iron industries in (5.29) at the initial prices in accordance with Sraffa's hypothesis. The wheat industry's receipts are $1 \cdot p_1^{\ 1} = 4/3$ and its costs are:

$$11/10 \cdot 1 \cdot p_2^{\ 1} + 1/2 \cdot w_y^{\ 2} = 1713/1260 > 4/3$$

So, the wheat industry is a 'deficit' industry. The iron industry's receipts are $1 \cdot p_2^{\ 1} = 5/6$ and its costs are:

$$11/10 \cdot 1/4 \cdot p_1^{\ 1} + 1/2 \cdot w_y^{\ 2} = 510/630 < 5/6$$

So, the iron industry is a 'surplus' industry. However, it is neither the wheat nor the iron industry which is supposed to break even but the Standard System. The Standard System's receipts are:

$$2/3 \cdot p_1^{\ 1} + 4/3 \cdot p_2^{\ 1} = 2$$

and its costs are:

$$11/10 \cdot (2/3 \cdot p_2^{\ 1} + 1/3 \cdot p_1^{\ 1}) + 1 \cdot w_y^{\ 2} = 1251/630 < 2$$

This implies that the Standard System is a 'surplus' industry. So, in this case, the Standard System does not appear to possess the invariance property claimed for it by Sraffa. The numerical example illustrates *Result 10*, for the w–r curve (5.33a) is not of the form (5.24).

There is one caveat. In both the general statement of the analysis, *Result 10*, and the numerical example, I have taken the second wage rate, $w_y^{\ 2}$, to be that on the w–r curve corresponding to the second rate of profit, r^2. Sraffa stated parenthetically in section 16: '*Nothing* is assumed at the moment as to what rate of profit corresponds to what wage reduction; all that is required at this stage is that there should be a uniform wage rate and a uniform rate of profits throughout the system' (emphasis added). In the example, it is possible to find a wage rate, w^2, such that the Standard System breaks even at r^2 $(= 1/10)$, w^2, $p_1^{\ 1}$ $(= 4/3)$, $p_2^{\ 1} = 5/6$. For:

$$\text{Receipts} = 2 = 11/10 \cdot (2/3 \cdot 5/6 + 1/3 \cdot 4/3) + 1 \cdot w^2$$
$$= \text{Costs}$$

implies $w^2 = 9/10$. Which wage rate should be chosen – $w_y{}^2$ or w^2 or any other feasible value of w between 0 and 1. If it is not to be $w_y{}^2$, Sraffa throws no light on the question.

5.6 Conclusion

In section 5.5, I have raised doubts about Sraffa's method of constructing the Standard Commodity. It cannot be done unless the system is already in the Standard proportions – in which case, of course, it does not need to be done. As any numeraire is, by definition, invariant, the usefulness of choosing a particular commodity basket depends on the properties that can be derived. For the Standard Commodity, it was shown in section 5.4 that the w–r curve has the simple form given in (5.18). However, this does not appear to be a more profound property than that illustrated in *Result 8.1*.

Commentary

This chapter is based on chapters III–V of PCMC. 'On an invariable measure of value', see chapter I of Ricardo's *Principles* (Ricardo, 1951) and Ricardo's essay on 'Absolute and Exchangeable Value' (Ricardo, 1952b).

For further discussion of The Standard System, see the review of PCMC by Harcourt and Massaro (1964); more mathematically demanding are Newman (1962), already referred to in Chapter 1, and Pasinetti (1977b). Levine (1974) is not concerned solely with the Standard System. Criticism of the Standard System, from two different points of view, is provided by Burmeister (1968, 1980), on the one hand, and Broome (1977) and Flaschel (1984), on the other.

The connection between Sraffa and Marx is discussed by Meek (1961), Eatwell (1975), Steedman (1977) and Kurz (1979).

Exercises

1. Establish (5.21).

2. Derive (5.32) and (5.33).

3. Consider the economy described in (5.4):
   (i) Solve the price equations with the actual net output as numeraire.
   (ii) Construct the Standard System.
   (iii) Does the Standard System satisfy Sraffa's hypothesis, stated in *Result 10*?

4. Repeat exercise 3 for the following economy:

   4/15 qr wheat ⊕ 4/5 t iron ⊕ 4/5 labour ⊖ 16/15 qr wheat
   2/15 qr wheat ⊕ 1/5 labour ⊖ 4/5 t iron.

5. Repeat exercise 3 for the following economy:

   9 qr wheat ⊕ 6 t iron ⊕ 2/3 labour ⊖ 18 qr wheat
   4 qr wheat ⊕ 16 t iron ⊕ 1/3 labour ⊖ 24 t iron

6. Repeat exercise 3 for the following economy:

   54 qr wheat ⊕ 36 t iron ⊕ 4 labour ⊖ 108 qr wheat
   36 qr wheat ⊕ 144 t iron ⊕ 3 labour ⊖ 216 t iron

7. 'Sraffa's main result is that when the numeraire is stated in terms of the Standard Commodity prices are invariant with respect to a wage change if and only if $r = R(1 - w)$.' Discuss.

8. 'Now let us consider the meaning and/or uses of the Standard Commodity. In any state of technology, there will be a subset of all commodities (the basic commodities) from which, when the economy is in equilibrium, one can construct a (weighted) composite whose rate of exchange with any given commodity will be invariant with respect to changes in the ratio of wages to the rate of profit' (Reder, 1961, pp. 691–2). Discuss this statement.

9. What is the relation between the wage rate and the rate of profit when the wage is advanced and the Standard Commodity is used as numeraire? (cf. exercise 18, Chapter 4.)

10. What is the relation between the total amount of labour embodied in the Standard Net Product and the amount of direct labour required to produce it?

11. Consider the following economy:

    1/3 qr wheat ⊕ 1/2 labour ⊖ 1 qr wheat
    2/3 qr wheat ⊕ 1/2 labour ⊖ 1 t iron

    (i) Which commodities are basic?
    (ii) What is the net output of the economy?

(iii) Do both wheat and iron form the Standard Commodity? If not, why not?
(iv) Let net output be the numeraire. Write down and solve the price equations.
(v) Suppose that $w_y = 1$, $r = 0$ initially. Find the corresponding prices. Next let $w_y = 4/5$. What is the corresponding value of r from the w–r curve? Following the method of section 5.5, determine whether the Standard Commodity is a surplus or deficit industry at $w_y = 4/5$, the corresponding r and the initial prices. Are the individual industries surplus or deficit industries?
(vi) Let the Standard Commodity be the numeraire. Solve the price equations.
(vii) What effect does changing the numeraire have on the surplus/deficit nature of each industry? (Use (v).)
(viii) Do you think that changing the numeraire should affect the surplus/deficit nature of an industry? Give reasons.

12. Solve the equations:

$$X_1^* = (1+r)(a_{11}X_1^* + a_{12}X_2^*) + F_1^*$$

$$X_2^* = (1+r)(a_{21}X_1^* + a_{22}X_2^*) + F_2^*$$

where F_1^* and F_2^* are in the proportions of the Standard Commodity. Are there any restrictions on r?

Notes to Chapter 5

1. As seen in Chapter 4.
2. Concomitant with which was his distinction between absolute and exchangeable value.
3. See exercise 20, Chapter 4, for the latter.
4. The numerical example in (5.4) may be of use in answering exercise 20, Chapter 4.

6 Choice of Technique

6.1 Introduction

In Chapters 2–5, I assumed that there was only one process available to each sector. Consequently, there was only one technique available to the economy as a whole. I now relax this assumption in the simplest possible way by assuming that just one sector, say the second, has two processes, denoted by (IIα) and (IIβ). With the first sector's process denoted by (I), there are two techniques of production:

(α) consists of (I) and (IIα); and

(β) consists of (I) and (IIβ).

For this simple model, choice of technique is equivalent to choice of process by the second industry. I devote sections 6.2–6.4 to the analysis of this model. Then, in section 6.5, I extend the model by permitting the second sector to have an arbitrary finite number of processes. A more substantial generalisation is made in section 6.6, where both sectors can have an arbitrary finite number of processes. In the two final sections, I draw some implications from the theory expounded in this chapter.

It is clearly necessary to state at the outset the criterion to be employed in choosing between techniques. Following Sraffa (PCMC, sections 92 and 93), I use the criterion of cost-minimisation. To illustrate its application, suppose that (α) is initially employed at a feasible rate of profit $\bar{r}$ ($< R^{\alpha}$, the maximum rate of profit of technique (α)), with corresponding real wage, $w^{\alpha}(\bar{r})$, and prices $p_1^{\alpha}(\bar{r}) = 1$, $p_2^{\alpha}(\bar{r})$ (the first commodity being numeraire as in Chapter 4). Suppose that process (IIβ) becomes available to the second sector. A capitalist in that sector would evaluate the process at the prevailing price system. There are three possibilities:

(i) (IIβ) is more expensive than (IIα), in which case there is no justification for switching to the new process;

(ii) (IIβ) reduces costs, in which case the capitalist switches his process of production because he can obtain a supernormal rate of profit, at least in the short run;

(iii) (IIβ) breaks even, so that it will be a matter of indifference to the capitalist whether he uses (IIα) or (IIβ).

I now examine each of these possibilities in more detail. In case (i), the capitalist has no reason to adopt process (IIβ). Technique (α) thus appears to be a cost-minimising technique at $\bar{r}$, $w^{\alpha}(\bar{r})$, $p_1^{\alpha}(\bar{r})$ and $p_2^{\alpha}(\bar{r})$. In case (ii), process (IIβ) reduces the second sector's costs at the prevailing price system: thus (α) cannot be a cost-minimising technique at the given rate of profit, prices and wage rate. Suppose that the switch from (IIα) to (IIβ) is effected. Assume, further, that (β)'s price system is established at the same rate of profit, $\bar{r}$. Now, the capitalist in the second sector evaluates (IIα) at the new price system – $\bar{r}$, $w^{\beta}(\bar{r})$, $p_1^{\beta}(\bar{r}) = 1$ and $p_2^{\beta}(\bar{r})$ – to see if it is more profitable than (IIβ). Clearly, the same three possibilities arise when (IIα) is evaluated at (β)'s price system as when (IIβ) is evaluated at (α)'s price system: that is, (IIα) is cheaper than, more expensive than or as cheap as (IIβ). If (IIα) is cheaper than (IIβ) at (β)'s prices, the capitalist would be justified in switching back to the original process: in such a situation, there would be continual switching between (IIα) and (IIβ), (that is, techniques (α) and (β)) implying that choice of technique is indeterminate. On the other hand, if (IIα) is more expensive than (IIβ) at (β)'s prices, there would be no justification in switching back to (IIα): thus, (β) appears to be a cost-minimising technique at $\bar{r}$, $w^{\beta}(\bar{r})$, $p_1^{\beta}(\bar{r})$ and $p_2^{\beta}(\bar{r})$. If (IIα) breaks even at (β)'s price system, the capitalist is indifferent between employing (IIα) and (IIβ); however, I supposed that (IIβ) reduced costs at (α)'s price system, implying that (IIβ) was preferred to (IIα). This creates another difficulty for the theory of choice of technique, as there appears to be indeterminancy. Having exhausted the possibilities that can arise with (i) and (ii), consider finally (iii). If (IIβ) breaks even at (α)'s price system, a capitalist in the second sector is indifferent between (IIα) and (IIβ). Suppose that the switch to (IIβ) is effected and (β)'s price system is established at the same rate of profit. When (IIα) is evaluated at (β)'s price system, the analogues of (i)–(iii) arise. If (IIα) is more expensive than (IIβ), there is no reason to switch back to the original process. Thus, there is an argument to support the view that (β) is a cost-minimising technique at $\bar{r}$, $w^{\beta}(\bar{r})$, $p_1^{\beta}(\bar{r})$ and $p_2^{\beta}(\bar{r})$. Such an argument should be qualified by the conclusion drawn from (iii) when (IIβ) was evaluated at (α)'s prices – namely, that it is a matter of indifference whether the capitalist employs (IIα) or (IIβ). This raises another question for the theory of choice of technique. A similar question arises if (IIα) reduces costs at (β)'s prices: for then, the capitalist has an incentive to switch back to (IIα) whereas, if that process were initially employed, he would be indifferent between the two. It is only when (IIα) breaks even at (β)'s prices that no potential contradiction arises with (IIβ)'s breaking even at (α)'s prices.

Each of (i)–(iii) can arise when (IIβ) is evaluated at (α)'s prices. The analogues of (i)–(iii) can arise when (IIα)is evaluated at (β)'s prices. So, there is a total of nine possibilities. The purpose of the theory of choice of technique is to establish which of these possibilities can occur and which cannot. Generally speaking, this means consideration of the following questions:

(a) Is choice of technique determinate at each feasible value of *r*?

(b) If so, how many cost-minimising techniques can there be at each feasible value of *r*?

(a) is recognised as the question of existence, (b) that of uniqueness.

In answering these questions, it is necessary to evaluate both techniques at both sets of prices. For if (IIβ) is cheaper than (IIα) at (α)'s prices, it does not immediately follow that (IIα) is more expensive than (IIβ) at (β)'s prices: this must be derived. The necessity of taking this approach will be appreciated once it is realised than (β) could equally be the original technique, with (IIα) the new technique that becomes available to the second sector: in such a situation, it would be necessary to evaluate (IIα) at (β)'s price system initially. There is a further point to be emphasised concerning the rate of profit at which the calculations are performed. It was assumed in the discussion above that r was fixed at $\bar{r}$ in the comparison between equilibria. This does not, of course, imply that the rate of profit is unaffected by the choice of technique. The particular assumption – that the rate of profit is constant – is made so that the question of choice of technique at a given rate of profit can be answered. This method of analysis is completely general. As will be seen in Chapters 9–11, it can be applied to *any* model where the question of choice of technique arises.

6.2 Preliminaries

It was implicitly assumed in section 6.1 that process (IIβ) produced the same commodity as (IIα) by means of the same inputs.[1] Technique (α) is thus described by the sextuple $(a_{11}, a_{21}, l_1; a_{12}^{\alpha}, a_{22}^{\alpha}, l_2^{\alpha}) \equiv (\text{I}; \text{II}\alpha)$, and (β) by the sextuple $(a_{11}, a_{21}, l_1; a_{12}^{\beta}, a_{22}^{\beta}, l_2^{\beta}) \equiv (\text{I}; \text{II}\beta)$. The theory developed in Chapter 4 can be applied to (α) and (β) separately, assuming that both are productive. So, I have with the first commodity as numeraire:

$$\begin{aligned} w^{\alpha} &= f^{\alpha}(r)/g^{\alpha}(r) \qquad & w^{\beta} &= f^{\beta}(r)/g^{\beta}(r) \\ p^{\alpha} &= h^{\alpha}(r)/g^{\alpha}(r) \qquad & p^{\beta} &= h^{\beta}(r)/g^{\beta}(r) \end{aligned} \tag{6.1}$$

where:

$$\begin{aligned} f^{\iota}(r) \equiv\ & (1 - (1 + r)a_{11})(1 - (1 + r)a_{22}^{\iota}) \\ & - (1 + r)^2 a_{12}^{\iota} a_{21} \end{aligned} \tag{6.2a}$$

$$g^{\iota}(r) \equiv l_1(1 - (1 + r)a_{22}^{\iota}) + (1 + r)l_2^{\iota} a_{21} \tag{6.2b}$$

$$h^{\iota}(r) \equiv l_2^{\iota}(1 - (1 + r)a_{11}) + (1 + r)l_1 a_{12}^{\iota} \tag{6.2c}$$

$$\iota = \alpha, \beta.$$

There are two sets of calculations, using (6.1) and (6.2), that will be employed in the analysis of choice of technique. First:

$$\begin{aligned} w^{\alpha} - w^{\beta} &= f^{\alpha}(r)/g^{\alpha}(r) - f^{\beta}(r)/g^{\beta}(r) \\ &= (1 + r)a_{21}(l_2^{\beta} f^{\alpha}(r) - l_2^{\alpha} f^{\beta}(r) \\ &\qquad - (1 + r)l_1 k(r))/g^{\alpha}(r)g^{\beta}(r) \end{aligned} \tag{6.3}$$

where

$$k(r) \equiv a_{12}^{\alpha}(1 - (1 + r)a_{22}^{\beta}) - a_{12}^{\beta}(1 - (1 + r)a_{22}^{\alpha}) \tag{6.4}$$

Second:

$$p^{\beta} - p^{\alpha} = h^{\beta}(r)/g^{\beta}(r) - h^{\alpha}(r)/g^{\alpha}(r)$$

$$= l_1(l_2^{\beta}f^{\alpha}(r) - l_2^{\alpha}f^{\beta}(r) - (1 + r)l_1k(r))/g^{\alpha}(r)g^{\beta}(r) \tag{6.5}$$

From (6.3) and (6.5):

$$p^{\beta} - p^{\alpha} = l_1(w^{\alpha} - w^{\beta})/(1 + r)a_{21} \tag{6.6a}$$

so that:[2]

$$\text{sign}(p^{\beta} - p^{\alpha}) = \text{sign}(w^{\alpha} - w^{\beta}) \tag{6.6b}$$

6.3 Choice of Technique: Part 1

Having completed the preliminaries, I can now attend to the question of choice of technique. As explained in section 6.1, I assume that (α) is initially employed at a feasible rate of profit $\bar{r}$, when (IIβ) becomes available to the second sector. Let $c_2(\beta\text{: }\alpha)$ denote the cost of operating (IIβ) at (α)'s prices, i.e.[3]

$$c_2(\beta{:}\alpha) \equiv (1 + \bar{r})(a_{12}^{\beta} + p^{\alpha}a_{22}^{\beta}) + w^{\alpha}l_2^{\beta} \tag{6.7}$$

Let $s_2(\beta{:}\alpha)$ denote the surplus or loss, relative to normal profits, of operating (IIβ) at (α)'s prices, i.e.

$$s_2(\beta{:}\alpha) \equiv p^{\alpha} - c_2(\beta{:}\alpha) \tag{6.8}$$

From (6.7) and (6.8):

$$s_2(\beta{:}\alpha) = p^{\alpha} - (1 + \bar{r})(a_{12}^{\beta} + p^{\alpha}a_{22}^{\beta}) - w^{\alpha}l_2^{\beta}$$

$$= (1 - (1 + \bar{r})a_{22}^{\beta})p^{\alpha} - (1 + \bar{r})a_{12}^{\beta} - w^{\alpha}l_2^{\beta} \tag{6.9}$$

The definitions (6.7) and (6.8) permit a proper specification of the problem to be considered. The criterion for choice of technique is cost-minimisation, a concept hitherto defined only informally. It is now time to offer:

Definition 3: A technique $(\theta) = (\text{I}, \text{II}\theta)$ is cost-minimising at a feasible rate of profit $\bar{r}$ $(< R^{\theta})$ if and only if:

$$s_2(\varphi{:}\theta) < 0 \tag{6.10}$$

for any other technique $(\varphi) = (\text{I}, \text{II}\varphi)$.

Inequality (6.10) states that the condition for (θ) to be cost-minimising is that any process $(\text{II}\varphi)$ makes losses at (θ)'s price system. In the model being analysed, the only choices for θ are α and β; similarly for φ.

Substituting from (6.1) into (6.9), I obtain after straightforward manipulations:

$$s_2(\beta{:}\alpha) = (l_2^{\alpha} f^{\beta}(\bar{r}) - l_2^{\beta} f^{\alpha}(\bar{r}) + (1 + \bar{r}) l_1 k(\bar{r}))/g^{\alpha}(\bar{r}) \tag{6.11}$$

From (6.3) and (6.11):

$$\text{sign } s_2(\beta{:}\alpha) = \text{sign}(w^{\beta} - w^{\alpha}) \tag{6.12}$$

as $g^{\iota}(r) > 0$ for feasible r, $\iota = \alpha, \beta$. Suppose that $s_2(\beta{:}\alpha) > 0$; then $(\text{II}\beta)$ reduces costs at (α)'s prices – clearly, (α) is not cost-minimising. Assume that the switch is made and (β)'s price system is established at $\bar{r}$. Now evaluate $(\text{II}\alpha)$ at (β)'s prices, i.e. calculate:

$$s_2(\alpha{:}\ \beta) \equiv p_2^{\beta} - c_2(\alpha{:}\ \beta) \tag{6.13}$$

where $c_2(\alpha{:}\beta)$ and $s_2(\alpha{:}\beta)$ are defined in the same way as $c_2(\beta{:}\alpha)$ and $s_2(\beta{:}\alpha)$ respectively. (6.13) becomes:

$$s_2(\alpha{:}\beta) = (1 - (1 + \bar{r}) a_{22}^{\alpha}) p^{\beta} - (1 + \bar{r}) a_{12}^{\alpha} - w^{\beta} l_2^{\alpha} \tag{6.14}$$

Substituting from (6.1), I obtain after straightforward manipulations:

$$s_2(\alpha{:}\beta) = (l_2^{\beta} f^{\alpha}(\bar{r}) - l_2^{\alpha} f^{\beta}(\bar{r}) - (1 + \bar{r}) l_1 k(\bar{r}))/g^{\beta}(\bar{r}) \tag{6.15}$$

From (6.3), it follows that:

$$\text{sign } s_2(\alpha{:}\beta) = \text{sign}(w^\alpha - w^\beta) \tag{6.16}$$

Note that, if $s_2(\beta{:}\alpha) > 0$, it follows from (6.12) and (6.16) that $s_2(\alpha{:}\beta) < 0$. Hence, (IIα) makes losses at (β)'s price system.

In general, I have from (6.11) and (6.16):

$$\text{sign } s_2(\beta{:}\alpha) = (-1)\text{sign } s_2(\alpha{:}\beta) \tag{6.17}$$

This is the fundamental equation for the theory of choice of technique in single-product industries, circulating capital models with only produced means of production.

Neither I nor a capitalist in the second sector know the sign of $s_2(\beta{:}\alpha)$ *a priori*.[4] It is necessary to perform the evaluation. If $s_2(\beta{:}\alpha) > 0$, it is clear that (α) cannot be cost-minimising. (6.17) tells me and a capitalist in the second sector that $s_2(\alpha{:}\beta) < 0$, that is, (IIα) neither breaks even nor reduces costs at (β)'s prices. In such a circumstance, (β) is the cost-minimising technique: note that it is the *unique* cost-minimising technique. Next, let $s_2(\beta{:}\alpha) < 0$. Then (α) is cost-minimising by *Definition 3*. (6.17) informs me and a capitalist in the second sector that (β) cannot also be cost-minimising: for, if (β) is employed, it follows from (6.17), in this case, that $s_2(\alpha{:}\beta) > 0$. So, if $s_2(\beta{:}\alpha) < 0$, (α) is the unique cost-minimising technique. Finally, suppose that $s_2(\beta{:}\alpha) = 0$. (α) is cost-minimising because (β) does not actually reduce costs at (α)'s prices. From (6.17), it follows that $s_2(\alpha{:}\beta) = 0$, which implies that (β) is also cost-minimising.

To summarise the discussion: there are three possibilities for the sign of $s_2(\beta{:}\alpha)$. If $s_2(\beta{:}\alpha) > 0$, (β) is the unique cost-minimising technique; if $s_2(\beta{:}\alpha) < 0$, (α) is the unique cost-minimising technique; if $s_2(\beta{:}\alpha) = 0$, both (α) and (β) are cost-minimising techniques. In each case, choice of technique is determinate, being unique in each of the first two. Questions (a) and (b), posed in section 6.1, have thus been answered. I have:

> *Result 11:* In the single-product industries, circulating capital model considered above, a cost-minimising technique exists at each feasible value of r. If $s_2(\varphi{:}\theta) >$ (resp. $<$) 0, (φ) (resp. (θ)) is the unique cost-minimising technique. If $s_2(\theta{:}\varphi) = 0$, both ($\varphi$) and ($\theta$) are cost-minimising, $\varphi, \theta = \alpha, \beta$.

To complete the derivation of this result, there are some technical points to be considered. First, $\bar{r}$ is feasible for (α), by assumption, but is it also feasible for (β)? Suppose that (α) is initially employed and that $s_2(\beta:\alpha) > 0$. This justifies the switch to (β). Could it happen that $\bar{r} > R^\beta$? I now examine this possibility. As $s_2(\beta:\alpha) > 0$, I have on evaluating both processes in (β) at (α)'s prices:

$$1 = w^\alpha l_1 + (1 + \bar{r})(a_{11} + p^\alpha a_{21}) \tag{6.18a}$$

$$p^\alpha > w^\alpha l_2 + (1 + \bar{r})(a^\beta_{12} + p^\alpha a^\beta_{22}) \tag{6.18b}$$

As $l_1 > 0$, $l^\beta_2 > 0$, (18) can be rewritten as:

$$1 > (1 + \bar{r})(a_{11} + p^\alpha a_{21})$$

$$p^\alpha > (1 + \bar{r})(a^\beta_{12} + p^\alpha a^\beta_{22})$$

or

$$(1 - (1 + \bar{r})a_{11}) > (1 + \bar{r})p^\alpha a_{21} \tag{6.19a}$$

$$(1 - (1 + \bar{r})a^\beta_{22})p^\alpha > (1 + \bar{r})a^\beta_{12} \tag{6.19b}$$

As r is feasible for (α), it follows from (6.19a) that:

$$(1 - (1 + \bar{r})a_{11}) > 0 \tag{6.20a}$$

(Equivalently, this inequality can be derived by noting that the right-hand side of (6.19a) is positive.) As the right-hand side of (6.19b) is positive and $p^\alpha > 0$, it follows that:

$$1 - (1 + \bar{r})a^\beta_{22} > 0 \tag{6.20b}$$

From (6.19b) and (6.20b), I obtain:

$$p^\alpha > (1 + \bar{r})a^\beta_{12}/(1 - (1 + \bar{r})a^\beta_{22})$$

which, when substituted into (19a), yields:

$$(1 - (1 + \bar{r})a_{11}) > (1 + \bar{r})^2 a^\beta_{12} a_{21}/(1 - (1 + \bar{r})a^\beta_{22})$$

or

$$(1 - (1 + \bar{r})a_{11})(1 - (1 + \bar{r})a^{\beta}_{22}) - (1 + \bar{r})^2 a^{\beta}_{12} a_{21} > 0 \tag{6.20c}$$

From (4.6) of Chapter 4, it is easily seen that (6.20a)–(6.20c) are the necessary and sufficient conditions for $\bar{r}$ to be feasible for technique (β). To conclude: if $s_2(\beta{:}\alpha) > 0$ at $\bar{r}$, $\bar{r}$ is feasible for (β). There are two other possibilities: $s_2(\beta{:}\alpha) = 0$ and $s_2(\beta{:}\alpha) < 0$. If $s_2(\beta{:}\alpha) = 0$, the argument in (6.18)–(6.20) can be repeated to yield: $\bar{r} < R^\beta$ if $w^\alpha > 0$; $\bar{r} = R^\beta$ if $w^\alpha = 0$. This leaves $s_2(\beta{:}\alpha) < 0$. If (α) is employed initially, there is no reason to switch to (β). However, my purpose is to demonstrate that, if (β) were chosen initially, (α) would be preferred to it. $s_2(\beta{:}\alpha) < 0$ at $\bar{r}$ is consistent with both $\bar{r} \leqslant R^\beta$ and $\bar{r} > R^\beta$. If $\bar{r} \leqslant R^\beta$, (β)'s price system is positive at $\bar{r}$; in particular, $g^\beta(\bar{r}) > 0$. Then, the theory developed in (6.7)–(6.17) and summarised in *Result 11* applies: if (β) is initially employed at $\bar{r}$, (α) reduces costs and is thus the cost-minimising technique. If $\bar{r} > R^\beta$, (β) cannot support positive prices and wage rate at $\bar{r}$. So, (β) could not be observed in the first place. In either case, (α) is the cost-minimising technique.

Discussion of these technicalities is necessary because the derivation of *Result 11* is based on the implicit assumption that $\bar{r}$ is feasible for both techniques. It is reasonable to suppose that $\bar{r} \leqslant R^\alpha$ in order to start the analysis. However, it is not known at the outset whether $\bar{r}$ is feasible for (β). The significance of (6.18)–(6.20) is that they ensure that $\bar{r} \leqslant R^\beta$ if $s_2(\beta{:}\alpha) > 0$ at $\bar{r}$. I have also examined the implications of $s_2(\beta{:}\alpha) \leqslant 0$. So, if $\bar{r} \leqslant \min(R^\alpha, R^\beta)$, it is feasible for both techniques. If $R^\beta < \bar{r} \leqslant R^\alpha$, the question of choice of technique does not arise, as $\bar{r}$ is feasible only for (α), which must therefore be the cost-minimising technique.

Result 11 is the fundamental theorem on choice of technique for single-product industries, circulating capital models. Having derived it, I can now characterise cost-minimising techniques. To illustrate, suppose that $s_2(\beta{:}\alpha) > 0$. Then from (6.12):

$$w^\beta > w^\alpha \tag{6.21}$$

In this case, (β) is the cost-minimising technique by *Result 11* and, from (6.21), supports the higher real wage. Next suppose that $s_2(\beta{:}\alpha) < 0$. Again from (6.12):

$$w^\beta < w^\alpha \tag{6.22}$$

In this case, (α) is the cost-minimising technique by *Result 11* and, by (6.22), supports the higher real wage. Finally, suppose that $s_2(\beta{:}\alpha) = 0$. From (6.12):

$$w^{\beta} = w^{\alpha} \tag{6.23}$$

In this case, both techniques are cost-minimising, each breaking even at the other's prices. From (6.23), they support the same real wage. It follows from *Result 11* and (6.21)–(6.23) that the cost-minimising technique supports the higher real wage. This provides one charaterisation of the optimal technique.

It is natural to enquire if the theory of choice of technique, and the characterisation just derived, depend on the choice of numeraire. To answer this question, examine the effect on $s_2(\beta{:}\alpha)$ of changing the numeraire from the first to the second commodity. With the first commodity as numeraire (indicated by the bracketed subscript '1', as in (4.24) of Chapter 4), I have in (6.9):

$$\begin{aligned} s_2(\beta{:}\alpha) &= (1 - (1 + \bar{r})a^{\beta}_{22})p^{\alpha}_{(1)} - (1 + \bar{r})a^{\beta}_{12} - w^{\alpha}_{(1)}l^{\beta}_{2} \\ &= p^{\alpha}_{(1)}((1 - (1 + \bar{r})a^{\beta}_{22})\cdot 1 - (1 + \bar{r})a^{\beta}_{12}/p^{\alpha}_{(1)} \\ &\qquad - w^{\alpha}_{(1)}l^{\beta}_{2}/p^{\alpha}_{(1)}) \end{aligned} \tag{6.24}$$

But:

$$1/p^{\alpha}_{(1)} = p^{\alpha}_{(2)},\ w^{\alpha}_{(1)}/p^{\alpha}_{(1)} = w^{\alpha}_{(2)} \tag{6.25}$$

where the bracketed subscript '2' denotes the fact that the second commodity is numeraire. From (6.24) and (6.25):

$$s_2(\beta{:}\alpha) = p^{\alpha}_{(1)}S_2(\beta{:}\alpha) \tag{6.26}$$

where $S_2(\beta{:}\alpha)$ is the surplus or loss, relative to normal profits, of operating process (IIβ) at (α)'s prices when the second commodity is numeraire. As $p^{\alpha}_{(1)} > 0$, it follows from (6.26) that:

$$\text{sign } s_2(\beta{:}\alpha) = \text{sign } S_2(\beta{:}\alpha) \tag{6.27a}$$

Similarly:

$$\text{sign } s_2(\alpha{:}\beta) = \text{sign } S_2(\alpha{:}\beta) \tag{6.27b}$$

Clearly, from (6.27), any conclusion drawn on choice of technique when the first commodity is numeraire is equally valid when the second commodity is numeraire. The cost-minimising technique is thus independent of the choice of numeraire.

I have shown above that, when the first commodity is numeraire, the cost-minimising technique supports the higher real wage. Is this valid when the second commodity is numeraire? Suppose that (α) is cheaper than (β) at $\bar{r}$. Then:

$$w^{\alpha}_{(1)} > w^{\beta}_{(1)} \quad \text{and} \quad p^{\beta}_{(1)} > p^{\alpha}_{(1)} \tag{6.28}$$

from *Result 11* and (6.6). The inequalities in (6.28) imply that:

$$w^{\alpha}_{(2)} = w^{\alpha}_{(1)}/p^{\alpha}_{(1)} > w^{\beta}_{(1)}/p^{\beta}_{(1)} = w^{\beta}_{(2)} \tag{6.29}$$

Thus, (α) supports the higher real wage regardless of the choice of numeraire.

The obverse of (6.28) and (6.29) is that the cost-minimising technique supports the lower labour-commanded prices. For, if (α) is cheaper than (β) at $\bar{r}$, it follows from (6.1) and (6.28) that:

$$f^{\alpha}(\bar{r})/g^{\alpha}(\bar{r}) > f^{\beta}(\bar{r})/g^{\beta}(\bar{r}) \tag{6.30a}$$

and from (6.1) and (6.29) that:

$$f^{\alpha}(\bar{r})/h^{\alpha}(\bar{r}) > f^{\beta}(\bar{r})/h^{\beta}(\bar{r}) \tag{6.30b}$$

(6.30a) and (6.30b) can be rewritten respectively as:

$$g^{\beta}(\bar{r})/f^{\beta}(\bar{r}) > g^{\alpha}(\bar{r})/f^{\alpha}(\bar{r}) \tag{6.31a}$$

$$h^{\beta}(\bar{r})/f^{\beta}(\bar{r}) > h^{\alpha}(\bar{r})/f^{\alpha}(\bar{r}) \tag{6.31b}$$

$g^{\alpha}(\bar{r})/f^{\alpha}(\bar{r})$ is the labour-commanded price of the first commodity in technique (α) at rate of profit $\bar{r}$; that is, the number of units of labour that can be bought with one unit of the first commodity. Similarly, $h^{\alpha}(\bar{r})/f^{\alpha}(\bar{r})$ is the labour-commanded price of the second commodity.

From the discussion above, I have two equivalent characterisations of a cost-minimising technique, summarised in:

Figure 6.1

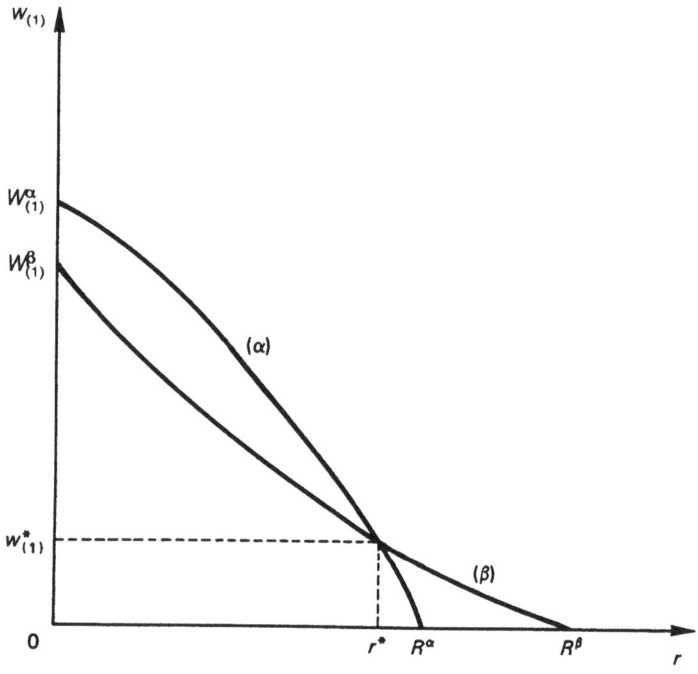

Corollary 11.1: The cost-minimising technique at a given feasible value of r is that which supports:

(a) the higher real wage in terms of any numeraire;
(b) the lower labour-commanded prices, as in (6.31).

I infer from *Corollary 11.1*(a) that the choice of technique can be determined by reference to the diagram of w–r curves, in terms of any numeraire. In Figure 6.1, (α) is cost-minimising for $0 \leqslant r < r^*$, (β) for $r^* < r \leqslant R^{\beta}$. Over the interval $R^{\alpha} < r \leqslant R^{\beta}$, only one technique is available. It follows from (6.12), (6.16) and (6.17) that both techniques are cost-minimising at r^*: this is called a switch-point value of r. From (6.12), $w^{\alpha}_{(1)} = w^{\beta}_{(1)}$ and from (6.6), $p^{\alpha}_{(1)} = p^{\beta}_{(1)}$: choice of numeraire is immaterial. Thus, I can characterise switch-points in:

Corollary 11.2: (α) and (β) have a switch-point at $\bar{r}$ if they share the same price system there (i.e. prices and real wage relative to any numeraire).

The same line of argument as that above can also be used to derive Okishio's Theorem, which I state as:

Corollary 11.3: For the single-product industries, circulating capital model above, the introduction of a cost-reducing process at a given feasible of r results in the new technique being employed with a higher real wage.

To establish this result, refer to Figure 6.1. Suppose that (β) is initially employed at $\bar{r}$ lying between 0 and r^*, with corresponding real wage $w^{\beta}_{(1)}$ and prices 1, $p^{\beta}_{(1)}$. If (IIα) becomes available, it is clear that $s_2(\alpha{:}\beta) > 0$ and $s_2(\beta{:}\alpha) < 0$. Then from (6.12) or (6.16):

$$w^{\alpha}_{(1)} > w^{\beta}_{(1)} \qquad (6.32)$$

as required.

As this section contains the essential theory on choice of technique, a brief summary is in order. Underlying section 6.3 and the rest of this chapter is *Result 11*, which states that choice of technique is determinate at each feasible value of r and unique except at switch-points. The cost-minimising technique is obtained through the operation of competitive forces – capitalists evaluate alternative processes of production, using an expression such as (6.8). If he can reduce his costs by changing his process, a capitalist will do so, thereby obtaining a supernormal rate of profit at least in the short run; these supernormal profits will be eliminated by other capitalists following his lead. It follows that the cost-minimising technique supports the higher real wage: the determination of choice of technique by reference to the diagram of w–r curves, as in Figure 6.1, has the logical status of a corollary, albeit a useful one.

For the model employed in this section, choice of technique is equivalent to choice of process in the second sector. Thus, the question raised is not about the selection of an individual input coefficient; rather, it concerns the choice of a set of input coefficients, or a process, in the second industry. Now, it was demonstrated in Chapter 4 that the price system depends on the conditions of production and the distribution of income. If the rate of profit is fixed, two techniques of production, differing in only one process, will in general have different price systems. So, with prices dependent on the conditions of production and different processes comparable only at a given price system, a question of indeterminacy, not to say circularity, arises. I have shown in *Result 11* that this question can be answered: the cost-minimising technique is the cheaper at each set of prices. This justifies Sraffa's assertion: 'It can however be shown that, while the *extent* of the cheapness of one method of production relatively to the other will vary according as the comparison is carried out in (technique (α)) or in (technique (β)), the *order* of the two methods as to cheapness must be the same in the two (techniques)' (PCMC, section 93, p. 83).

In sections 6.5 and 6.6, I discuss how far the propositions derived above can be extended to single-product industries models where first one sector and then both sectors can have an arbitrary finite number of processes.

6.4 Switching of Techniques

In this section, I analyse the particular question of switching of techniques for the three-process model above. In section 6.3, I identified a switch-point between (α) and (β) as that value of r at which $w^{\alpha}_{(1)} = w^{\beta}_{(1)}$ (alternatively, $w^{\alpha}_{(2)} = w^{\beta}_{(2)}$). Equivalently, a switch-point occurs where $p^{\alpha}_{(1)} = p^{\beta}_{(1)}$ using (6.6b) of section 6.2. (6.3) of section 6.2 is:

$$w^{\alpha}_{(1)} - w^{\beta}_{(1)} = (1 + r)a_{21}(l^{\beta}_{2}f^{\alpha}(r) - l^{\alpha}_{2}f^{\beta}(r) - (1 + r)l_{1}k(r))/ g^{\alpha}(r)g^{\beta}(r) \tag{6.33}$$

$w^{\alpha}_{(1)} = w^{\beta}_{(1)}$ for those values of r at which the bracketed term on the right-hand side of (6.33) is zero. As $f^{\alpha}(r)$ and $f^{\beta}(r)$ are quadratic functions of r and $k(r)$ is a linear function of r, it follows that the bracketed term is also a quadratic in r. $w^{\alpha}_{(1)} - w^{\beta}_{(1)} = 0$ can have at most two real roots. It is demonstrated in the Exercises that there can be two switch-points in the range $0 \leqslant r \leqslant \min(R^{\alpha}, R^{\beta})$, the relevant one for choice of technique. Alternatively, the switch-points can be calculated from (6.5) of section 6.2 by putting $p^{\alpha}_{(1)}$ −

$p^{\beta}_{(1)} = 0$, with the same quadratic term, $(l^{\beta}_{2}f^{\alpha}(r) - l^{\alpha}_{2}f^{\beta}(r) - (1 + r)l_{1}k(r))$, recurring.

From the Exercises, it will be seen that there can be no, one or two switch-points between (α) and (β) in the positive quadrant. In section 4.4, I demonstrated that the *w–r* curve can assume any of three forms. It might therefore be imagined that any pair of combinations of *w–r* curves can occur, giving rise say to Figures 6.2–6.4. In fact, none of these cases can occur in this model, as demonstrated in the following:

> *Result 12:* (i) (Non-Switching Theorem) There are no switch-points between (α) and (β) if each of them exhibits a uniform capital–labour ratio.
>
> (ii) (No-Reswitching Theorem) The possibilities illustrated in Figures 6.3 and 6.4 cannot arise.
>
> (iii) If $w^{\alpha}_{(1)}$ and $w^{\beta}_{(1)}$ have different curvature, there is at most one switch-point between (α) and (β).

Figure 6.2

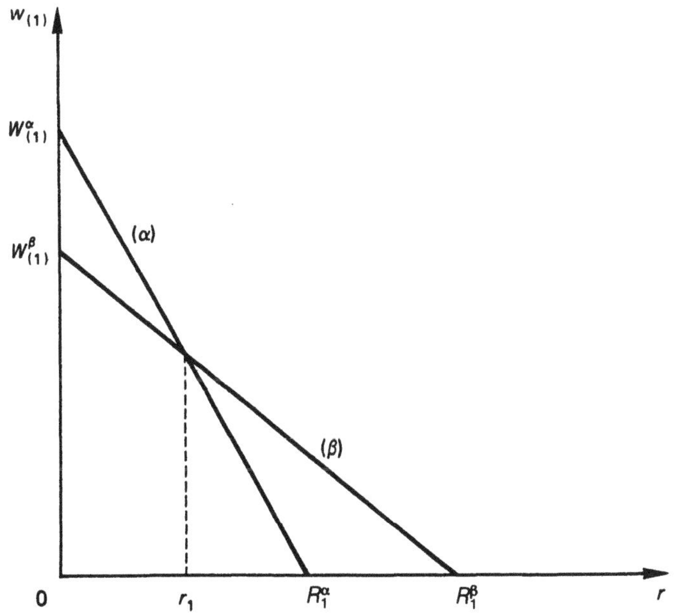

Figure 6.3

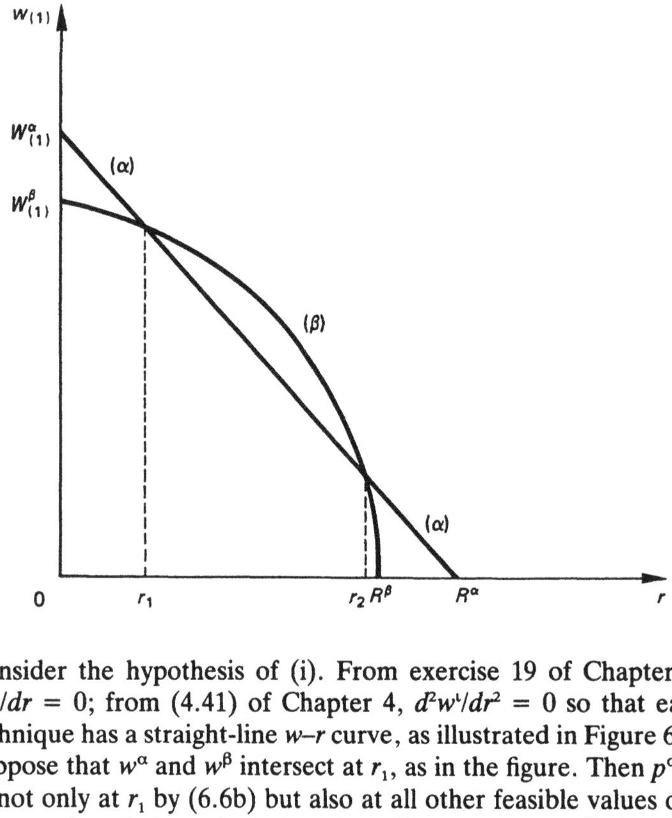

Consider the hypothesis of (i). From exercise 19 of Chapter 4, $dp^{\iota}/dr = 0$; from (4.41) of Chapter 4, $d^2w^{\iota}/dr^2 = 0$ so that each technique has a straight-line w–r curve, as illustrated in Figure 6.2. Suppose that w^{α} and w^{β} intersect at r_1, as in the figure. Then $p^{\alpha} = p^{\beta}$ not only at r_1 by (6.6b) but also at all other feasible values of r because the relative price is invariant. However, $p^{\alpha} \neq p^{\beta}$ when $r \neq r_1$. So, there is a contradiction. It then follows that there cannot be any switch-points between (α) and (β). This proves the Non-Switching Theorem.

To derive the No-Reswitching Theorem, suppose that the arrangement in Figure 6.3 is possible, where $dp^{\alpha}/dr = 0$ and $dp^{\beta}/dr > 0$. From (6.6b), $p^{\alpha} = p^{\beta}$ at both r_1 and r_2. Clearly, this is impossible as p^{α} is constant and p^{β} is a monotonically increasing function of r. The only remaining question is whether any switch-point resembles r_1 – in the sense that (α) is chosen for values of r less than r_1 – or r_2 – in the sense that (β) is chosen for values of r less than r_2. Suppose that the switch-point is r_1. From (6.6b), it follows that $p^{\beta} > p^{\alpha}$ for $0 \leqslant r < r_1$. As $dp^{\alpha}/dr = 0$ and $dp^{\beta}/dr > 0$, it follows that p^{β}

Figure 6.4

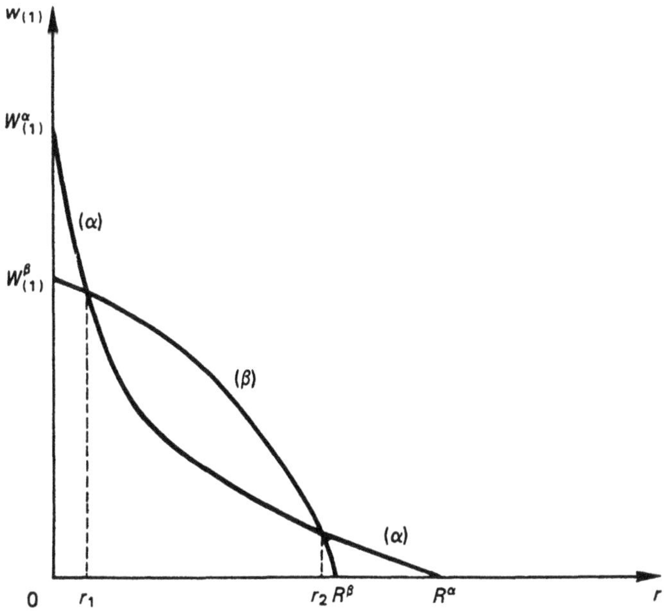

$> p^{\alpha}$ at r_1. This contradicts the definition of a switch-point. Hence, any switch-point between straight-line and concave w–r curves must be of the same type as r_2. If there is a switch-point, that technique with the concave w–r curve ((β) in Figure 6.3) is chosen over the lower range of values of r, that with the straight-line w–r curve ((α) in Figure 6.3) over the higher range. A similar line of argument holds if w^{β} is convex and w^{α} is a straight line. First, there cannot be reswitching. Second, if there is a switch-point, (α) is chosen over the lower range of values of r, (β) over the higher range. To complete the proof of (ii), suppose that w^{α} and w^{β} are as illustrated in Figure 6.4. $dp^{\alpha}/dr < 0$ and $dp^{\beta}/dr > 0$. From (6.6b), $p^{\alpha} = p^{\beta}$ at r_1 and r_2. Clearly, this is a contradiction, as p^{α} is decreasing and p^{β} is increasing in r. By the same line of argument as above, if there is a switch-point between the two techniques, (β) must be chosen over the lower range of values of r, (α) over the upper range.

It is known from *Result 8* of Chapter 4 that each w–r curve can be either convex, concave or a straight line – this is what is meant by curvature. The proof of (iii) then follows from the same line of argument as that used to derive (i) and (ii).

Result 12 provides sufficient conditions for no switching and no reswitching. When can reswitching occur? The answer is provided in the following:

> *Result 13:* A necessary condition for reswitching between (α) and (β) is that w^α and w^β have the same non-zero curvature.

A straight-line w–r curve has zero curvature: thus *Result 13* states that reswitching can occur only if either w^α and w^β are convex or w^α and w^β are concave. Consider Figure 6.5, where $dp^\iota/dr < 0$, $\iota = \alpha, \beta$. Then, it is possible that, if they are equal at r_1, p^α and p^β can also be equal at r_2. In Figure 6.6, $dp^\iota/dr > 0$, $\iota = \alpha, \beta$. As both p^α and p^β are increasing functions of r, it is possible that they can be equal at r_1 and r_2. The other possibilities can be excluded by an appeal to *Result 12*.

Note that the curvature condition in *Result 13* is not sufficient

Figure 6.5

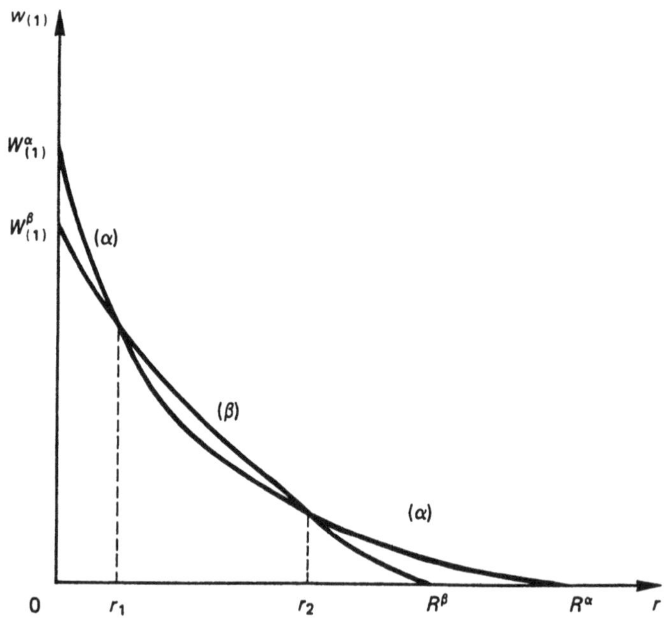

Figure 6.6

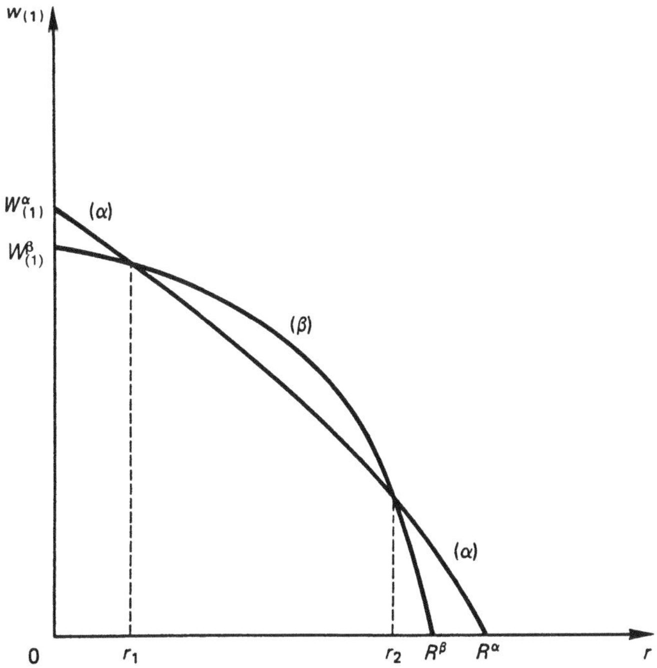

for reswitching, as illustrated in Figure 6.7 and the Exercises. $dp^{\iota}/dr < 0$, $\iota = \alpha, \beta$, but there is only one switch-point between (α) and (β) in the positive quadrant. Indeed, it is possible to construct a numerical example where w^{α} and w^{β} do not intersect in the positive quadrant. Figure 6.7 overleaf also illustrates a sufficient condition for switching: $R^{\alpha} < R^{\beta}$ and $W^{\alpha} > W^{\beta}$. These inequalities imply that there is an odd number of switch-points between (α) and (β). As there can be at most two, it follows that there is just one switch-point in the positive quadrant.

Though my main concern in this chapter, as in the rest of this book, is with models in which there are at least two capital goods, it is a useful application of the theory developed above to examine the question of switching for a model in which there is only one capital good or, more generally, only one basic commodity. Suppose that $a^{\iota}_{12} = 0$, $\iota = \alpha, \beta$, which implies that iron is the only basic commodity, though wheat may be used to produce itself. As this

Figure 6.7

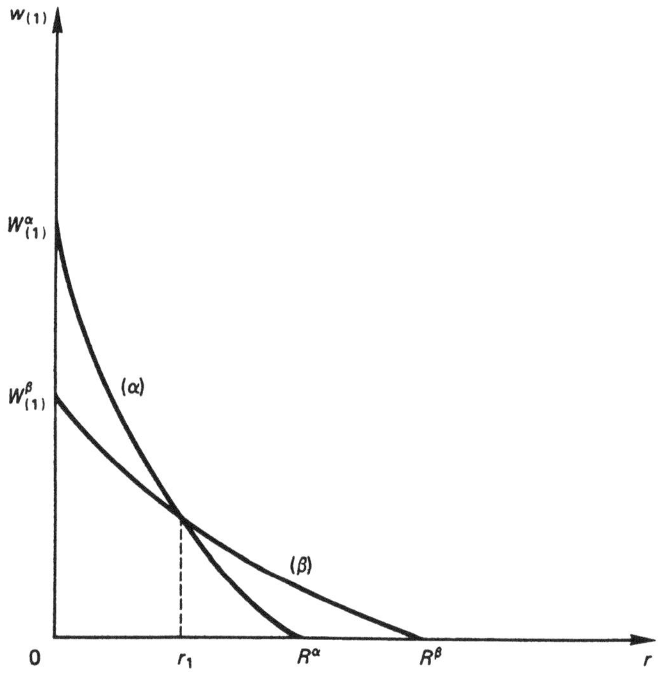

model is a special case of that analysed in sections 6.2 and 6.3, it follows that the theory developed for the latter applies to the former. In particular, choice of technique is determinate at each feasible value of r and is independent of the numeraire. Let the second commodity be the numeraire, so that the price equations are:

$$p^{\iota}_{(2)} = w^{\iota}_{(2)}l_1 + (1 + r)\,(p^{\iota}_{(2)}\,a_{11} + a_{21}) \tag{6.34a}$$

$$1 = w^{\iota}_{(2)}l^{\iota}_2 + (1 + r)\,a^{\iota}_{22} \tag{6.34b}$$

$\iota = \alpha, \beta$. From (6.34b):

$$w^{\iota}_{(2)} = (1 - (1 + r)a^{\iota}_{22})/l^{\iota}_2 \tag{6.35}$$

(6.35), the real wage rate–rate of profit curve for technique (ι) in terms of the second commodity, is a straight line. So, if $w^{\alpha}_{(2)}$ and $w^{\beta}_{(2)}$ intersect in the positive quadrant, they can do so only once.

From *Corollary 11.1*, it follows that there cannot be reswitching between (α) and (β) if there is only one basic commodity in the model. I call this:

> *Result 14*: In the two-sector, three-process model, reswitching cannot occur if there is only one basic commodity common to both techniques.

Care should be taken in the application of *Result 14*. It does not follow, for example, that reswitching cannot occur between two techniques each of which has only one basic commodity. Suppose, for the sake of illustration, that wheat is not used in either industry as means of production and that the second industry's processes produce different commodities, say iron and copper, which are not interchangeable. If the second industry produces iron, by means of iron and labour, the first industry produces its commodity, wheat, by means of iron and labour. However, should the second industry produce copper, by means of copper and labour, the first industry must produce wheat by means of copper and labour. Immediately, it is evident that such a model differs from those considered above for the simple reason that a change in the second sector's process necessitates a change in the first sector's process also. *Result 14 cannot* be applied to this model where there are two basic commodities, each specific to one technique. This type of model, where a capital good is specific to a technique, has proved a popular vehicle for the discussion of issues in capital theory – see, for example, Robinson (1953–4), Champernowne (1953–4), Samuelson (1961–2) and Garegnani (1970). While essentially the same theory as derived above applies,[5] this type of model suffers from at least two deficiencies: first, it does not permit full interdependence between commodities within one technique – in this sense, the alternative type of model is too simple; secondly, a change of technique requires a switch of process in both industries – in this sense, the alternative type of model is more complicated than necessary for the problem at hand.

In this section and the last, I have been considering questions on choice of technique (including switching) for the three-process model introduced in section 6.1. In sections 6.5 and 6.6, I extend this theory to models where first one sector and then both can have an arbitrary finite number of processes.

6.5 Choice of Technique: Part 2

In this section, I relax the assumption of sections 6.2–6.4 that the second sector has only two processes. Instead, I assume that the second sector has an arbitrary finite number of processes – denoted by (IIα), (IIβ), . . ., (IIτ) – while the first sector still has only one process, denoted by (I). Retain all the other assumptions of sections 6.1–6.4: in particular, that all techniques produce and use the same two commodities and that each technique is productive; unproductive techniques can be deleted by the argument used in *Result 11*.

The theory developed in section 6.3 can be applied to this model. List the productive techniques: (α), (β), . . ., (τ). Let (α) be initially employed at a feasible rate of profit $\bar{r} < R^{\alpha}$. Then (α) and (β) can be compared in the manner described in section 6.3. Unless $\bar{r}$ is a switch-point, one of the techniques is cost-minimising, say (α). Then (α) can be compared with the next technique in the list, (γ), again using the method of section 6.3 because (α) and (γ) differ with respect to only one process. Assuming that $\bar{r}$ is not a switch-point between (α) and (γ), the cheaper of these two techniques is in fact the cheapest of the three considered so far; let it be (γ). Then (γ) can be compared with (δ). And so on until all techniques have been considered. The cheaper technique from the last comparison, involving (τ), will be the cheapest among all the techniques; let it be (θ). Then, under the assumption that $\bar{r}$ is not a switch-point between (θ) and any other technique, it follows that:

$$w^{\theta}_{(i)} > w^{\iota}_{(i)} \text{ for all } \iota \neq \theta,\ i = 1,2 \tag{6.36a}$$

and

$$\begin{aligned} g^{\theta}(r)/f^{\theta}(r) &< g^{\iota}(r)/f^{\iota}(r) \\ h^{\theta}(r)/f^{\theta}(r) &< g^{\iota}(r)/f^{\iota}(r) \end{aligned} \tag{6.36b}$$

(θ) supports the highest real wage by (6.36a) and the lowest labour-commanded prices by (6.36b). If $\bar{r}$ is a switch-point between (θ) and (σ), say, then the inequalities (6.36) are replaced by equations for (θ) and (σ).

This exhaustive procedure, which generalises the theory developed in section 6.3, can be simplified somewhat. Let (α) be initially employed at $\bar{r}$. The capitalist in the second sector can evaluate all the alternative processes at (α)'s price system: suppose that he does this systematically by considering (IIβ), (IIγ), . . ., (IIτ) in that order. Only if one of the processes reduces costs does he need to consider switching. Suppose that (IIβ) is more expensive but (IIγ) is cheaper than (IIα). Then (γ) is cheaper than (α) by the argument used to derive *Result 11*; note, in particular, that $\bar{r}$ is feasible for (γ) if (IIγ) reduces costs at (α)'s prices. As (α) is cheaper than (β), (γ) is also cheaper than (β). The switch to (γ) can be made and successive processes can be evaluated at (γ)'s prices. Only those processes reducing costs at a given price system are candidates to form a cost-minimising technique: those processes more expensive at any given price system can be discarded. Eventually, by applying this procedure, the cost-minimising technique (θ) is obtained. The point of this argument is that it is unnecessary to consider techniques pairwise as above: using *Result 11*, it suffices to consider a technique that reduces costs at the prevailing price system. To summarise: let (α) be employed initially. Evaluate the successive processes (IIβ), (IIγ), . . . at (α)'s prices until a cost-reducing one, say (IIγ), is found. Switch from (IIα) to that process to form the new prevailing technique, (γ). Evaluate successive processes (IIδ), (IIε), . . . at (γ)'s prices until a cost-reducing one is found, say (IIφ). Then (φ) forms the new prevailing technique. The structure of the algorithm to locate the cost-minimising technique is by now clear. The prevailing technique at the beginning of each stage in the algorithm is the cheapest among all considered thitherto; likewise, the new prevailing technique (at the end of each step) is the cheapest among all considered thitherto. As there is only a finite number of techniques, there can be only a finite numbers of stages in the algorithm: the maximum number is equal to the number of processes in the second sector. These points about the algorithm should be noted. First, the algorithm terminates (i.e. a cost-minimising technique is found) when the technique entering any stage as the prevailing technique also emerges from that stage as the prevailing technique. Second, a technique which is prevailing at some stage but is subsequently discarded cannot then resume its status as a prevailing technique. Third, it may happen that each of the processes (IIβ), (IIγ), . . ., (IIτ) is more expensive than (IIα) at (α)'s prices: then (α) would be the cost-minimising technique and the algorithm would terminate after one stage. Fourth, the ordering of processes is immaterial to the outcome of the algorithm: that is, the algorithm locates a cost-minimising technique regardless of the order in which the second sector's processes are considered.

All the results on choice of technique from sections 6.3 and 6.4 carry over to this model. In particular, choice of technique is determinate at each feasible value of r (as in *Result 11*) and can be obtained by reference to the outer envelope of w–r curves (*Corollary 11.1*). The reswitching phenomenon exhibited above can occur in this model. Recurrence of techniques can arise in this model, as illustrated in Figures 6.8 and 6.9. Reswitching occurs when two techniques are both equally profitable at two distinct switch-points. Recurrence occurs when a technique is cost-minimising over at least two disjoint intervals but does not share two switch-points with the same technique. In Figure 6.8, there is no reswitching on the outer envelope of w–r curves. The ordering of cost-minimising techniques as r increases from 0 to R^α is (α), (β), (γ), (α). Technique (α) 'recurs', being cost-minimising over low

Figure 6.8

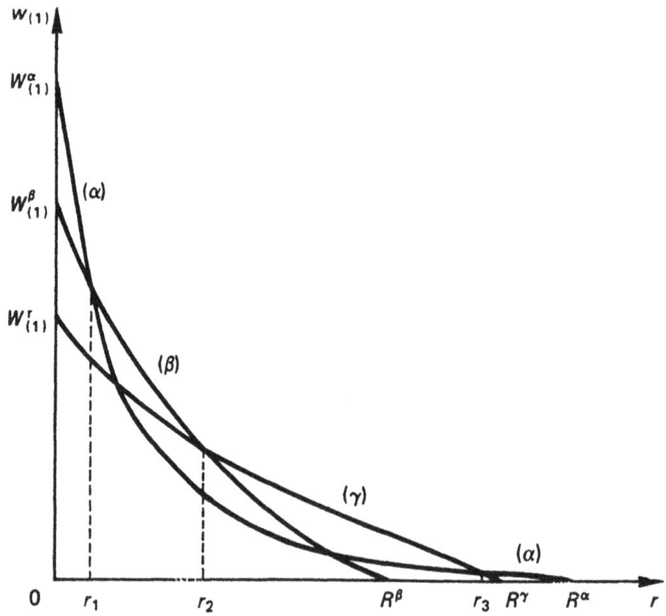

Figure 6.9

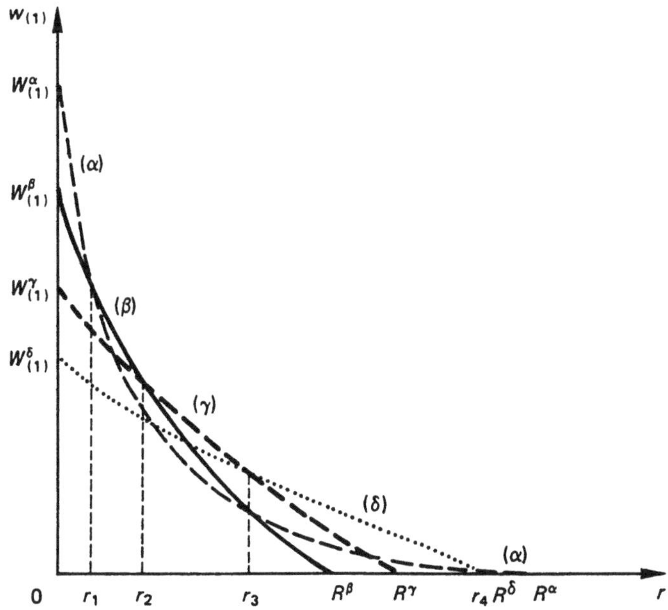

and high values of r. In Figure 6.9, there is again no reswitching between any pair of techniques on the frontier. (α) is cost-minimising for $0 \leqslant r < r_1$ and $r_4 < r \leqslant R^{\alpha}$; (β) for $r_1 < r < r_2$; (γ) for $r_2 < r < r_3$; (δ) for $r_3 < r < r_4$. There are four switch-points and technique (α) recurs.

6.6 Choice of Technique: Part 3

I now relax the assumption of sections 6.3–6.5 that only the second industry has alternative processes of production. Instead, I assume that the first sector has n_1 processes, the second sector n_2; there is a maximum number of $N = n_1 n_2$ possible techniques, obtained by taking one process from each sector.[6] Denote the techniques by (α), (β), (γ), . . ., (ω). No generality is lost in assuming that all these techniques are productive, or that all unproductive techniques have been deleted, for an unproductive technique cannot be cost-minimising.

Let the processes in each sector be listed in any given order.[7]

Suppose that (α) is initially employed at $\bar{r}$. I now propose an algorithm for locating a cost-minimising technique at this value of r.[8,9] This algorithm consists of a finite number of stages, indexed by arabic numerals, each of which has two steps, indexed by lower-case roman letters.

1.i (α) ≡ (Iα, IIα) is given. The process in the second industry is fixed. The capitalist in the first industry searches for a cost-reducing process by working his way through his book of blueprints. Suppose that (Iβ) is the first process encountered which reduces costs. The first industry switches from (Iα) to (Iβ). By the theory in section 6.3, (Iβ, IIα) is cheaper than (α): in particular, $\bar{r}$ is feasible for (Iβ, IIα), a comment applicable to any cost-reducing technique.

1.ii (Iβ, IIα) is given, with its corresponding price system, and now the process in the first industry is fixed. The capitalist in the second industry searches for a cost-reducing process by working his way through his book of blueprints. Let (IIμ) be the first process encountered which reduces costs. By the theory in section 6.3, (Iβ, IIμ) is the cheapest among all techniques considered so far, because it is cheaper than (Iβ, IIα) which, in turn, is cheaper than those considered in 1.i.

2.i (Iβ, IIμ) is given, with corresponding price system, and now (IIμ) is fixed. The capitalist in the first industry searches for a cost-reducing process. Let (Iλ) be the first process encountered which reduces costs. Then (Iλ, IIμ) is the cheapest among all those considered so far.

2.ii (Iλ, IIμ) is given, with corresponding price system, and now (Iλ) is fixed. The capitalist in the second sector searches for a cost-reducing process; let (IIϱ) be the first such process encountered. (Iλ, IIϱ), the cheapest among all techniques considered so far, is advanced to the third stage.

I have described the first two stages in detail. The algorithm terminates when the same technique emerges from a stage as entered it, for then there are no more opportunities for cost reduction. The technique obtained from that terminal stage will be the cheapest of all; it will support the highest real wage and the lowest labour-commanded prices. These properties follow from the fact that techniques in each step differ from each other in only one process: thus, I can apply the theory developed in sections 6.3 and 6.4.

This algorithm presents a formal, not to say idealised, solution to the question of choice of technique. It might be argued that the underlying approach is inapplicable because the two sectors are not controlled by the same capitalist; new processes could therefore be introduced simultaneously, a possibility not considered above. To discuss this question, I take two techniques $(\alpha) \equiv (\mathrm{I}\alpha, \mathrm{II}\alpha)$ and $(\beta) \equiv (\mathrm{I}\beta, \mathrm{II}\beta)$ which differ in both processes. Let (α) be initially employed at $\bar{r}$. There are five cases to be examined:

(a) $s_1(\beta{:}\alpha) = 0$ (6.37a)

$s_2(\beta{:}\alpha) = 0$ (6.37b)

where $s_1(\beta{:}\alpha)$ is defined in a similar way to $s_2(\beta{:}\alpha)$. Thus, (β) breaks even at (α)'s prices. It is a straightforward matter to show that $\bar{r}$ is feasible for (β), $w^\beta = w^\alpha$ and $p^\beta = p^\alpha$. Hence, $\bar{r}$ is a switch-point between (α) and (β).

(b) $s_1(\beta{:}\alpha) \leqslant 0$ (6.38a)

walosi

$s_2(\beta{:}\alpha) \leqslant 0$ (6.38b)

As neither process in (β) reduces costs at (α)'s prices, there is no reason to switch from (α) to (β). It can be shown that $w^\beta < w^\alpha$ and that (α) supports the lower labour-commanded prices, even if there is only one strict inequality in (6.38). In this case, (α) is unambiguously preferred to (β).

(c) $s_1(\beta{:}\alpha) \geqslant 0$ (6.39a)

walosi

$s_2(\beta{:}\alpha) \geqslant 0$ (6.39b)

In this case, there is reason to switch to (β), for at least one process reduces costs and neither is more expensive than the corresponding process in (α). It follows from (6.39) that $\bar{r} < R^\beta$, $w^\beta > w^\alpha$ and (β) supports the lower labour-commanded prices. Hence, (β) is preferred to (α).

(d) $s_1(\beta:\alpha) > 0$ (6.40a)

$s_2(\beta:\alpha) < 0$ (6.40b)

Here, a capitalist in the first sector can make supernormal profits by switching to (Iβ); a capitalist in the second sector who switched to (IIβ) would make losses. So, consider (γ) ≡ (Iβ, IIα). From (6.40):

$s_1(\gamma:\alpha) > 0$ (6.41a)

$s_2(\gamma:\alpha) = 0$ (6.41b)

Then (γ) is preferred to (α) by the argument in (c).

(e) $s_1(\beta:\alpha) < 0$ (6.42a)

$s_2(\beta:\alpha) > 0$ (6.42b)

This is essentially similar to (d). From (6.42), there is another technique (δ) ≡ (Iα, IIβ) which is preferred to (α).

(a)–(e) represent a sketch of the proof that choice of technique is determinate. The problem that arises when two techniques differ in both processes can perhaps best be understood by reconsidering the analysis of sections 6.3 and 6.4, where techniques differ in only one process. There, it was possible to prove that, if it was cheaper than (IIα) at (α)'s prices, (IIβ) was also cheaper at (β)'s prices. Suppose, for the sake of argument that (6.38) holds. It does not follow that:

$s_1(\alpha:\beta) \geqslant 0$ (6.43a)

walosi

$s_2(\alpha:\beta) \geqslant 0$ (6.43b)

The possibilities illustrated in (d) and (e) can also occur. This necessarily complicates the analysis because the comparison between two techniques may yield ambiguous results. However, this problem can be overcome. Suppose that (6.38) holds: then $w^\beta < w^\alpha$. Now evaluate (α) at (β)'s prices: the same five possibilities, (a)–(e), arise. (a) cannot obtain for, if it did, $w^\beta = w^\alpha$, a contradiction. Can (b) hold? i.e.

$$s_1(\alpha:\beta) \leqslant 0 \tag{6.44a}$$

walosi

$$s_2(\alpha:\beta) \leqslant 0 \tag{6.44b}$$

Clearly not, as (6.44) imply that $w^\beta > w^\alpha$. (c) can hold, as the implications of

$$s_1(\alpha:\beta) \geqslant 0 \tag{6.45a}$$

$$s_2(\alpha:\beta) \geqslant 0 \tag{6.45b}$$

are consistent with (6.38). Also, (d) can hold, i.e.

$$s_1(\alpha:\beta) > 0 \tag{6.46a}$$

$$s_2(\alpha:\beta) < 0 \tag{6.46b}$$

(6.46) is consistent with (6.38), as it leads to a new technique (Iα, IIβ) which supports a higher real wage than (α) and, *a fortiori*, (β). Similarly:

$$s_1(\alpha:\beta) < 0 \tag{6.47a}$$

$$s_2(\alpha:\beta) > 0 \tag{6.47b}$$

is consistent with (6.38). The conclusion is that:

> *either* one technique is cheaper than another at both sets of prices;
> *or*, if not, there is a third technique supporting a higher real wage than the first two.

The introduction of cost-reducing processes results in a higher real wage at the given rate of profit (Okishio's Theorem). So, once a technique is discarded in favour of another, it can never reappear as a cost-reducing technique. For, if there were such a technique, say (ε), I would necessarily obtain a chain of inequalities such as the following:

$$\ldots < w^\varepsilon < w^\varphi < \ldots\ldots < w^\varepsilon < \ldots$$

which clearly cannot occur. As there is only a finite number of alternative processes, there can be only a finite number of cost-reducing techniques. Hence, the procedure described in (a)–(e) will eventually yield the cost-minimizing technique. That is, it will yield the same answer as the algorithm presented at the outset. I summarise this discussion in:

> *Result 15:* Let each sector have alternative processes of production. At a given feasible rate of profit, there is at least one cost-minimising technique. Such a technique supports the highest real wage and the lowest labour-commanded prices.[10]

I conclude this section by investigating the nature of switch-points in this model. In sections 6.3 and 6.4, a switch-point was a value of r at which two techniques, differing in only one process, were both cost-minimising: by construction, the techniques could differ by only one process. For the model analysed in this section, techniques can differ by two processes. Take two such techniques $(\alpha) \equiv (\mathrm{I}\alpha, \mathrm{II}\alpha)$ and $(\beta) \equiv (\mathrm{I}\beta, \mathrm{II}\beta)$ with a switch-point $\bar{r}$. By definition at $\bar{r}$:

$$s_1(\beta{:}\alpha) = 0 \tag{6.48a}$$

$$s_2(\beta{:}\alpha) = 0 \tag{6.48b}$$

and

$$s_1(\alpha{:}\beta) = 0 \tag{6.49a}$$

$$s_2(\alpha{:}\beta) = 0 \tag{6.49b}$$

It follows from (6.48) and (6.49) that techniques $(\eta) \equiv (\mathrm{I}\alpha, \mathrm{II}\beta)$ and $(\mu) \equiv (\mathrm{I}\beta, \mathrm{II}\alpha)$ must also share the same switch-point, as illustrated in Figure 6.10. For:

$$s_1(\eta{:}\alpha) = s_1(\alpha{:}\alpha) = 0 \tag{6.50a}$$

$$s_2(\eta{:}\alpha) = s_2(\beta{:}\alpha) = 0 \tag{6.50b}$$

Similarly for (μ). So, if (α) and (β) differ with respect to both processes at the switch-point $\bar{r}$, there are four equally profitable techniques there.

Figure 6.10

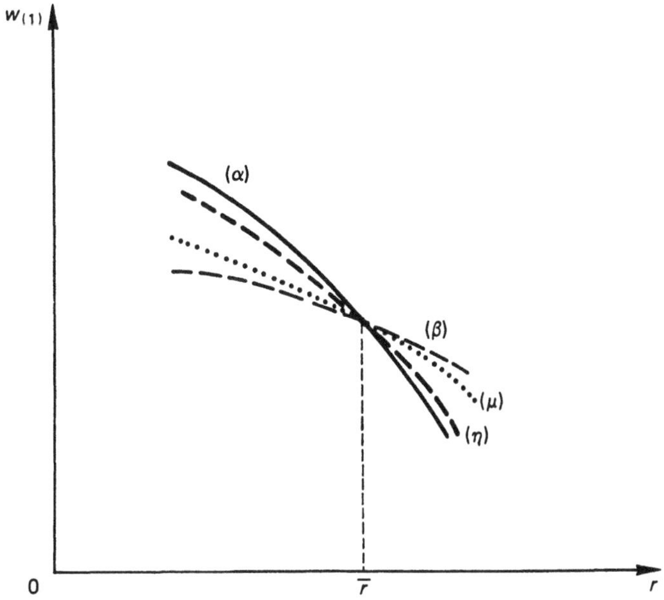

Suppose that (α) is cost-minimising for $\bar{r}-e < r < \bar{r}$, (β) is cost-minimising for $\bar{r} < r < \bar{r}+e$, where e is a sufficiently small positive number. In this model, the transition from (α) to (β) can be described as being between techniques which differ with respect to only one process, thereby providing a justification for the algorithm described at the beginning of this section. For at $\bar{r}$, (α) is equally profitable with (η) (or (μ)), the two techniques differing only in their second (or first) process. (η) (or (μ)) and (β), which are also equally profitable there, differ only in their first (or second) process. The transition can thus be described as follows: (α) to (η) and then (η) to (β).

The configuration illustrated in Figure 6.10 can be described as unusual, but not impossible. Normally, two techniques having a switch-point, $\bar{r}$, will differ with respect to only one process, there being a simple reason for this. If (α) and (β) above have a switch-point at $\bar{r}$, (6.48) must be satisfied, i.e. *two* equations. If (α) and (η) above have a switch-point at $\bar{r}$, (6.50) must be satisfied, i.e. *one* equation. It is more likely that one equation and one identity will be satisfied, as in (6.50), than two equations, as in (6.48). So, it is reasonable to expect that 'adjacent' techniques on the outer envelope of w–r curves[11] will in general differ by only one process; and, if they differ in both, an intermediate technique can be substituted, as in Figure 6.10.

The essential result in this section confirms the theory of choice of technique developed in sections 6.3 and 6.4. Choice of technique is determinate at each feasible value of r. The cost-minimising technique supports the highest real wage and the lowest labour-commanded prices: the continued use of w–r curves as indicators of efficiency in choice of technique is thus justified.

6.7 Choice of Technique and Microeconomics

In this section, I discuss some implications for microeconomics of the theory of choice of technique derived above. To be specific, I shall concentrate on the relationship between the quantity of an input used in an industry and its price. This analysis will be conducted within the simplest possible framework – that of sections 6.1–6.3. Any negative conclusions drawn from such a model apply *a fortiori* to more general systems (e.g. section 6.6). I consider, first of all, four numerical examples.

Example 1: Let (α) and (β) be constructed from these processes:

$$(\text{I}) \equiv (1/2,\ 2/5;\ 1) \tag{6.51a}$$

$$(\text{II}\alpha) \equiv (1/10,\ 1/2;\ 1) \tag{6.51b}$$

$$(\text{II}\beta) \equiv (1/5,\ 1/4;\ 1) \tag{6.51c}$$

Using the first commodity as numeraire and noting that:

$$(l_1 a^\iota_{12} + l^\iota_2 a^\iota_{22})/l^\iota_2 < (l_1 a_{11} + l^\iota_2 a_{21})/l_1 \tag{6.52}$$

$\iota = \alpha, \beta$, it follows from sections 4.3 and 4.4 that:

$$dp^\iota/dr < 0,\ d^2w^\iota/dr^2 > 0 \tag{6.53}$$

Also:

$$s^\alpha_1 = 7/10 > (15 + \sqrt{153})/40 = s^\beta_1 \tag{6.54a}$$

so that:

$$R^{\alpha} \simeq 0.429 < 0.462 \simeq R^{\beta} \qquad (6.54b)$$

$$W^{\alpha} \simeq 0.233 > 0.219 \simeq W^{\beta} \qquad (6.54c)$$

From (6.54b) and (6.54c), (α) and (β) have one switch-point, $\bar{r} \simeq$ 0.204, as illustrated in Figure 6.11a. Straightforward calculations yield the following:

$$\text{at } r = 0, \quad p = p^{\alpha} \simeq 0.667 \qquad (6.55a)$$

$$\text{at } r = 0.20, p = p^{\alpha} \simeq 0.591 \qquad (6.55b)$$

$$\text{at } r = 0.21, p = p^{\beta} \simeq 0.586 \qquad (6.55c)$$

$$\text{at } r = 0.45, p = p^{\beta} \simeq 0.466 \qquad (6.55d)$$

The relation between the quantity of commodity two used in the second industry, a_{22}, and its price is shown in Figure 6.11b – the arrows indicate the direction of change in p as r increases. A decrease in p is associated with a decrease in a_{22}, contrary to what might have been expected. Nonetheless, a_{22}^{β} is the cost-minimising input of commodity two when p lies between $p^{\beta}(R^{\beta}) \simeq$ 0.466 and $p^{\beta}(\bar{r}) \simeq 0.586$. Choice in this model is particularly simple, there being only two processes: hence either a_{22}^{α} or a_{22}^{β} is used. This input is not chosen in isolation, being a component of a process, either (IIα) or (IIβ).

The choice of numeraire restricts the analysis to some extent: for, if I wish to investigate the relations between the quantity of the first commodity used in industry two and its price, I find that the latter is by definition constant. This problem can be circumvented by choosing the second commodity as numeraire. Then, from (6.53), I have:

$$dp_{(2)}^{\iota}/dr > 0 \quad \iota = \alpha, \beta \qquad (6.56)$$

It is then possible to construct a diagram similar to Figure 6.11b relating a_{12} to $p_{(2)}$: the essential point is that a rise in $p_{(2)}$, the price of the first commodity in terms of the second, is associated with a rise in a_{12} from 1/10 to 1/5.

Alternatively, labour-commanded prices can be used: let $P_i \equiv$

Figure 6.11a

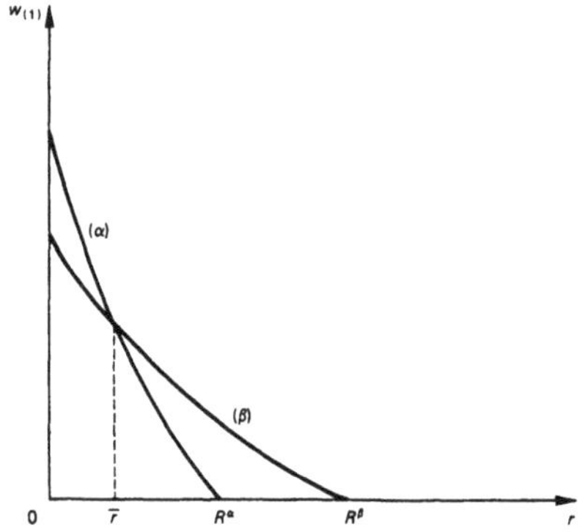

Figure 6.11b

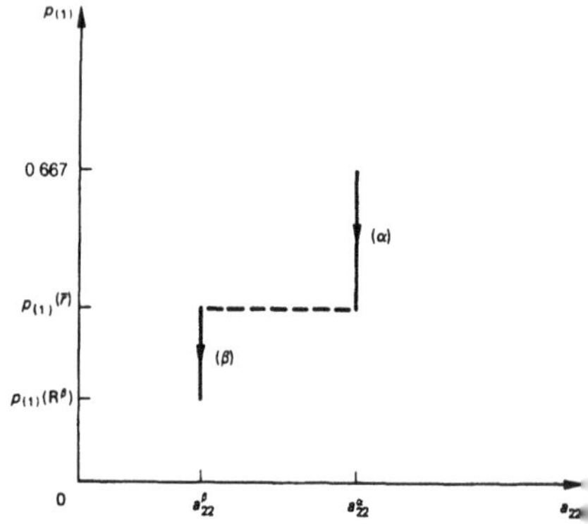

Figure 6.11c

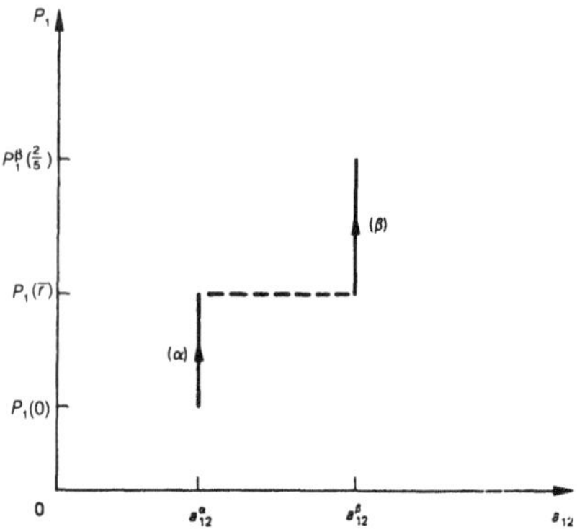

Figure 6.11d

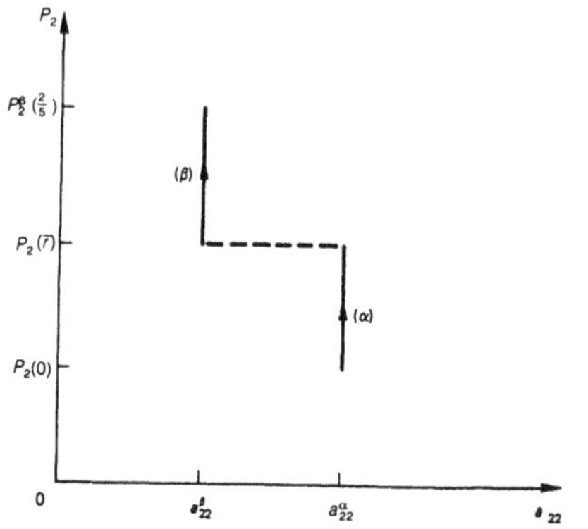

p_i/w, $i = 1,2$, be the price of commodity i in terms of the wage rate. Then:

$$\text{at } r = 0, \quad P_1^{\alpha} \bumpeq 4.286, \quad P_2^{\alpha} \bumpeq 2.857 \tag{6.57a}$$

$$\text{at } r = 0.20, \quad P_1^{\alpha} \bumpeq 8.594, \quad P_2^{\alpha} \bumpeq 5.078 \tag{6.57b}$$

$$\text{at } r = 0.21, \quad P_1^{\beta} \bumpeq 8.988, \quad P_2^{\beta} \bumpeq 5.269 \tag{6.57c}$$

$$\text{at } r = 0.40, \quad P_1^{\beta} \bumpeq 39.005, \quad P_2^{\beta} \bumpeq 19.110 \tag{6.57d}$$

Both labour-commanded prices increase without limit as r tends towards R^{β}. From the fact that choice of technique is independent of the numeraire, I have from (6.51), (6.57) and Figure 6.11a, the relations between P_1 and a_{12}, illustrated in Figure 6.11c, and between P_2 and a_{22}, illustrated in Figure 6.11d. It can be seen that there is a positive, monotonic relation between the price of commodity one (whether in terms of commodity two or labour) and a_{12}. On the other hand, I conclude from Figures 6.11b and 6.11d that the relation between a_{22} and the price of the second commodity depends on the choice of numeraire: it is positive monotonic in terms of commodity one and inverse monotonic in terms of the labour-commanded price of commodity two. The general conclusion to be drawn is that the relation between the use of a commodity and its price is not necessarily inverse monotonic, as might have been supposed.

Example 2: Let (α) and (β) be constructed from:

$$(\text{I}) \equiv (1/2,\ 2/5;\ 1) \tag{6.58a}$$

$$(\text{II}\alpha) \equiv (2/5,\ 3/10;\ 1) \tag{6.58b}$$

$$(\text{II}\beta) \equiv (1/5,\ 1/3;\ 3) \tag{6.58c}$$

With the first commodity as numeraire, I have from (6.58):

$$dp^{\iota}/dr < 0, \ d^2w^{\iota}/dr^2 > 0 \tag{6.59}$$

Straightforward calculations show that:

$$s_1^{\alpha} \bumpeq 0.812 > 0.712 \bumpeq s_1^{\beta} \tag{6.60a}$$

which implies that:

$$R^{\alpha} \triangleq 0.231 < 0.405 \triangleq R^{\beta} \quad (6.60b)$$

$$W^{\alpha} \triangleq 0.173 > 0.136 \triangleq W^{\beta} \quad (6.60c)$$

From (6.60b) and (6.60c), it follows that there is a single switch-point, $\bar{r} \triangleq 0.145$, between (α) and (β), as illustrated in Figure 6.12a. It can be shown that:

$$\text{at } r = 0, \quad p = p^{\alpha} \triangleq 0.818 \quad (6.61a)$$

$$\text{at } r = 0.14, p = p^{\alpha} \triangleq 0.795 \quad (6.61b)$$

$$\text{at } r = 0.15, p = p^{\beta} \triangleq 0.754 \quad (6.61c)$$

$$\text{at } r = 0.40, p = p^{\beta} \triangleq 0.533 \quad (6.61d)$$

From this data, I obtain the relation between p and a_{22} summarised in Figure 6.12b. Here, as the relative price of the second commodity falls, there is a switch to a process requiring more of that commodity as input per unit of output. If the second commodity is chosen as numeraire, it follows that:

$$dp^{\iota}_{(2)}/dr > 0, \; d^2w^{\iota}_{(2)}/dr^2 < 0 \quad \iota = \alpha, \beta \quad (6.62)$$

I can then obtain a relation between a_{12} and $p_{(2)}$ resembling that in Figure 6.12c. Figures 6.12b and 6.12c suggest that there are no 'perverse' relationships for this model. However, by working in terms of labour-commanded prices, I obtain Figures 6.12d and 6.12e. Note that, as P_2 increases through $P_2(\bar{r})$, the amount of commodity two used, a_{22}, increases.

In the first two examples, both w^{α} and w^{β} have the same curvature. In the next example, one curve is convex, the other concave.

Example 3: Let (α) and (β) be constructed from:

$$(\text{I}) \equiv (0, 1/2; 1) \quad (6.63a)$$

$$(\text{II}\alpha) \equiv (1/2, 0; 1/2) \quad (6.63b)$$

$$(\text{II}\beta) \equiv (1/8, 0; 3) \quad (6.63c)$$

Figure 6.12a

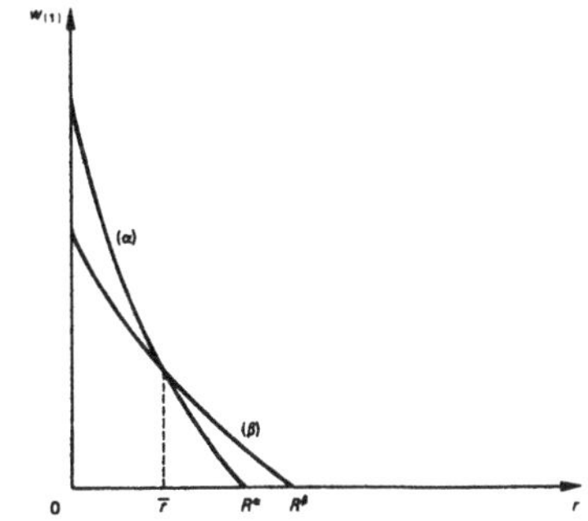

Figure 6.12b

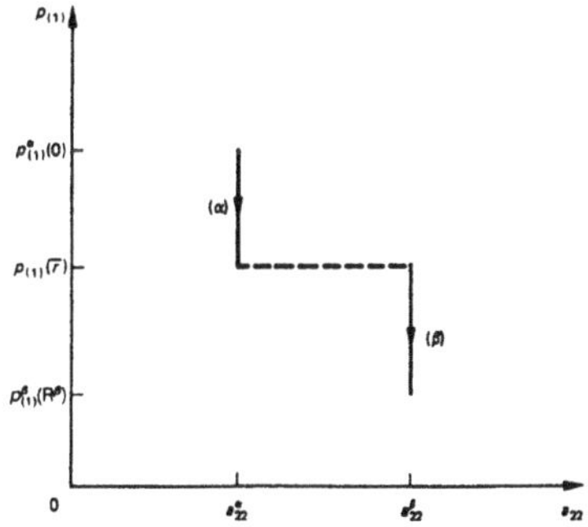

Figure 6.12c

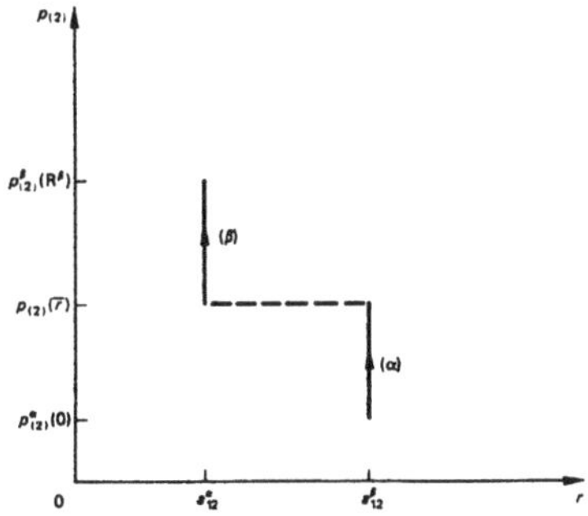

Figure 6.12d

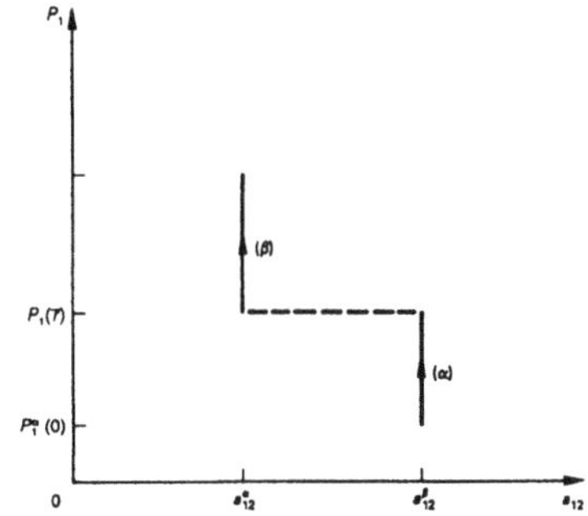

Figure 6.12e

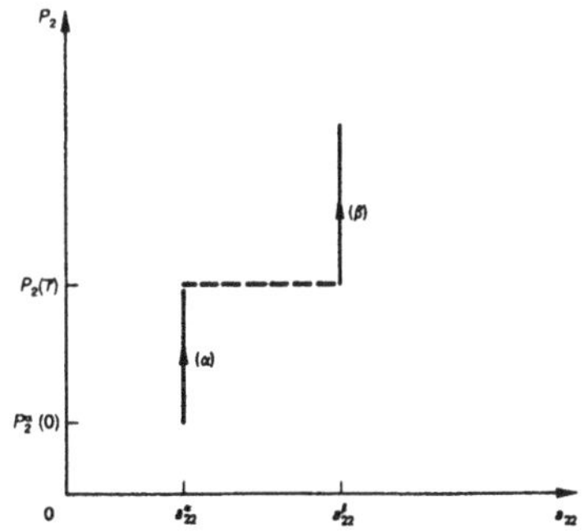

Choose the second commodity as numeraire; as $a^{\iota}_{22} = 0$, there is no relation to be drawn between this input and $p\ (\equiv p_{(1)})$. Straightforward calculations establish the following:

$$dp^{\alpha}_{(2)}/dr < 0,\ d^2w^{\alpha}_{(2)}/dr^2 > 0 \quad (6.64a)$$

$$dp^{\beta}_{(2)}/dr > 0,\ d^2w^{\beta}_{(2)}/dr^2 < 0 \quad (6.64b)$$

$$R^{\alpha} = 1 < 3 = R^{\beta} \quad (6.65c)$$

$$W^{\alpha}_{(2)} = 3/4 > 3/10 = W^{\beta}_{(2)} \quad (6.65d)$$

Hence, there is one switch-point, $\bar{r} \simeq 0.622$ between (α) and (β), as illustrated in Figure 6.13a. Then:

$$\text{at } r = 0,\ p_{(2)} = p^{\alpha}_{(2)} = 1.25 \quad (6.66a)$$

$$\text{at } r = \bar{r},\ p_{(2)} = p^{\alpha}_{(2)} = p^{\beta}_{(2)} \simeq 1.072 \quad (6.66b)$$

$$\text{at } r = 3,\ p_{(2)} = p^{\beta}_{(2)} = 3 \quad (6.66c)$$

On the basis of this data, I can construct Figure 6.13b. This differs from the relations derived above in that it is not monotonic – either increasing or decreasing – a conclusion attributable to the fact that $p_{(2)}$ is itself not a monotonic function of r: see Figure 6.13c. If $p_{(2)}$ rather than r is taken as exogenous, it is not immediately evident which is the cost-minimising technique when $1.072 < p_{(2)} < 1.25$; (α) supports such a price for $0 \leqslant r < \bar{r}$, (β) for $\bar{r} < r \leqslant 1.046$. If labour-commanded prices are used, the relation between a_{12} and $p_{(2)}$ resembles that in Figure 6.13d.

Example 4: Let (α) and (β) be derived from:

$$(\text{I}) \equiv (1/12,\ 1/3;\ 1) \quad (6.67a)$$

$$(\text{II}\alpha) \equiv (1/6,\ 1/6;\ 1) \quad (6.67b)$$

$$(\text{II}\beta) \equiv (137/546,\ 19/273;\ 92/91) \quad (6.67c)$$

With the first commodity as numeraire, I obtain:

$$dp^{\iota}/dr < 0,\ d^2w^{\iota}/dr^2 > 0 \quad \iota = \alpha, \beta \quad (6.68)$$

(α) and (β) have switch-points $\bar{r} = 1/3$, $\bar{\bar{r}} = 1/2$, as illustrated in

Figure 6.13a

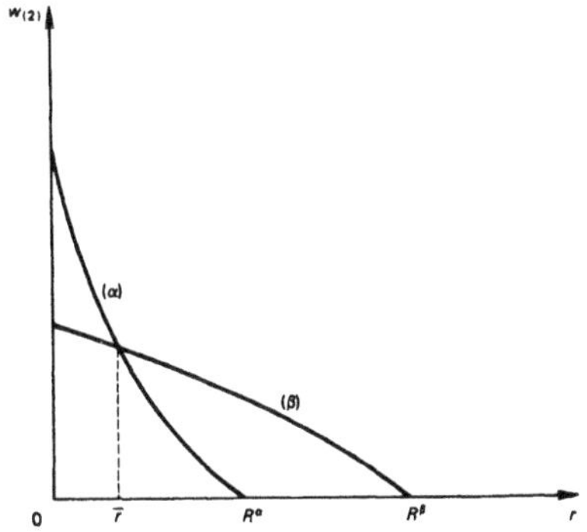

Figure 6.13b

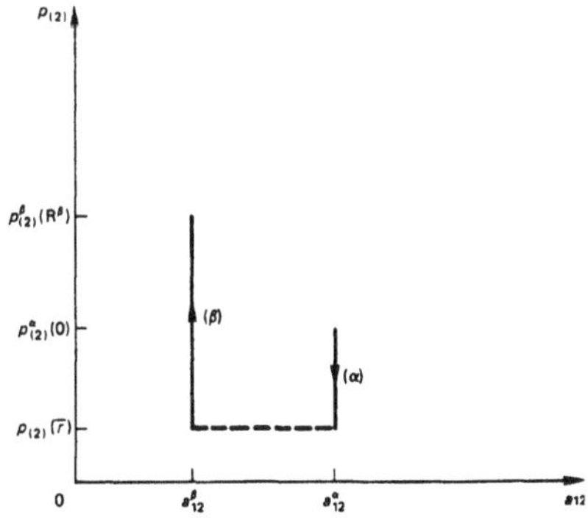

Figure 6.13c

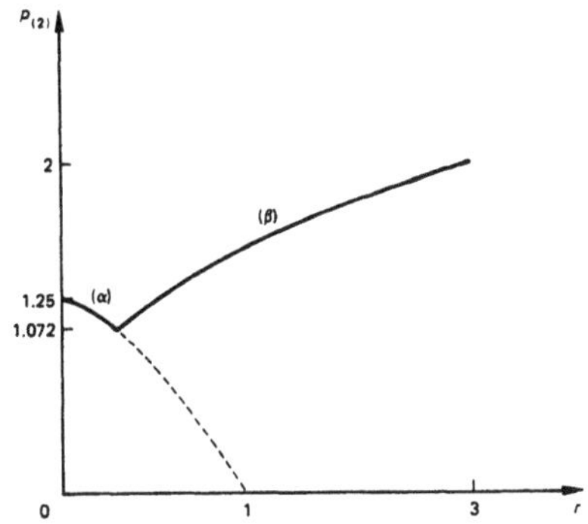

Figure 6.13d

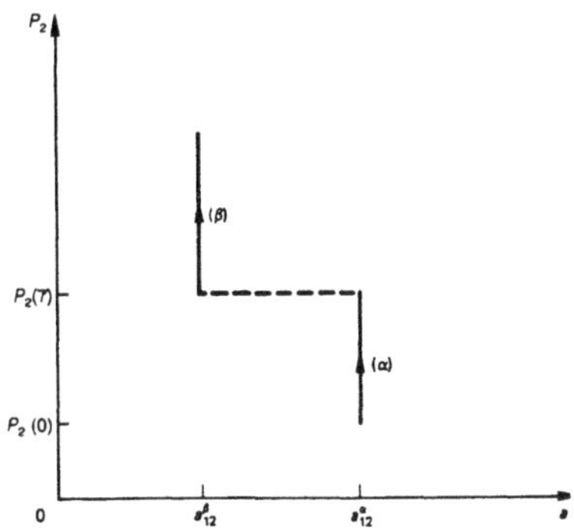

Figure 6.14a. The relation between a_{22} and p is shown in Figure 6.14b. Though p is a monotonically decreasing function of r, a_{22} is not a monotonic function of p. As p increases from its value at $r = 0$, there is at $\bar{r}$ a fall in a_{22} from 1/6 to 19/273 and then, at $\bar{\bar{r}}$, a rise from 19/273 to 1/6. If the second commodity had been chosen as numeraire, I would have obtained a relation between a_{12} and $p_{(2)}$ resembling that in Figure 6.14c. From (6.68), $dp^{\iota}_{(2)}/dr > 0$, $\iota = \alpha$, β. Again, there is no monotonic relation between the produced input and its price. Non-monotonicity is also obtained in Figures 6.14d and 6.14e, where labour-commanded prices are used.

The discussion so far has concentrated on the relation between the input of a *produced* commodity and its price. Consider, next, the relation between the labour input, l_2, and the real wage. In each of *Examples 1–3*, l_2 is a monotonically decreasing function of $w \equiv w_{(1)}$ (or $w_{(2)}$). In Figure 6.15, I have drawn the relation between l_2 and the wage rate for techniques (α) and (β) in *Example 4*. The existence of reswitching and, more generally, recurrence implies that l_2 is not a monotonically decreasing function of the wage, however it is measured.

This line of analysis can be extended. By taking the second commodity as numeraire when there are alternative processes only in the second industry, I have as the w–r curve for technique (ι):

$$w^{\iota}_{(2)} = \frac{(1 - (1+r)a_{11})(1 - (1+r)a^{\iota}_{22}) - (1+r)^2 a^{\iota}_{12}a_{21}}{l^{\iota}_2(1- (1+r)a_{11}) + (1+r)l_1 a^{\iota}_{12}} \qquad (6.69)$$

When $r = 0$:

$$w^{\iota}_{(2)} = W^{\iota}_{(2)} = \frac{(1 - a_{11})(1 - a^{\iota}_{22}) - a^{\iota}_{12}a_{21}}{l^{\iota}_2(1 - a_{11}) + l_1 a^{\iota}_{12}} \qquad (6.70)$$

$$= 1/v^{\iota}_2$$

where v^{ι}_2 is the labour embodied in a unit of the second commodity when technique (ι) is operated. When $r = -1$:

$$w^{\iota}_{(2)} = 1/l_2 \qquad (6.71)$$

Suppose that there are only two techniques, (α) and (β) having

Figure 6.14a

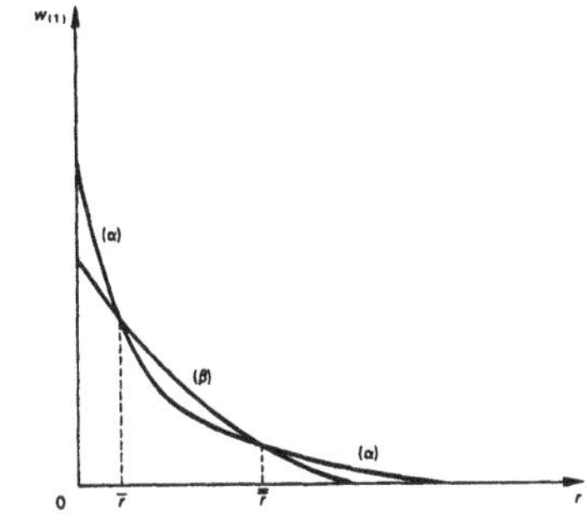

Figure 6.14b

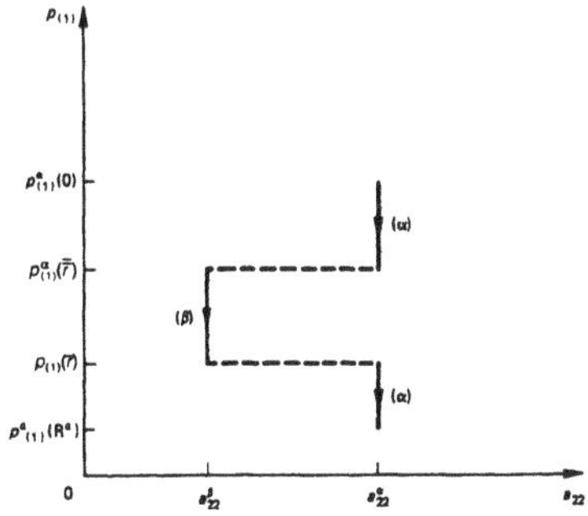

Figure 6.14c

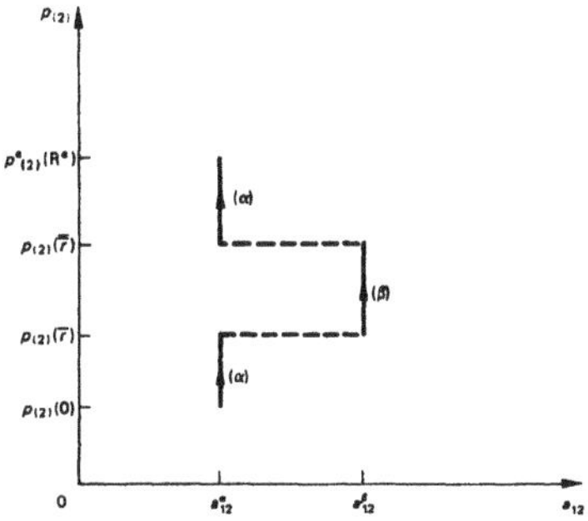

Figure 6.14d

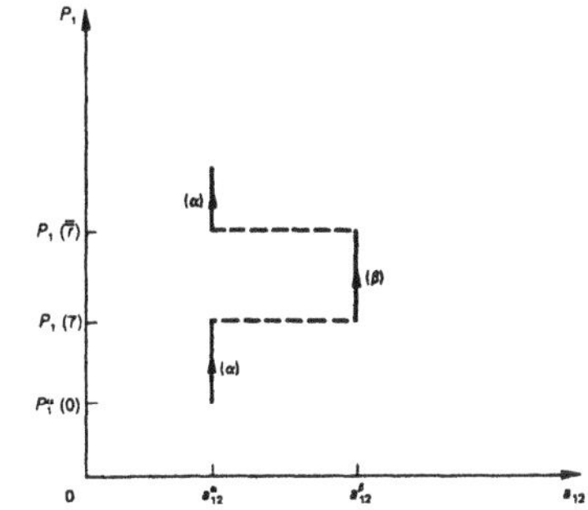

Figure 6.14e

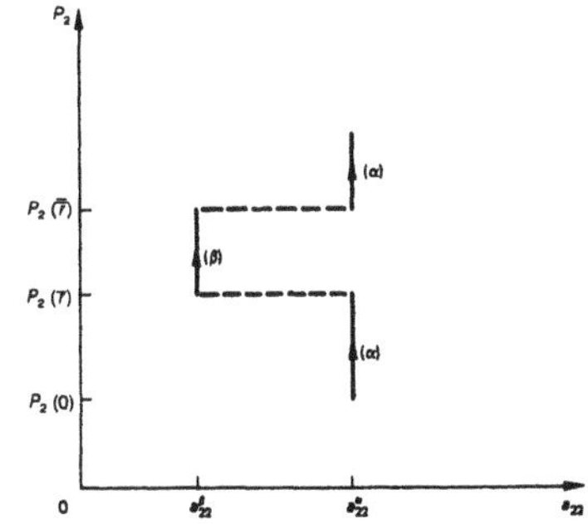

Figure 6.15

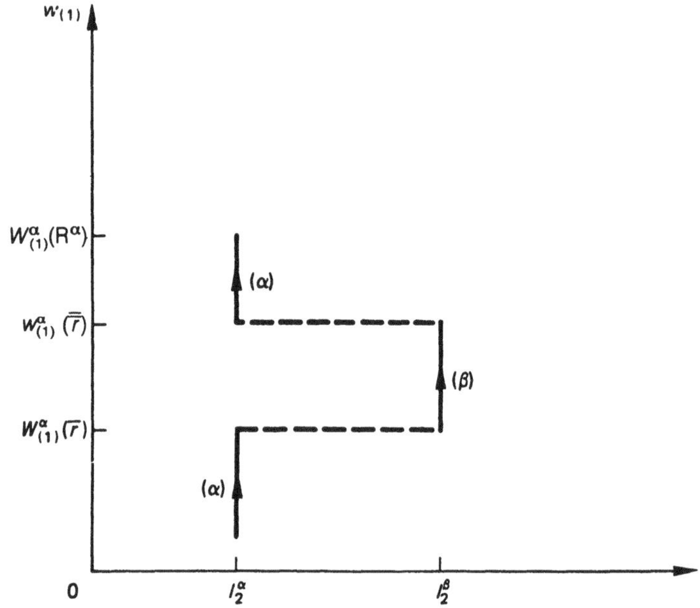

only one switch-point in the positive quadrant and no points of intersection between $r = 0$ and $r = -1$. Such a case is illustrated in Figure 6.16a. Using (6.70) and (6.71), it follows from the intercepts at $r = 0$ and $r = -1$ that:

$$l^{\beta}_{2} > l^{\alpha}_{2},\ v^{\beta}_{2} > v^{\alpha}_{2} \tag{6.72}$$

This explains the arrangement on the horizontal axis in Figure 6.17a, where the relations between l_2 and $w_{(2)}$, and v_2 and $w_{(2)}$ are exhibited. (α) is chosen for $W^{\alpha}_{(2)} \geqslant w_{(2)} > \bar{w}_{(2)}$, (β) for $\bar{w}_{(2)} > w_{(2)} \geqslant 0$.

Consider next Figure 6.16b where there is a point of intersection between $w^{\alpha}_{(2)}$ and $w^{\beta}_{(2)}$ at $\underline{r}$, $0 > \underline{r} > -1$, in addition to that in the positive quadrant. (β) is chosen for $W^{\beta}_{(2)} \geqslant w_{(2)} > \bar{w}_{(2)}$, (α) for $\bar{w}_{(2)} > w_{(2)} \geqslant 0$. From (6.70), (6.71) and Figure 6.16b, it follows that:

$$l^{\beta}_{2} > l^{\alpha}_{2},\ v^{\beta}_{2} < v^{\alpha}_{2} \tag{6.73}$$

The existence of the point of intersection $\underline{r}$ implies that, even in the absence of reswitching, there is not necessarily an inverse monotonic relation between l_2 and the real wage – this point is demonstrated in Figure 6.17b. Note that there is an inverse monotonic relation between v_2 and the real wage.

In the final case, illustrated in Figure 6.16c, there is reswitching between (α) and (β). From (6.70), (6.71) and Figure 6.16c, I have:

$$l_2^\beta > l_2^\alpha, \; v_2^\beta > v_2^\alpha \tag{6.74}$$

Figure 6.17c resembles Figure 6.15 as there is not an inverse monotonic relation between l_2 and the real wage; indeed, there is not a monotonic relation between the two: similarly, for v_2 and the real wage.

The main conclusion to be drawn from this section is a negative one: there is not necessarily an inverse monotonic relation between the cost-minimising quantity of an input and its price. This has been demonstrated with respect to produced commodities in *Examples 1–4* and non-produced inputs in *Example 4* and the subsequent discussion. Thus, the proposition that the cost-minimising quantity of an input is inversely related to its price is invalid. It might have been presupposed that the failure of this proposition could be attributed to the possibilities of reswitching and recurrence. Support for such a view could be sought in *Example 4*: the fact that (α) is cost-minimising over two disjoint intervals implies that the relation between prices and quantities cannot even be monotonic (see Figures 6.14b–e). Yet the proposition fails in models where there is no reswitching. *Examples 1–3* have very simple technologies, there being only one switch-point in each case: apparently 'perverse' results can be obtained in 'reasonable' technologies. Clearly, the failure of the proposition has nothing to do with reswitching or recurrence.

The theory developed in this chapter relates to choice of technique, i.e. a whole set of input coefficients, rather than of a particular input coefficient. In the simplest case, where only one industry has alternative processes, choice of technique is equivalent to choice of a process: even here, the case illustrated in *Examples 1–4*, the proposition does not hold. In so far as it relies on the proposition, traditional theory can be criticised on the basis of the conclusions drawn from the examples and the discussion

Figure 6.16a

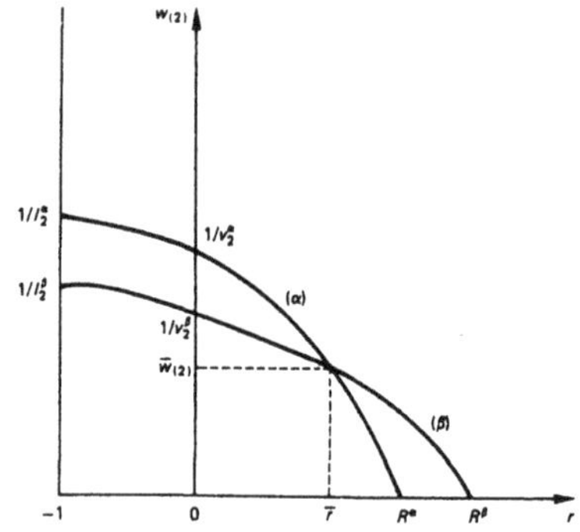

Figure 6.17a

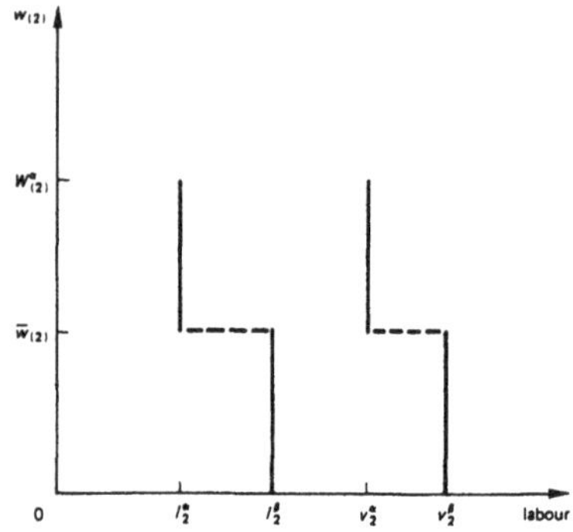

Figure 6.16b

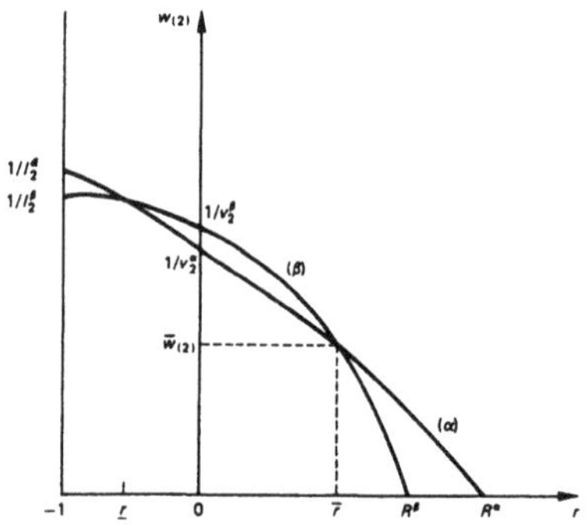

Figure 6.17b

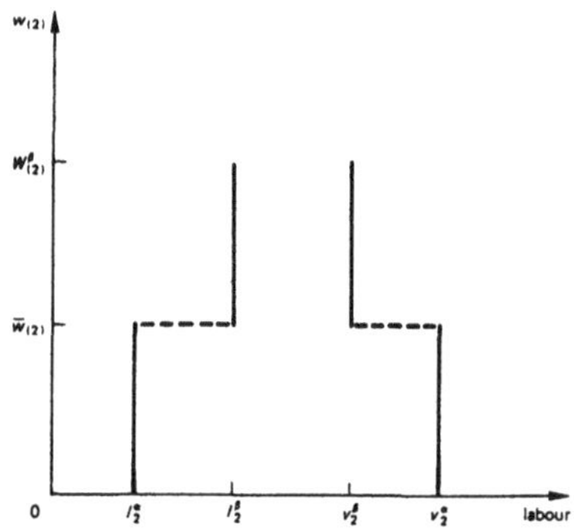

Figure 6.16c

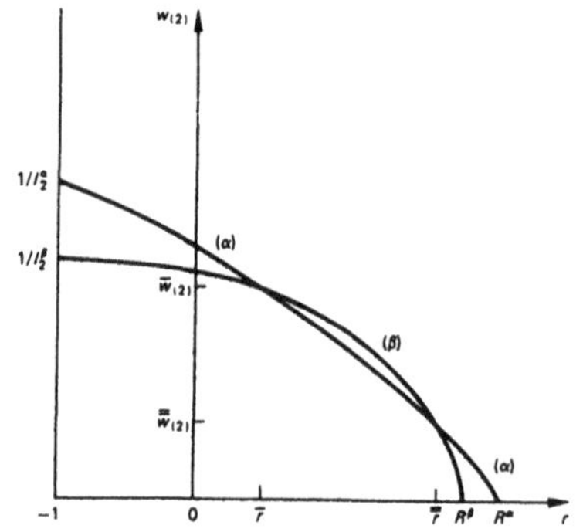

Figure 6.17c

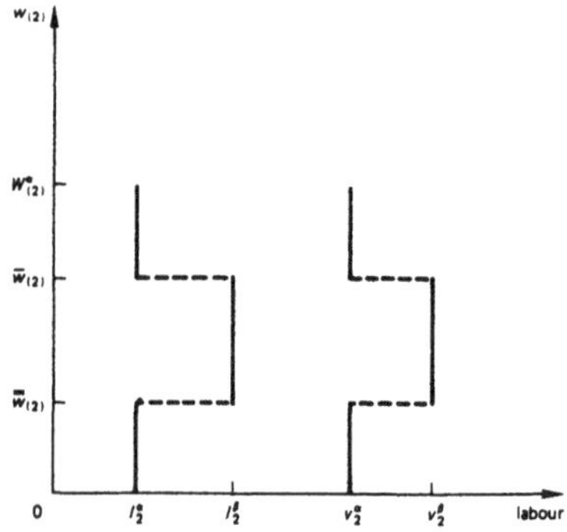

above. In particular, the notion of substitution – which seems to rely on the changes in input quantities being in the opposite direction to the respective price changes – is called into question.[12]

Though this section has been devoted to microeconomic implications of the theory of choice of technique, it is appropriate to conclude with a brief discussion of a macroeconomic implication, especially as it arises from the same analysis. Figures 6.17a–6.17c can be interpreted as demand curves for labour. The relation between l_2 and $w_{(2)}$ is a microeconomic demand curve for labour, that of the second industry. The relation between v_2 and $w_{(2)}$ can be interpreted as a macroeconomic demand curve for labour, which would occur if there were a net output of only the second commodity. In Figure 6.17a, both the sectoral and aggregate demand curves for labour are downward-sloping; in Figure 6.17b, the aggregate demand curve is downward-sloping while the sectoral demand curve is upward-sloping. In a two-sector, three-process model, the aggregate demand curve is necessarily downward-sloping in the absence of reswitching. I have shown in Figure 6.17c that the aggregate demand curve is not downward-sloping in the presence of reswitching: indeed, like the sectoral curve, it is not even monotonic. Reswitching is sufficient, not necessary, for the aggregate demand curve for labour not to be downward-sloping: to see this, consider Figure 6.18. It is clear from Figure 6.18a that there is no reswitching, though there are two points of intersection between $w^{\alpha}_{(2)}$ and $w^{\beta}_{(2)}$ in the positive quadrant. The relations between l^{ι}_2 and $w_{(2)}$, v^{ι}_2 and $w_{(2)}$ are exhibited in Figure 6.18b: neither is monotonic.

In Figure 6.17b, it was shown that the sectoral demand curve for labour was not necessarily downward-sloping, even in the absence of reswitching and recurrence of techniques. In Figure 6.18b, it has been shown that this negative conclusion can be extended to the aggregate demand curve for labour. Of course, this raises doubts about the validity of the aggregate demand curve for labour as traditionally employed in macroeconomic models.

6.8 Conclusions

Three conclusions present themselves from the analysis of this chapter. First, the choice of technique, under the hypothesis of cost-minimisation, is determinate at each feasible value of r; the

Figure 6.18a

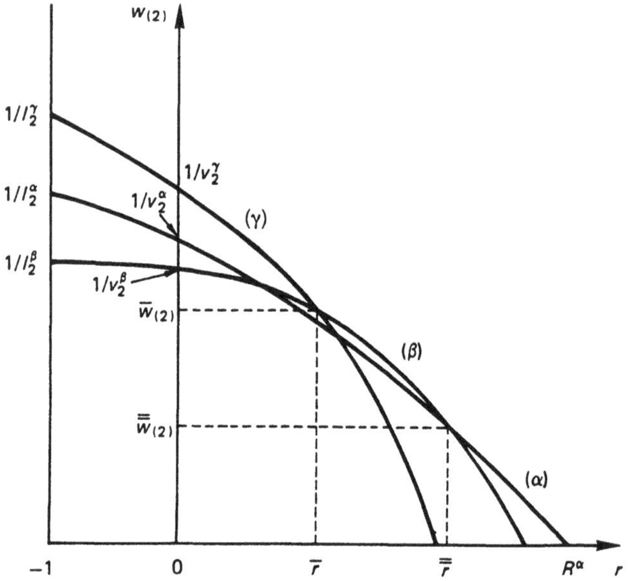

Figure 6.18b

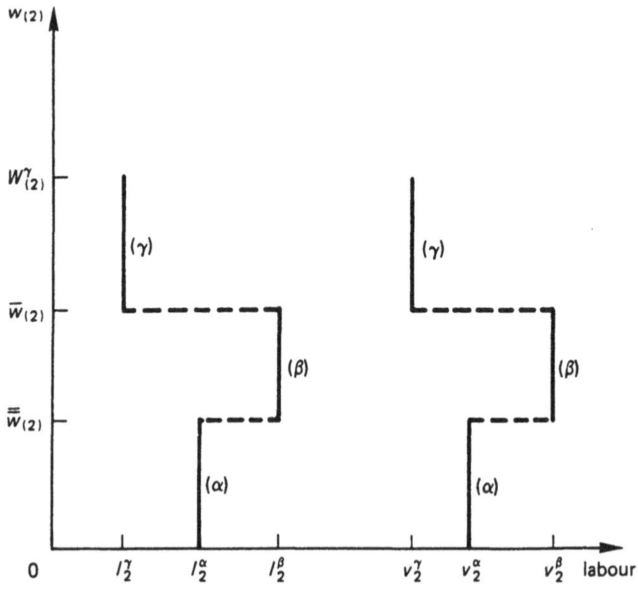

range of feasible values of r is endogenously determined. As a corollary, the cost-minimising technique at a given value of r is that supporting the highest real wage. Second, the ordering of techniques by the rate of profit at which each is cost-minimising is not necessarily unique, in the sense that a particular technique can be most profitable over two disjoint intervals of r; this is established from the existence of the reswitching and recurrence phenomena. The notion of reswitching is usually applied to techniques, not to individual processes – of course, if there is reswitching between (α) and (β), as in section 6.3, there is reswitching at the sectoral level between (IIα) and (IIβ). On the other hand, it is possible to have reswitching of a process without reswitching of a technique. Suppose that the first sector has processes (Iα) and (Iβ), the second processes (IIα) and (IIβ). Then, if the ordering of techniques as r increase from 0 to its maximum value is (Iα, IIα), (Iβ, IIα), (Iβ, IIβ), (Iα, IIβ), it is clear that reswitching of techniques does not occur, though process (Iα) is employed at low and high values of r. The final conclusion concerns the microeconomic implications of the theory of choice of technique. The set of available processes, the technology, is usually taken as given. Though there are restrictions on the possibilities of switching – as explained in section 6.4 – it does not follow that changes in input proportions are systematically related to changes in the corresponding prices.

The theory of choice of technique is based on a simple idea: a capitalist evaluates alternative processes at the prevailing price system, with a switch being made if costs can be reduced. By the assumption that the same commodities are common to all techniques, the method of analysis can be presented in the simplest possible terms. Once established, the essential principle can be extended to models where capital goods are specific to particular techniques.

Appendix

The purpose of this Appendix is to analyse a simple model in which capital goods can differ between techniques. As an example of the model to be studied, consider the following:

Technique (α)

$$a_{11}^{\alpha} \text{ qr wheat} \oplus a_{21}^{\alpha} \text{ t iron} \oplus l_1^{\alpha} \text{ labour} \ominus 1 \text{ qr wheat} \qquad (6.\text{A1a})$$

$$a_{12}^{\alpha} \text{ qr wheat} \oplus a_{22}^{\alpha} \text{ t iron} \oplus l_2^{\alpha} \text{ labour} \ominus 1 \text{ t iron} \qquad (6.\text{A1b})$$

Technique (β)

$$a_{11}^{\beta} \text{ qr wheat} \oplus a_{21}^{\beta} \text{ t copper} \oplus l_1^{\beta} \text{ labour} \ominus 1 \text{ qr wheat} \quad (6.A2a)$$

$$a_{12}^{\beta} \text{ qr wheat} \oplus a_{22}^{\beta} \text{ t copper} \oplus l_2^{\beta} \text{ labour} \ominus 1 \text{ t copper} \quad (6.A2b)$$

The first industry has two process, (Iα) and (Iβ), described in (6.A1a) and (6.A2a) respectively; each process produces the same output, wheat. The second industry also has two processes, (IIα) and (IIβ), described in (6.A1b) and (6.A2b) respectively, but these produce different commodities, iron and copper. Clearly, (Iα) must be combined with (IIα), (Iβ) with (IIβ); it is impossible to combine (Iα) with (IIβ) or (Iβ) with (IIα). Though there are four processes in the technology, two to each sector, there are only two techniques for the economy as a whole: (α) ≡ (Iα, IIα) and (β) ≡ (Iβ, IIβ).[a1] The model described in (6.A1) and (6.A2) is the simplest that can be constructed in which: (a) there are only two techniques; (b) both produced commodities in each technique are basic; and (c) capital goods can be specific to a technique.[a2]

The theory originally developed in Chapter 4 can be applied to each technique so that:

$$w^{\iota} = \frac{(1-(1+r)a_{11}^{\iota})(1-(1+r)a_{22}^{\iota}) - (1+r)^2 a_{12}^{\iota} a_{21}^{\iota}}{l_1^{\iota}(1-(1+r)a_{22}^{\iota}) + (1+r) l_2^{\iota} a_{21}^{\iota}} \equiv \frac{f^{\iota}(r)}{g^{\iota}(r)} \quad (6.A3)$$

$$p^{\iota} = \frac{l_2^{\iota}(1-(1+r)a_{11}^{\iota}) + (1+r) l_1^{\iota} a_{12}^{\iota}}{l_1^{\iota}(1-(1+r)a_{22}^{\iota}) + (1+r) l_2^{\iota} a_{21}^{\iota}} \equiv \frac{h^{\iota}(r)}{g^{\iota}(r)} \quad (6.A4)$$

$\iota = \alpha, \beta$, with the first commodity, wheat, as numeraire.

The existence of different capital goods in different techniques can cause a problem for the theory of choice of technique. To see this, refer to the model discussed in sections 6.3 and 6.4. Suppose that (α) is initially employed: then (IIβ) can be evaluated at (α)'s prices. Now, in the model above, (IIβ) cannot be evaluated at (α)'s price system because the former contains (as input and output) copper for which the latter has no corresponding price. This is not to say that (α)'s price system should be discarded; it is merely that copper inputs and outputs should not be evaluated by the price of iron.

Alternative processes exist and the question of choice of technique must be faced. Consider a capitalist in the second industry, faced with the choice between (IIα) and (IIβ): (α) is the prevailing technique initially. As he purchases wheat inputs from the first industry, he will pay for them at the prevailing price (which is 1 in (α)'s price system); similarly, he will pay each labourer a wage of w^{α}. He decides to set the price of copper by:

$$p_2^{(\beta)} = w^{\alpha} l_2^{\beta} + (1+r)(a_{12}^{\beta} + p_2^{(\beta)} a_{22}^{\beta}) \quad (6.A5)$$

$p_2^{(\beta)}$ is the price of copper at the given rate of profit, r, when wheat and labour inputs are evaluated at (α)'s prices. The capitalist in the second sector is thus obtaining the rate of profit prevailing hitherto. Assuming that there is at least one capitalist producing copper rather than iron, a capitalist can now consider the choice between (Iα) and (Iβ). To answer this, a capitalist evaluates (Iβ) at the prevailing prices: this means using the price of wheat and the real wage from (α) and the price of copper from (6.A5), i.e.

$$s_1(\beta:\alpha) \equiv 1 - (1+r)(\alpha_{11}^{\beta} + p_2^{(\beta)}a_{21}^{\beta}) - w^{\alpha}l_1^{\beta} \qquad (6.A6)$$

Substituting from (6.A5) into (6.A6), I obtain:

$$s_1(\beta:\alpha) \equiv f^{\beta}(r)(1 - w^{\alpha}g^{\beta}(r)/f^{\beta}(r))/(1 - (1+r)a_{22}^{\beta}) \qquad (6.A7)$$

Assuming that r is feasible for (β), otherwise there is no question of choice of technique, I have:

$$\begin{aligned} 1 - (1+r)a_{22}^{\beta} &> 0 \\ f^{\beta}(r) &> 0 \end{aligned} \qquad (6.A8)$$

From (6.A3), (6.A7) and (6.A8), I obtain:

$$\begin{aligned} \text{sign } s_1(\beta:\alpha) &= \text{sign}(1 - w^{\alpha}/w^{\beta}) \\ &= \text{sign}(w^{\beta} - w^{\alpha}) \end{aligned} \qquad (6.A9)$$

Suppose that $w^{\beta} > w^{\alpha}$, so that the capitalist switches from (Iα) to (Iβ). Will the capitalist ever switch from (Iβ) to (Iα)? To answer this, suppose that (β) is initially employed. A capitalist in the second industry sets the price of his output, iron, using process (IIα) as follows:

$$p_2^{(\alpha)} = w_{(1)}^{\beta}l_2^{\alpha} + (1+r)(a_{12}^{\alpha} + p_2^{(\alpha)}a_{22}^{\alpha}) \qquad (6.A10)$$

by analogy with (6.A5). A capitalist in the first industry evaluates (Iα) using the price of wheat and the real wage from (β), together with $p_2^{(\alpha)}$ from (6.A10). He calculates the following surplus or loss relative to normal profits:

$$s_1(\alpha:\beta) \equiv 1 - (1+r)(a_{11}^{\alpha} + p_2^{(\alpha)}a_{21}^{\alpha}) - w^{\beta}l_1^{\alpha} \qquad (6.A11)$$

From (6.A3), (6.A10) and (6.A11), it follows that:

$$\text{sign } s_1(\alpha:\beta) = \text{sign }(w^{\alpha} - w^{\beta}) \qquad (6.A12)$$

So, from (6.A9) and (6.A12), I conclude that:

$$\text{sign } s_1(\beta:\alpha) = (-1)\text{sign } s_1(\alpha:\beta) \qquad (6.A13)$$

This is the analogue of (6.17) for the three-process, two-technique model.

(6.A13) establishes determinacy and uniqueness in the choice of technique. For, if $s_1(\beta:\alpha) > 0$, so that the switch is made from (α) to (β), it follows from (6.A13) that $s_1(\alpha:\beta) < 0$, implying that there is no need to switch back to (α). Hence, if $s_1(\beta:\alpha) > 0$, (β) is the cost-minimising technique. Similarly, if $s_1(\beta:\alpha) < 0$, (α) is the cost-minimising technique. From (6.A9) or (6.A12), the cost-minimising technique supports the higher real wage. The final case to be considered is $s_1(\beta:\alpha) = 0$. Clearly, (α) and (β) are equally profitable. The given value of r is a switch-point, characterised from (6.A9) or (6.A12) by $w^{\alpha} = w^{\beta}$.[a3]

I can now offer the following conclusions on choice of technique:

(1) the theory developed in Chapter 4 can be applied to each technique: in particular *Result 8* holds;
(2) at a given feasible value of r, there is a cost-minimising technique;
(3) it is possible that, at a given feasible value of r, two techniques, (α) and (β), are equally profitable: such a switch-point is characterised by $w^{\alpha} = w^{\beta}$;
(4) if r is not switch-point, there is a unique cost-minimising technique, characterised as that supporting the higher real wage.

(1)–(4) resemble the theory derived in section 6.3 for the three-process, two-technique model. It should be noted that some results from Chapter 6, especially section 6.4, do not extend to the four-processes, two-technique model of the Appendix. *Result 12* is inapplicable to the four-process model: for example, the possibilities illustrated in Figures 6.2–6.4 can now arise. The proofs in *Result 12* relied on the relative prices in the two techniques being equal at a switch-point; but, as observed above, there is no reason why the relative price of iron should equal the relative price of copper at a switch-point. This argument indicates the inapplicability of *Result 12* to the new model, not that (i)–(iii) are themselves invalid.

There is one relatively minor point to be made in conclusion. In the three-process model of sections 6.3 and 6.4, there were at most two switch-points between any two techniques. For the model described in this Appendix, the maximum number of switch-points between two techniques is three, equal to the number of basic commodities (wheat, iron and copper). Not much additional significance can be attached to this extra switch-point.

Commentary

Sraffa treats the question of choice of technique for single-product industries models in sections 92–95, chapter XII, of PCMC.

The theory of choice of technique was initially developed to provide the basis for aggregate growth and capital theory. Indeed, recent interest in the problems of choice of technique can be traced to Robinson (1953–4), which was concerned with 'The Production Function and the Theory of Capital'. In his 'Comment' on this article, Champernowne (1953–4) alerted economists to the reswitching and recurrence phenomena. His assumption (viii) – 'There is never more than one food-wage rate at which two given basic equipments are both competitive' (p. 116) – can be rewritten in the terminology of this book as 'There is at most one switch-point on the w–r frontier between any two techniques'. His assumption (ix) – 'Every set of values of the (food wage) for which a given set of basic equipments is competitive is a closed connected set' (p. 116) – can be rewritten as 'Each technique can be cost-minimising over only one interval of values of *r*'. Champernowne is thus excluding reswitching and recurrence – by assumption. The subsequent literature (e.g. Swan, 1956; Solow, 1955–6) dealt mainly with technical questions of aggregation (except Robinson, 1956). In Part III of PCMC, Sraffa *raised* the question of choice of technique (see his chapter XII, 'Switch in Methods of Production'). This particular issue lay dormant until Levhari (1965) claimed that reswitching could not occur in economies with only basic commodities (or 'indecomposable technologies', as he put it). In a later issue of *The Quarterly Journal of Economics* (1966), entitled 'Paradoxes in Capital Theory', it was conclusively proved that Levhari's Non-Switching Theorem was false. In that issue:

(1) Pasinetti (1966), who first questioned Levhari's Theorem, produced an example of reswitching in an economy with non-basic commodities (i.e. a decomposable technology);
(2) Garegnani (1966) and Bruno, Burmeister and Sheshinski (1966) provided counter-examples to Levhari's Theorem for a model with only basic commodities (i.e. an indecomposable technology).

The implications of reswitching discussed by Levhari were essentially those of Champernowne. The desirability of a no-reswitching theorem was evident. Despite the conclusive counter-examples to Levhari's Theorem, the idea that sufficient conditions could be found for the absence of reswitching proved irresistible. Gallaway and Shukla (1974) claimed to have discovered such a condition, only for Garegnani (1976a) and Sato (1976) to provide numerical counter-examples. The material in section 6.4 is taken from Woods (1988). The Non-Switching Theorem was independently discovered by Salvadori and Steedman (1987).

Harcourt (1969, 1972, 1975, 1976, 1983) discusses the nature and implications for economics of reswitching and other phenomena, as well as providing extensive bibliographies.

The two capital models discussed in this chapter have been extensively employed in the literature. The one analysed in the Appendix can be found in Robinson (1953–4), Champernowne (1953–4), Samuelson (1961–2) and Garegnani (1970), among many. It is obviously possible to construct a hybrid model from the two dealt with in this chapter: there would be some capital goods common to all techniques and others specific to a technique. Such a model has been analysed by Bharadwaj (1970) and Pasinetti (1977).

Section 6.7 is based on Garegnani (1970) and Steedman (1985a).

Exercises

1. Prove that, if $a_{i2}^{\beta} \leqslant a_{i2}^{\alpha}$, $i = 1,2$, $l_2^{\beta} \leqslant l_2^{\alpha}$, walosi, ($\beta$) is the cost-minimising technique for all feasible values of r.

2. Construct numerical examples satisfying $a_{i2}^{\beta} \leqslant a_{i2}^{\alpha}$, $i = 1,2$, walosi, $l_2^{\beta} > l_2^{\alpha}$, such that:
   (a) (β) is the cost-minimising technique for all feasible values of r;
   (b) (β) is the cost-minimising technique for some feasible values of r.

3. Analyse this model:

   (I) 5/12 qr wheat ⊕ 1/4 t iron ⊕ 3/7 labour ⊖ 1 qr wheat
   (IIα) 1/3 qr wheat ⊕ 1/2 t iron ⊕ 4/7 labour ⊖ 1 t iron
   (IIβ) 1/4 qr wheat ⊕ 1/2 t iron ⊕ 6/7 labour ⊖ 1 t iron

   i.e. Calculate the real wage rate–rate of profits curve, the maximum wage rate and rate of profit, and the relative price for each technique. Find the range of values of r over which each technique is cost-minimising. Show that choice of technique is independent of the numeraire.

4. Analyse this model:

   (I) 1/2 qr wheat ⊕ 2/5 t iron ⊕ 1 labour ⊖ 1 qr wheat
   (IIα) 1/10 qr wheat ⊕ 1/2 t iron ⊕ 1 labour ⊖ 1 t iron
   (IIβ) 1/5 qr wheat ⊕ 1/4 t iron ⊕ 1 labour ⊖ 1 t iron

   (See *Example 1*, section 6.7)

5. Analyse this model:

   (I) 1/2 qr wheat ⊕ 2/5 t iron ⊕ 1 labour ⊖ 1 qr wheat
   (IIα) 2/5 qr wheat ⊕ 3/10 t iron ⊕ 1 labour ⊖ 1 t iron
   (IIβ) 1/5 qr wheat ⊕ 1/3 t iron ⊕ 3 labour ⊖ 1 t iron

   (See *Example 2*, section 6.7.)

6. Analyse this model:

   (I) 1/2 t iron ⊕ 1 labour ⊖ 1 qr wheat
   (IIα) 1/2 qr wheat ⊕ 1/2 labour ⊖ 1 t iron
   (IIβ) 1/8 qr wheat ⊕ 3 labour ⊖ 1 t iron

   (See *Example 3*, section 6.7.)

7. Analyse this model:

   (I) 1/6 qr wheat ⊕ 1/3 t iron ⊕ 1 labour ⊖ 1 qr wheat
   (IIα) 1/6 qr wheat ⊕ 1/6 t iron ⊕ 1 labour ⊖ 1 t iron
   (IIβ) 137/546 qr wheat ⊕ 19/273 t iron ⊕ 92/91 labour ⊖ 1 t iron

(See *Example 4*, section 6.7.) This exercise is due to Garegnani (1976).

8. Analyse this model:

   (I) 1/5 qr wheat ⊕ 2/5 t iron ⊕ 1 labour ⊖ 1 qr wheat
   (IIα) 2/5 qr wheat ⊕ 1/5 t iron ⊕ 3/2 labour ⊖ 1 t iron
   (IIβ) 0.5205 qr wheat ⊕ 0.08 t iron ⊕ 1.55 labour ⊖ 1 t iron

   This exercise is due to Sato (1976).

9. In each of exercises 4–8, determine the switch-points by solving:

   (*a*) $p^{\alpha}_{(1)} = p^{\beta}_{(1)}$; (*b*) $w^{\alpha}_{(2)} = w^{\beta}_{(2)}$; (*c*) $p^{\alpha}_{(2)} = p^{\beta}_{(2)}$.

10. Construct a numerical example to illustrate the Non-Switching Theorem, *Result 12*(i).

11. Combine a technique having concave *w–r* curve with one of the techniques in exercise 10 to illustrate the No-Reswitching Theorem, *Result 12*(ii).

12. Construct a two-technique model in which one *w–r* curve is convex, the other concave and there is one switch-point – to illustrate the No-Reswitching Theorem, *Result 12*(ii).

13. Construct two-technique examples in which there are no switch-points and:

    (a) both *w–r* curves are straight lines;
    (b) both *w–r* curves are convex;
    (c) both *w–r* curves are concave;
    (d) one *w–r* curve is a straight line, the other convex;
    (e) one *w–r* curve is a straight line, the other concave;
    (f) one *w–r* curve is convex, the other concave.

14. Consider the model analysed in section 6.3.

    (i) Let $s_2(\beta{:}\alpha) = 0$ at $\bar{r}$. Prove that : (a) if $w^{\alpha} > 0$, $\bar{r} < R^{\beta}$; (b) if $w^{\alpha} = 0$, $\bar{r} = R^{\beta}$.
    (ii) Let $s_2(\beta{:}\alpha) < 0$ at $\bar{r}$. Show, by means of examples, that this is consistent with (a) $\bar{r} \leqslant \mathrm{R}^{\beta}$ and (b) $\bar{r} > R^{\beta}$.

15. Prove that the following constitute a sufficient condition for no switching:
    w^{α} and w^{β} have different curvature, and $R^{\alpha} < R^{\beta}$, $W^{\alpha} < W^{\beta}$ or $R^{\alpha} > R^{\beta}$, $W^{\alpha} > W^{\beta}$.

16. Provide a numerical example to illustrate Figure 6.7, i.e. two tech-

niques with w–r curves of the same curvature and only one switch-point.

17. Prove that, if $W^{\alpha} > W^{\beta}$ and $R^{\alpha} < R^{\beta}$ or $W^{\alpha} < W^{\beta}$ and $R^{\alpha} > R^{\beta}$, there is one switch-point between (α) and (β). Provide numerical examples with w–r curves having different curvature and only one switch-point.

18. Consider the algorithm presented in section 6.5. Prove that:
(a) the algorithm terminates when the technique entering any stage as the prevailing technique emerges from it in the same state;
(b) a technique once discarded cannot re-emerge as a prevailing technique.

19. Consider the algorithm presented in section 6.6. Prove that:
(a) if (6.37) holds at $\bar{r}$, this value is a switch-point;
(b) if (6.38) holds at $\bar{r}$, (α) is preferred to (β).

20. Prove that *Result 15* is unaffected by a change of numeraire.

21. Given techniques (α) and (β), a convex combination of them is given by $c(\alpha) + (1-c)(\beta)$, $0 \leqslant c \leqslant 1$. Write down the technical coefficients of the convex combination. When can a convex combination be cost-minimising?

22. Consider the technology:

(Iα) 2/5 t iron $\oplus$ 1/2 labour $\ominus$ 1 qr wheat
(Iβ) 1/5 t iron $\oplus$ 3/5 labour $\ominus$ 1 qr wheat
(IIα) 2/5 qr wheat $\oplus$ 1/2 labour $\ominus$ 1 t iron
(IIβ) 1/10 qr wheat $\oplus$ 1/10 labour $\ominus$ 1 t iron

With wheat as numeraire, evaluate the four w–r curves. Hence, find the ordering of techniques. Show that there is just one switch-point, r^*, on the frontier, where $r^* < R^{\alpha,\alpha}$ ($R^{\alpha,\alpha}$ being the maximum rate of profit of the technique (Iα, IIα). Suppose that (Iα, IIα) is initially employed at a value of r lying between r^* and $R^{\alpha.\alpha}$. Then let (Iβ) and (IIβ) become available. Show that:

$$w^{\alpha,\alpha} < w^{\beta,\alpha} < w^{\beta,\beta} < w^{\alpha,\beta}$$

This example, due to Fujimoto (1983), proves that, though a process such as (Iβ) may be cost-reducing initially, it is not necessarily employed when both sectors have alternative processes. Note that this example is consistent with the choice of technique algorithm advanced in section 6.6.

23. Analyse the following model:

(Iα) 2/3 t iron ⊕ 1 labour ⊖ 1 qr wheat
(Iβ) 1/2 t iron ⊕ 2 labour ⊖ 1 qr wheat
(IIα) 2/3 qr wheat ⊕ 1 labour ⊖ 1 t iron
(IIβ) 1/2 qr wheat ⊕ 2 labour ⊖ 1 t iron

This exercise, due to Salvadori and Steedman (1987), should be studied in connection with section 6.4. In this model, there is a switch-point on the outer envelope at $r = 1/5$ between (Iα, IIα) and (Iβ, IIβ). This example demonstrates the possibility that there can be a switch-point on the outer envelope between two techniques each having a uniform capital–labour ratio if they do not share a common process.

24. Analyse the following model:

(I) 379/423 t iron ⊕ 89/10 labour ⊖ 1 qr wheat
(IIα) 1/2 qr wheat ⊕ 1/10 t iron ⊕ 9/50 labour ⊖ 1 t iron
(IIβ) 1/4 qr wheat ⊕ 5/12 t iron ⊕ 3/2 labour ⊖ 1 t iron

This example is due to Garegnani (1966).

25. Consider the following model:

(I) 1/10 t iron ⊕ 1 labour ⊖ 1 qr wheat
(IIα) 1/50 qr wheat ⊕ 3/10 t iron ⊕ 33/50 labour ⊖ 1 t iron
(IIβ) 71/100 qr wheat ⊕ 1/100 labour ⊖ 1 t iron

This example is due to Bruno, Burmeister and Sheshinski (1966).

26. Analyse the following model:

(Iα) 1/10 qr wheat ⊕ 1/5 t iron ⊕ 1 labour ⊖ 1 qr wheat
(Iβ) 1/10 qr wheat ⊕ 1/5 t iron ⊕ 1/2 labour ⊖ 1 qr wheat
(IIα) 1/10 qr wheat ⊕ 1/10 t iron ⊕ 4/5 labour ⊖ 1 t iron
(IIβ) 1/20 qr wheat ⊕ 1/10 t iron ⊕ 9/10 labour ⊖ 1 t iron
(IIγ) 1/100 qr wheat ⊕ 1/10 t iron ⊕ 1 labour ⊖ 1 t iron

This example is due to Salanti (1984). Construct the diagram of w–r curves and hence discuss the choice of technique.

27. Consider this model:

(I) 1/5 t iron ⊕ 1 labour ⊖ 1 qr wheat
(IIα) 1/10 qr wheat ⊕ 1/2 t iron ⊕ 1/2 labour ⊖ 1 t iron
(IIβ) 1 qr wheat ⊕ 1/5 labour ⊖ 1 t iron.

This example is due to Morishima (1966). Does it exhibit reswitching?

28. '*Result 12*(i) shows that equal capital–labour ratios in the two sectors rules out reswitching.' Do you agree?

29. Consider the two-technique model of section 6.3. If (α) is preferred to (β), prove that $p^{\alpha} < p^{\beta}$, $w^{\alpha} > w^{\beta}$.

30. Can reswitching occur in this model?

    71/144 qr wheat ⊕ 7/8 labour ⊖ 1 qr wheat
    1/6 qr wheat ⊕ 1/6 t iron ⊕ 1 labour ⊖ 1 qr wheat
    1 qr wheat ⊕ 1 labour ⊖ 1 t iron

    This example is due to Broome (1983).

31. Consider the decomposable model (6.34).
    (a) Find conditions for the *w–r* curve to be a straight line. Do they depend on choice of numeraire? Contrast with the conditions (4.33) of Chapter 4. Can these conditions ever hold in (6.34)?
    (b) Is *Result 14* consistent with *Result 12*(i), the Non-Switching Theorem?
    (c) Choose values for a_{22}^{ι} and l_2^{ι} in (6.34) such that $W_{(2)}^{\alpha} > W_{(2)}^{\beta}$, $R^{\alpha} < R^{\beta}$ (or vice versa). Solve the price equations and determine the switch-point.
    (d) For your numerical example in (c), examine the effect on choice of technique of changing the numeraire from the second to the first commodity.

Exercises 32–36 refer to the model in the Appendix.

32. Analyse the following model:

    ($I\alpha$) 1 qr wheat ⊕ 2.8 t iron ⊕ 0.6 labour ⊖ 1 qr wheat
    ($II\alpha$) 1 qr wheat ⊕ 1.2 t iron ⊕ 0.4 labour ⊖ 1 t iron
    ($I\beta$) 0.9 qr wheat ⊕ 2.088 t copper ⊕ 0.6 labour ⊖ 1 qr wheat
    ($II\beta$) 0.684 qr wheat ⊕ 1.224 t copper ⊕ 0.4 labour ⊖ 3.312 t copper

    Use this example to comment on the Non-Switching Theorem, *Result 12*(i).

33. Analyse the following model:

    ($I\alpha$) and ($II\alpha$) as in exercise 32.
    ($I\beta$) 0.4 qr wheat ⊕ 1.6 t copper ⊕ 7/9 labour ⊖ 1.98 qr wheat
    ($II\beta$) 0.6 qr wheat ⊕ 2.4 t copper ⊕ 2/9 labour ⊖ 4 t copper

    Use this example to comment on the No-Reswitching Theorem, *Result 12*(ii).

34. Analyse the following model:

    ($I\alpha$) 14/9 qr wheat ⊕ 20/9 t iron ⊕ 4/5 labour ⊖ 10/3 qr wheat
    ($II\alpha$) 7/9 qr wheat ⊕ 10/9 t iron ⊕ 1/5 labour ⊖ 10/3 t iron
    ($I\beta$) 0.48663 qr wheat ⊕ 0.48663 t copper ⊕ 0.48663 labour ⊖ 2.046 qr wheat

(IIβ) 0.55934 qr wheat ⊕ 0.76336 t copper ⊕ 0.51773 labour ⊖ 1.245 t copper

Are there *three* switch-points between (α) and (β)?

Exercises 32–34 are due to Robinson and Naqvi (1967).

35. Examine the question of the maximum number of switch-points in the four-process, two technique model. Refer to Bharadwaj (1970), Pasinetti (1977a), Robinson and Naqvi (1967) and the previous exercise.

36. A special case of (6.A1) and (6.A2) has been used in the literature: namely, $a^{\iota}_{1j} = 0$, $j = 1,2$, $\iota = \alpha, \beta$. So, wheat is a pure consumption good. Construct numerical examples to illustrate the various switching possibilities for this special case. (Adopt a taxonomic approach as in exercise 13.)

37. 'The *w–r* frontier is obtained by taking the inner envelope of feasible *w–r* curves.' Is this true?

38. 'The non-substitution theorem (i.e. *Result 11*) is invalid for the single-product industries, circulating capital model.' Do you agree?

39. A technology is a convex cone if:
    (i) each technique exhibits constant returns to scale;
    (ii) given two techniques (α) and (β), a third technique (γ) = c(α) + (1 − c)(β) can be constructed for any real number *c* between 0 and 1. (So: $a^{\gamma}_{ij} = ca^{\alpha}_{ij} + (1-c)a^{\beta}_{ij}$, $l^{\gamma}_{j} = cl^{\alpha}_{j} + (1-c)l^{\beta}_{j}$, $i,j = 1,2$.)

    'The theory of choice of technique (presented in this chapter) is invalid because it does not allow for a convex cone of production possibilities.' Discuss.

40. 'If a single-product industry uses only produced inputs, the theory (presented in this chapter) implies a choice of technique which locates industry output on the industry's technological or factor rewards frontier.' Is this true?

41. Consider a special case of the model analysed in this chapter where there is only one capital good (say $a^{\iota}_{1j} \neq 0$, $a^{\iota}_{2j} = 0$, $j = 1,2$, for all ι). Can reswitching and/or capital reversing occur?

42. Consider a special case of the model analysed in the Appendix where there is only one capital good in each technique, but a capital good is specific to a technique. Can reswitching and/or capital reversing occur?

Notes to Chapter 6

1. See the Appendix to this chapter for discussion of models where capital goods can differ between techniques.
2. (6.6) can be obtained directly from the first equations in (α) and (β):

$$1 = w^{\iota} l_1 + (1+r)(a_{11} + p^{\iota} a_{21})$$

(6.3) and (6.5) will also be used later.

3. For ease of notation, I drop the bracketed suffix, $(\bar{r})$, from p^{α} and w^{α}.
4. Except in the trivial case where

$$a^{\beta}_{i2} \geqslant a^{\alpha}_{i2},\ l^{\beta}_2 \geqslant l^{\alpha}_2 \text{ walosi}$$

or $$a^{\beta}_{i2} \leqslant a^{\alpha}_{i2},\ l^{\beta}_2 \leqslant l^{\alpha}_2 \text{ walosi}$$

5. See the Appendix to this chapter.
6. Each technique produces and uses the same two commodities, wheat and iron.
7. Once chosen, each ordering is fixed, an assumption made to facilitate the exposition. Each industry has its own 'book of blueprints'.
8. The algorithm is a generalisation of that exhibited in section 6.5.
9. If r is a switch-point on the outer envelope of w–r curves, there will be at least two cost-minimising techniques; otherwise, there will be a unique cost-minimising technique.
10. I have operated throughout this section with the first commodity as numeraire. The conclusions are unaffected by changing the numeraire.
11. That is, techniques sharing a switch-point on the w–r frontier.
12. See Pasinetti (1977a, chapter 6) and (1977b).

a1. Compare this model with that employed in Chapter 6. There, a four-process model, with two to each sector, would yield four techniques.

a2. Some slight simplification can be achieved by having $a^{\iota}_{11} = a^{\iota}_{22} = 0$, $\iota = \alpha,\beta$; (a)–(c) would still be satisfied.

a3. Contrast this definition of a switch-point, namely:

$$s_1(\beta{:}\alpha) = s_1(\alpha{:}\beta) = 0$$
$$w^{\beta}_{(1)} = w^{\alpha}_{(1)}$$

with that for the model in sections 6.3 and 6.4:

$$s_2(\beta{:}\alpha) = s_2(\alpha{:}\beta) = 0$$
$$p^{\beta}_{(1)} = p^{\alpha}_{(1)}$$
$$w^{\beta}_{(1)} = w^{\alpha}_{(1)}$$

The prices of the second commodities (iron and copper) are in general not equal at a switch-point between (α) and (β) in the model of the Appendix: there is no reason why they should be.

7

The Quantity Equations and Duality

7.1 Introduction

So far, I have considered productive economies in a stationary state. At the end of each production period, the value of the physical surplus (over and above inter-industry requirements to maintain next period's outputs at this period's levels) is allocated between wages and profits, all of which is consumed. That is, the level of new investments (in the form of advances of means of production) is zero. Retain all the assumptions made in the stationary state analysis except that referring to a constant labour force or population; instead, assume that the labour force grows at rate ϱ in each period. Hitherto, the net outputs, F_1 and F_2 (which, in a stationary state, can be thought of as consumption) have been taken as exogenous; I now assume not only exogeneity but also constancy of consumption, the latter in the sense of consumption per head. Thus, I shall concentrate on those features resulting solely from the introduction of a growing labour force with a constant technology and constant consumption per head. To maintain constant consumption per head with a growing labour force, production of each commodity must be expanded at rate ϱ. If next period's production has to be $(1+\varrho)$ times this period's, it follows that the advances of means of production made at the end of this period (for inter-industry uses next period) must be $(1+\varrho)$ times the advances made at the end of last period (for uses this period). It is clear that by introducing growth in the labour force as the sole dynamic element in the economy, I have to modify the stationary state analysis only to the extent that all physical variables now grow absolutely at rate ϱ, whereas previously they were constant. Note that the relations between the physical variables remains constant which implies that the physical variables in per capita terms remain constant. The model I have in mind is thus a quasi-stationary state.

In section 7.2, I derive the quantity equations for the model: it will be seen that they are structurally similar to the price (and quantity) equations extensively analysed in earlier chapters. This duality is exploited in section 7.3 to permit the calculation of aggregate variables. Then, in section 7.4, I combine this analysis with that of choice of technique to study the effect of switches of technique on the aggregate variables. This leads naturally in section 7.5 to an examination of the aggregate production function, a familiar concept in macroeconomics.

7.2 The Quantity Equations

Let $X_i(t)$ and $F_i(t)$ denote the gross and net output respectively of commodity i at the end of period t. The net output of a commodity is equal to the gross output minus the total amount used up as means of production in both industries. So, the quantity equations are:

$$X_1(t) = X_{11}(t) + X_{12}(t) + F_1(t) \tag{7.1a}$$

$$X_2(t) = X_{21}(t) + X_{22}(t) + F_2(t) \tag{7.1b}$$

which are identical to those of Chapters 2 and 3, except that a time suffix has been added.[1] Given the technique of production, the relations between inputs and outputs are known so that (7.1) can be written as:

$$X_1(t) = a_{11}X_1(t) + a_{12}X_2(t) + F_1(t) \tag{7.2a}$$

$$X_2(t) = a_{21}X_1(t) + a_{22}X_2(t) + F_2(t) \tag{7.2b}$$

The net output of each commodity is now allocated between consumption and net, or new, investments. Let $C_i(t)$ denote the quantity of commodity i consumed at the end of period t, or during period $(t+1)$, from period t's output. Let $I_i(t)$ denote the amount of commodity i that is allocated to new investments out of period

t's output. By the circulating capital assumption, new investments consist of increases in inter-industry advances at the end of period t over the levels in period $(t-1)$. So:

$$F_1(t) = C_1(t) + I_1(t) \tag{7.3a}$$

$$F_2(t) = C_2(t) + I_2(t) \tag{7.3b}$$

Assuming a constant relation between consumption and the size of the labour force:

$$C_1(t) = c_1 L(t) \tag{7.4a}$$

$$C_2(t) = c_2 L(t) \tag{7.4b}$$

where c_i is the consumption of commodity i per head. By the hypothesis made about the labour force:

$$L(t) = (1+\varrho)^t L(0) \tag{7.5}$$

ϱ being the growth rate of the labour force, $L(t)$ the size of the labour force at time t. As the structure of consumption per head is constant, total consumption of each commodity increases each period at rate ϱ. To meet this increased consumption demand next period, productive capacity has to be enlarged by extra inter-industry advances from this year's gross output, over and above that required to keep capacity constant (i.e. to replace circulating capital in a stationary state). To maintain full utilisation of capacity, the inter-industry advances from sector i to sector j for use in period $(t+1)$ are equal to $(1+\varrho)$ times the same inter-industry advances in period t. That is, the new investments of commodity i are ϱ times the total inter-industry advances of commodity i in a stationary state, or:

$$I_1(t) = \varrho X_{11}(t) + \varrho X_{12}(t) \tag{7.6a}$$

$$I_2(t) = \varrho X_{21}(t) + \varrho X_{22}(t) \tag{7.6b}$$

Substituting from (7.3), (7.4) and (7.6) into (7.2), I obtain:

$$X_1(t) = (1+\varrho)(a_{11}X_1(t) + a_{12}X_2(t)) + c_1 L(t) \tag{7.7a}$$

$$X_2(t) = (1+\varrho)(a_{21}X_1(t) + a_{22}X_2(t)) + c_2L(t) \tag{7.7b}$$

Dividing (7.7) by $L(t)$ and denoting $X_i(t)/L(t)$ by $x_i(t)$, $i = 1,2$, I have:

$$x_1(t) = (1+\varrho)(a_{11}x_1(t) + a_{12}x_2(t)) + c_1 \tag{7.8a}$$

$$x_2(t) = (1+\varrho)(a_{21}x_1(t) + a_{22}x_2(t)) + c_2 \tag{7.8b}$$

As the technical coefficients, the growth rate and the components of consumption per head are constant, there is a constant solution to (7.8):

$$x_i(t) = x_i \quad i = 1,2 \tag{7.9}$$

Then (7.8) becomes:

$$x_1 = (1+\varrho)(a_{11}x_1 + a_{12}x_2) + c_1 \tag{7.10a}$$

$$x_2 = (1+\varrho)(a_{21}x_1 + a_{22}x_2) + c_2 \tag{7.10b}$$

(7.10) is structurally similar to (4.5) of Chapter 4. By *Result 6*, there is a positive solution to (7.10), with $c_i \geqslant 0$, $i = 1,2$, walosi, if and only if:

$$1 - (1+\varrho)a_{11} > 0 \tag{7.11a}$$

$$1 - (1+\varrho)a_{22} > 0 \tag{7.11b}$$

$$(1 - (1+\varrho)a_{11})(1 - (1+\varrho)a_{22}) - (1+\varrho)^2a_{12}a_{21} > 0 \tag{7.11c}$$

By the same argument as in section 4.2, there is a positive value of ϱ, denoted by ϱ^*, at which:

$$f(\varrho) \equiv (1 - (1+\varrho)a_{11})(1 - (1+\varrho)a_{22}) - (1+\varrho)^2a_{12}a_{21} = 0 \tag{7.12}$$

and (7.11a) and (7.11b) are satisfied. Clearly, $\varrho^* = R$, the maximum rate of profit. When ϱ assumes this value, it follows from (7.10)–(7.12) that $c_1 = c_2 = 0$. So, for $0 \leqslant \varrho < R$, I have from (7.10):

$$x_1 = (c_1(1 - (1 + \varrho)a_{22}) + c_2(1 + \varrho)a_{12})/f(\varrho) \tag{7.13a}$$

$$x_2 = (c_1(1 + \varrho)a_{21} + c_2(1 - (1 + \varrho)a_{11}))/f(\varrho) \tag{7.13b}$$

When $\varrho = R$:

$$\begin{aligned} x_1/x_2 &= (1 + R)a_{12}/(1 - (1 + R)a_{11}) \\ &= (1 - (1 + R)a_{22})/(1 + R)a_{21} \end{aligned} \tag{7.14}$$

7.3 The Consumption–Growth Curve and Duality

Suppose that only the first commodity is consumed: then $c_2 = 0$ in section 7.2. From the definitions:

$$\begin{aligned} l_1x_1 + l_2x_2 &= \frac{L_1}{X_1} \cdot \frac{X_1}{L} + \frac{L_2}{X_2} \cdot \frac{X_2}{L} \\ &= (L_1 + L_2)/L = L/L = 1 \end{aligned} \tag{7.15}$$

Multiplying (7.13a) by l_1, (7.13b) by l_2, I obtain:

$$\begin{aligned} l_1x_1 + l_2x_2 &= (l_1c_1(1 - (1 + \varrho)a_{22}) + l_2c_1(1 + \varrho)a_{21})/f(\varrho) \\ &= c_1g(\varrho)/f(\varrho) \end{aligned} \tag{7.16}$$

where $g(\varrho)$ is defined as in (4.27) of Chapter 4. So, from (7.15) and (7.16), I have:

$$c_1 = f(\varrho)/g(\varrho) \tag{7.17}$$

(7.17), the consumption–growth curve, is identical to $w_{(1)} = f(r)/g(r)$, the wage rate–rate of profits curve in terms of the first commodity. In particular, consumption per head is at its maximum when $\varrho = 0$, its minimum when $\varrho = R$, with $dc_1/d\varrho < 0$. The relation between c_1 and ϱ, illustrated in Figure 7.1, is dual to that between $w_{(1)}$ and r.

As an application of this duality, consider Figure 7.1, where r and ϱ are measured on the horizontal axis, $w_{(1)}$ and c_1 on the vertical axis. I have superimposed the $c_1 - \varrho$ curve on the $w_{(1)} - r$ curve; as these two are identical, only one – given by $w_{(1)}DBR$ – appears in the figure. Let the rate of profit be given by $\bar{r}$, the rate of growth by $\bar{\varrho}$. Then, from the $w_{(1)} - r$ curve, the real wage is given by $\bar{w}_{(1)}$; and, from the $c_1 - \varrho$ curve, the level of consumption per head is $\bar{c}_1$. Denote the value of net output per head by y and the

Figure 7.1

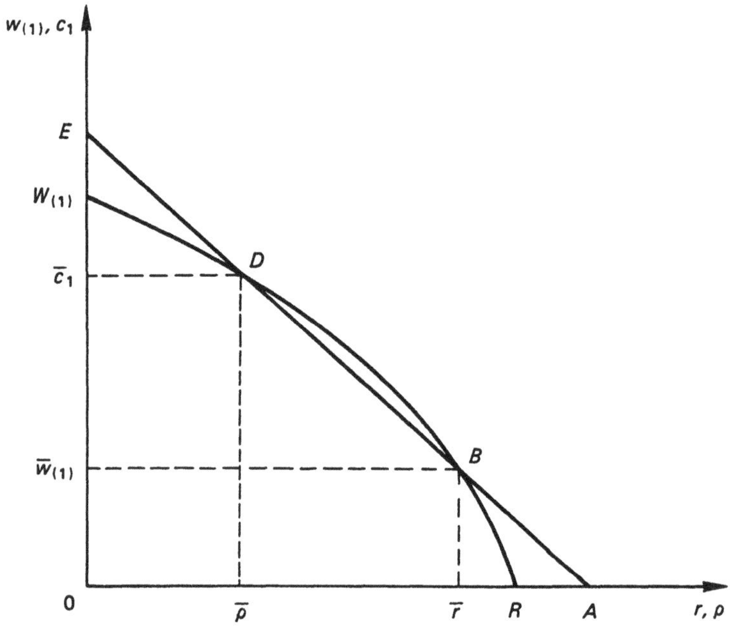

value of capital per head by k; as both net output and capital per head in general consist of quantities of both commodities, they must be measured in value terms if a scalar rather than a vector representation is required. These identities hold:

$$y \equiv rk + w_{(1)} \equiv \varrho k + c_1 \qquad (7.18)$$

That is, the value of net output per head (y) is equal to the value of consumption per head (c_1) plus the value of net investment per head (ϱk). The value of net output per head (that is, net income per head) must be distributed as wages ($w_{(1)}$) and profits per head (rk). From (7.18), I obtain if $r \neq \varrho$:

$$k = (c_1 - w_{(1)})/(r - \varrho) \qquad (7.19)$$

When $r = \bar{r}$, $\varrho = \bar{\varrho}$, $\bar{c}_1 - \bar{w}_{(1)} = DF$ and $\bar{r} - \bar{\varrho} = FB$. So, the value of capital per head is given by the slope of the line DB, or the line AE:

$$k = \tan 0AE = \tan \bar{w}_{(1)}BE \tag{7.20}$$

Profits per head are equal to the rate of profit times the value of capital per head:

$$\begin{aligned}\text{Profits per head} &= 0\bar{r}\cdot\tan\bar{w}_{(1)}BE \\ &= \bar{w}_{(1)}B\cdot\tan\bar{w}_{(1)}BE = \bar{w}_{(1)}E\end{aligned} \tag{7.21}$$

When $r = \bar{r}$, the wage rate is equal to $0\bar{w}_{(1)}$. So:

$$\begin{aligned}0\bar{w}_{(1)} + \bar{w}_{(1)}E &= \text{wage rate plus profits per head} \\ &= 0E \\ &= \text{value of net output per head}\end{aligned} \tag{7.22}$$

Alternatively, as $\tan\bar{w}_{(1)}BE = \tan c_1DE$, it follows that the value of net investment per head is equal to the rate of growth times the value of capital per head. When $\varrho = \bar{\varrho}$:

$$\begin{aligned}\text{Value of net investment per head} &= 0\bar{\varrho}\cdot\tan\bar{c}_1DE \\ &= \bar{c}_1E\end{aligned} \tag{7.23a}$$

$$\text{Value of consumption per head} = 0\bar{c}_1 \tag{7.23b}$$

So:

$$\begin{aligned}0\bar{c}_1 + \bar{c}_1E &= \text{value of net investment per head plus} \\ &\quad\ \text{value of consumption per head} \\ &= 0E \\ &= \text{value of net output per head}\end{aligned} \tag{7.24}$$

Thus, the w–r and c–ϱ curves can be used to calculate the values of net output and capital per head, if r and ϱ are known.[2] Also, the capital–output ratio, measured in value terms, can be calculated from the triangle $0AE$. For:

$$\begin{aligned}0A = 0E\cdot 0A/0E &= y/\tan 0AE \\ &= y/k \text{ the output–capital ratio.}\end{aligned} \tag{7.25}$$

Figure 7.2a

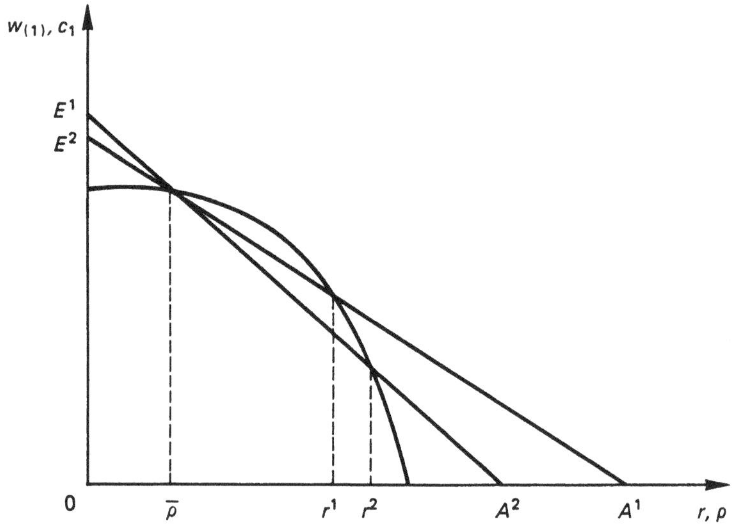

As a further exercise in duality theory, the effects of changes in either r or ϱ on the aggregate variables can be determined. From Chapter 4, the w–r curve, and hence the c– ϱ curve, can assume one of only three forms. Consider first the case where $d^2w_{(1)}/dr^2 < 0$, as in Figure 7.2a and the growth rate is fixed at $\bar{\varrho}$. If r increases from r^1 to r^2, the value of net output increases from $0E^1$ to $0E^2$, the value of capital per man increases from tan$0A^1E^1$ to tan $0A^2E^2$ and the capital–output ratio increases from $1/0A^1$ to $1/0A^2$. As the growth rate is constant, only the value variables have altered as a result of the change in r: yet, this suffices to affect the values of net output per head, capital per head and the capital–output ratio. These changes are referred to as *negative* price Wicksell effects because the increase in r results in an increase in each of the aggregate variables (hence, it is a negative effect), with the actual physical outputs constant (hence, it is a price effect). Now consider Figure 7.2b, where $d^2w_{(1)}/dr^2 > 0$. The increase in r from r^1 to r^2 results in a decrease in the value of net output per head from $0E^1$ to $0E^2$, a decrease in the value of capital per head from tan$0A^1E^1$ to tan$0A^2E^2$ and a decrease in the capital–output ratio from $1/0A^1$ to $1/0A^2$. These changes are referred to as *positive* price Wicksell

Figure 7.2b

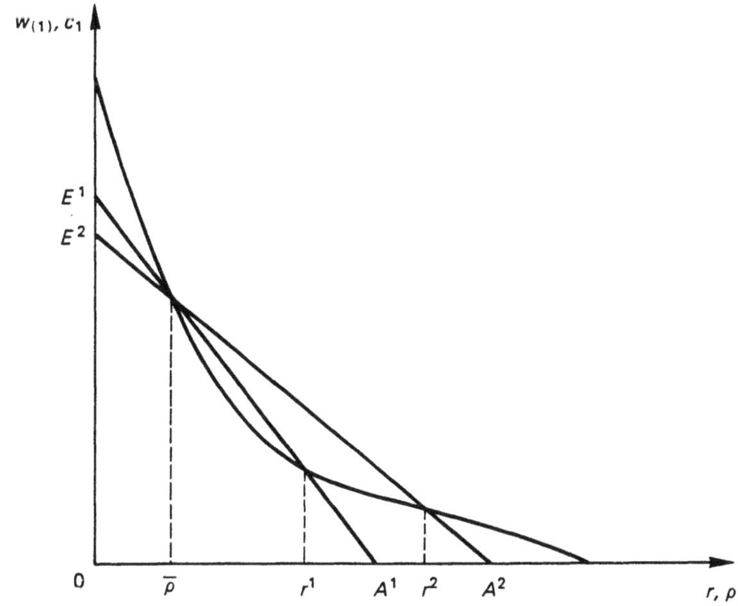

effects because an increase in r results in a decrease in each of the aggregate variables (hence, it is a positive effect), with physical outputs constant (hence, it is a price effect).[3] Finally, consider Figure 7.2c, where $d^2w_{(1)}/dr^2 = 0$ and the w–r curve is given by AE. As changes in r do not affect the three aggregate variables, this case exhibits *neutral* price Wicksell effects. The study of two-sector models so far in this book establishes that a preconception in favour of positive price Wicksell effects is unjustified. There is no *a priori* reason why the positive effect should be considered normal or the negative effect abnormal. Ultimately, these effects are governed by the conditions of production and there is no reason to suppose that one sector is more capital-intensive than the other.

On the basis of Figures 7.2a–c, Figures 7.3a–c can be constructed. For example, Figure 7.3a is obtained from Figure 7.2a by plotting the values of k and y at each value of r between $\bar{\rho}$ and R; similarly, for Figures 7.3b and 7.3c. The upper panels of Figure 7.3 might be interpreted as production functions because each exhibits a relation between the value of net output per head and the value of capital per head. However, it should be remembered that the

Figure 7.2c

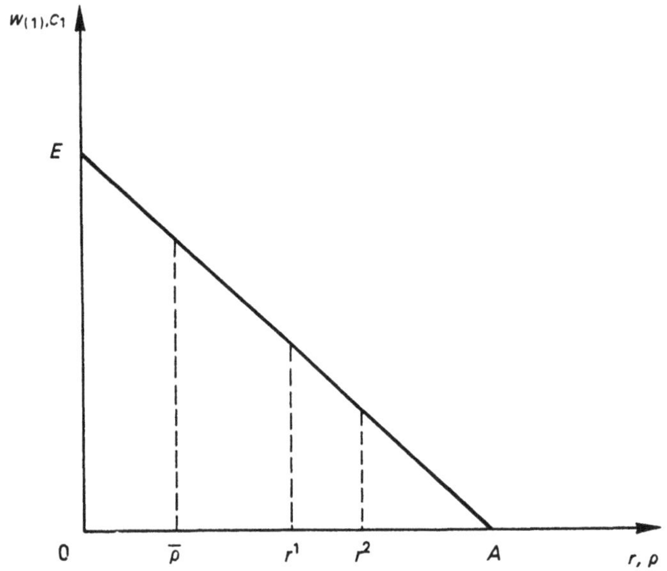

variations in both k and y are due solely to price changes – the physical components of both means of production (or capital) and net output per head are constant. Figures 7.3a–c present a summary of the aggregate relationships in the economy for a given growth rate. Two arguments can be advanced against the interpretation of the upper panels in Figure 7.3 as production functions. First, in none of the cases is there a concave relation between y and k. Second, and more important, a production function is usually considered to be a physical relation in the sense that output changes if and only if capital changes.

The discussion above has been conducted under the assumption that there is only one technique. In section 7.4, I examine the implications of relaxing this assumption.

7.4 Alternative Techniques and Duality

Suppose now that there are two techniques, as illustrated in Figure 7.4a: let (α) and (β) differ only with respect to their second processes. The duality theory of sections 7.2 and 7.3 can be

Figure 7.3a

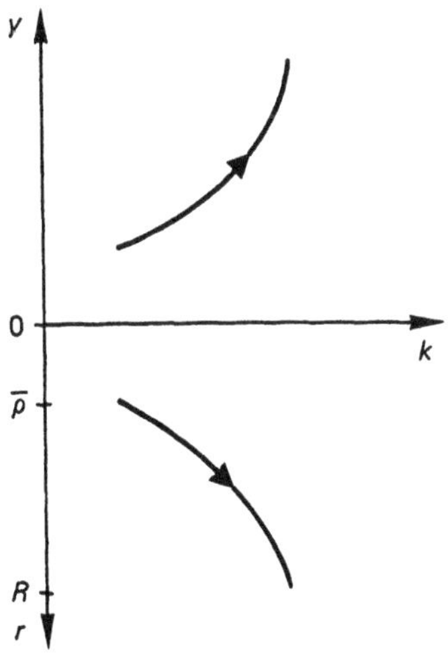

Figure 7.3b

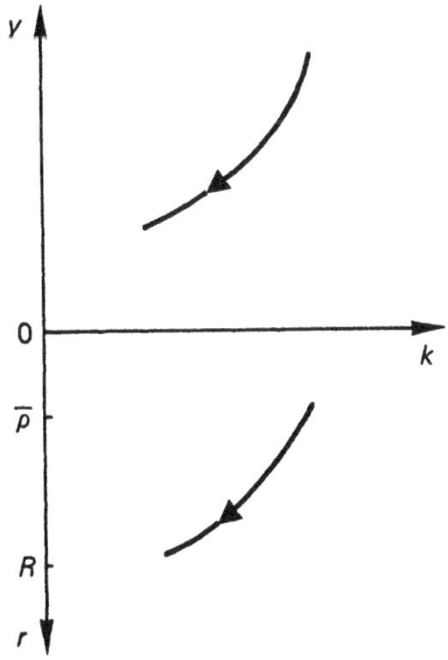

Figure 7.3c

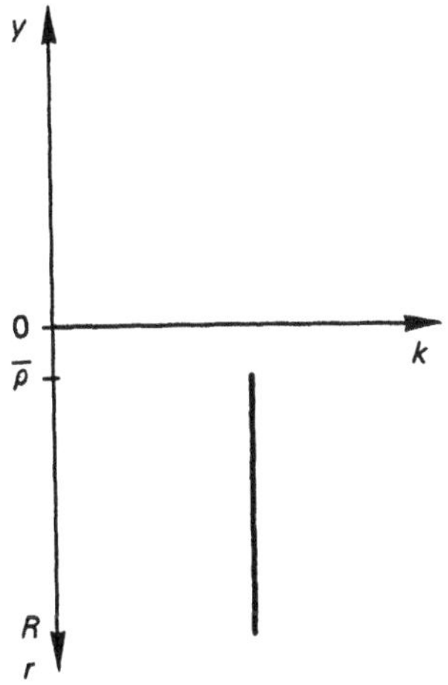

applied to (α) and (β) separately. (α) is employed for $\bar{\varrho} \leqslant r < \bar{r}$, (β) for $\bar{r} < r \leqslant R^{\beta}$, with $\bar{r}$ a switch-point between the two. As r increases towards $\bar{r}$, y, k and k/y are all decreasing. Applying the theory of section 7.3, it can easily be seen that at $\bar{r}$:

Figure 7.4a

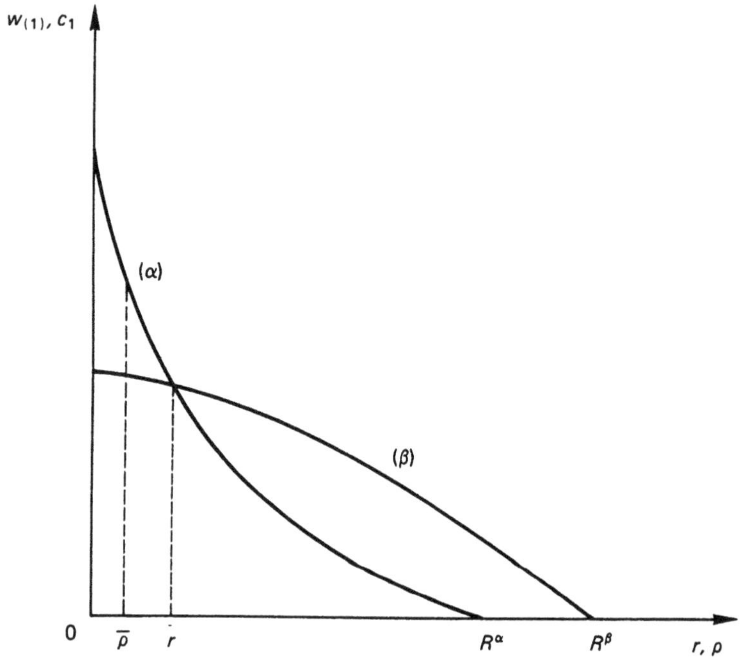

$$
\begin{aligned}
&y^\alpha(\bar{r}) > y^\beta(\bar{r}) \\
&k^\alpha(\bar{r}) > k^\beta(\bar{r}) \qquad (7.26) \\
&k^\alpha(\bar{r})/y^\alpha(\bar{r}) > k^\beta(\bar{r})/y^\beta(\bar{r})
\end{aligned}
$$

That is, as r increases through $\bar{r}$, there is a switch to the technique with the lower values of net output per head, capital per head and the capital–output ratio. Such a switch is called a positive real Wicksell effect – 'positive' because the inverse monotonic relation between each aggregate variable and r is preserved; 'real' because there is a change in the proportions of the means of production, with the switch from (IIα) to (IIβ). Then, as r increases from $\bar{r}$ towards R^β, y, k and k/y are increasing in r. I can summarise Figure 7.4a as follows: as r increases from $\bar{\rho}$ towards $\bar{r}$, there is a positive price Wicksell effect; at $\bar{r}$, there is a positive real Wicksell effect; as r increases from $\bar{r}$ to R^β, there is a negative price Wicksell effect. A price Wicksell effect is merely a revaluation of the means of production and outputs with constant technique; a real Wicksell

Figure 7.4b

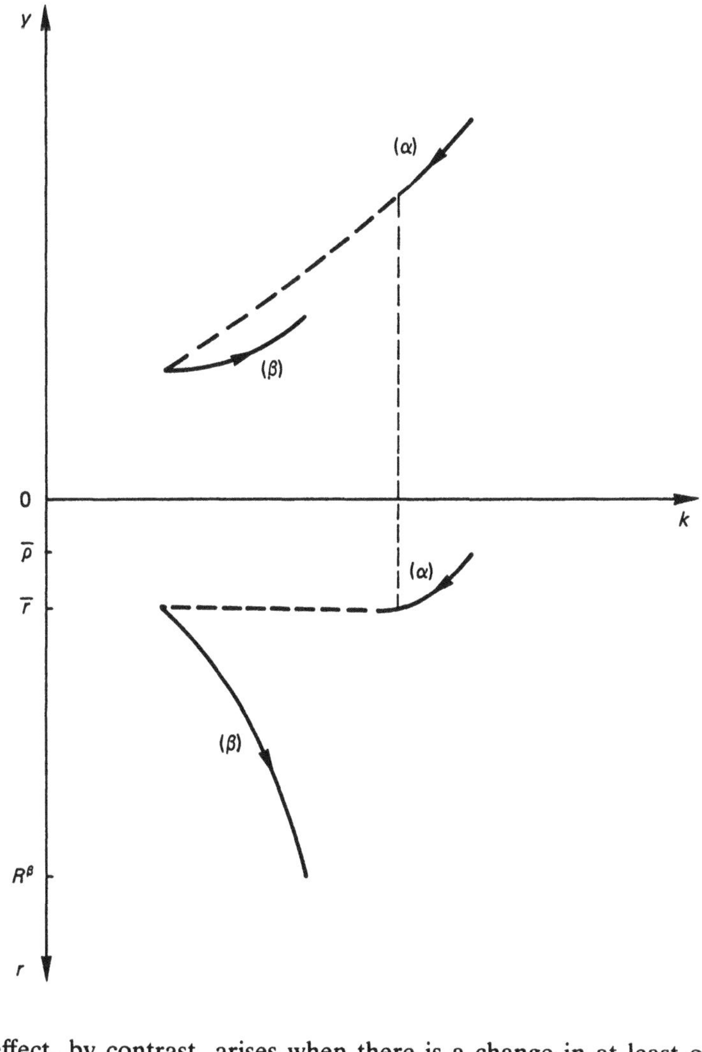

effect, by contrast, arises when there is a change in at least one process of production at a constant price vector (i.e. a switch-point). Corresponding to Figure 7.4a, I can construct Figure 7.4b. For $\bar{\varrho} \leqslant r < \bar{r}$, I can apply the theory of section 7.3 to obtain the curves marked (α); for $\bar{r} < r \leqslant R^\beta$, I obtain the curves marked (β). At $\bar{r}$, either (α) or (β) or a convex combination of both can be chosen, as indicated by the dotted line in Figure 7.4b.

Figure 7.5a

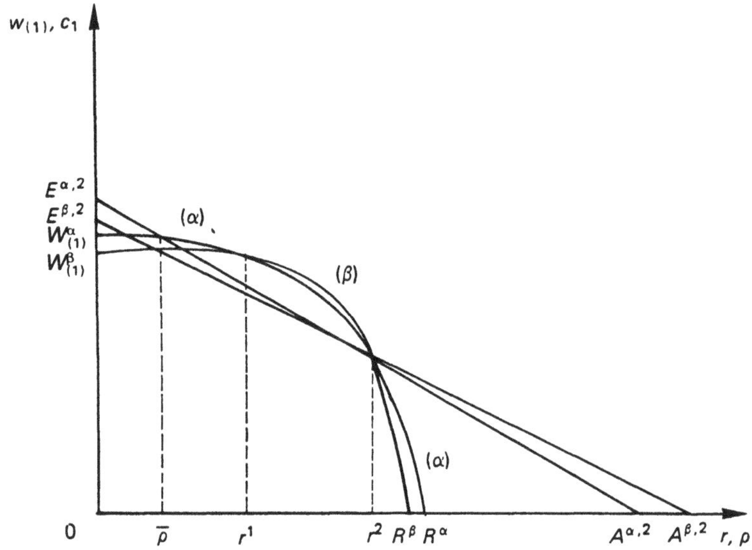

It is a straightforward matter to demonstrate that, if there is only one switch-point between (α) and (β), a positive real Wicksell effect occurs, regardless of the price Wicksell effects. So, consider next Figure 7.5a, where there are two switch-points and the price Wicksell effect is negative in both (α) and (β). It is easily seen that a positive real Wicksell effect occurs at r^1. Applying the duality theory at r^2, I have:

$$\begin{aligned} y^{\beta}(r^2) &= 0E^{\beta,2} < 0E^{\alpha,2} = y^{\alpha}(r^2) \\ k^{\beta}(r^2) &= \tan 0A^{\beta,2}E^{\beta,2} < \tan 0A^{\alpha,2}E^{\alpha,2} = k^{\alpha}(r^2) \\ k^{\beta}(r^2)/y^{\beta}(r^2) &= 1/0A^{\beta,2} < 1/0A^{\alpha,2} = k^{\alpha}(r^2)/y^{\alpha}(r^2) \end{aligned} \tag{7.27}$$

So, there is a switch, as r increases through r^2, from the technique with the lower values of y, k and k/y to the technique with the higher values – that is, from (β) to (α). This is called a negative real Wicksell effect or capital-reversing, because the change is in an unexpected direction: it was thought that, if higher values of r effected a change of technique, it would be to one with lower values of y, k and k/y. So, in Figure 7.5a, there is a negative price Wicksell effect for $\bar{\varrho} \leqslant r < r^1$, a positive real Wicksell effect at r^1, a

Figure 7.5b

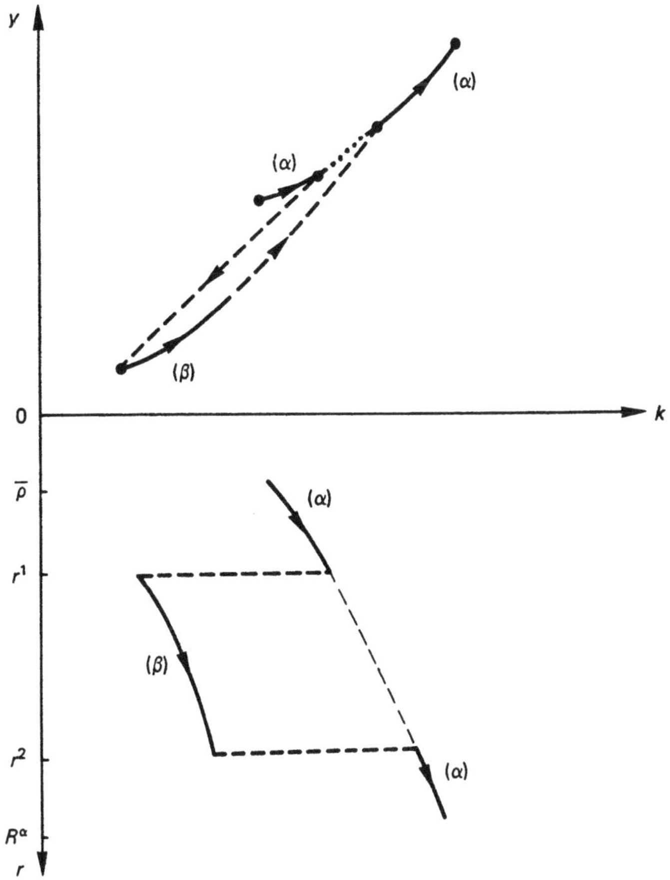

negative price Wicksell effect for $r^1 < r < r^2$, a negative real Wicksell effect at r^2 and a negative price Wicksell effect for $r^2 < r \leqslant R^{\alpha}$. Applying duality theory to this example, I obtain Figure 7.5b. In the upper panel, the arcs labelled '(α)' are obtained from technique (α) by evaluating k and y over those ranges for which this technique is cost-minimising (these can be read from the lower panel). In effect, I erase that part of (α)'s k–r curve between r^1 and r^2 and the corresponding part of (α)'s y–k curve. The dotted lines indicate convex combinations which can be chosen at switch-points. I conclude discussion of the case illustrated in Figure 7.5a by referring to Figure 7.5b, which should be read as follows: choose a value of r between $\bar{\varrho}$ and R^α; the corresponding value of k, in the cost-minimising technique, can then be obtained from the lower panel, with the corresponding value of y from the upper panel. If none of Figures 7.3a–c resembles a traditional production function, the same comment applies with more force to Figure 7.5b (and Figure 7.4b).

Before taking up the quest for the aggregate production function, it is appropriate to consider at greater length the new phenomenon exhibited in Figure 7.5. The reswitching and recurrence phenomena were demonstrated in Chapter 6. Now, from Figure 7.5, it can be seen that reswitching has implications for the relations between macroeconomic variables on the one hand (namely y, k and k/y) and the rate of profit, on the other: briefly, reswitching implies capital reversing. However, the latter does not imply the former, as can be seen by the simplest modification of Figure 7.5a. In Figure 7.6, I have introduced a third process, (IIγ), giving rise to a new technique, (γ), which is cost-minimising over the interval $\bar{\varrho} \leqslant r < r^3$. The switch-point r^1 between (α) and (β) becomes irrelevant for the choice of technique. At r^3, there is a positive real Wicksell effect. The negative real Wicksell effect at r^2 remains. So, capital reversing can occur in the absence of reswitching.

There are two points to be made in this preliminary discussion of the application of duality theory. First, it is a straightforward matter to show that recurrence of techniques implies, but is not implied by, capital reversing. Second, the capital reversing phenomenon is itself dependent on the growth rate. In Figure 7.5, the growth rate is fixed at $\bar{\varrho}$ and the rate of profit is allowed to vary. If the growth rate lies between r^1 and r^2, it can be seen that the capital reversing phenomenon is eliminated at r^2 – that is, there is a positive, not a negative, real Wicksell effect at r^2 if $r^1 < \varrho < r^2$. This emphasises the fact that the valuations of net income and capital per head depend on the growth rate: y and k are functionally dependent on r and ϱ.

Comparison of the cases illustrated in Figures 7.4 and 7.5 indicates the additional problems which can arise when there are alternative techniques. Clearly, these two cases do not exhaust all possibilities. Other examples can be constructed by the reader.

7.5 The Aggregate Production Function

Contrast Figure 7.3, on the one hand, with Figures 7.4 and 7.5, on the other. In the upper panel of Figure 7.3, changes in y and k are brought about solely by price changes. However, there are two types of change occurring in the upper panels of Figures 7.4b and 7.5b. First, if r is not a switch-point, changes in income distribution result in price changes, with constant technique; second, at a switch-point value of r, there is a change of technique at constant prices, i.e. a purely physical change. In so far as an aggregate production function is interpreted as a physical construct, it is necessary to eliminate the effects of price changes, caused by changes in income distribution. The natural way of achieving this is to construct chain-indices of capital and net output per head. The idea behind a chain-index is that its value changes if and only if its physical constituents change: so, a chain-index of capital, for example, would assume a different value only at a switch-point.

To illustrate the method of constructing a chain-index, consider Figure 7.7a, where (α) is chosen for $\bar{\varrho} \leqslant r < r^1$, ($\beta$) for $r^1 < r < r^2$ and (γ) for $r^2 < r < R^\gamma$. So, there will be one amount of capital for $\bar{\varrho} < r < r^1$, another for $r^1 < r < r^2$ and a third for $r^2 < r < R^\gamma$. Denote the amount of capital in (α) by $\varkappa_\alpha \equiv 1$ (or any other positive number). At r^1, there is a switch to (β). I now need a method of calculating the amount of capital in (β) which reflects, in some sense, the relative amounts of capital in the first two techniques. As it is the value of r at which (α) and (β) are equally profitable, where their price systems are identical, r^1 is the appropriate place to calculate the index: for differences in the quantities of capital can be ascribed to physical, not value, changes. The quantity of capital in (β) is given by the ratio of the cost of capital in (β) to its cost in (α), times the quantity of capital in (α), the calculations being performed at r^1. The cost of capital in (α) is simply the value of capital in (α); similarly, for (β). From section 7.3, these values can be calculated using duality theory. Figure 7.7b is extracted from Figure 7.7a. The value of capital in (α) at r^1 is equal to $\tan w^1_{(1)} P^1 E^{\alpha,1}$ which is greater than $\tan w^1_{(1)} P^1 E^{\beta,1}$, the value of capital in (β) at r^1. So, the quantity of capital in (β) is given by:

$$\varkappa_{\alpha\beta} = \frac{\tan w^1_{(1)} P^1 E^{\beta,1}}{\tan w^1_{(1)} P^1 E^{\alpha,1}} \cdot (\text{index of capital in } (\alpha))$$

$$= \frac{\tan w^1_{(1)} P^1 E^{\beta,1}}{\tan w^1_{(1)} P^1 E^{\alpha,1}} = \frac{w^1_{(1)} E^{\beta,1}}{w^1_{(1)} E^{\alpha,1}} < 1 = \varkappa_\alpha \quad (7.28)$$

$\varkappa_{\alpha\beta}$ is the quantity of capital in (β) for $r^1 < r < r^2$. At r^2, there is a switch to (γ). From Figure 7.7c, extracted from Figure 7.7a with (α) deleted, I have:

$$\text{value of capital in } (\beta) \text{ at } r^2 = \tan w^2_{(1)} P^2 E^{\beta,2}$$

$$> \tan w^2_{(1)} P^2 E^{\gamma,2}$$

$$= \text{value of capital in } (\gamma) \text{ at } r^2.$$

So, the quantity of capital in (γ) is given by:

$$\varkappa_{\beta\gamma} = \frac{(\text{value of capital in } (\gamma) \text{ at } r^2)}{(\text{value of capital in } (\beta) \text{ at } r^2)} \cdot (\text{index of capital in } (\beta))$$

$$= \frac{\tan w^2_{(1)} P^2 E^{\gamma,2}}{\tan w^2_{(1)} P^2 E^{\beta,2}} \cdot \varkappa_{\alpha\beta} = \frac{w^2_{(1)} E^{\gamma,2}}{w^2_{(1)} E^{\beta,2}} \cdot \varkappa_{\alpha\beta}$$

$$< \varkappa_{\alpha\beta} \quad (7.29)$$

Note that, for the arrangement of techniques in Figure 7.7a, $\varkappa_\alpha > \varkappa_{\alpha\beta} > \varkappa_{\beta\gamma}$.[4] So, as r increases from zero to its maximum value, each switch that occurs is to a technique with a lower chain-index value of capital. This regular, or inverse monotonic, relation between $\varkappa$ and r can be attributed to the absence of reswitching, recurrence and capital reversing, as will become clear below. However, before demonstrating this, it is necessary to explain the construction of the capital price index corresponding to the capital quantity index outlined above.

Denote the price index by π. Then, by definition, the following should be satisfied:

$$y = r\pi\varkappa + w \quad (7.30)$$

The product of π and $\varkappa$ should be equal to k, the value of capital per head. By assumption, $\varkappa$ assumes different values only at a switch-point. As k varies between switch-points for a given technique, it follows that π must also vary between switch-points so that $\pi\varkappa = k$. Let K_1^ι and K_2^ι be the quantities per head of the first and second commodities in technique (ι)'s capital stock (i.e. means of production advanced at the beginning of each period). With p_1^ι and p_2^ι the prices of the two commodities in technique (ι), I have as the value of capital in (ι):

$$\tau^\iota(r) = p_1^\iota K_1^\iota + p_2^\iota K_2^\iota \tag{7.31}$$

From Figure 7.7, (α) is employed for $\bar{\varrho} \leqslant r < r^1$. So, over this range:

$$\tau^\alpha(r) = p_1^\alpha K_1^\alpha + p_2^\alpha K_2^\alpha \tag{7.32}$$

is the value of capital per head. As the quantity of capital per head in (α), $\varkappa_\alpha$, is 1 by definition, it follows that I can sensibly define:

$$\pi(r) = \tau^\alpha(r) \quad \text{for } \bar{\varrho} \leqslant r < r^1 \tag{7.33}$$

At r^1, there is a switch to (β). Over the interval $r^1 \leqslant r < r^2$, the variation in the value of capital is captured by:

$$\frac{\tau^\beta(r)}{\tau^\beta(r^1)} = \frac{p_1^\beta(r)K_1^\beta + p_2^\beta(r)K_2^\beta}{p_1^\beta(r^1)K_1^\beta + p_2^\beta(r^1)K_2^\beta} \tag{7.34}$$

So, define:

$$\pi(r) = \tau^\alpha(r^1)\cdot\frac{\tau^\beta(r)}{\tau^\beta(r^1)} \quad \text{for } r^1 \leqslant r \leqslant r^2 \tag{7.35}$$

Note that, at r^1, $\pi(r^1) = \tau^\alpha(r^1)$ from both (7.33) and (7.35).

At r^2, there is a switch to (γ). The variation in the value of capital in (γ) over the interval $r^2 \leqslant r \leqslant R^\gamma$ is captured by:

$$\tau^\gamma(r)/\tau^\gamma(r^2) \tag{7.36}$$

Then define:

$$\pi(r) = \tau^\alpha(r^1)\cdot\frac{\tau^\beta(r^2)}{\tau^\beta(r^1)}\cdot\frac{\tau^\gamma(r)}{\tau^\gamma(r^2)} \quad \text{for } r^2 \leqslant r \leqslant R^\gamma \tag{7.37}$$

Figure 7.6

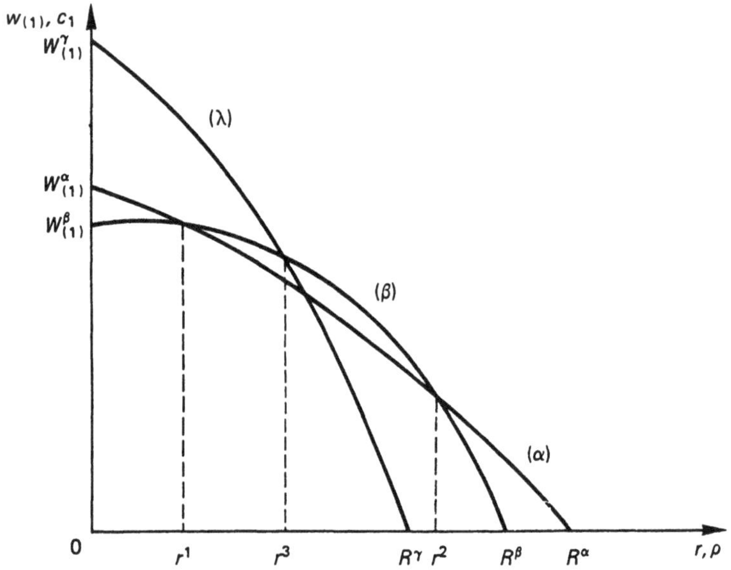

It is a straightforward matter to show that the quantity and price indices of capital are consistent in the sense that, at any value of r between $\bar{\varrho}$ and R^{γ}:

$$k(r) = \pi(r)\varkappa(r) \tag{7.38}$$

using (7.28), (7.29), (7.33), (7.35) and (7.37). This completes the exposition of the method of constructing the capital price and quantity indices.

Quantity and price indices of net output are constructed in a similar way. With reference to Figure 7.7a, let the amount of net output in (α) be 1. Then, at r^1, there is a switch to (β). From Figure 7.7b, the ratio of values of net output is given by $0E^{\beta,1}/0E^{\alpha,1}$. When multiplied by the chain-index of output in (α), this ratio gives the amount of output in (β), i.e.

$$\chi_{\alpha\beta} = \frac{0E^{\beta,1}}{0E^{\alpha,1}} \cdot \chi_{\alpha} \tag{7.39a}$$

$$\chi_{\alpha} = 1 \tag{7.39b}$$

Figure 7.7a

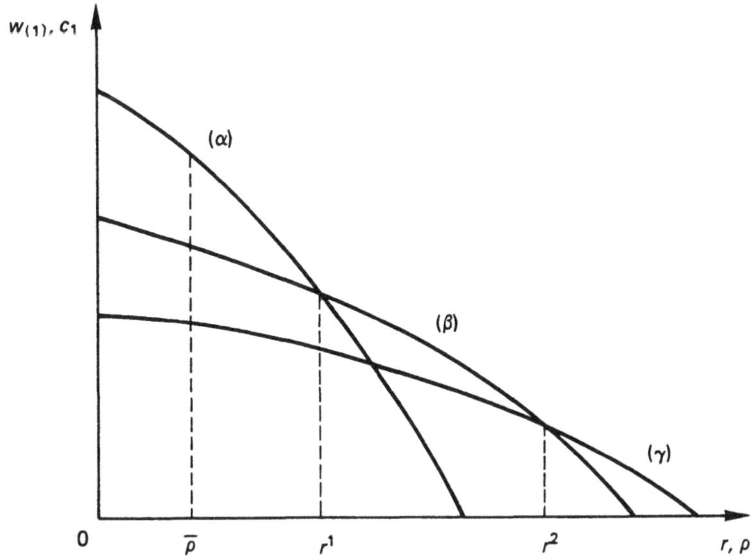

At r^2, there is a switch to (γ). From Figure 7.7c, the ratio of values of net output is given by $0E^{\gamma,2}/0E^{\beta,2}$. So:

$$\chi_{\beta\gamma} = \frac{0E^{\gamma,2}}{0E^{\beta,2}} \cdot \chi_{\alpha\beta}$$

$$= \frac{0E^{\gamma,2}}{0E^{\beta,2}} \cdot \frac{0E^{\beta,1}}{0E^{\alpha,1}} \cdot 1 \qquad (7.39c)$$

A price index of output, $\sigma(r)$, can be constructed in a similar way to $\pi(r)$ so that:

$$y = \sigma(r)\chi(r) \qquad (7.40)$$

Applying the method outlined above for the construction of capital and net output indices, I obtain Figure 7.7d from Figure 7.7a. If $\bar{\varrho} \leqslant r < r^1$, (α) is the unique cost-minimising technique, with capital index $\varkappa_\alpha$ and output index χ_α, denoted by the blob marked '(α)' in the upper panel. If $r^1 < r < r^2$, (β) is the cost-

Figure 7.7b

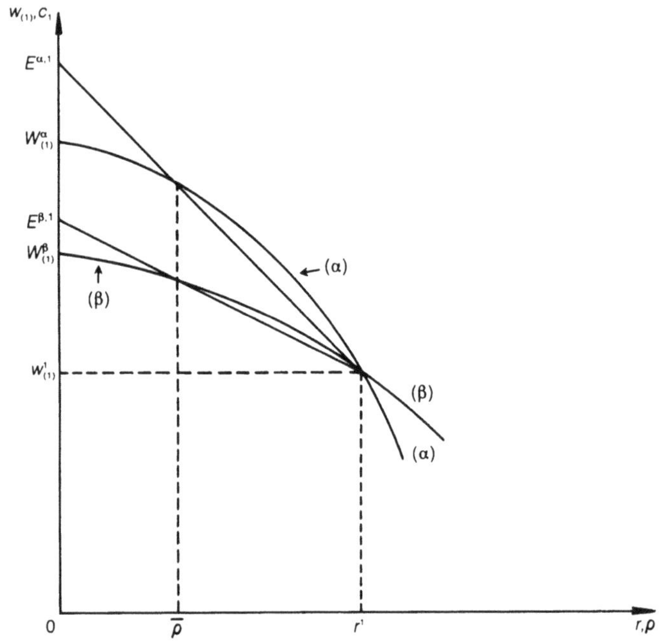

minimising technique, with capital index $\varkappa_{\alpha\beta}$ and output index $\chi_{\alpha\beta}$, indicated by the blob marked '(β)' in the upper panel. The line joining (α) and (β) represents all convex combinations of these two techniques which are cost-minimising at the switch-point r^1. Similarly, for (γ) and the line joining (β) and (γ). In the absence of reswitching, recurrence and capital reversing, these two conclusions can be drawn:

(1) $\varkappa$ is an inverse monotonic function of r;
(2) χ is a concave function of $\varkappa$.

For purposes of exposition, I have examined a technology with only three techniques. Suppose that other techniques are added to the outer envelope in Figure 7.7a and that the three phenomena are still absent. I would then obtain Figure 7.7e, in which conclusions (1) and (2) remain valid. The upper panel in this figure is a better discrete approximation to a traditional concave aggregate production function than the upper panel in Figure 7.7d.

Figure 7.7c

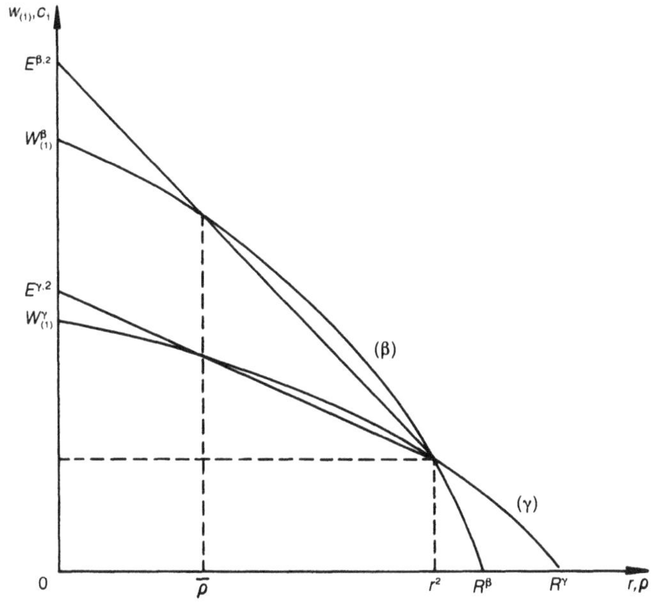

The two conclusions drawn above depend essentially on the absence of the three phenomena, as I shall explain at greater length in section 7.6. If there is neither reswitching nor recurrence, the ordering of techniques by the rate of profit at which each is most profitable, is necessarily unique: each technique is cost-minimising over only one range of values of *r*. Non-concavities are introduced to the aggregate production function by capital reversing, as will be seen below. So, in the absence of the three phenomena, the cost-minimising technique at the lowest values of *r* is that with the highest values of both capital and net output per head and the highest capital–output ratio. With increases in *r*, there are switches to techniques with lower values of capital and net output per head and lower capital–output ratios. As a final remark, it should be noted that the only restrictions placed on the *w*–*r* curves in Figure 7.7a and that underlying Figure 7.7e are those imposed by the results of section 6.4, in addition to the absence of the three phenomena.

Figure 7.7d

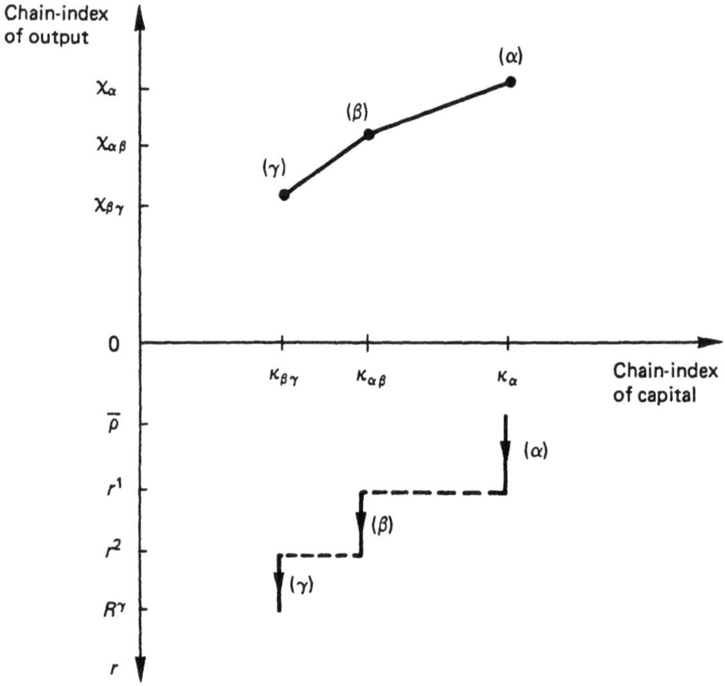

7.6 The Aggregate Production Function and the Three Phenomena

In this section, I investigate how robust the aggregate production function is to the introduction of the three phenomena. First, as an example of reswitching, reconsider Figure 7.5. Applying the method of section 7.5 for constructing chain-indices of capital and net output per head, I obtain the following:

for $\overline{r} \leqslant r < r^1$, (α) is chosen with capital index $\varkappa_\alpha$ and output index χ_α;

for $r^1 < r < r^2$, (β) is chosen with capital index $\varkappa_{\alpha\beta} < \varkappa_\alpha$ and output index $\chi_{\beta\alpha} < \chi_\alpha$;

for $r^2 < r \leqslant R^\alpha$, (α) is chosen with capital index $\varkappa_{\beta\alpha} > \varkappa_{\alpha\beta}$ and output index $\chi_{\beta\alpha} > \chi_{\alpha\beta}$.

Figure 7.7e

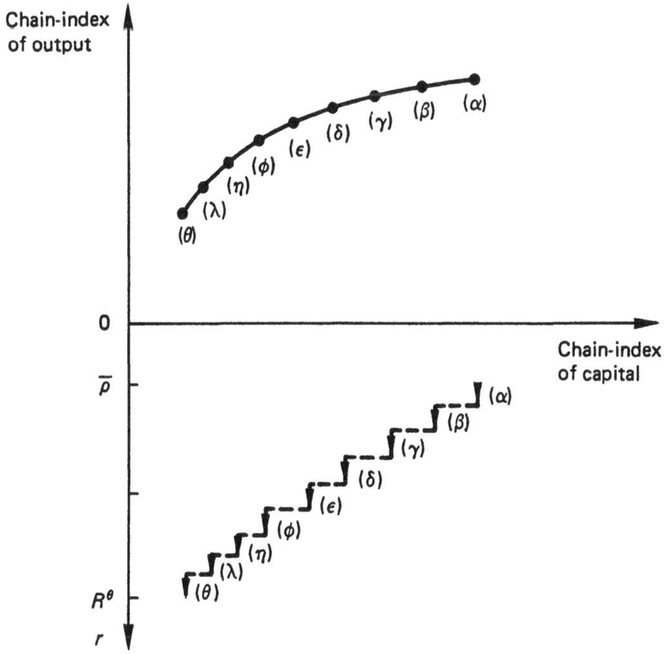

This is illustrated in Figure 7.8. As r increases from $\bar{\varrho}$, (α) is employed until, at r^1, there is a switch to (β), which has the lower values of capital and net output per head (i.e. there is a positive real Wicksell effect at r^1). However, at r^2, there is a switch back to (α), which has higher values of capital and net output per head (there is a negative real Wicksell effect at r^2). The upper panel of Figure 7.8 does not resemble that in either Figure 7.7d or Figure 7.7e. Part of the downward line (α)–(β) representing convex combinations of (α) and (β) which are cost-minimising at r^1, lies beneath the upward line (β)–(α), representing convex combinations of which are cost-minimising at r^2. This does not imply that the relevant part of the downward line (α)–(β) is inefficient. Rather, the conclusion to be drawn is that the aggregate production function, as represented in the upper panel of Figure 7.8, is not concave.

As a further illustration of the effects of reswitching, introduce a third technique into Figure 7.5a; let (γ) be cost-minimising for $r^3 < r < R^\gamma$, where $R^\gamma > R^\alpha > r^3 > r^2$. So, the ordering of techniques

Figure 7.8

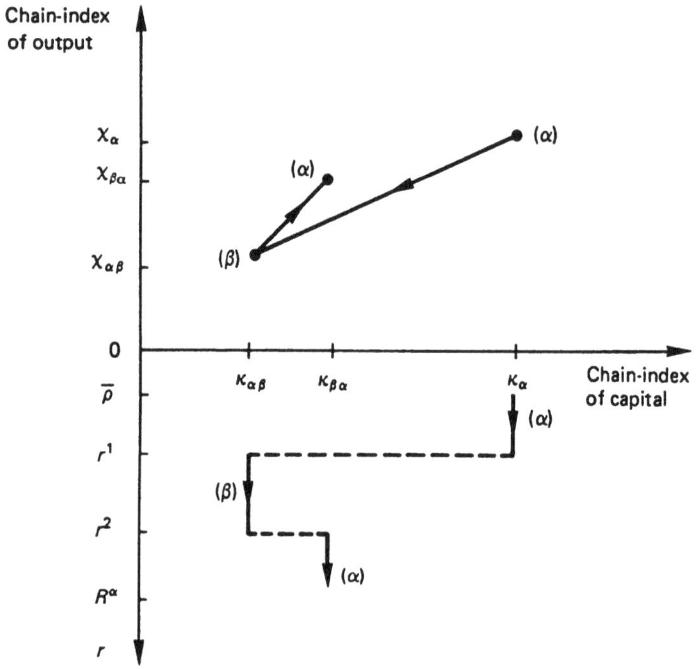

is: (α) for $\bar{\varrho} \leqslant r < r^1$, (β) for $r^1 < r < r^2$, (α) for $r^2 < r < R^\beta$, (γ) for $r^3 < r \leqslant R^\gamma$. Assuming, for ease of exposition, that (γ) has only one switch-point in the positive quadrant with each of the other techniques, I obtain Figure 7.9 by applying the method of section 7.5. Clearly, the function in the upper panel is not concave.[5] Here, the upward line (β)–(α) dominates parts of two downward lines (α)–(β) and (α)–(γ). As with Figure 7.8, this does not imply that the dominated parts are inefficient: for the downward line (α)–(β) represents convex combinations of (α) and (β) which are cost-minimising at r^1; similarly, the downward line (α)–(γ) represents convex combinations of (α) and (γ) which are cost-minimising at r^3.

The effects of recurrence of techniques are similar to those of reswitching. From Figure 6.8 of Chapter 6, I obtain Figure 7.10. The recurrence of (α) at r^3 induces the non-concavity in the upper panel.

Figure 7.9

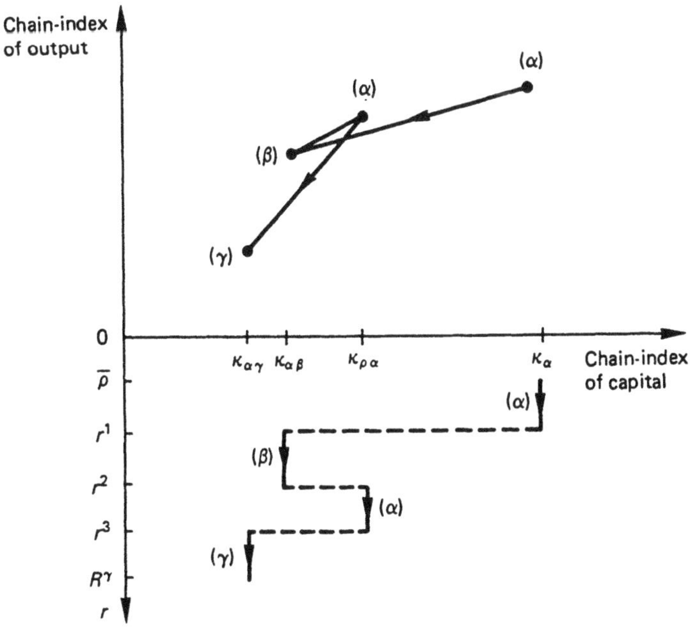

Consider finally an example where capital reversing occurs in the absence of the other two phenomena. In Figure 7.11, (α) is chosen for $\bar{\varrho} \leqslant r < r^1$, (β) for $r^1 < r < r^2$ and (γ) for $r^2 < r \leqslant R^\gamma$. Applying the method of section 7.5, I obtain: $\varkappa_{\alpha\beta} < \varkappa_\alpha$, $\chi_{\alpha\beta} < \chi_\alpha$ and $\varkappa_{\beta\gamma} > \varkappa_{\alpha\beta}$, $\chi_{\beta\gamma} > \chi_{\alpha\beta}$, as illustrated in Figure 7.11b. Capital reversing suffices for non-concavity of the aggregate production function.

It is clear from Figures 7.8–7.11 that the non-concavities are induced by the presence of capital reversing. Significance can be attached to reswitching and recurrence because both of these phenomena imply capital reversing. However, it is capital reversing that is seen to play the more fundamental role, at least as regards concavity of the aggregate production function. In this respect, capital reversing can be interpreted as the most damaging of the three. Contrast Figures 7.8–7.10, on the one hand, with Figure 7.11, on the other. Though a non-concavity occurs in the latter, each technique is cost-minimising over only one range of values of r; hence, each technique occurs only once in the aggregate

Figure 7.10

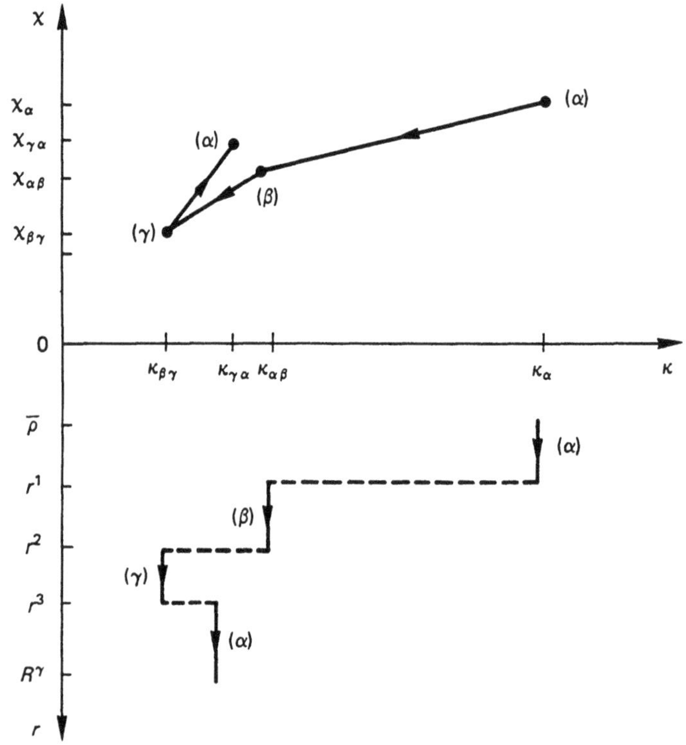

production function. Compare this with Figure 7.8, where (α) occurs twice, with quantities of capital $\varkappa_\alpha$ and $\varkappa_{\beta\alpha}$. Consequently, it might be argued that the chain-index method cannot be applied because its essence is that there should be one value of capital associated with each technique. This is a matter of interpretation, not construction. Figures 7.8–7.10 can be constructed; that (α) has two values of capital associated with it, in each of Figures 7.8–7.10, reflects the fact that it is chosen over two disjoint ranges of income distributions. As a final remark, I emphasise that the construction of capital and output indices is based on the theory of choice of technique and, hence, the specification of the technology. If it has two switch-points with (β), as in Figure 7.5, (α) will have two corresponding values of capital; if it has only one switch-point, (α) will have only one value of capital. Thus, there is generally not one intrinsic value of capital associated with each technique.

Figure 7.11a

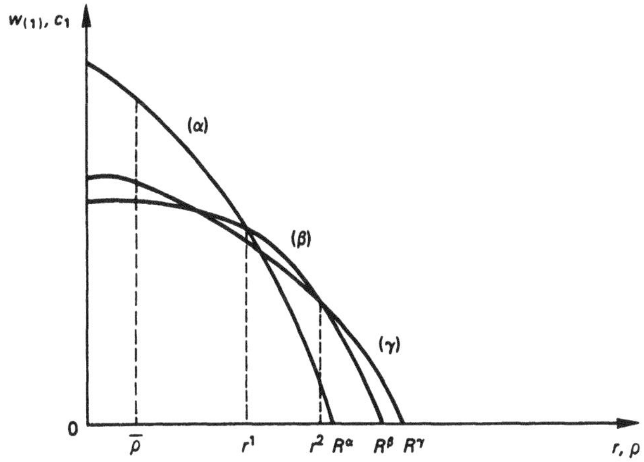

Figure 7.11b

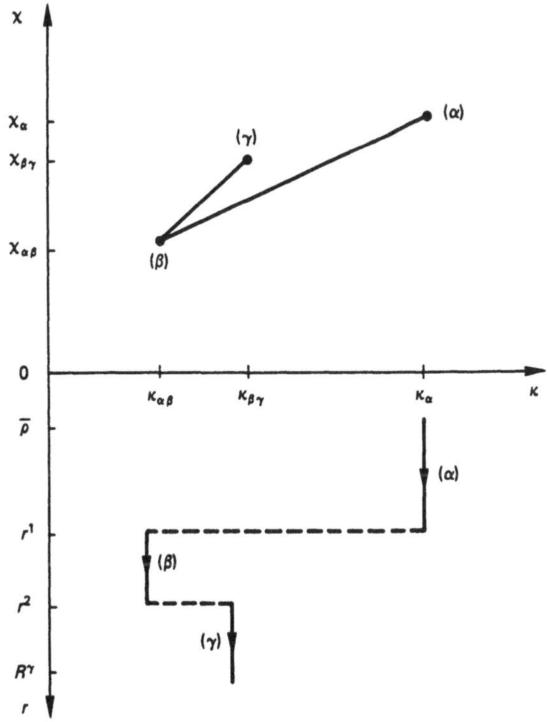

7.7 Conclusion

Sections 6.7 and 7.4–7.6 have been devoted to applications of the theory of choice of technique. In section 6.7, I drew attention mainly to microeconomic implications of the theory, concentrating on the relationships between prices and quantities of inputs. In this chapter, I have dealt with macroeconomic implications.

The construction of a concave aggregate production function depends on the absence of the three phenomena – reswitching, recurrence and capital reversing – from the underlying technology, a point explicitly recognised by Champernowne (1953–4). Indeed, a major outcome of the recent capital theory debates, as discussed, for example, in Harcourt (1972), is that this particular point is now generally understood: the conditions under which a concave aggregate production function exists are very restrictive. Hence, those areas of economic theory depending on the assumption of such a function, such as macroeconomics and aggregate growth theory, are called into question. Nor is this the only weakness in traditional theory to have been exposed by the methods employed here.

It was shown in section 6.7 that if there is either reswitching or recurrence of techniques, the aggregate demand function for labour is not necessarily downward-sloping: *a fortiori*, this negative conclusion extends to the case of capital reversing. Furthermore, it has been shown in sections 7.4 and 7.6 that the relation between the value of capital and the rate of profit is not necessarily inversely monotonic. Now, in a circulating capital model, the demand for capital is identical to the demand for investment. So, I can conclude that the relation between the amount of investment and the rate of profit is not necessarily downward-sloping. This relation surfaces in macroeconomics as the marginal efficiency of investment, or capital.

Much of the argument in the capital theory debates centred on the aggregate production function. I have suggested above that this is not the only concept in macroeconomics for which the theory of choice of technique has implications: the demand function for labour is not necessarily downward-sloping with respect to the real wage, nor is demand for capital an inversely monotonic function of the rate of profit, as usually asserted. In so far as it relies on these properties of the two demand functions and the aggregate production function, traditional macroeconomic theory is thereby called into question.

Commentary

In PCMC, Sraffa does not consider the question of constructing an aggregate production function, nor does he explicitly examine the marginal efficiency of capital. The nearest he comes to it is in chapter VI, where he shows that 'reversals in the direction of movement of relative prices, in face of unchanged methods of production, cannot be reconciled with *any* notion of capital as a measurable quantity independent of distribution and prices' (PCMC, section 48, p. 38). A similar view was expressed in Sraffa (1962) in which he concluded that 'it is not possible to define the quantity of capital . . . in a way that makes [it] independent of the rate of interest . . . One can only wonder what is the good of a quantity of capital . . . which, since it depends on the rate of interest, cannot be used for its traditional purpose, which is to determine the rate of interest' (pp. 478–9). Evidently, Sraffa is referring here to the theory in which the rate of interest, or rather profit (see footnote (1), Sraffa, 1962, p. 478), is determined by the marginal product of capital.

Robinson (1953–4) expressed views similar to those of Sraffa quoted above from section 48 of PCMC in her article which effectively started the recent capital theory debates:

> Should capital be valued according to its future earning power or its past costs? When we know the future expected rate of output associated with a certain capital good, and expected future prices and costs, then, if we are given a rate of interest, we can value a capital good as a discounted stream of future profit which it will earn. But to do so, we have to begin by taking the rate of interest as given, whereas the main purpose of the production function is to show how wages and the rate of interest (regarded as the wages of capital) are determined by technical conditions and the factor ratio. (Robinson, 1953–4, p. 115).

It is interesting to note that both Sraffa and Robinson do not employ any of the three phenomena in their respective critiques of the traditional theory of capital measurement. Nor should it be supposed that all neoclassical economists were unaware of the difficulties inherent in the treatment of capital in their professed approach. For example, Wicksell (1934) was able to prove that, even under perfect competition, the rate of interest was not equal to the marginal product of capital. Wicksell's line was repeated by Metzler (1950), who argued that the divergence between the marginal product of capital and the rate of interest 'is attributable to the fact that it is impossible to find an invariant unit in which to measure the social quantity of capital' (Metzler, 1950, p. 293). Two observations can be made here. First, that Metzler's views are not dissimilar from Robinson's. After reviewing alternative methods of measuring capital as a quantity of goods in terms of their cost of production, their value in terms of some unit of purchasing power and their productivity, she concluded that 'The ambiguity of the conception of capital is connected with a profound methodological error, which makes the major part of neo-classical doctrine spurious' (Robinson, 1953–4, p. 117). Second, that Metzler's views are not dissimilar from Sraffa's, or even Ricardo's, on the need for an invariable standard of value. Metzler continues his argument as follows:

> To put the matter another way, we may say that a change in the supply of capital – arising, for example, from new voluntary savings – alters the units in which all the previously existing capital is measured; and it is therefore incorrect to say that the supply of capital as a whole has increased by the amount of the voluntary saving. It is important to emphasise that this problem of measuring the quantity of capital is not an index-number problem. There are, to be sure, numerous index-number problems of the greatest complexity in the theory of capital. But the problem to which I now refer would exist even in the simplest economy in which all output consisted of a single type of consumer's good and all firms were exactly alike. (Metzler, 1950, p. 293)

The capital reversing phenomenon was called by Joan Robinson (1965) the 'Ruth Cohen Curiosum' (pp. 109–10); incidentally, she described it in a footnote there as 'a somewhat intricate piece of analysis which is not of great importance'. (It is worth mentioning here that Levhari thought that the Ruth Cohen Curiosum referred 'to the possibility that as we change the interest rate producers switch the (technique) of production from α to β, but as we change it further in the same direction they return to α' (Levhari, 1965, p. 99); according to Bruno, Burmeister and Sheshinski (1966, p. 526), 'The "Ruth Cohen Curiosum" may be considered a special case where only a *single* activity recurs.') It had been noticed earlier by Champernowne (1953–4).

> It may seem intuitively obvious that the function . . . expressing output as a function of labour and capital must be single-valued. But our assumptions are not sufficient to ensure this . . . Contrary to our intuitive expectation, our assumptions do not ensure that a graph of (output against capital) is a single-valued curve sloping upward to the right. For example, a graph of the form shown in Figure 7.9 is quite possible. The further assumption that is needed in order to eliminate this possibility is that of two techniques (α) and (β) (equally profitable at $\bar{r}$), (α) (that cost-minimising for $r < \bar{r}$) will have the higher productivity, i.e. the higher ratio of net output to labour input. Under this assumption a gradual fall in the rate of (profit) would entail increases in both productivity and in the quantity of capital per head. (Champernowne, 1953–4, p. 118, with minor amendments to make terminology consistent with that employed here)

It is clear that Champernowne's 'further assumption' is simply that capital reversing does not occur. See the Commentary to Chapter 6 for discussion of Champernowne's other assumptions. What reason could be advanced to support this assumption? Champernowne was quite clear on this point:

> But although this (i.e. no capital reversing) may fit in well with our preconceived notions, there is no logical justification for the assumption. It is logically possible that over certain ranges of the rate of (profit), a fall in (the rate of profit) and rise in (the real wage) will be accompanied by a *fall* in output per head and a *fall* in the quantity of capital per head. (ibid., emphasis in original)

It will have become clear by now that Champernowne (1953–4) is an essential reference in the theory of choice of technique and its applications. In this chapter, I have essentially given an account of Champernowne's chain-index method of aggregating capital following Woods (1979). A further reference on the chain-index method is Bliss (1975).

Capital-reversing has come to play an important role in the capital theory literature: see, for example, Pasinetti (1969), Garegnani (1970, 1978, 1979), Harcourt (1972, 1983), Eatwell and Milgate (1983).

The dynamic model analysed in this chapter is a special case of one due to von Neumann (1945–6). Champernowne's commentary (1945–6) should be consulted. A further reference is Pasinetti (1977a).

Exercises

1. Prove that, if there is only one switch-point between (α) and (β), a positive real Wicksell effect occurs.

2. Construct a numerical example to illustrate Figure 7.6 (use the exercises of Chapter 6).

3. Prove that recurrence of a technique implies capital reversing, if the rate of growth lies in a certain interval.

4. Consider Figure 7.5. Prove that, if the growth rate lies between r^1 and r^2, there is a positive, not a negative, real Wicksell effect at r^2.

5. Construct examples, additional to those shown treated in Figures 7.4 and 7.5, to illustrate the other possibilities when there are alternative techniques.

6. Prove that the price and quantity indices of capital are consistent in the sense that (7.38) holds.

7. Construct a price index of output, $\sigma(r)$, such that (7.40) is satisfied.

8. Establish conclusions (1) and (2) in section 7.5 regarding the aggregate production function.

9. Apply the theory of section 7.5, with $\bar{\varrho} = 0.1$, to the following technology:

   (I) 1/2 t iron ⊕ 1/2 labour ⊖ 1 qr wheat
   (IIα) 1/4 qr wheat ⊕ 1/3 t iron ⊕ 1/4 labour ⊖ 1 t iron
   (IIβ) 1/2 qr wheat ⊕ 1/2 labour ⊖ 1 t iron
   (IIγ) 1/8 qr wheat ⊕ 1/10 t iron ⊕ 2 labour ⊖ 1 t iron.

10. Apply the theory of sections 7.5–7.6 to your numerical example constructed in exercise 2. (Select an appropriate value for $\bar{\varrho}$. See Figure 7.11.)

11. Apply the chain-index method to exercises 3–8, 22–27 and 30 of Chapter 6.

12. Explain how the chain-index method can be applied to the model analysed in the Appendix to Chapter 6.

13. Consider the model analysed in the Appendix to Chapter 6. Suppose that there are many techniques, in each of which wheat and a specific capital good are produced. Suppose further that wheat is a pure consumption good, i.e. $a^{\iota}_{1j} = 0, j = 1,2$, for all techniques ι, and that, in a typical technique:

$$a^{\iota}_{21}/l^{\iota}_{1} = a^{\iota}_{22}/l^{\iota}_{2} \quad \iota = a, \beta, \gamma, \ldots, \omega$$

   Prove that a concave production function can be obtained by the chain-index method. Interpret the condition above. This exercise is due to Samuelson (1961–2).

14. (Generalisation of 13.) Prove that a concave production function can be constructed if:

$$a^{\iota}_{11}/a^{\iota}_{21} = a^{\iota}_{12}/a^{\iota}_{22}$$
$$a^{\iota}_{11}/l_{1} = a^{\iota}_{12}/l^{\iota}_{2}$$

   This exercise is due to Zarembka (1975).

15. (Generalisation of 13 and 14.) Prove that a concave production function can be constructed if:

$$(l^{\iota}_{1}a^{\iota}_{12} + l^{\iota}_{2}a^{\iota}_{22})/l^{\iota}_{2} = (l^{\iota}_{1}a^{\iota}_{11} + l^{\iota}_{2}a^{\iota}_{21})/l^{\iota}_{1}$$

   Interpret this condition. Show that it implies but is not implied by the conditions in exercises 14 and 15.

16. Apply the chain-index method to exercises 32–34 of Chapter 6.

17. Construct a numerical example to illustrate Figure 7.9.

18. Does the capital reversing phenomenon depend on the growth rate? Consider a two-technique model with switch-points r_1 and r_2; examine the effects of ϱ lying in each of the intervals $(0, r_1)$, (r_1, r_2) and (r_2, r_{max}).

19. Consider the following comments:

   (i) 'When provision has to be made for growth, the net outputs from the original activities will change and so will the w–r curve.'
   (ii) 'Adding growth merely transforms the linear coefficients, but cannot exclude them being of a character which admits the "perverse" cases.'

   Are they true?

20. 'Since relative prices are affected by the rate of growth, so is the relationship between the value of output and the value of capital.' Is this true?

Notes to Chapter 7

1. Note that the means of production on the right-hand side of (7.1) are advanced out of period $(t-1)$'s output.
2. Or if either w or r and either c or ϱ are known.
3. The definitions of these price Wicksell effects are confusing: a negative effect occurs when an increase in r results in an increase in each of the aggregate variables, a positive effect when an increase in r results in a decrease in each of the aggregate variables. Surely, they should be the other way around? However, it was initially supposed that there was a general inverse monotonic relation between r and each of the aggregate variables. So, an increase in r associated with a decrease in each of the aggregate variables confirmed the presupposition: hence, such an association was described as a positive effect. An increase in r associated with an increase in each of the aggregate variables, considered to be contrary to expectations, was thus described as a negative effect. To add to the confusion, these are called Wicksell effects, even though Ricardo (in chapter I of *The Principles*) was the first to analyse the effect of changes in income distribution on relative prices.
4. The ordering of subscripts indicates the ordering of techniques: (α) is chosen for low values of r; then there is a switch from (α) to (β) and finally from (β) to (γ).
5. Strictly speaking, the relation between output and capital is not a function at all. For $\varkappa_{\alpha\beta} < \varkappa < \varkappa_{\beta\alpha}$, there are at least two corresponding values of χ.

8
Introduction to Multiple-Product Industries Models

8.1 Fixed Capital and Land

The models analysed in Chapters 2–7 are without doubt very unrealistic. Absent from consideration were durable capital goods, non-produced means of production and intrinsic joint production of the wool-and-mutton variety – an impressive list of omissions. Yet the models in Chapters 2–7 embody the important feature that means of production are advanced, with profits paid at a uniform rate on their value. Furthermore, the study of these simpler models provides the foundation for the analysis of multiple-product industries models in the sense that the principles established for the former apply *mutatis mutandis* to the latter. This remark can best be appreciated by considering a particular example.

Suppose that, in the two-sector model, one of the commodities, say the first, is a machine which has a maximum physical lifetime of one year when employed in the first industry and two years when employed in the second. The machine is thus a circulating capital good in the machine sector and a fixed capital good in the other, say the iron, sector;[1] assume that iron is used as circulating capital in both sectors. As the machine can be used for two years in the iron sector, there are two corresponding processes. In the first, a new machine is combined with iron and labour inputs to produce as gross output a quantity of iron and a one-year-old machine. This one-year-old machine can then enter the second process with iron and labour inputs (possibly different from those in the first process) to produce a quantity of iron (again, possibly different from that in the first process). There are two points to be made about this model, which is the simplest multi-sector model that can be constructed with fixed capital. There is joint production in the first process, with iron and the ageing machine as outputs. More importantly though, it should be recognised that the item of fixed capital is analysed as two circulating capital goods – a new machine in the first process which becomes a one-year-old machine in the second process. This brief discussion suggests similarities between the analyses of fixed and circulating capital goods – a proper treatment of the former should be in terms of the framework provided by the latter. This is not to say that results on single-product industries, circulating capital models can be immediately applied to fixed capital models: for, in the first process of the example above, joint production necessarily arises.

Two points have been established above: explicitly, that the analysis of circulating capital is relevant to the analysis of fixed capital; and, implicitly, that fixed capital must be treated within a joint production framework. Similar conclusions apply if a non-produced means of production such as land is employed. By way of example, suppose that the first sector produces iron, the second wheat on homogeneous land which is unaffected by production. Then, in this case of intensive rent, there will be room for two processes operating on the land, determining a uniform rent per acre. In each process, land enters as means of production with the circulating capital and labour inputs to emerge as part of the gross output with wheat.

8.2 Arrangement of Chapters 9–11

In Chapter 9, I deal with fixed capital, concentrating on the simple model used for illustrative purposes in section 8.1. Having established the basic results for this case, I describe how the model can be generalised to permit, inter alia, the use of fixed capital in both sectors. Next, in Chapter 10, I analyse models with non-produced means of production, the emphasis being mainly on the familiar cases of extensive and intensive rent. It will be seen that some of the results from Chapter 6 cannot be extended to the models of Chapters 9 and 10. In Chapter 11, I relax the assumptions of Chapters 2–7 in a different way by examining pure joint production, circulating capital models – both industries produce, say, wheat and iron by means of wheat, iron and labour inputs. The peculiarities of joint production, compared with the regularities of single-product industries models, are exposed.

Commentary

The material in Chapters 9–11 corresponds broadly to that in chapters VII–XI of PCMC. However, it is not covered in the same order. I deal first with fixed capital, then land and finally joint production. Sraffa devotes the first three chapters of Part II of PCMC to pure joint production before treating fixed capital in chapter X and land in chapter XI.

Note to Chapter 8

1. The reason for considering this particular example will become evident in section 9.3.

9
Fixed Capital

9.1 Introduction

In section 8.1, I suggested that the appropriate way to generalise the analysis of circulating capital to the fixed capital case was within a joint production framework – indeed, the provision of such an analysis is the main purpose of this chapter. However, it should be recognised that the treatment of fixed capital within a joint production framework is not the only possible generalisation. In section 9.2, I present an alternative to the joint production approach, suggesting its properties and indicating its weaknesses. The study of this alternative – in itself a useful exercise in the application of concepts discussed in Chapters 4 and 6 – is a preliminary to the proper treatment of fixed capital in sections 9.3–9.11.

9.2 *A Priori* Specified Mortality Coefficients

Reconsider the price equations for the circulating capital model:

$$p_1 = wl_1 + (p_1a_{11} + p_2a_{21}) + r(p_1a_{11} + p_2a_{21}) \qquad (9.1a)$$

$$p_2 = wl_2 + (p_1a_{12} + p_2a_{22}) + r(p_1a_{12} + p_2a_{22}) \qquad (9.1b)$$

In (9.1a), wl_1 is the wage cost and $(p_1a_{11} + p_2a_{21})$ the value of means of production that must be advanced, both per unit of output of the first commodity. By assumption, the means of production that are advanced are entirely used up in the production process; hence, their value must be recovered from the sale proceeds of the first commodity.[1] The final term on the right-hand side of (9.1a) refers to profits, paid at a uniform rate on the value of capital advanced. So, the price of the first commodity is equal to wage costs plus cost of capital used up plus profits at the prevailing rate, all per unit of output.

Now relax the assumption that all capital is circulating. a_{ij} is still the amount of commodity i that must be advanced as means of production per unit of output of the j-th commodity, but it is no longer the amount of commodity i that is used up in each period in producing commodity j. A simple way to treat durable means of production, which have just been introduced, is to define mortality, or depreciation, coefficients thus:

d_{ij} = proportion of commodity i advanced as means of production that is used up in one period in producing commodity j, $j = 1,2$.

If $d_{ij} = 1$, commodity i is circulating capital when used in the production of commodity j. At the other extreme, $d_{ij} = 0$ implies that commodity i is unaffected when used as means of production in the j-th industry: that is, commodity i is an everlasting machine that always operates at constant efficiency. One consequence of the introduction of mortality coefficients should be noted when $d_{ij} < 1$. Clearly, commodity i is durable when used in industry j; that is, it lasts for more than one period. However, it is unnecessary to distinguish between commodities i of different ages employed in industry j because an 'old' commodity i can be reduced to an equivalent amount of a new commodity i.[2] Define:

$$\underline{a}_{ij} = a_{ij}d_{ij}$$

$\underline{a}_{ij}$ is the amount of commodity i used up (as distinct from advanced) in producing one unit of commodity j. The price equations can now be written as:

$$p_1 = wl_1 + (p_1\underline{a}_{11} + p_2\underline{a}_{21}) + r(p_1a_{11} + p_2a_{21}) \tag{9.2a}$$

$$p_2 = wl_2 + (p_1\underline{a}_{12} + p_2\underline{a}_{22}) + r(p_1a_{12} + p_2a_{22}) \tag{9.2b}$$

The price of commodity one is equal to wage costs, wl_1, plus the cost of capital used up, $(p_1\underline{a}_{11} + p_2\underline{a}_{21})$, plus profits, $r(p_1a_{11} + p_2a_{21})$, which are paid at a uniform rate on the value of capital advanced; similarly, for the second commodity. Once mortality coefficients are introduced, it becomes necessary in specifying the price equations to distinguish between the value of means of production advanced and the value of means of production used up in each period. It can be seen from (9.2) that I enjoy the best of both worlds by introducing mortality coefficients: I can treat fixed capital while remaining within the realm of single-product industries.

(9.2) are the most general price equations for a model with *a priori* specified mortality coefficients. Other special cases, apart from the two mentioned above of $d_{ij} = 1$ and $d_{ij} = 0$ are: first, $d_{ij} = d_i$, $j = 1,2$ for both i, which means that each capital good has the same rate of depreciation regardless of its sector of employment; and second, $d_{ij} = d_j$, $i = 1,2$ for both j, which means that capital goods employed in the same sector have the same rate of depreciation. In the first case, different capital goods employed in the same sector can have different rates of depreciation while, in the second case, the same capital good can have different depreciation rates according to its sector of employment.

In (9.2), all four mortality coefficients can be different. The only restriction to be placed on the coefficients, d_{ij}, is that the system should be productive. It will be recalled from Chapter 4 that the analysis of the price equations (9.1) was based on the following productiveness condition:

There are $X_1 > 0$, $X_2 > 0$ such that:

$$a_{11}X_1 + a_{12}X_2 < X_1 \tag{9.3a}$$

$$a_{21}X_1 + a_{22}X_2 < X_2 \tag{9.3b}$$

The essence of (9.3) is that the total quantity of each commodity used up as means of production is less than the gross output. The appropriate productiveness condition for the fixed capital model with price equations (9.2) can be written as:

There are $X_1 > 0$, $X_2 > 0$ such that:

$$\underline{a}_{11}X_1 + \underline{a}_{12}X_2 < X_1 \tag{9.4a}$$

$$\underline{a}_{21}X_1 + \underline{a}_{22}X_2 < X_2 \tag{9.4b}$$

Conditions (4.4) of Chapter 4 apply, with a_{ij} replaced by $\underline{a}_{ij}$.

If (9.4) is satisfied, it can be shown that (9.2) has a positive solution for $0 \leqslant r \leqslant R_F$, where $R_F = 1/s_1$ and s_1 is the smallest positive root of:

$$s^2 - s(c_{11} + c_{22}) + c_{11}c_{22} - c_{12}c_{21} = 0 \tag{9.5}$$

where:

$$\begin{aligned}
c_{11} &= (a_{11}(1 - \underline{a}_{22}) + a_{12}\underline{a}_{21})/D \\
c_{12} &= (a_{11}\underline{a}_{12} + a_{12}(1 - \underline{a}_{11}))/D \\
c_{21} &= (a_{21}(1 - \underline{a}_{22}) + a_{22}\underline{a}_{21})/D \\
c_{22} &= (a_{21}\underline{a}_{12} + a_{22}(1 - \underline{a}_{11}))/D \\
D &= (1 - \underline{a}_{11})(1 - \underline{a}_{22}) - \underline{a}_{12}\underline{a}_{21}
\end{aligned} \tag{9.6}$$

That is:

$$\begin{array}{ll}
p_1 > 0, p_2 > 0 & \text{if } 0 \leqslant r \leqslant R_F \\
w_{(i)} > 0 & \text{if } 0 \leqslant r < R_F \\
w_{(i)} = 0 & \text{if } r = R_F \\
dw_{(i)}/dr < 0 & \text{if } 0 \leqslant r \leqslant R_F
\end{array} \tag{9.7}$$

So far, I have assumed that each sector has only process of production. If there are alternative processes, different techniques can be constructed in the usual way; clearly, corresponding mortality coefficients can differ between techniques. The theory of choice of technique developed in Chapter 6 can be extended to this fixed capital model. In particular, the cost-minimising technique at a given feasible value of r is that which supports the highest real wage. Hence, choice of technique can be determined from the outer envelope of feasible w–r curves.

Two reasons can be advanced for the study of fixed capital by means of *a priori* specified mortality coefficients. First, it is a simple way of accommodating durable means of production without the attendant difficulties of joint production. In other words, the model is both relatively tractable and possesses properties familiar from the analysis of single-product industries models. The second is a corollary to the first. In performing the analysis above, the problems peculiar to fixed capital – such as the determination of the optimal economic lifetime of machinery – can be perceived by their absence. The question about the economic lifetime of machinery is evaded by the assumption on mortality: necessarily so, as underlying this treatment of capital is the hypothesis that an old capital good is equivalent to a smaller quantity of a new capital good. Of course, this hypothesis is satisfactory if capital goods depreciate in this fashion: but problems arise if this is offered as a general way of treating capital. To appreciate this point, consider the following simple example. Suppose that a capitalist has an old machine in its last year of life; next year, this capital good will no longer exist. However, if he owned a supposedly equivalent quantity of new machinery, he would have capital goods next year and throughout the machinery's lifetime. The assumption on mortality is theoretically inadequate, for problems arise associated with the age-structure and scrapping of machinery. This simple example illustrates the inherent difficulty in attempting to reduce qualitative differences in machinery to quantitative differences. The latter depend on the price system which varies in general with income distribution. To impose *a priori* specified mortality coefficients as part of a general treatment of fixed capital cannot be justified on theoretical grounds because the profitability of a machine, and hence its economic lifetime, depend on prices; the imposition of mortality coefficients means that the lifetime of each machine in each sector has been specified at the outset without regard to essential economic considerations.

9.3 A Proper Fixed Capital Model: Introduction

In the remaining sections of this chapter, I develop an acceptable treatment of fixed capital. At first, for ease of exposition, I assume that there is only one type of durable capital good; furthermore, it is durable when employed in only one sector. Having expounded the principles of the model, I relax this assumption in section 9.8 to permit fixed capital in both sectors.

I retain the asumption from Chapters 2–7 that each sector produces only one final, or marketable, commodity – the first sector iron, the second new machines. When employed in the first sector, a new machine lasts for only one period but, when used in the second sector, it can last for two periods: the new machine is thus a circulating capital good in the iron sector, a fixed capital good in the machine sector. Iron is a circulating capital good in both sectors. The treatment of fixed capital in a joint production framework is most easily illustrated by the specification of the conditions of production:

Iron

$$X_{11} \text{ t iron} \oplus X_{21} \text{ new machines} \oplus L_1 \text{ labour} \ominus X_1 \text{ t iron} \qquad (9.8a)$$

Machines

$$X_{12} \text{ t iron} \oplus X_{22} \text{ new machines} \oplus L_2 \text{ labour}$$

$$\ominus X_2 \text{ new machines} \oplus X_{22} \text{ old machines} \qquad (9.8b)$$

$$X_{13} \text{ t iron} \oplus X_{22} \text{ old machines} \oplus L_3 \text{ labour}$$

$$\ominus X_3 \text{ new machines} \qquad (9.8c)$$

In (9.8b), new machines enter the production process with circulating capital and labour inputs, to emerge a year older as part of the output of the process.

> We shall regard durable instruments of production as part of the annual intake of a process, on the same footing as such means of production (e.g. raw materials) as are entirely used up in the course of a year; while what is left of them at the end of the year will be treated as a portion of the annual joint product of the industry, of which the more conspicuous part consists of the marketable commodity that is the primary object of the process. (PCMC, section 73, p. 63)

The old machines emerging from (9.8b) can then enter the second process in the machine sector.

> This point of view implies that the same machine, at different ages, should be regarded as so many different products, each with its own price . . . Accordingly, an industry which employs a durable instrument of production must be regarded as being subdivided into as many separate processes as are the years of the total life of the instrument in question. Each of these processes is distinguished by the fact that it uses an instrument of a different age; and each of them 'produces', jointly with a quantity of a marketable commodity, an instrument a year older than the one which it uses – with the exception of the process using the expiring instrument in its last year, which produces singly the marketable commodity. (ibid., section 74, pp. 63–4)

It is easily seen that the model summarised in (9.8) above is the simplest that can be constructed in which it is necessary to treat capital in this way.[3] By assuming that an instrument is durable in only one sector, the question of the treatment of fixed capital arises. By assuming that the durable instrument has a maximum physical lifetime of only two years, it is necessary to specify just two processes in the machine sector in addition to the one in the iron sector. The result is a two-sector, three-process, fixed capital, single-product industries model which is sufficiently complex to accommodate the question of the optimal economic lifetime of the machine when employed in one sector.

Before deriving the price equations, there is one final comment on the technology (9.8a)–(9.8c). Once it has been decided that new machines are durable in only one sector, no generality is lost in assuming that it is the machine sector which employs fixed capital: I could equally have assumed that it is the iron sector which employs fixed capital.

I number commodities as follows: 1 iron, 2 a new machine, 3 an old machine. Then, the price equations corresponding to (9.8a)–(9.8c) are:

$$(1+r)\ (p_1X_{11} + p_2X_{21}) + wL_1 = p_1X_1 \tag{9.9a}$$

$$(1+r)\ (p_1X_{12} + p_2X_{22}) + wL_2 = p_2X_2 + p_3X_{22} \tag{9.9b}$$

$$(1+r)\ (p_1X_{13} + p_3X_{22}) + wL_3 = p_2X_3 \tag{9.9c}$$

> These processes [i.e. (9.9b) and (9.9c)] need not be separate in ownership or in operation, and will often be run side by side in the same shed; all that is necessary is that the amounts of means of production and labour employed by each should be separately ascertainable by use of measures of quantity, without need of knowing the values – so that an independent equation can be set up for each. Nor is it necessary that the instruments belonging to successive age-groups should actually be marketed for their prices to be effective; since even though these are only book-values, they are the basis for correctly allocating the profits and making allowance for depreciation in the case of each age-group: 'correctly' in the sense of just fulfilling the original condition of making possible the replacement of the means of production and the payment of a uniform rate of profits. (ibid., section 74, p. 64)

If I follow Sraffa in assuming that the old machine is not marketed, p_3 is interpreted as an 'accounting' price. To see this, consider (9.9b) which can be rewritten as:

$$p_2X_2 = wL_2 + (p_1X_{12} + (p_2 - p_3)X_{22}) + r(p_1X_{12} + p_2X_{22}) \qquad (9.9b')$$

The receipts from operating the first process in the machine sector are p_2X_2, because the old machine is not traded. This is equal to the wage costs, wL_2, plus the cost of means of production used up, $(p_1X_{12} + (p_2 - p_3)X_{22})$, plus profits paid at a uniform rate on the value of means of production advanced, $r(p_1X_{12} + p_2X_{22})$. p_1X_{12} is the value of iron inputs used up to produce X_2 new machines; $(p_2 - p_3)X_{22}$ is the change in the value of the machine (i.e. depreciation) when used in the first process of the machine industry; $(p_1X_{12} + p_2X_{22})$ is the value of means of production advanced (both circulating and fixed capital) in the first process of the machine industry.

> The price at any given age of a durable instrument of production or fixed capital asset, as it results from the equations, represents its correct book-value after depreciation. The difference between the values of the asset at two consecutive ages gives the allowance to be made for depreciation for that year. And this latter amount ($(p_2 - p_3)X_{22}$ in (9.9b)) added to the profit at the general rate on the value of the asset at the beginning of the year (p_2X_{22} in (9.9b)) gives the annual charge for that year. This charge will in general not be constant but changing, and probably falling, with the ageing of the instrument or asset. (ibid., section 77, p. 66)

(9.9b′) can be rewritten as:

$$p_2X_2 = wL_2 + (1+r)p_1X_{12} + ((p_2 - p_3)X_{22} + rp_2X_{22}) \qquad (9.9b'')$$

where the right-hand side is the sum of wage costs, circulating capital charges and fixed capital charges. No further comment is required on (9.9c), as both iron and the old machine are circulating capital.

Having derived the price equations, (9.9), I can now attend to their solution.

9.4 Solution of the Price System

The fundamental condition to be imposed on (9.8) is that it is productive. This means that the gross output of each marketable commodity is at least as great as the total inter-industry requirements. So, I have:

Iron

$$X_1 \geqslant X_{11} + X_{12} + X_{13} \tag{9.10a}$$

New Machines

$$X_2 + X_3 \geqslant X_{21} + X_{22} \tag{9.10b}$$

walosi.

The price equations, (9.9), cannot be solved in the same way as (4.5) of Chapter 4 because of the presence of joint production. The analysis of (9.9) under the productiveness condition, (9.10), proceeds by the elimination of the old machine. Multiply (9.9b) by $(1+r)$ and add the resulting equation to (9.9c) to obtain:

$$\begin{aligned}(1+r)p_1((1+r)X_{12} + X_{13}) + (1+r)p_2((1+r)X_{22})\\ + w((1+r)L_2 + L_3) = p_2((1+r)X_2 + X_3)\end{aligned} \tag{9.11}$$

The old machine price is absent from (9.11). Dividing through (9.9a) by X_1 and (9.11) by $((1+r)X_2 + X_3)$, I obtain respectively:

$$(1+r)\ (p_1A_{11} + p_2A_{21}) + wA_1 = p_1 \tag{9.12a}$$

$$(1+r)\ (p_1A_{12}(r) + p_2A_{22}(r)) + wA_2(r) = p_2 \tag{9.12b}$$

where:[4]

$$A_{i1} = X_{i1}/X_1,\ A_1 = L_1/X_1, \quad i = 1,2 \tag{9.13a}$$

$$\begin{aligned}A_{12}(r) &= ((1+r)X_{12} + X_{13})/((1+r)X_2 + X_3)\\ A_{22}(r) &= ((1+r)X_{22})/((1+r)X_2 + X_3)\\ A_2(r) &= ((1+r)L_2 + L_3)/((1+r)X_2 + X_3)\end{aligned} \tag{9.13b}$$

The coefficients in (9.12a) are similar to those encountered in Chapters 4–7. However, those in (9.12b) differ from those in (9.12a) in being functionally dependent on r, as is clear from (9.13b). While (9.12) bears a superficial resemblance to (9.2) of Chapter 4, the theory developed for the latter cannot be mechanically applied to the former because all the coefficients in (9.12) are not constant. Note that (9.12a) and (9.12b) are structurally similar to (3.5a) and (3.5b) of Chapter 3, with $(1+r)A_{11}$ playing the role of a_{11}, $(1+r)A_{21}$ that of a_{12}, $(1+r)A_{12}(r)$ that of a_{21}, $(1+r)A_{22}(r)$ that of a_{22}, A_1 that of F_1 and $A_2(r)$ that of F_2. By *Result 3*, (9.12) has a positive solution if and only if the analogues of (3.8a), (3.8b) and (3.11) of Chapter 3 are satisfied, namely:

$$1 - (1+r)A_{11} > 0 \tag{9.14a}$$

$$1 - (1+r)A_{22}(r) > 0 \tag{9.14b}$$

$$(1 - (1+r)A_{11})(1 - (1+r)A_{22}(r)) - (1+r)^2 A_{12}(r)A_{21} > 0 \tag{9.14c}$$

When evaluated at $r = 0$, (9.14a) states that the output of iron is greater than the input of iron into the iron industry, and (9.14b) that the gross output of new machines from the machine sector's two processes is greater than the input of new machines into the first process of the machine sector.[5] The productiveness conditions, (9.10a) and (9.10b), then imply (9.14c). So, under (9.10), (9.14a)–(9.14c) are satisfied at $r = 0$. As each of the functions on the left-hand sides of (9.14a)–(9.14c) is continuous, the inequalities will be satisfied for a sufficiently small range of positive values of r. The immediate problem is to discover whether there is an upper limit to those values of r for which (9.14a)–(9.14c) are satisfied. The analogous question for the circulating capital model of Chapters 3 and 4 was answered by analysing the quadratic equation:

$$f(r) \equiv (1 - (1+r)a_{11})(1 - (1+r)a_{22}) - (1+r)^2 a_{12}a_{21} = 0 \tag{9.15}$$

Note the resemblance between the expression on the left-hand side of (9.14c) and the quadratic $f(r)$. By the same line of argument as used in section 4.2, the inequality (9.14c) is the first that will fail to be satisfied: that is, if either (9.14a) or (9.14b) does not hold at a given value of r, say r^1, (9.14c) will already have ceased to hold at a value $r^2 < r^1$. As both $(1 - (1+r)A_{11})$ and $(1 - (1+r)A_{22}(r))$ become negative for sufficiently large positive values of r, it follows that the expression on the left-hand side of (9.14c) must also become negative at a positive value of r. So, I concentrate on the rational polynomial:

$$F(r) \equiv (1 - (1+r)A_{11})(1 - (1+r)A_{22}(r)) - (1+r)^2 A_{12}(r)A_{21} \tag{9.16}$$

Arguing by analogy with the circulating capital case of Chapters 3 and 4, I seek the smallest positive value of r, denoted by R, for which $F(r) = 0$. Now (9.16) can be rewritten as:

$$F(r) \equiv (1+r)^2((s - A_{11})(s - A_{22}(r)) - A_{12}(r)A_{21})$$

by defining $s \equiv 1/(1+r)$; so, $F(r) = 0$ if and only if:

$$G(s) \equiv s^2 - s(A_{11} + A_{22}(r)) + A_{11}A_{22}(r) - A_{12}(r)A_{21} = 0 \tag{9.17}$$

By the argument above, there must be at least one positive value of r at which $F(r) = 0$ and hence at least one corresponding value of s at which $G(s) = 0$. The relevant solution, R, is obtained from:

$$1/(1+R) = S_1 = (A_{11} + A_{22}(R) + \sqrt{(A_{11} + A_{22}(R))^2 - 4(A_{11}A_{22}(R) - A_{12}(R)A_{21})})/2 \tag{9.18}$$

as can easily be shown by substitution for s from (9.18) into (9.17). This arguments *suggests* the existence of a positive value of the rate of profit, R, such that (9.14a)–(9.14c) are satisfied for $0 \leqslant r \leqslant R$. The difficulty with this model, compared with the circulating capital model of Chapters 3 and 4, is that the coefficients are functions of r, not constants: a change in the value of r alters the coefficients in (9.16) or (9.17). To prove the existence of R, consider separately these two functions:

$$d(r) = 1/(1+r) \tag{9.19a}$$

$$e(r) = (A_{11} + A_{22}(r) + \sqrt{(A_{11} + A_{22}(r))^2 - 4(A_{11}A_{22}(r) - A_{12}(r)A_{21})})/2 \tag{9.19b}$$

From (9.18), R is the smallest positive value of r at which $d(r) = e(r)$. I now derive the properties of $d(r)$ and $e(r)$.

> When $r = 0$, $d(r) = 1$; as $r \to \infty$, $d(r) \to 0$. $d(r)$ is a continuous function for all $r \geqslant 0$.

> When $r = 0$, $e(0) < 1$, by the productiveness conditions, (9.10) – a proof by contradiction, similar to the one in section 4.2, suffices. As $r \to \infty$:

$$A_{22}(r) \to X_{22}/X_2 \equiv A_{22}^* \qquad (9.20a)$$

$$A_{12}(r) \to X_{12}/X_2 \equiv A_{12}^* \qquad (9.20b)$$

and

$$e(r) \to (A_{11} + A_{22}^* + \sqrt{(A_{11} + A_{22}^*)^2 - 4(A_{11}A_{22}^* - A_{12}^*A_{21})})/2 = e^* \qquad (9.20c)$$

$e(r)$ is also a continuous function for all $r \geqslant 0$. Two possible configurations are illustrated in Figure 9.1. It follows from the properties of $d(r)$ and $e(r)$ that there must be at least one intersection in the positive quadrant and there can be at most three.[6] In Figure 9.1a, there is only one point of intersection which necessarily gives the value R. In Figures 9.1b and 9.1c, there are three points of intersection: it is the smallest of R, $\bar{r}$ and $\underline{r}$ that is relevant. The qualitative information in (9.19) and (9.20), together with the productiveness condition, permits me to derive the existence of the value R. It is not necessary to know the relation between $e(0)$ and e^* or the sign of the derivative de/dr. So, it could happen that $e^* > e(0)$, without affecting the conclusions; also, $e(r)$ can be increasing in r over part of its range.

To summarise so far: (9.12a) and (9.12b) have a positive solution for each r lying between 0 and R, the latter being determined as the smallest positive value of r for which (9.16) is zero. When $r = R$, $w = 0$ in (9.12) and $p_1 > 0$, $p_2 > 0$ by the same argument as in section 4.2. Hence, either marketable commodity, or a basket of both, can be chosen as numeraire. Note that I have proved that only marketable commodity prices are positive for $0 \leqslant r \leqslant R$.

Figure 9.1a

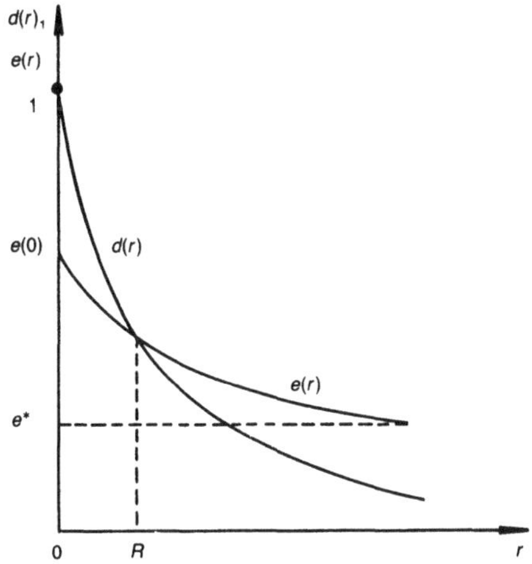

Figure 9.1b

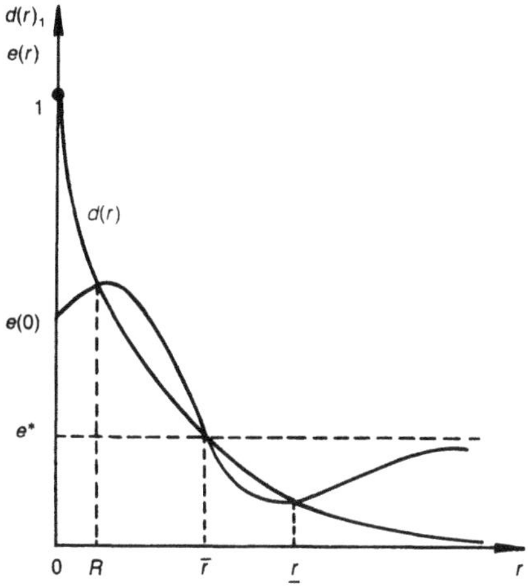

Figure 9.1c

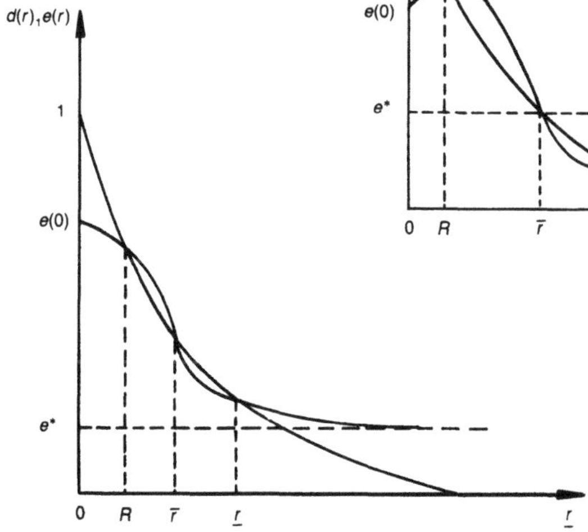

Does it follow that the ageing machine price is also positive over the same range? To answer this question, consider the following numerical examples:

Example 1

1 t iron ⊕ 1 new machine ⊕ 1 labour ⊖ 3 t iron (9.21a)

1 t iron ⊕ 1 new machine ⊕ 1 labour ⊖ 3 new machines

⊕ 1 old machine (9.21b)

1/2 t iron ⊕ 1 old machine ⊕ 1 labour ⊖ 2 new machines (9.21c)

$$\text{Then } A_{11} = 1/3 = A_{21} = A_1 \tag{9.22a}$$

$$A_{12} = ((1+r) + 1/2)/((1+r)3 + 2)$$

$$A_{22} = (1+r)/((1+r)3 + 2) \tag{9.22b}$$

$$A_2 = ((1+r) + 1)/((1+r) + 2)$$

Substituting these values into (9.16), I obtain R as the smallest positive solution of:

$$13 - 12r - 13r^2 = 0$$

$$\text{i.e. } R = (-6+\sqrt{205})/13 \simeq 0.64 \tag{9.23}$$

With iron as numeraire, expressions for p_2 and w can be obtained by solving (9.12) after substituting from (9.22). Then from either (9.9b) or (9.9c), the following expression can be obtained for p_3:

$$p_3 = 3(3r+1)/4(2r + 3) \tag{9.24}$$

In this case, $p_3 > 0$ for $0 \leqslant r \leqslant R$.

Example 2

1 t iron ⊕ 1 new machine ⊕ 1 labour ⊖ 3 t iron (9.25a)

1 t iron ⊕ 1 new machine ⊕ 1 labour ⊖ 3 new machines

⊕ 1 old machine (9.25b)

1 t iron ⊕ 1 old machine ⊕ 1 labour ⊖ 1 new machine (9.25c)

Straightforward calculations from (9.16) and (9.25) show that R is the solution of:

$$-7r^2 - 6r + 4 = 0$$

$$\text{i.e. } R = (-3 + \sqrt{37})/7 \simeq 0.44 \qquad (9.26)$$

Then, following the same procedure as in *Example 1*, I have:

$$p_3 = 3(r - 1)/(4r + 5) \qquad (9.27)$$

Clearly, in this case, $p_3 < 0$ for $0 \leqslant r \leqslant R$.

In section 9.3, I observed that no generality was lost by assuming that only the machine sector employed durable capital. In the remaining four examples, I suppose that it is the iron sector which employs fixed capital: hence, it will be the iron sector which uses the ageing machine and has two processes. *Example 3–6* will provide the reader with an opportunity to solve a system structurally similar to but slightly different from (9.9).

Example 3

2 t iron ⊕ 1 new machine ⊕ 2 labour ⊝ 15 t iron

⊕ 1 old machine (9.28a)

3 t iron ⊕ 1 old machine ⊕ 3 labour ⊝ 12 t iron (9.28b)

1 t iron ⊕ 1 labour ⊝ 1 new machine (9.28c)

The corresponding price equations are, with iron as numeraire:

$$(1+r)(2+p_2) + 2w = 15 + p_3 \qquad (9.29a)$$

$$(1+r)(3+p_3) + 3w = 12 \qquad (9.29b)$$

$$(1+r) + w = p_2 \qquad (9.29c)$$

p_3 can be eliminated from (9.29a) and (9.29b) in the usual way to yield:

$$(1+r)(2r+5) + (1+r)^2 p_2 + w(2r+5) = 15r + 27 \qquad (9.29d)$$

(9.29c) and (9.29d) are analogous to (9.12a) and (9.12b). Straightforward calculations show that R is the smallest positive solution of:

$$-r^3 - 5r^2 + 5r + 21 = 0 \quad (9.30a)$$

i.e. $R \simeq 2.1$

An expression for w can be obtained from (9.29c) or (9.29d) which, when substituted into (9.29b), yields:

$$p_3 = (4r - 3)/(r^2 + 4r + 6) \quad (9.31)$$

So, the price of the old machine is negative for some values of r $(0 \leqslant r < 3/4)$ and positive for others $(3/4 < r \leqslant R)$.

Example 4

6 t iron ⊕ 1 new machine ⊕ 3 labour ⊖ 20 t iron

⊕ 1 old machine (9.32a)

9 t iron ⊕ 1 old machine ⊕ 2 labour ⊖ 16 t iron (9.32b)

1 t iron ⊕ 1 labour ⊖ 1 new machine (9.32c)

For this model, R is obtained as the smallest positive solution of:

$$-r^3 - 9r^2 - 4r + 20 = 0 \quad (9.33a)$$

i.e. $R \simeq 1.21$ (9.33b)

The expression for the ageing machine price is:

$$p_3 = (1 - 7r)(2 + r)/(6 + 5r + r^2) \quad (9.34)$$

So, the old machine price is positive for low values of r $(0 \leqslant r < 1/7)$ and negative for higher values of r $(1/7 < r \leqslant R)$.

Example 5

1/16 t iron ⊕ 1 new machine ⊕ 43/40 labour ⊖ 1 t iron

⊕ 1 old machine (9.35a)

1/4 t iron ⊕ 1 old machine ⊕ 1 labour ⊖ 1 t iron (9.35b)

1/16 t iron ⊕ 1/10 labour ⊖ 1 new machine (9.35c)

R is the smallest positive solution of:

$$-r^3 - 4r^2 + 7r + 26 = 0 \tag{9.36a}$$

i.e. $R \doteq 2.6$ (9.36b)

The expression for the old machine price is:

$$p_3 = (6r^2-5r+1)/2(8r^2+102r+174) \tag{9.37}$$

As $6r^2 -5r+1 = (3r-1)(2r-1)$, if follows that $p_3 > 0$ for $0 \leqslant r < 1/3$ and $1/2 < r \leqslant R$, and $p_3 < 0$ for $1/3 < r < 1/2$. Here, the old machine price is positive for low and high values of r and negative over an intermediate range ($1/3 < r < 1/2$).

Example 6

6 t iron ⊕ 1 new machine ⊕ 2 labour ⊖ 20 t iron

⊕ 1 old machine (6.38a)

8.5 t iron ⊕ 1 old machine ⊕ 3 labour ⊖ 20 t iron (6.38b)

1 t iron ⊕ 1 labour ⊖ 1 new machine (6.38c)

R is the smallest positive solution of:

$$-2r^3 - 18r^2 - 7r + 49 = 0 \tag{9.39a}$$

i.e. $R \doteq 1.38$

The expression for the old machine price is:

$$\begin{aligned} p_3 &= (-11r^2 + 20r - 9)/(2r^2 + 8r + 12) \\ &= (r - 1)(9 - 11r)/(2r^2 + 8r + 12) \end{aligned} \tag{9.40}$$

So, $p_3 < 0$ for $0 \leqslant r < 1$ and $1.22 \doteq 11/9 < r \leqslant R$, and $p_3 > 0$ for $1 < r < 11/9$. Here, in contrast to *Example 5*, the ageing machine price is negative for low and high values of r and positive over an intermediate range $(1 < r < 11/9)$.

The following conclusions can be immediately drawn from these examples:

1. the old machine price is not necessarily positive over the interval $0 \leqslant r \leqslant R$, as demonstrated by *Examples 2 – 6*;
2. there is not necessarily any relation between p_3 and the rate of profit; in particular, the old machine price is not necessarily an inverse monotonic function of r, as is clear from *Examples 3,5* and *6*.

In precluding the derivation of a general result on the relation between p_3 and r, these examples raise the question of the nature and implications of a negative ageing machine price. Before investigating this question in section 9.5, I summarise the analysis of this section in

> *Result 16:* The productive single-product industries, fixed capital model has a maximum rate of profit, R, such that, for $0 \leqslant r \leqslant R$, marketable commodity prices are positive, and the wage in terms of either marketable commodity is positive if $0 \leqslant r < R$ and zero if $r = R$. The old machine price can be negative over a feasible range of values of r; furthermore, there is no generally valid relation between p_3 and r.

9.5 Negative Old Machine Price

The purpose of this section is to provide an interpretation of a negative old machine price when it occurs at a feasible value of r. A machine can be valued according to its future earning power or the costs incurred in its construction. In deriving the price equations, (9.9), I have essentially adopted the latter approach. In an equilibrium, the two methods of evaluation should be equivalent.[7] Recognition of this provides a clue to the interpretation of a negative old machine price, which cannot be due to other negative costs of production. From (9.9b), define:

$$z_2(1) \equiv p_2X_2 - (1 + r)\, p_1X_{12} - wL_2 \tag{9.41a}$$

$$z_2(2) \equiv p_2X_3 - (1 + r)\, p_1X_{13} - wL_3 \tag{9.41b}$$

$z_2(\tau)$ is the return on a machine of age $(\tau - 1)$ at rate of profit r in the τ-th process available to the second industry, $\tau = 1,2$. Using (9.41a) and (9.41b), (9.9b) and (9.9c) can be rewritten respectively as:

$$(1+r)p_2X_{22} = z_2(1) + p_3X_{22} \tag{9.42a}$$

$$(1+r)p_3X_{22} = z_2(2) \tag{9.42b}$$

From (9.42b):

$$p_3 = z_2(2)/(1+r)X_{22} \tag{9.43a}$$

which, when substituted into (9.42a), yields:

$$\begin{aligned} p_2 &= z_2(1)/(1+r)X_{22} + z_2(2)/(1+r)^2X_{22} \\ &= (z_2(1)/(1+r) + z_2(2)/(1+r)^2)/X_{22} \end{aligned} \tag{9.43b}$$

From (9.43a), p_3 is the discounted profit obtained by operating a one-year-old machine; and from (9.43b), p_2 is the discounted profit obtained by operating a new machine throughout its lifetime. In both (9.43a) and (9.43b), the rate of discount is the prevailing rate of profit.

There is now straightforward interpretation of a negative ageing machine price. From (9.43a), it follows that $p_3 < 0$ if and only if the receipts from operating the second process in the machine industry are insufficient to cover circulating capital and labour costs, the former being compounded: that is, the old machine is inefficient at the prevailing price system. The implication of a negative old machine price is that the machine should be scrapped before the end of its physical lifetime and the corresponding process not operated: in this model, the machine should be scrapped after one year and the second process in the machine sector should not be operated. If this is done, only processes (9.8a) and (9.8b) are activated. This means that a technique, different from that in (9.8a)–(9.8c), is being operated. Implicit in the technology are two techniques – the first, which I have already considered and which I now call '(2)', consists of the only process in the iron industry and both processes in the machine industry; the second, the existence of which has just been revealed and which I call '(*1*)', consists of the only process in the iron industry and the first process in the machine industry.[8] Assuming that the old machine can be scrapped costlessly, I have as the processes constituting technique (*1*):

$$X_{11} \text{ t iron} \oplus X_{21} \text{ new machines} \oplus L_1 \text{ labour}$$

$$\ominus X_1 \text{ t iron} \tag{9.44a}$$

$$X_{12} \text{ t iron} \oplus X_{22} \text{ new machines} \oplus L_2 \text{ labour}$$

$$\ominus X_2 \text{ new machines} \tag{9.44b}$$

Clearly, the theory developed in Chapter 4 can be applied to this technique.

It may seem from (9.43a) that the ageing machine price, and the corresponding second process in the machine industry, can be treated as residuals. However, it is clear from (9.43b) that the profitability of this process affects the price of the new machine. Thus, it is impossible to analyse the ageing machine price in a partial equilibrium framework by examining only the second process (or even both processes) in the machine industry. Rather, it is necessary to consider both processes together with that in the iron sector; in other words, the analysis must be conducted within a general framework. It might have been thought, by comparing (9.12) and (9.9), that the old machine was not a basic commodity: although the second process in the machine sector can be deleted, both iron and new machines can still be produced. Perhaps, the correct comparison here involves the deletion of the process producing the old machine. If the first process in the machine sector is deleted, neither new machines nor iron can be produced. Thus, I conclude that the old machine is a basic commodity.[9]

The general conclusion to be drawn from this section is that the question of choice of technique is implicit in any properly specified fixed capital model. Though possibly unrecognised during the construction of the model, this problem necessarily arises when attention is drawn to the old machine price (as occurs if numerical examples are considered).

9.6 Choice of Technique in a Fixed Capital Model: Part 1

From the examination of the two-sector, three-process model in sections 9.3–9.5, there are two techniques, (2) and (*1*): the price equations of the former have been analysed in sections 9.3 and 9.4, those of the latter in Chapter 4. I now deal with the question of choice of technique for this model.

The solution of (9.9a)–(9.9c), with iron as numeraire, is given by:

$$p_2^{(2)} = [L_1(1+r)((1+r)X_{12} - X_{13}) + L_2(1+r)(X_1 - (1+r)X_{11}) + L_3(X_1 - (1+r)X_{11})]/$$
$$[L_1((1+r)(X_2 - (1+r)X_{22}) + X_3) + L_2 (1+r)^2X_{21} + L_3(1+r)X_{21}]$$
$$= [(1+r)L_1((1+r)X_{12} - X_{13}) + (X_1 - (1+r)X_{11}) (L_2(1+r) + L_3)]/q_2^{(2)} \qquad (9.45a)$$

$$p_3^{(2)} = [(1+r)L_1(X_{12}X_3 - X_{13}(X_2 - (1+r)X_{22})) + L_2(X_3(X_1 - (1+r)X_{11}) - (1+r)^2X_{21}X_{13}) + L_3((1+r)^2X_{21}X_{13} - (X_1 - (1+r)X_{11}) (X_2 - (1+r) X_{22}))]/q_2^{(2)} \qquad (9.45b)$$

$$w^{(2)} = [X_3(X_1 - (1+r)X_{11}) - (1+r)^2X_{13}X_{21} + (1+r)((X_1 - (1+r)X_{11})(X_2 - (1+r)X_{22}) - (1+r)^2X_{12}X_{21})]/q^{(2)}(r) \qquad (9.45c)$$

where $q^{(2)}(r)$ is the denominator in (9.45a). (9.45a) and (9.45b) can be obtained by solving (9.12a) and (9.12b); $p_3^{(2)}$ can then be obtained by substitution from (9.9b) or (9.9c).

Technique (*1*)'s price equations are, with iron as numeraire:

$$(1+r)(X_{11} + p_2^{(1)}X_{21}) + w^{(1)}L_1 = X_1 \qquad (9.46a)$$

$$(1+r)(X_{12} + p_2^{(1)}X_{22}) + w^{(1)}L_2 = p^{(1)}X_2 \qquad (9.46b)$$

Hence:

$$p_2^{(1)} = \frac{(L_1(1+r)X_{12} + L_2(X_1 - (1+r)X_{11}))}{(L_1(X_2 - (1+r)X_{22}) + L_2(1+r)X_{21})} \qquad (9.47a)$$

$$w^{(1)} = \frac{(X_1 - (1+r)X_{11})(X_2 - (1+r)X_{22}) - (1+r)^2X_{12}X_{21}}{L_1(X_2 - (1+r)X_{22}) + L_2(1+r)X_{21}} \tag{9.47b}$$

There is one final calculation to be performed. From (9.45b), (9.45c) and (9.46b), I have after straightforward but lengthy manipulations:

$$\begin{aligned} w^{(2)} - w^{(1)} = {} & (1+r)X_2X_{22}p_3^{(2)}/(L_1(X_2 - (1+r)X_{22}) \\ & + L_2(1+r)X_{21}) \end{aligned} \tag{9.48}$$

This equation will be used below in deriving a corollary on choice of technique.

Suppose that technique (*1*) is initially employed at a feasible rate of profit, r, with price system $(1, p_2^{(1)}, 0)$ and $w^{(1)}$. That is, in technique (*1*), the old machine has a zero implicit price. The capitalist in the second sector, faced with the question of whether to scrap the machine after the first year or use it until the end of its physical lifetime, evaluates his second process at the prevailing, i.e. (*1*)'s, prices. That is, he calculates:

$$s_3(2{:}1) \equiv p_2^{(1)}X_3 - (1+r)X_{13} - w^{(1)}L_3 \tag{9.49}$$

remembering that the old machine has a zero price in the prevailing technique. Substituting from (9.47a) and (9.47b) into (9.49), I obtain:

$$\begin{aligned} s_3(2{:}1) = {} & [(1+r)L_1(X_{12}X_3 - X_{13}(X_2 - (1+r)X_{22})) \\ & + L_2(X_3(X_1 - (1+r)X_{11}) - (1+r)^2X_{13}X_{21}) \\ & + L_3((1+r)^2X_{12}X_{21} \\ & - (X_1 - (1+r)X_{11})\,(X_2 - (1+r)X_{22}))]/ \\ & \quad [L_2(X_2 - (1+r)X_{22}) + L_2(1+r)X_{21}] \\ = {} & p_3^{(2)}X_{22}q^{(2)}(r)/(L_1(X_2 - (1+r)X_{22} + L_2(1+r)X_{21}) \end{aligned} \tag{9.50}$$

For feasible values of r, both $q^{(2)}(r)$ and the denominator of (9.50) are positive. So:

$$\text{sign } s_3(2{:}1) = \text{sign } p_3^{(2)} \qquad (9.51)$$

That is, the second process in the machine sector makes super-normal profits at technique (*1*)'s prices if and only if the old machine price is positive. However, if technique (*1*) is initially employed, $p_3^{(2)}$ is unknown. Suppose that $s_3(2{:}1) > 0$, so that the capitalist is justified in using the machine for the second year. Let technique (*2*)'s prices be established at the same rate of profit. Evaluating the only process of technique (*1*), in which the machine the scrapped at the end of the first year, the capitalist calculates:

$$s_2(1{:}2) \equiv p_2^{(2)}X_2 - (1+r)(X_{12} + p_2^{(2)}X_{22}) - w^{(2)}L_2 \qquad (9.52)$$

Using (9.9b), it follows from (9.52) that:

$$s_2(1{:}2) = -p_3^{(2)}X_{22} \qquad (9.53a)$$

so that:

$$\text{sign } s_2(1{:}2) = (-1)\text{sign } p_3^{(2)} \qquad (9.53b)$$

Hence, if $s_3(2{:}1) > 0$, it follows from (9.51) that $p_3^{(2)} > 0$ so that $s_2(1{:}2) < 0$. This means that, if he decided to operate the machine for two years, instead of one as before, the capitalist would not then decide to switch back to operating it for only one year. From (9.51) and (9.53b):

$$\text{sign } s_3(2{:}1) = (-1)\text{sign } s_2(1{:}2) \qquad (9.54)$$

Similarly, if $s_3(2{:}1) < 0$, the capitalist will operate only the first process in the machine industry. If he initially operated both processes in the machine sector when $p_3^{(2)} < 0$, the capitalist would find it more profitable to scrap the machine after one year. Finally, if $s_3(2{:}1) = 0$, the machine can be operated equally profitably for one or both processes. I summarise this discussion as:

Result 17: There is a cost-minimising technique for the two-sector, three-process fixed capital model at each feasible value of r, i.e. $0 \leqslant r \leqslant \max(R^{(1)}, R^{(2)})$. Choice of technique is unique except at a switch-point, which is defined as a value of r at which

$$s_3(2{:}1) = s_2(1{:}2) = 0.$$

This is the analogue for the fixed capital model of *Result 11* on the circulating capital model. As with the latter, there are two technical points to be raised. First, if (*1*) is initially employed at $\bar{r}$, and the second process in the machine industry is cost-reducing in the sense that $s_3(2{:}1) > 0$, does it follow that $\bar{r}$ is also feasible for technique (2)? For if $s_3(2{:}1) > 0$ and $\bar{r} > R^{(2)}$, there is no cost-minimising technique because (2), which is cheaper than (*1*), would not support a positive price system. $s_3(2{:}1) > 0$ implies that:

$$p_1^{(1)}X_1 = (1+\bar{r})(p_1^{(1)}X_{11} + p_2^{(1)}X_{21}) + w^{(1)}L_1 \qquad (9.54a)$$

$$p_2^{(1)}X_2 = (1+\bar{r})(p_1^{(1)}X_{12} + p_2^{(1)}X_{22}) + w^{(1)}L_2 \qquad (9.54b)$$

$$p_2^{(1)}X_3 > (1+\bar{r})(p_1^{(1)}X_{13} + w^{(1)}L_3 \qquad (9.54c)$$

Multiplying (9.54b) by $(1+\bar{r})$ and adding the resulting equation to (9.54c), I obtain:

$$p_2^{(1)}((1+\bar{r})X_2 + X_3) > (1+\bar{r})p_1^{(1)}((1+\bar{r})X_{12} + X_{13})$$
$$+ (1+\bar{r})p_2^{(1)}(1+\bar{r})X_{22} + w^{(1)}((1+\bar{r})L_2 + L_3) \qquad (9.54d)$$

Employing the notation introduced in (9.13), (9.53a) and (9.53d) can be rewritten respectively as:

$$p_1^{(1)} = (1+\bar{r})(p_1^{(1)}A_{11} + p_2^{(1)}A_{21}) + w^{(1)}A_1 \qquad (9.55a)$$

$$p_2^{(1)} > (1+\bar{r})(p_1^{(1)}A_{12}(\bar{r}) + p_2{}^{(1)}A_{22}(\bar{r})) + w^{(1)}A_2(\bar{r}) \qquad (9.55b)$$

By deleting the wage terms in (9.55a) and (9.55b), I obtain a pair of inequalities from which (9.14) can be derived. This implies that $\bar{r} \leqslant R^{(2)}$, as required.

The second technical point is related to the first. The proof of *Result 17* was based on the implicit assumption that r was feasible for both techniques. An argument must be added to deal with the case where r is feasible for only one technique – this is left as an exercise.

It is clear from (9.51) and (9.53b) that the old machine price is an indicator of efficiency in the choice of technique. For, if $p_3^{(2)} > 0$, it is cost-minimising to operate both processes in the machine sector, i.e. use the machine for the whole of its physical lifetime. If $p_3^{(2)} < 0$, the machine should be scrapped after its first year of operation. An alternative indicator of efficiency is provided by the real wage rate. From (9.48), it follows that:

$$\text{sign}\ (w^{(2)} - w^{(1)}) = \text{sign}\ p_3^{(2)} \tag{9.56}$$

Hence, if $p_3^{(2)} > 0$, so that technique (*2*) is cost-minimising, $w^{(2)} > w^{(1)}$ from (9.56), i.e. technique (2) supports the higher real wage. I can summarise this in:

> *Corollary 17.1:* Choice of technique can be determined by reference to either:
>
> (a) the sign of the old machine price; or
> (b) the outer envelope of *w–r* curves.

Obviously, *Corollary 17.1*(a) has no counterpart in the circulating capital case. *Corollary 17.1*(b) is the analogue of *Corollary 11.1* for the simpler model. If the cost-minimising technique supports the higher real wage (measured in terms of marketable commodities), it follows that it must also support the lower labour-commanded prices. So, *Corollary 17.1*(b) is equivalent to the two statements in *Corollary 11.1*.

In *Corollary 17.1*, I have obtained a characterisation of the cost-minimising technique in terms of *w–r* curves, without first needing to derive properties of $w^{(1)}$ and $w^{(2)}$. As technique (*1*) is a circulating capital model, the theory of Chapter 4 applies so that $dw^{(1)}/dr < 0$: hence, the outer envelope is a downward-sloping function of r when technique (*1*) is optimal. Consider now technique (*2*). Rewrite (9.9) as:

$$P_1X_1 = (1+r)(P_1X_{11} + P_2X_{21}) + L_1 \tag{9.57a}$$

$$P_2X_2 + P_3X_{22} = (1+r)(P_1X_{12} + P_2X_{22}) + L_2 \tag{9.57b}$$

$$P_2X_3 = (1+r)(P_1X_{13} + P_3X_{22}) + L_3 \tag{9.57c}$$

where $P_i \equiv p_i^{(2)}/w$ is the labour-commanded price of commodity i. Differentiate (9.57) with respect to r to obtain:

$$\frac{dP_1X_1}{dr} = (1+r)\left(\frac{dP_1X_{11}}{dr} + \frac{dP_2X_{21}}{dr}\right) + (P_1X_{11} + P_2X_{21}) \qquad (9.58a)$$

$$\frac{dP_2X_2}{dr} + \frac{dP_3X_{22}}{dr} = (1+r)\left(\frac{dP_1X_{12}}{dr} + \frac{dP_2X_{22}}{dr}\right) + (P_1X_{12} + P_2X_{22}) \qquad (9.58b)$$

$$\frac{dP_2X_3}{dr} = (1+r)\left(\frac{dP_1X_{13}}{dr} + \frac{dP_3X_{22}}{dr}\right) + (P_1X_{13} + P_3X_{22}) \qquad (9.58c)$$

Multiply (9.58b) by $(1+r)$ and add the resulting equation to (9.58c). Employing the notation in (9.13), I obtain this pair of equations:

$$\frac{dP_1}{dr} = (1+r)\left(\frac{dP_1}{dr}A_{11} + \frac{dP_2}{dr}A_{21}\right) + c_1 \qquad (9.59a)$$

$$\frac{dP_2}{dr} = (1+r)\left(\frac{dP_1}{dr}A_{12} + \frac{dP_2}{dr}A_{22}\right) + c_2 \qquad (9.59b)$$

where c_1 and c_2 are the residuals from the right-hand side of (9.58a) and the combination of the right-hand sides of (9.58b) and (9.58c). As I am interested in technique (2) when it is cost-minimising, $p_3^{(2)}$ and hence P_3 are positive, which means that both c_1 and c_2 are positive. (9.59) is analogous to (9.12) with dP_i/dr replacing p_i, $i = 1,2$. As the given r is feasible for technique (2), it follows that (9.59) has positive solution:

$$dP_i/dr > 0 \qquad i = 1,2 \qquad (9.60)$$

If each labour-commanded marketable commodity price is an increasing function of r, it follows that the real wage (in terms of any basket of marketable commodities) is a decreasing function of r. So, I have:

> *Corollary 17.2:* The outer envelope of real wage rate–rate of profit curves for the fixed capital model is downward-sloping.

In this section, I have presented the essential theory of choice of technique for fixed capital models. In the next two sections, I generalise this theory: first, by allowing the machine to have a maximum physical lifetime longer than two years and, second, by allowing fixed capital in both industries.

9.7 Choice of Technique in a Fixed Capital Model: Part 2

In this section, I relax the assumption that the machine has a maximum physical lifetime of two years when employed in the machine sector – I permit the machine to last for three years! This extension is not trivial, introducing new questions on choice of technique. So, I deal with them before permitting fixed capital in both sectors in section 9.8. Instead of processes (9.8a)–(9.8c), I now have:

Iron

$$X_{11} \text{ t iron} \oplus X_{21} \text{ new machines} \oplus L_1 \text{ labour} \ominus X_1 \text{ t iron} \tag{9.61a}$$

Machines

$$X_{12} \text{ t iron} \oplus X_{22} \text{ new machines} \oplus L_2 \text{ labour}$$
$$\ominus\, X_2 \text{ new machines} \oplus X_{22} \text{ one-year-old machines} \tag{9.61b}$$

$$X_{13} \text{ t iron} \oplus X_{22} \text{ one-year-old machines} \oplus L_3 \text{ labour}$$
$$\ominus\, X_3 \text{ new machines} \oplus X_{22} \text{ two-year-old machines} \tag{9.61c}$$

$$X_{14} \text{ t iron} \oplus X_{22} \text{ two-year-old machines} \oplus L_4 \text{ labour}$$
$$\ominus\, X_4 \text{ new machines} \tag{9.61d}$$

As the machine is used for three years in the machine sector, I call this technique (*3*). The basic productiveness condition is stated in these two inequalities:

Iron

$$X_1 \geqslant X_{11} + X_{12} + X_{13} + X_{14} \tag{9.62a}$$

Machines

$$X_2 + X_3 + X_4 \geqslant X_{21} + X_{22} \tag{9.62b}$$

walosi.

The price equations corresponding to (9.61a)–(9.61d) are, with iron as numeraire:

$$(1+r)(X_{11} + p_2^{(3)}X_{21}) + w^{(3)}L_1 = X_1 \tag{9.63a}$$

$$(1+r)(X_{12} + p_2^{(3)}X_{22}) + w^{(3)}L_2 = p_2^{(3)}X_2 + p_3^{(3)}X_{22} \tag{9.63b}$$

$$(1+r)(X_{13} + p_3^{(3)}X_{22}) + w^{(3)}L_3 = p_2^{(3)}X_3 + p_4^{(3)}X_{22} \tag{9.63c}$$

$$(1+r)(X_{14} + p_4^{(3)}X_{22}) + w^{(3)}L_4 = p_2^{(3)}X_4 \tag{9.63d}$$

where $p_i^{(3)}$ is the price of the (i–2)-year-old machine, i = 2,3,4, the bracketed superscript referring to technique (*3*). Eliminating ageing machines by (9.63b)–(9.63d) by multiplying the first equation by $(1+r)^2$, the second by $(1+r)$ and the resulting equations to the third, I obtain:

$$\begin{aligned}&(1+r)((1+r)^2X_{12} + (1+r)X_{13} + X_{14}) + (1+r)p_2((1+r)^2X_{22})\\ &+w((1+r)^2L_2 + (1+r)L_3 + L_4)\\ &= p_2((1+r)^2X_2 + (1+r)X_3 + X_4)\end{aligned} \tag{9.64a}$$

or

$$(1+r)(A_{12}^{(3)}(r) + p_2^{(3)}A_{22}^{(3)}(r)) + w^{(3)}A_2^{(3)}(r) = p_2^{(3)} \tag{9.64b}$$

where

$$A_{12}^{(3)}(r) = \frac{(1+r)^2X_{12} + (1+r)X_{13} + X_{14}}{(1+r)^2X_2 + (1+r)X_3 + X_4}$$

$$A_{22}^{(3)}(r) = \frac{(1+r)^2X_{22}}{(1+r)^2X_2 + (1+r)X_3 + X_4}$$

$$A_2^{(3)}(r) = \frac{(1+r)^2L_2 + (1+r)L_3 + L_4}{(1+r)^2X_2 + (1+r)X_3 + X_4}$$

Dividing through (9.63a) by X_1, I obtain:

$$(1+r)(A_{11}^{(3)} + p_2^{(3)}A_{21}^{(3)}) + w^{(3)}A_1^{(3)} = 1 \tag{9.64d}$$

Collect (9.64b) and (9.64d) as the price equations:

$$(1+r)(A_{11}^{(3)} + p_2^{(3)}A_{21}^{(3)}) + w^{(3)}A_1^{(3)} = 1 \tag{9.65a}$$

$$(1+r)(A_{12}^{(3)}(r) + p_2^{(3)}A_{22}^{(3)}(r)) + w^{(3)}A_2^{(3)}(r) = p_2^{(3)} \tag{9.65b}$$

(9.65a) and (9.65b) are analogous to (9.12a) and (9.12b). Following the method adopted in section 9.4, the maximum rate of profit, $R^{(3)}$, is obtained as the smallest positive solution of:

$$f^{(3)}(r) \equiv (1 - (1+r)A_{11}^{(3)})(1 - (1+r)A_{22}^{(3)}(r)) - (1+r)^2A_{12}^{(3)}(r)A_{21}^{(3)}) = 0 \tag{9.66}$$

$R^{(3)}$ exists on the basis of (9.62). *Result 16* applies:

$p_2^{(3)} > 0$ for $0 \leqslant r \leqslant R^{(3)}$; $w^{(3)} > 0$ if $0 \leqslant r < R^{(3)}$,

$w^{(3)} = 0$ if $r = R^{(3)}$. (9.65) has solution:

$$p_2^{(3)} = \frac{(1+r)A_1^{(3)}A_{12}^{(3)}(r) - A_2^{(3)}(r)(1 - (1+r)A_{11}^{(3)})}{A_1^{(3)}(1 - (1+r)A_{22}^{(3)}(r)) + (1+r)A_2^{(3)}(r)A_{21}^{(3)}} \tag{9.67a}$$

$$w^{(3)} = \frac{(1 - (1+r)A_{11}^{(3)})(1 - (1+r)A_{22}^{(3)}(r)) - (1+r)^2A_{12}^{(3)}(r)A_{21}^{(3)}}{A_1^{(3)}(1 - (1+r)A_{22}^{(3)}(r)) + (1+r)A_2^{(3)}(r)A_{21}^{(3)}} \tag{9.67b}$$

The ageing machine prices can then be obtained from (9.63b)–(9.63d).

The interpretation of ageing machine prices, advanced in section 9.5, applies *mutatis mutandis* to technique (*3*). Defining $z_2^{(3)}(\tau)$ for (9.63b)–(9.63d) in the same way as $z_2(\tau)$ in section 9.5, it is straightforward matter to show that:

$$p_4^{(3)} = z_2^{(3)}(3)/(1+r)X_{22} \tag{9.68a}$$

$$p_3^{(3)} = [z_2^{(3)}(2)/(1+r) + z_2^{(3)}(3)/(1+r)^2)]/X_{22} \tag{9.68b}$$

$$p_2^{(3)} = [z_2^{(3)}(1)/(1+r) + z_2^{(3)}(2)/(1+r)^2 + z_2^{(3)}(3)/(1+r)^3)]/X_{22} \quad (9.68c)$$

The price of a machine of given age is then the sum of discounted profits that can be obtained by operating it for the remainder of its physical lifetime. As with the model of sections 9.3–9.6, the possibility of a negative ageing machine price arises.

Implicit in (9.63a)–(9.63d) are *three* techniques – not only (*3*), to which I have already referred, but also (*1*) and (*2*) of section 9.6. The analysis of the last section was particularly simple because there were only two techniques – (*2*) was either cheaper than, more expensive than or equally costly as (*1*). This simplicity is now lost for, as will be seen below, there is another possibility that can arise when two techniques are compared. I adopt a taxonomic approach, assuming that each technique in turn is initially employed, evaluating the others at its prices. To simplify the presentation, I employ this notation, familiar from section 9.6 and Chapter 6:

$s_i(j{:}k)$ = surplus or loss relative to normal profits of operating process i in technique (j) at (k)'s prices, $i = 2,3,4$; $j,k = 1,2,3$.

Assuming that technique (*1*) is initially employed, there are two possibilities when technique (*2*) is evaluated at (*1*)'s prices:

(1.i) $\quad s_3(2{:}1) < 0 \quad$ (9.69a)

On the basis of (9.69a), the capitalist should not use the machine for a second year; for, if he did, he would not obtain the prevailing rate of profit. It follows from (9.69a), using the argument of section 9.6, that:

$$w^{(1)} > w^{(2)},\ p_3^{(2)} < 0 \quad (9.69b)$$

(1.ii) $\quad s_3(2{:}1) > 0 \quad$ (9.70a)

From (9.70a), the capitalist can reduce his costs by using the machine for a second year, i.e. switching from technique (*1*) to technique (*2*). It follows from section 9.6 that:

$$w^{(1)} < w^{(2)},\ p_3^{(2)} > 0 \quad (9.70b)$$

In (1.i) and (1.ii), I am merely repeating the analysis of section 9.6. Now consider technique (*3*) at (*1*)'s prices. As there are no ageing machines in (*1*), it is necessary to assume that they are assigned zero prices in order to perform the evaluation.

(1.iii) $$s_3(3{:}1) < 0 \tag{9.71a}$$

$$s_4(3{:}1) < 0 \tag{9.71b}$$

As both processes make losses at (*1*)'s prices, there is no reason for the capitalist to operate either. To examine the implications of (9.71), I write down all the expressions involved when (*3*) is evaluated at (*1*)'s prices:

$$(1+r)(X_{11} + p_2^{(1)}X_{21}) + w^{(1)}L_1 = X_1 \tag{9.72a}$$

$$(1+r)(X_{12} + p_2^{(1)}X_{22}) + w^{(1)}L_2 = p_2^{(1)}X_2 \tag{9.72b}$$

$$(1+r)X_{13} \qquad + w^{(1)}L_3 > p_2^{(1)}X_3 \tag{9.72c}$$

$$(1+r)X_{14} \qquad + w^{(1)}L_4 > p_2^{(1)}X_4 \tag{9.72d}$$

(9.72a) and (9.72b) are technique (*1*)'s price equations, while (9.72c) and (9.72d) correspond to (9.71a) and (9.71b) respectively: ageing machines are absent from the last two expressions as each has a zero price in technique (*1*). Multiply (9.72b) by $(1+r)^2$, (9.72c) by $(1+r)$ and add the resulting expressions to (9.72d) to obtain:

$$(1+r)(A_{12}^{(3)} + p_2^{(1)}A_{22}^{(3)}) + w^{(1)}A_2^{(3)} > p_2^{(1)} \tag{9.73a}$$

Combine this with (9.72a), rewritten as:

$$(1+r)(A_{11}^{(3)} + p_2^{(1)}A_{21}^{(3)}) + w^{(1)}A_1^{(3)} = 1 \tag{9.73b}$$

It is a straightforward matter to show from (9.73) that:

$$w^{(1)} > w^{(3)} \tag{9.74}$$

(i.iv) $$s_3(3{:}1) > 0 \tag{9.75a}$$

$$s_4(3{:}1) > 0 \tag{9.75b}$$

As he can obtain super-normal profits by operating each of these processes, the capitalist is justified in employing the machine until the end of its physical lifetime. It then follows, by the same line of argument as in (1.iii), that:

$$w^{(3)} > w^{(1)} \tag{9.76}$$

(1.iii) and (1.iv) are the analogues for technique (*3*) of (1.i) and (1.ii) for technique (*2*). There are, however, two other possibilities for (*3*) having no counterpart for (*2*).

(1.v) $$s_3(3{:}1) > 0 \tag{9.77a}$$

$$s_4(3{:}1) < 0 \tag{9.77b}$$

As the third process makes a super-normal profit but the fourth process makes a loss, the capitalist is justified in operating the machine for an extra year and then scrapping it, i.e. a switch from (*1*) to (*2*). This case then becomes analogous to (1.ii), so that (9.70b) holds.

(1.vi) $$s_3(3{:}1) < 0 \tag{9.78a}$$

$$s_4(3{:}1) > 0 \tag{9.78b}$$

The inference in this case is less obviously clear cut. As the third process makes a loss, there is an argument for scrapping the machine after its first year. Such a policy necessarily ignores the super-normal profit from the fourth process (which can be obtained, of course, only if the third process is operated). The correct procedure in deciding whether to operate the machine for the whole of its physical lifetime is to offset the compounded losses from (9.78a) against the super-normal profits from (9.78b). If the losses outweigh the profits, the capitalist is justified in remaining with technique (*1*). Then, by following the procedure outlined in (1.iii), I would obtain (9.73b) which, when combined with (9.73a), yields (9.74). On the other hand, if the profits outweigh the losses, I would obtain instead of (9.73b):

$$(1+r)(A_{12}^{(3)} + p_2^{(1)}A_{22}^{(3)}) + w^{(1)}A_2^{(3)} < p_2^{(1)} \tag{9.79}$$

Combined with (9.73a), this yields (9.76). (1.vi) differs from each of (1.i)–(1.v) in that there is not one definite conclusion to be drawn. It is clear from (9.78a) that the capitalist should not extend the use of the machine for just one year. Whether the machine is operated for one or three years depends on the compounded sum of (9.78a) and (9.78b), the sign of which cannot in general be determined *a priori*.

Having exhausted the possibilities that can arise when (*1*) is initially employed, I now suppose that (*2*) is chosen.

(2.i) $s_2(1{:}2) < 0$ (9.80a)

This case, where the second process makes losses at (*2*)'s prices, has been considered in section 9.6. On the basis of (9.80a), the capitalist would not be justified in scrapping his machine after one year. It follows from (9.80a) that:

$$w^{(2)} > w^{(1)} \tag{9.80b}$$

(2.ii) $s_2(1{:}2) > 0$ (9.81a)

As the second process makes super-normal profits, the capitalist is justified in scrapping the machine after its first year, i.e. switching from (*2*) to (*1*).[10] It follows from (9.81a) that:

$$w^{(1)} > w^{(2)} \tag{9.81b}$$

(2.iii) $s_4(3{:}2) < 0$ (9.82a)

(9.82a) is derived under the assumption that a zero price for a two-year-old machine is appended to (*2*)'s price system. As (9.82a) means that losses are incurred by operating the machine for another year, it follows that the capitalist is justified in scrapping the machine after two years. By the same argument as in section 9.6, I conclude that:

$$w^{(2)} > w^{(3)} \tag{9.82b}$$

(2.iv) $s_4(3{:}2) > 0$ (9.83a)

In this case, the fourth process makes super-normal profits. So, the capitalist would be justified in extending the life of the machine by one year. (9.83a) implies:

$$w^{(3)} > w^{(2)} \tag{9.83b}$$

This exhausts the possibilities which arise when (*2*) is initially chosen. I now assume that (*3*) is employed.

(3.i) $$s_2(1{:}3) < 0 \tag{9.84a}$$

This inequality implies that the capitalist should not scrap the machine at the end of its first year. It is a straightforward matter to show that (9.84a) implies:

$$w^{(3)} > w^{(1)} \tag{9.84b}$$

(3.ii) $$s_2(1{:}3) > 0 \tag{9.85a}$$

This implies that the capitalist can obtain super-normal profits by scrapping the machine after its first year. (9.85a) implies that $p_3^{(3)} < 0$. Using (9.85a), it can be shown that:

$$w^{(1)} > w^{(3)} \tag{9.85b}$$

(3.iii) $$s_2(2{:}3) > 0 \tag{9.86a}$$

$$s_3(2{:}3) > 0 \tag{9.86b}$$

In this case, the capitalist makes super-normal profits by operating the second and third processes: $p_4^{(3)} < 0$ from (9.86). It follows from (9.86) that:

$$w^{(2)} > w^{(3)} \tag{9.86c}$$

(3.iv) $$s_2(2{:}3) < 0 \tag{9.87a}$$

$$s_3(2{:}3) < 0 \tag{9.87b}$$

As both second and third processes make losses, there is no reason to scrap the machine before the end of its lifetime. (9.87) implies:

$$\begin{aligned} w^{(3)} &> w^{(2)} \\ w^{(3)} &> w^{(1)} \end{aligned} \tag{9.87c}$$

(3.v) $s_2(2:3) > 0$ (9.88a)

$s_3(2:3) < 0$ (9.88b)

As the third process makes losses, there is no reason for the capitalist to scrap the machine after the second year. (9.88a) implies that he can obtain super-normal profits by scrapping the machine after its first year. Hence, as in (3.ii):

$$w^{(1)} > w^{(3)} \quad (9.88c)$$

(3.vi) $s_2(2:3) < 0$ (9.89a)

$s_3(2:3) > 0$ (9.89b)

This case is analogous to (1.vi). The outcome depends on whether the compounded loss from (9.89a) is greater or less than the super-normal profits from (9.89b). If it is greater, the capitalist should operate all processes so that:

$$w^{(3)} > w^{(2)} \quad (9.89c)$$

If it is less, the capitalist should scrap the machine after its second year, implying:

$$w^{(2)} > w^{(3)} \quad (9.89d)$$

In (1.i)–(3.vi), I have covered all the possibilities that can arise for the model (9.61a)–(9.61d). To derive definite results on choice of technique, I need to know that, if it is cheaper than (k) at (k)'s prices, technique (j) is also cheaper at its own prices. It is clear from (1.vi) and (3.vi) that the definition of the concept of cheapness is more complicated for this model than for the circulating capital models treated in earlier chapters. Technique (j) is cheaper than technique (k) at (k)'s prices if:

(a) each process in (j) breaks even, with one or more making super-normal profits;
(b) when one fixed capital process in (j) makes a loss, the compounded sum of losses and profits from all fixed capital pro-

cesses is positive. (The fixed capital processes are (9.61b)–(9.61d).)

It follows from (1.i)–(3.vi) that, if (j) is cheaper than (k) at (k)'s prices:

$$w^{(j)} > w^{(k)} \tag{9.90}$$

Now can (k) be cheaper than (j) at (j)'s prices? If it were:

$$w^{(k)} > w^{(j)} \tag{9.91}$$

which contradicts (9.90). The method of analysis employed above and in Chapter 6 – whereby techniques are evaluated at the prevailing prices and a switch is made if there is a cost reduction – yields a determinate result on choice of technique.

Suppose that (j) is initially employed. When another technique (say (k), is evaluated at (j)'s prices, there are two possibilities:

(A) (k) is more expensive than (j), in which case the capitalist stays with (j) and $w^{(j)} > w^{(k)}$;

(B) (k) is cheaper than (j), in which case the capitalist switches to (k) and $w^{(k)} > w^{(j)}$.

If (A), the capitalist then evaluates another technique, (h), at (j)'s prices, with the same two alternatives. The outcome of each stage of the process is that the cost-minimising technique is chosen among all those considered thitherto. As there is only a finite number of techniques (three), it follows that after a finite number of steps (at most two), the overall cost-minimising technique will be obtained. I summarise this discussion as:

Result 18: If r is feasible, i.e. $r \leqslant \max_j R^{(j)}$, there is a cost-minimising technique of production for the model described in (9.60a)–(9.60d). Unless r is a switch-point, choice of technique is unique.

In section 9.6, I suggested two characterisations of the cost-minimising technique in the simplest fixed capital model – in terms of the wage rate and the ageing machine price. The former extends immediately to the model analysed in this section. So, I have:

Corollary 18.1: The cost-minimising technique at any feasible value of *r* is that which supports:

(a) the highest real wage, in terms of any numeraire consisting of marketable commodities;

(b) the lowest labour-commanded marketable commodity prices.

The second characteristic does not permit such an immediate extension, for the simple reason that there is more than one ageing machine price. I can derive:

Corollary 18.2: (i) If its price system is positive at *r*, (*3*) is the unique cost-minimising technique; (ii) if its price system is positive at *r*, (*2*) is cheaper than (*1*).

It does not follow that, if its price system is positive, (*2*) is the cost-minimising technique, for (*3*) may be cheaper. (1) or (2) is the cost-minimising technique if and only if (*3*) has a negative ageing machine price, when the rate of profit is feasible.

I conclude this section by discussing five numerical examples.

Example 1

$$6 \text{ t iron} \oplus 1 \text{ new machine} \oplus 2 \text{ labour} \ominus 20 \text{ t iron} \oplus 1 \text{ one-year-old machine} \quad (9.91a)$$

$$8.5 \text{ t iron} \oplus 1 \text{ one-year-old machine} \oplus 3 \text{ labour} \ominus 20 \text{ t iron} \oplus 1 \text{ two-year-old machine} \quad (9.91b)$$

$$10 \text{ t iron} \oplus 1 \text{ two-year-old machine} \oplus 1.9 \text{ labour} \ominus 20 \text{ t iron} \quad (9.91c)$$

$$1 \text{ t iron} \oplus 1 \text{ labour} \ominus 1 \text{ new machine} \quad (9.91d)$$

Straightforward calculations yield the following:

$$W^{(3)} \simeq 4.37 \qquad 1.30 < R^{(3)} < 1.34$$
$$W^{(2)} \simeq 3.75 \qquad 1.37 < R^{(2)} < 1.38 \tag{9.92}$$
$$W^{(1)} \simeq 4.33 \qquad 1.38 < R^{(1)} < 1.39$$

(*1*) supports the largest rate of profit, (*3*) the largest real wage. Techniques (*1*) and (*2*) are taken from *Example* 6 in section 9.4. (*1*) and (*2*) have switch-points $r = 1$, $r = 11/9$. As $w^{(3)} > w^{(1)}$ at $r = 1$ and $w^{(3)} < w^{(1)}$ at $r = 11/9$, it follows that the ordering of techniques as r increases from 0 to $R^{(1)}$ is (*3*), (*2*), (*1*).

Example 2

6 t iron ⊕ 1 new machine ⊕ 2 labour ⊖ 20 t iron
⊕ 1 one-year-old machine (9.93a)
8.5 t iron ⊕ 1 one-year-old machine ⊕ 3 labour
⊖ 20 t iron ⊕ 1 two-year-old machine (9.93b)
12 t iron ⊕ 1 two-year-old machine ⊕ 1.4 labour
⊖ 20 t iron (9.93c)
1 t iron ⊕ 1 labour ⊖ 1 new machine (9.93d)

This differs from *Example 1* only in the third process. Straightforward calculations yield:

$$W^{(3)} \simeq 4.39 \qquad R^{(3)} < 1.35 \tag{9.94a}$$
$$w^{(3)} < w^{(1)} \text{ at } r = 1 \text{ and } r = 11/9 \tag{9.94b}$$

This suggests the following ordering of techniques as r increases from 0 to $R^{(1)}$: (*3*), (*1*), (*2*), (*1*).

Example 3

Again only the third process differs from *Example 1*. I now have:

4 t iron ⊕ 1 two-year-old machine ⊕ 10 labour
⊖ 20 t iron (9.95)

Then:

$$W^{(3)} \simeq 2.53 \qquad 1.5 > R^{(3)} > 1.4 \tag{9.96a}$$

and

$$w^{(3)} > w^{(1)} \text{ at } r = 1 \text{ and } r = 11/9 \tag{9.96b}$$

This suggests the following ordering of techniques as r increases from 0 to $R^{(3)}$: (*1*), (*3*).

Example 4

Once again, only the third process differs from *Example 1*. I now have:

$$\begin{aligned}&2 \text{ t iron} \oplus 1 \text{ two-year-old machine} \oplus 100 \text{ labour}\\&\ominus 20 \text{ t iron}\end{aligned} \tag{9.97}$$

Then:

$$W^{(3)} \simeq 0.4 \qquad 1.6 > R^{(3)} > 1.5 \tag{9.98a}$$

$$w^{(3)} < w^{(1)} \text{ at } r = 1 \text{ and } r = 11/9 \tag{9.98b}$$

This suggests that the ordering of techniques as r increases from 0 to $R^{(3)}$ is: (*1*), (*2*), (*1*), (*3*).

Example 5

The third process is

$$\begin{aligned}&18 \text{ t iron} \oplus 1 \text{ two-year-old machine} \oplus 0.1 \text{ labour}\\&\ominus 20 \text{ t iron}\end{aligned} \tag{9.99}$$

the other processes being the same as in *Example 1*.
Then:

$$W^{(3)} \simeq 4.34 \qquad 1.1 > R^{(3)} > 1.0 \tag{9.100a}$$

$$w^{(3)} < w^{(1)} \text{ at } r = 1 \qquad (9.100b)$$

So, the ordering of techniques as r increases from 0 to $R^{(1)}$ is (*3*), (*1*), (2), (*1*). In this respect, *Example 5* resembles *Example 1*, though the iron and labour combination in the third process is different.

The conclusions to be drawn from these examples are similar to those drawn from the six examples of section 9.4. There is no necessary relation between the optimal economic lifetime of machinery and r. Furthermore, it can happen, as seen in *Examples 2–5*, that the optimal economic lifetime of a machine in adjacent techniques on the outer envelope of w–r curves (i.e. successive cost-minimising techniques as r increases) can differ by more than one year.

In this section, I have established three results for the model described by (9.61). First, the choice of technique is determinate at each feasible value of r; in fact, choice of technique is unique unless r is a switch-point. Second, choice of technique can be determined by reference to the outer envelope of w–r curves. Third, ageing machine prices are indicators of efficiency in choice of technique. These results can be extended to a model in which the machine is durable for an arbitrary finite number of years in one sector.

9.8 Choice of Technique in a Fixed Capital Model: Part 3

So far, I have assumed that fixed capital is employed in only one industry. I now relax this assumption by supposing that a new machine is durable in both industries: it has a maximum physical lifetime of two years in the iron sector and three years in the machine sector. The technology is thus described by these five processes:

Iron

$$X_{11} \text{ t iron} \oplus X_{21} \text{ new machines} \oplus L_1 \text{ labour}$$

$$\ominus X_1 \text{ t iron} \oplus X_{21} \text{ one-year-old } i\text{-machines} \qquad (9.101a)$$

$$X_{12} \text{ t iron} \oplus X_{21} \text{ one-year-old } i\text{-machines} \oplus L_2 \text{ labour}$$

$$\ominus X_2 \text{ t iron} \qquad (9.101b)$$

Machines

X_{13} t iron ⊕ X_{23} new machines ⊕ L_3 labour

⊖ X_3 new machines ⊕ X_{23} one-year-old *m*-machines (9.101c)

X_{14} t iron ⊕ X_{23} one-year-old *m*-machines ⊕ L_4 labour

⊖ X_4 new machines ⊕ X_{23} two-year-old *m*-machines (9.101d)

X_{15} t iron ⊕ X_{23} two-year-old *m*-machines ⊕ L_5 labour

⊖ X_5 new machines (9.101e)

This is the simplest model in which fixed capital can be employed in both sectors with different maximum physical lifetimes. It is necessary to distinguish between machines of the same type and age employed in different sectors.

> The depreciation of a machine, however, is not determined exclusively by its employment in one particular industry . . . The same type of machine may be used in several industries and it may be subject to greater wear and tear when employed in one than in the other and have a shorter life; or, even if the total life is the same, its efficiency may fall at different rates from year to year or require more repairs. (PCMC, section 78, p. 66)

So, I distinguish between one-year-old *i*- and *m*-machines. Indeed, the reason for considering (9.101a)–(9.101e), rather than a model in which the maximum physical lifetimes are identical in both sectors, is to ensure that this distinction is made. Then, if a new machine had a maximum physical lifetime of two years in both industries, it would still be necessary to distinguish between one-year-old *i*- and *m*-machines.

There are five commodities in (9.101a)–(9.101e): the two marketable commodities, iron and new machines; and the three non-marketable commodities, a one-year-old *i*-machine, one- and two-year-old *m*-machines. I number the commodities, 1,2,3,4,5 in this order. Then, with p_i denoting the price of commodity i, the price equations corresponding to (9.101a)–(9.101e) are with iron as numeraire:

$$(1+r)(X_{11} + p_2X_{21}) + wL_1 = X_1 + p_3X_{21} \qquad (9.102a)$$

$$(1+r)(X_{12} + p_3X_{21}) + wL_2 = X_2 \tag{9.102b}$$

$$(1+r)(X_{13} + p_2X_{23}) + wL_3 = p_2X_3 + p_4X_{23} \tag{9.102c}$$

$$(1+r)(X_{14} + p_4X_{23}) + wL_4 = p_2X_4 + p_5X_{23} \tag{9.102d}$$

$$(1+r)(X_{15} + p_5X_{23}) + wL_5 = p_2X_5 \tag{9.102e}$$

The only restriction placed on the inputs and outputs is a familiar productiveness condition:

Iron

$$X_1 + X_2 \geqslant X_{11} + X_{12} + X_{13} + X_{14} + X_{15} \tag{9.103a}$$

Machines

$$X_3 + X_4 + X_5 \geqslant X_{21} + X_{23} \tag{9.103b}$$

walosi. So, I permit any combination of relations between X_{11} and X_{12}, L_1 and L_2, X_1 and X_2, e.g. $X_{11} > X_{12}$, $L_1 < L_2$, $X_2 > X_1$; and similarly for inputs and outputs in the machine sector.

In section 9.5, I argued that a properly specified fixed capital model already embodied alternative techniques. For the technology described in (9.101), the new machine in the iron sector has a maximum physical lifetime of two years, that in the machine sector three years. From (9.101), I can construct six techniques – (*1*, *1*), (*1*, 2), (*1*, *3*), (2, *1*), (2, 2), (2, *3*) – where (j, k) denotes that technique in which the machine is employed for j years in the iron industry and k years in the machine industry. (2, *3*) is described by (9.101). (*1*, *2*) is described by:

X_{11} t iron ⊕ X_{21} new machines ⊕ L_1 labour ⊖ X_1 t iron (9.104a)

X_{13} t iron ⊕ X_{23} new machines ⊕ L_3 labour
⊖ X_3 new machines ⊕ X_{23} one-year-old *m*-machines (9.104b)

X_{14} t iron ⊕ X_{23} one-year-old *m*-machines ⊕ L_4 labour
⊖ X_4 new machines (9.104c)

The one-year-old *i*-machine and the two-year-old *m*-machine have been scrapped. (9.104) resembles the model analysed in sections 9.3–9.6. Before treating the question of choice of technique – that is, determining the optimal economic lifetime of machinery in both sectors – I consider (*2, 3*)'s price system.

To solve (9.102), first of all eliminate ageing machines. Add $(1+r)$ times (9.102a) to (9.102b) to obtain:

$$(1+r)(A_{11} + p_2A_{21}) + wA_1 = 1 \tag{9.105a}$$

Add $(1+r)^2$ times (9.102c) to $(1+r)$ times (9.102d) to (9.102e) to yield:

$$(1+r)(A_{12} + p_2A_{22}) + wA_2 = p_2 \tag{9.105b}$$

Compared with sections 9.6 and 9.7, I have been lax with respect to notation in (9.102) and (9.105). The former should contain bracketed superscripts (2,3) on prices and the wage rate; similarly, A_{ij}, A_i, $i,j = 1,2$ w and p_2 in (9.105) should have a bracketed superscript. It is for ease of notation that I have omitted them. A_{ij}, and A_i are defined in a similar way to (9.13): the coefficients in (9.105a) are rational linear functions of r, those in (9.105b) are rational quadratics. Following the same line of argument as in section 9.4, the maximum rate of profit for (*2, 3*), $R^{(2,3)}$, is obtained as the smallest positive solution of:

$$F(r) \equiv (1 - (1+r)A_{11})(1 - (1+r)A_{22}) - (1+r)^2A_{12}A_{21} = 0 \tag{9.106}$$

By the productiveness conditions, (9.103), (9.106) has a positive solution. Then (9.105) can be solved to yield:

$$p_2 = \frac{A_1(1+r)A_{12} + A_2(1 - (1+r)A_{11})}{A_1(1 - (1+r)A_{22}) + A_2(1+r)A_{21}} \tag{9.107a}$$

$$w = \frac{(1 - (1+r)A_{11})(1 - (1+r)A_{22}) - (1+r)^2A_{12}A_{21}}{A_1(1 - (1+r)A_{22}) + A_2(1+r)A_{21}} \tag{9.107b}$$

p_3 can then be obtained from (9.102a) or (9.102b); p_4 and p_5 from (9.102c)–(9.102e).

To summarise so far: if it is productive, (*2*, *3*) has a positive maximum rate of profit, R, such that $p_2 > 0$ for $0 \leqslant r \leqslant R$, $w > 0$ for $0 \leqslant r < R$ and $w = 0$ if $r = R$. Ageing machine prices can be negative over the range $0 \leqslant r \leqslant R$.

The analysis of section 9.5 can be applied to machinery in both sectors. Choice of technique is thus equivalent to determining the optimal economic lifetime of machines in both sectors. The principles underlying the choice have already been expounded in sections 9.6 and 9.7. Suppose, for the sake of illustration, that (*1*, *1*) is initially employed. Each capitalist evaluates his alternatives at the prevailing prices: if he can reduce his costs by extending the economic lifetime of his machine beyond one year, the capitalist will effect a switch of technique. Let (9.101b) make losses, (9.101d) make super-normal profits at (*1*, *1*)'s prices. Then, there is reason to switch to (*1*, *2*) and, by the same line of argument as used in (1.i)–(3.vi) of section 9.7, I obtain:[11]

$$w^{(1,2)} > w^{(1,1)} > w^{(2,1)} \tag{9.108}$$

If (*1*, *2*) is established, there cannot be a switch back to (*1*, *1*) for, if (*1*, *1*) were cheaper than (*1*, *2*) at the latter's prices, I would obtain:

$$w^{(1,1)} > w^{(1,2)} \tag{9.109}$$

which contradicts (9.108). I have considered only three techniques so far. Hence, after (*1*, *2*)'s price has been established, it is necessary for each capitalist to evaluate his remaining alternatives, summarised in the techniques (*2*, *2*), (*2*, *3*), (*1*, *3*).

It is evident that more complicated patterns of surpluses and losses can arise for this model than for those in earlier sections. None the less, the basic principle remains valid and transitivity in comparison between techniques is preserved by the relationships between real wage rates: as a simple example, if (*1*, *2*) is cheaper than (*1*, *1*), the first inequality in (9.108) follows and (*1*, *1*) cannot be cheaper than (*1*, *2*) or any other technique which is in turn cheaper than (*1*, *2*). If a technique (h, j) is cheaper than (t, u) at (t, u)'s prices in the manner described in (A) and (B) of section 9.7, there will be a switch to (h, j) and

$$w^{(h,j)} > w^{(t,u)} \tag{9.110}$$

If alternative techniques are evaluated at (h, j)'s prices, the outcome will be the cheapest technique among those considered so far (and the one supporting the highest real wage). As there is only a finite number of techniques, and intransitivity is excluded by the inequalities between wage rates, it follows that, after a finite number of stages, the overall cost-minimising technique will be obtained. *Result 18* and *Corollaries 18.1* and *18.2* apply to this model, *mutatis mutandis*. Also, the general conclusion drawn at the end of section 9.7, can be extended to the fixed capital model of this section.

9.9 Two Special Cases

In this section, I investigate two special cases, primarily as applications of the theory developed in sections 9.6–9.8. Suppose, first, that $(2, 3)$ operates with constant efficiency, which means that:

$$X_{11} = X_{12},\ L_1 = L_2,\ X_1 = X_2 \tag{9.111a}$$

$$X_{13} = X_{14} = X_{15},\ L_3 = L_4 = L_5,\ X_3 = X_4 = X_5 \tag{9.111b}$$

Subtracting (9.102b) from (9.102a), I have:

$$(1+r)p_2 - p_3 = (1+r)p_3$$

or

$$(1+r)p_2/(1 + (1+r)) = p_3 \tag{9.112}$$

So $p_3 > 0$ if $p_2 > 0$. Now each marketable commodity price is positive for $0 \leqslant r \leqslant R$. So, $p_3 > 0$ over this range. Similarly, it can be shown from (9.102c)–(9.102e) that $p_4 > 0$, $p_5 > 0$ for $0 \leqslant r \leqslant R$. Hence, as all prices are positive at each r between 0 and R, it follows by the analogue of *Corollary 18.2*(i) that both machines are always operated until the end of their physical lifetimes, i.e. $(2, 3)$ is the cost-minimising technique for $0 \leqslant r \leqslant R$.

The second case is when machines operate with increasing efficiency, that is:

$$X_{11} \geqslant X_{12},\ L_1 \geqslant L_2,\ X_1 \leqslant X_2 \text{ walosi} \tag{9.113a}$$

$$X_{13} \geqslant X_{14} \geqslant X_{15},\ L_3 \geqslant L_4 \geqslant L_5,\ X_3 \leqslant X_4 \leqslant X_5 \text{ walosi} \tag{9.113b}$$

(9.113) can be interpreted as involving an initial period of 'running-in', after which net outputs increase. From (9.102a) and (9.102b), I have:

$$(1+r)(X_{11} - X_{12}) + X_{21}((1+r)(p_2 - p_3) - p_3) + w(L_1 - L_2)$$
$$= X_1 - X_2 \tag{9.114a}$$

Using (9.113a), it follows from (9.114a) that:

$$(1+r)(p_2 - p_3) < p_3$$

or

$$(1+r)(p_2/(1 + (1+r)) < p_3 \tag{9.114b}$$

As $p_2 > 0$ for $0 \leqslant r \leqslant R$, I conclude from (9.114b) that $p_3 > 0$ also. From (9.102c)–(9.102e), I conclude that, if (9.113b) holds, $p_4 > 0$ and $p_5 > 0$ for $0 \leqslant r \leqslant R$. So, if there is increasing physical efficiency, in the sense of (9.113), each machine is operated for the whole of its physical lifetime for $0 \leqslant R \leqslant R$.

9.10 Fixed Capital: Other Cases

In concluding this chapter, I mention a number of directions in which the model for section 9.8 can be generalised, also evaluating some of the assumptions I have made.

I have assumed that each sector has available to it only one set of processes, each involving an ageing machine. Then, the question of choice of technique is disguised as that of determining the optimal economic lifetime of each machine. Now suppose that there is an alternative pair of processes available to the iron industry in addition to (9.101a) and (9.101b):

$$X^{\beta}_{11} \text{ t iron} \oplus X^{\beta}_{21} \text{ new machines} \oplus L^{\beta}_1 \text{ labour} \ominus X^{\beta}_1 \text{ t iron}$$

$$\oplus\ X^{\beta}_{21} \text{ one-year-old machines} \tag{9.115a}$$

$$X^{\beta}_{12} \text{ t iron} \oplus X^{\beta}_{21} \text{ one-year-old machines} \oplus L^{\beta}_{2} \text{ labour}$$
$$\ominus\ X_2 \text{ t iron} \tag{9.115b}$$

The new machine in (9.115a) is of the same type as in (9.101a), only the proportions differ. An (α) superscript can be inserted into (9.101a) and (9.101b) so that (9.101a)–(9.101e) can be described as the α-technology. (9.115a), (9.115b), (9.101c)–(9.101e) is the β-technology. Choice of technique now consists of determining the optimal economic lifetime of each time machine when there is a choice between the α- and β-technologies. As a one-year-old β-machine in the iron industry differs from the corresponding α-machine, it follows that all commodities are not common to both techniques. In this sense, the model resembles that discussed in the Appendix to Chapter 6. Choice of technique in these circumstances is made by reference to the common marketable commodities produced by the two technologies – see the Appendix to Chapter 6 for the analysis of a much simpler model embodying a similar characteristic. As explained above, cost minimisation results in the selection of that technique with the lowest labour-commanded marketable commodity prices or, equivalently, the highest real wage. So, given a feasible value of r, the cost-minimising technique is that on the outer envelope of w–r curves (of both α- and β-technologies).

Throughout this chapter, I have considered models having only one type of fixed capital – a machine. Now suppose that both sectors produce durable means of production, the first sector a tractor, the second a machine as before. Let the tractor and the new machine be circulating capital in their own sectors but fixed capital in each other's.[12] If the tractor lasts for at most three years and the machine two, I obtain a five-process model similar to that in section 9.8. The commodities in such a model are a new tractor, a new machine, a one-year-old machine and one- and two-year-old tractors.[13] The ageing machine prices, and hence the optimal economic lifetime of each machine, are endogenously determined in the same way as in section 9.8. The extension to two durable capital goods does not present any essentially new theoretical problem.[14]

Having introduced a second fixed capital good, it is natural to enquire if the model can accommodate both types being employed in the same sector. As an example, suppose that tractors and new machines have the same maximum physical lifetime, three years, in the tractor industry. The different types of fixed capital can be interpreted as constituting a *t*-outfit, so that the three production processes can be described by:

$$X_{11} \text{ tractors} \oplus X_{21} \text{ new machines} \oplus L_1 \text{ labour}$$
$$\ominus X_1 \text{ tractors} \oplus Y_1 \text{ one-year-old } t\text{-outfits} \qquad (9.116a)$$

$$Y_1 \text{ one-year-old } t\text{-outfits} \oplus L_2 \text{ labour}$$
$$\ominus X_2 \text{ tractors} \oplus Y_1 \text{ two-year-old } t\text{-outfits} \qquad (9.116b)$$

$$Y_1 \text{ two-year-old } t\text{-outfits} \oplus L_2 \text{ labour} \ominus X_3 \text{ tractors} \qquad (9.116c)$$

If both machines and tractors have a maximum physical lifetime of, say, two years in the machine industry, I can likewise introduce a one-year-old *m*-outfit into the production equations for that sector. So, I obtain a five-process, five-commodity model, the commodities being a tractor, a new machine, one- and two-year-old *t*-outfits and a one-year-old *m*-outfit. The prices of the outfits are determined in the same way as the prices of the ageing machines in section 9.8

It is necessary now to relax the assumption that the different types of capital good have the same maximum physical lifetimes when employed in the same sector. Suppose that a tractor can last for at most three years in the tractor industry, a new machine at most two. I then have to specify six processes:

$$X_{11} \text{ new tractors} \oplus X_{21} \text{ new machines} \oplus L_1 \text{ labour}$$
$$\ominus X_1 \text{ new tractors} \oplus X_{11} \text{ one-year-old tractors}$$
$$\oplus X_{21} \text{ one-year-old machines} \qquad (9.117a)$$

$$X_{11} \text{ one-year-old tractors} \oplus X_{21} \text{ one-year-old machines}$$
$$L_2 \text{ labour} \ominus X_2 \text{ new tractors} \oplus X_{21} \text{ two-year-old tractors}$$
$$(9.117b)$$

$$X_{13} \text{ new tractors} \oplus X_{21} \text{ two-year-old tractors} \oplus L_3 \text{ labour}$$
$$\ominus X_3 \text{ new tractors} \oplus X_{13} \text{ one-year-old tractors} \qquad (9.117c)$$

X_{13} one-year-old tractors $\oplus$ X_{24} new machines $\oplus$ L_4 labour

$\ominus$ X_4 new tractors $\oplus$ X_{24} one-year-old machines (9.117d)

X_{15} new tractors $\oplus$ X_{24} one-year-old tractors $\oplus$ L_5 labour

$\ominus$ X_5 new tractors $\oplus$ X_{15} one-year-old tractors

$\oplus$ X_{24} two-year-old machines (9.117e)

X_{15} one-year-old tractors $\oplus$ X_{24} two-year-old machines

$\oplus$ L_6 labour $\ominus$ X_6 new tractors (9.117f)

The outputs of these six processes consist of six commodities: one marketable commodity, new tractors, and five different non-marketable outputs, as given by the right-hand sides of (9.117a)–(9.117e). When combined with the equations for the machine sector, it is easily seen that equality is preserved between numbers of processes and commodities, the latter including the various outfits. Then the prices of the outfits can be determined in the usual way.

Throughout this chapter, I have assumed that fixed capital goods are not traded.[15] To examine the implications of relaxing this assumption, consider the following very simple example:

X_{11} t iron $\oplus$ 1 old machine $\oplus$ L_1 labour $\ominus$ X_1 t iron (9.118a)

X_{12} t iron $\oplus$ 1 new machine $\oplus$ L_2 labour

$\ominus$ X_2 new machines $\oplus$ 1 old machine (9.118b)

The machine sector sells its ageing machine to the iron sector, which uses it in its only process of production. Immediately the price equations are written down, it can be seen that difficulties will arise for this model:

$$(1+r)(X_{11} + p_3) + wL_1 = X_1 \quad (9.119a)$$

$$(1+r)(X_{12} + p_2) + wL_2 = p_2X_2 + p_3 \quad (9.119b)$$

There are three commodities but only two processes. Eliminating the ageing machine by the usual method, I obtain from (9.119):

$$(1+r)((1+r)X_{12} + X_{13}) + (1+r)^2p_2 + w(L_2\,(1+r) + L_1)$$

$$= X_1 + (1+r)p_2X_2 \tag{9.120}$$

which consists of one equation in three unknowns. While one unknown has been eliminated from (9.119), there are still two degrees of freedom in (9.120). Contrast this with the simple model described in (9.8). Eliminating the ageing machine from (9.9b) and (9.9c), I obtain (9.12a) and (9.12b), which are analogous to the equations for the single-product industries models of Chapters 2–7: there is one price equation for each marketable commodity. Clearly, this is not true for (9.119). Thus, there are difficulties with the price equations if an ageing machine from one sector can be employed in the other. These difficulties are not peculiar to fixed capital, for there is nothing in (9.118) to require that the second commodity on the right-hand side of (9.118b) be interpreted as an old machine: it could, for example, be cement. As exactly the same problems arise in (9.119) and (9.120), it should be clear that the difficulties are caused by joint production. Can they be avoided by amending the technology so that there is equality between numbers of processes and commodities? Consider this example:

$$X_{11} \text{ t iron} \oplus 1 \text{ old machine} \oplus L_1 \text{ labour} \ominus X_1 \text{ t iron} \tag{9.121a}$$

$$X_{13} \text{ t iron} \oplus 1 \text{ new machine} \oplus L_3 \text{ labour} \ominus X_3 \text{ t iron} \tag{9.121b}$$

$$X_{12} \text{ t iron} \oplus 1 \text{ new machine} \oplus L_2 \text{ labour}$$
$$\ominus X_2 \text{ new machines} \oplus 1 \text{ old machine} \tag{9.121c}$$

This differs from (9.118) by the introduction of the second process, (9.121b), for the iron sector. Equality between numbers of processes and commodities is restored but two problems remain. First, it needs to be shown that it is cost minimising to operate all processes rather than, say, (9.121a) and (9.121c) or (9.121b) and (9.121c). Second, the difficulty exposed in (9.119) and (9.120) still exists, as can be seen by manipulating the price equations corresponding to (9.121).

9.11 Conclusion

The main purpose of this chapter has been to demonstrate that, by adopting Sraffa's approach, fixed capital can be treated properly. When durable means of production are distinguished by type, age and sector of employment, it becomes possible to formulate a model in which the depreciation of each machine, and hence its optimal economic lifetime, can be determined endogenously. It is no longer necessary to assume *a priori* specified depreciation coefficients, that is, to treat depreciation as a technical rather than an economic phenomenon. Even if it were not already evident from the solution of (9.9), consideration of Examples 1–6 in section 9.4 makes clear that prices of production in a fixed capital model, and *a fortiori* the depreciation charges and the optimal economic lifetime of each machine, depend on income distribution.

The single-product industries, fixed capital models analysed in this chapter resemble the single-product industries, circulating capital models of earlier chapters in two respects; first, for a given technique, there is a maximum value of the rate of profit, R, such that over the interval $0 \leqslant r \leqslant R$, marketable commodity prices are positive and the real wage is a non-negative decreasing function of r; second, choice of technique is determinate at each feasible value of r, the cost-minimising technique being that on the outer envelope of w–r curves.

Commentary

Sraffa deals with fixed capital in a joint production framework in chapter X of PCMC: also see appendix D for references to early treatments along similar lines. I have ignored Sraffa's analysis of the Standard System with fixed capital (PCMC, section 84). Those wishing to construct the Standard Commodity can synthesise the relevant material from Chapters 5 and 9. A more advanced analysis of fixed capital can be found in Pasinetti (1980) and Woods (1984a).

The fixed capital model discussed briefly in section 9.2 was the main, not to say sole, vehicle for discussion in the capital theory debates, mentioned in the Commentaries on Chapters 6 and 7. See, for example, Samuelson (1961–2, pp. 191–2) and Garegnani (1970). Garegnani was well aware of the deficiencies of this approach: 'This way of dealing with fixed capital evades the problems specific to *fixed* capital, which are problems of joint production . . . (T)he assumption of a "rate of mortality" $d = 1$ gives the correct treatment of circulating capital' (ibid., footnote 1, p. 408).

Exercises

1. Prove that, if (9.4) is satisfied, there exists a positive value of r, R_F, such that (9.2) has a positive solution, (9.7), if $0 \leqslant r \leqslant R_F$.

2. To see that the approach in section 9.2 is a generalisation of that in earlier chapters, put $\underline{a}_{ij} = a_{ij}$ in (9.2), (9.5) and (9.6).

3. Investigate the curvature of the w–r curve for the model in section 9.2. Are there conditions similar to those in 1.3 of *Result 8*, Chapter 4?

4. Consider the model in section 9.2. The labour value of commodity i (or the labour embodied in a unit of it), v_i, is defined by:

$$v_1 = v_1\underline{a}_{11} + v_2\underline{a}_{21} + l_1$$
$$v_2 = v_1\underline{a}_{12} + v_2\underline{a}_{22} + l_2$$

Solve for v_1 and v_2. (See exercise 11, Chapter 4.)

5. Prove that the relative price in section 9.2 is constant if and only if:

$$(v_1c_{11} + v_2c_{21})/v_1 = (v_1c_{12} + v_2c_{22})/v_2$$

where c_{ij} are defined in (9.6). If this condition is satisfied, show that $p_i = \alpha v_i$, $i = 1,2$. Is $p_i = \beta l_i$, $i = 1,2$?

6. Prove that the relative price in section 9.2 is constant if and only if there is, at each feasible value of r, a uniform:

   (i) value–capital/labour ratio;

   (ii) value–capital/output ratio;

   (iii) labour share in the value of net output.

   Is uniformity of the labour share in the value of gross output ever a necessary and/or sufficient condition for relative price invariance? (See exercises 13–18 of Chapter 4.)

7. Can you find an underlying (mathematical) condition for relative price invariance for the model in section 9.2 analogous to that of (4.33) in Chapter 4?

8. Prove that, in the model of section 9.2, the cost-minimising technique at a feasible value of r is that supporting the highest real wage.

9. Solve (9.9), i.e. p_2, p_3, w in terms of r. In particular, prove that $p_2 > 0$, $p_3 > 0$, $w = 0$ if $r = R$.

10. Interpret conditions (9.10) when $r = 0$.

11. Prove that (9.14c) is the first inequality of (9.14) that fails to be satisfied.

12. Prove that both $(1 - (1+r)A_{11})$ and $(1 - (1+r)A_{22}(r))$ become negative for sufficiently large values of r.

13. Prove that the maximum rate of profit, R, satisfies (9.18).

14. Consider $d(r)$ and $e(r)$ defined in (9.19). Prove that $e(0) < 1$. Derive (9.20a)–(9.20c).

15. Solve each of Examples 1–6 in section 9.4. Also, find an expression in each case for the depreciation charge on a machine (as a function of r).

16. Analyse this model:

    5 t iron ⊕ 1 new machine ⊕ 2 labour ⊖ 20 t iron ⊕ 1 old machine

    8 t iron ⊕ 1 old machine ⊕ 3 labour ⊖ 20 t iron

    1 t iron ⊕ 1 labour ⊖ 1 new machine.

17. Analyse the model obtained from exercise 16 by substituting 2 as the labour input in the second process.

18. Prove that, if (9.55) hold, $\bar{r} < R^{(2)}$.

19. Derive *Result 17* when r is feasible for only one technique. (E.g. Let $R^{(1)} < r < R^{(2)}$; prove that (*1*) cannot reduce costs at (*2*)'s prices.)

20. Derive (9.59) and confirm *Corollary 17.2*.

21. Derive (9.67a) and (9.67b).

22. Define $z_2^{(3)}(\tau)$ so that (9.68) can be derived.

23. Prove that (9.73) implies (9.74).

24. Prove that the hypothesis of (2.iii), namely (9.82a), implies (9.82b).

25. Prove that (9.83a) implies (9.83b).

26. Prove that (9.84a) implies (9.84b).

27. Prove that (9.85a) implies that $p_3^{(3)} < 0$ and (9.85b).

28. Prove that (9.86a) implies that $p_4^{(3)} < 0$ and (9.86b).

29. Solve each of Examples 1–5 in section 9.7. Also, obtain an expression for depreciation (as a function of r) or each machine in each example.

30. Consider each of the cases (1.i)–(3.vi) in section 9.7. What inferences can be drawn in each case about:

    (a) the relations between the real wage rates of the techniques?

    (b) ageing machine prices in the different techniques?

31. Derive (9.107).

32. Extend *Result 18* and *Corollaries 18.1* and *18.2* to the model of section 9.8.

33. Prove that, if (9.11) holds, both p_4 and p_5 are positive. Also, is $R^{(2,3)}$ the maximum among $R^{(j,k)}$, $j = 1,2$, $k = 1,2,3$?

34. Prove that, if (9.113) holds, both p_4 and p_5 are positive. What is the maximum of $R^{(j,k)}$?

35. Construct examples to illustrate the possibilities that can arise with decreasing physical efficiency, (i.e. inequalities (9.113) are reversed). Can a machine be employed for the whole of its physical lifetime?

36. Consider a fixed capital model with marketable commodities iron and new machines. Suppose that the machine can be scrapped as iron or converted into iron by another process. Examine the effect of each of these alternatives on the specification of production processes. What is the effect of these amendments on choice of technique?

37. Investigate the conditions for relative price invariance in the single-product industries, fixed capital models of sections 9.3–9.10.
    Prove that relative prices are invariant if and only if there is in each industry a uniform:

    (a) value–capital/labour ratio;

    (b) labour share in the value of output (gross or net);

    (c) value–capital/output ratio (gross or net).

    Find the underlying (mathematical) condition analogous to (4.34) of Chapter 4.

38. Consider the fixed capital models of sections 9.7 or 9.8. Derive general expressions for the depreciation charges. Can these be simplified under relative price invariance?

39. Consider a fixed capital model where each machine operates with constant physical efficiency throughout its lifetime. Derive expressions for the depreciation charges. What can you say about depreciation when $r = 0$?

40. Consider the following model:

    1 new machine ⊕ 1 labour ⊖ b new machines ⊕ 1 old machine

    1 old machine ⊕ 1 labour ⊖ b new machines

    1 new machine ⊕ 1 labour ⊖ c t iron ⊕ 1 old machine

    1 old machine ⊕ 1 labour ⊖ c t iron

    Solve the price system. Contrast with Samuelson's Surrogate Production Function model.

41. Continuation of 40.
    Let there be two techniques of the type described in exercise 40, with coefficients (b_1, c_1) and (b_2, c_2) respectively. Prove that there is at most one switch-point.

42. Analyse the following two-technique model.

    Technique 1 is a fixed capital model as in exercise 40 with $b = 19/6$, $c = 19$.

    Technique 2 is:

    1 new machine ⊕ 1 labour ⊖ 4 new machines

    1 new machine ⊕ 1 labour ⊖ 22 t iron

    Prove that reswitching can occur.

    (Exercises 40–42 are due to Steedman, (1979b.)

43. Discuss the application of the chain-index method of Chapter 7 to the construction of an aggregate production function for a technology containing proper fixed capital techniques.

44. Apply exercise 43 to various numerical examples and exercises from this chapter.

45. Construct the Standard System for a fixed capital technique.

46. Consider the most general fixed capital technique of this chapter, i.e. $(2, 3)$. Can (i, j) have a positive price system even though it is not cost minimising? $(i = 1,2, j = 1,2,3, (i,j) \neq (2,3))$

47. Analyse this model:

    1 labour ⊖ 1 new machine

    1 new machine ⊕ 1 labour ⊖ 1 t iron ⊕ 1 old machine

    1 old machine ⊕ 1 labour ⊖ 1 cwt coal

    (This exercise is due to Bliss, 1975.)

48. Consider the following maturing-labour inputs model, taken from section 48 of PCMC:

    (α) 20 units of labour applied 8 years ago produces 1 unit of output this year;

    (β) 1 unit of labour 25 years ago and 19 units of labour this year produce 1 unit of output this year.

    (a) Write down the price equations for (α) and (β).
    (b) Determine choice of technique at any feasible value of r.

49. (Extension of 48.) Consider the following model due to Samuelson (1966):

    (α) 7 units of labour ⊖ 1 litre of brandy

    1 litre of brandy ⊖ 1 litre of champagne

    (β) 2 units of labour ⊖ 1 litre of grape juice

    1 litre of grape juice ⊖ 1 litre of wine

    1 litre of wine ⊕ 6 units of labour ⊖ 1 litre of champagne.

    (a) Write down the price equations for (α) and (β).
    (b) Determine choice of technique at each feasible value of r.

Notes to Chapter 9

1. Alternatively, their value is transferred to that of the first commodity.
2. d_{ij} can be interpreted as the inverse of the average lifetime of commodity i when employed in industry j.
3. See note 1 of Chapter 8.
4. The A_{ij} and A_i in (9.12) denote coefficients, as defined in (9.13), and not absolute quantities. See (i) in note 1 of Chapter 2 about the use of capital letters in the notation up to Chapter 8.
5. (9.14b) is consistent with $X_{22} > X_2$, as would arise when $X_2 = 0$. In such a case, the production period for new machines is two years, as against one year for iron. The point of this example is to illustrate the fact that a properly specified fixed capital model, such as (9.8), can accommodate industries with different production periods.
6. Because $F(r)=0$ can be reduced to a cubic equation.
7. See Robinson (1953–4).
8. The numbers in brackets defining the technique refers to the number of processes operated by the machine industry.
9. I take up the question of basic commodities in multiple-product industries models in Chapter 11. The old machine would be non-basic if it were eliminated by a constant linear transformation of (9.9b) and (9.9c). Note that the transformation from (9.9b) and (9.9c) to (9.11) involves r: so the transformation at one feasible value of r differs from that at another. The old machine is basic.

10. From section 9.6, it follows that $p_3^{(2)} < 0$ if (9.81a) holds. The capitalist should not be operating the third process in the first place! Note that I am examining *all* possibilities.
11. Clearly, it is now necessary to introduce bracketed superscripts.
12. The tractor is made from tractor, machine and labour inputs, the machine being durable. The machine is also made from tractor, machine and labour inputs, the tractor being durable. Such a model is unrealistic to the extent that iron inputs have been deleted: a realistic treatment of two types of fixed capital good requires at least three sectors. The essential point in this tractor-machine model is that each commodity is durable in at least one sector.
13. It is necessary to distinguish between capital goods according to type, age and sector of employment.
14. Aside from the need, noted above, to increase the number of sectors. Suppose a three-sector model, producing tractors, machines and iron, were constructed. The same principles as described above would apply to its solution.
15. This is stronger than assuming that they are not marketed. For a capital good could be specific to a sector once installed but marketed at the end of each period, where it would be purchased by its seller or another capitalist from the same sector. The purpose of the market is to establish the prices of production for all commodities, though, as demonstrated earlier in the chapter, such an institutional structure is unnecessary if each capitalist constructs his accounts properly. (See section 74 of PCMC.)

10
Land

10.1 Introduction

So far, I have assumed that only produced means of production are used in each process.[1] In this chapter, I relax this assumption by permitting one sector – the agricultural sector producing wheat – to employ a durable non-produced means of production, which I shall call land. Following Ricardo and Sraffa, I examine two cases: in the first, there are two (or more) qualities of land, giving rise to extensive rent; in the second, land is homogeneous, implying that rent is of the intensive variety.

The first point to be made is that land must be in short supply for rent to be payable. In the extensive case, there are given acreages of the two (or more) qualities of land: if the final demand can be met by operating on only one land, the question of rent cannot arise as neither quality is scarce. To make the problem non-vacuous, it is necessary to assume that the given final demand requires the utilisation of all the available acreage of one type of land. Then, the question to be faced is: which quality of land is marginal? An analogous question to the determination of the extensive margin arises when land is homogeneous. Let there be two processes for use on homogeneous land. If the given final demand can be satisfied by operating either process alone, the question of intensive rent does not arise. So, assume that final demand can be met if the second process, but not the first, is operated by itself. It is then necessary to determine whether just the second process is employed or both processes should be activated. 'While the scarcity of lands thus provides the background from which rent arises, the only evidence of this scarcity to be found in the process of production is the duality of methods: if there were no scarcity, only one method, the cheapest, would be used on the land and there could be no rent' (PCMC, section 88, p. 76).

There is an analogy to be drawn between the ways in which the question of choice of technique arises in fixed capital and land models. I demonstrated in Chapter 9 that this question can be disguised as that of determining the optimal economic lifetime of machinery. In the land models of this chapter, it will be seen that the determination of the margin – extensive or intensive – is one way in which the question of choice of technique can be posed. There are two further similarities between the models of the previous chapter and this. First, land is treated in the same way as fixed capital, the difference arising from the fact that the former is non-produced.[2] So, in describing production processes below, I include land among the inputs and outputs: that is, I am treating land within the general framework provided by joint production. This leads naturally to the second similarity: each industry produces only one marketable commodity. The joint production framework is required solely to accommodate the durable non-produced means of production.

As the introduction of a non-produced means of production does create some analytical problems, it is as well to state, at the outset, the assumptions to be employed in this chapter. First, each industry produces one marketable commodity by means of circulating capital, labour and possibly land inputs; in each process, there are constant returns to scale subject to the land constraint, if relevant. Second, land is used as a direct input only in the agricultural sector producing wheat such that: (a) in the extensive case, a process of production is uniquely associated with a particular quality of land; or (b) in the intensive case, there is more than one process that can be operated on homogeneous land. Third, land is unaffected by any process in which it is used as input. Fourth, there is only one process for producing the industrial commodity, iron (i.e. a commodity produced without land as a direct input). Fifth, there is a given final demand for each commodity, which is at such a level that the question of rent, extensive or intensive, arises. Sixth, each technique is productive: that is, each technique can produce a positive net output vector in any proportions subject to the land constraint.

The method of analysis in determining the relevant margin will be the same as that employed in Chapters 6 and 9, when the question of choice of technique previously arose. I deal first with the question of extensive rent in sections 10.2–10.4 before treating the intensive case.

10.2 Extensive Rent: The Alternative Techniques

In this section, I show how alternative techniques arise in the simplest extensive rent model. The question of choice of technique will then be addressed in the next two sections. I assume that there are two types of land, to be called quality-one and quality-two.[3] There are now four commodities in the model: iron, wheat, quality-one land and quality-two land (this ordering indicates the numbering of commodities). If there are two processes available to the agricultural sector, the technology is described by these three processes:

Iron

$$a_{11} \text{ t iron} \oplus a_{21} \text{ qr wheat} \oplus l_1 \text{ labour} \ominus 1 \text{ t iron} \qquad (10.1a)$$

Wheat

$$a_{12} \text{ t iron} \oplus a_{22} \text{ qr wheat} \oplus a_{32} \text{ acres quality-one land}$$

$$\oplus\, l_2 \text{ labour} \ominus 1 \text{ qr wheat} \oplus a_{32} \text{ acres quality-one land} \qquad (10.1b)$$

$$a_{13} \text{ t iron} \oplus a_{23} \text{ qr wheat} \oplus a_{43} \text{ acres quality-two land}$$

$$\oplus\, l_3 \text{ labour} \ominus 1 \text{ qr wheat} \oplus a_{43} \text{ acres quality-two land} \qquad (10.1c)$$

By the fourth assumption of section 10.1, I can normalise each process so that there is one unit of output of the marketable commodity.

Let there be T_1 acres of quality-one land, T_2 acres of quality-two land. Suppose that final demand is at such a level that it cannot be met by using only one type of land, but that it can be met by using both. Consider, first, the possibility that (10.1b) and (10.1c) are operated but that there is unused acreage of both qualities of land. Consequently, neither quality of land is scarce. As both qualities of land are free, it follows that (10.1a)–(10.1c) describe the type of model analysed in Chapters 3–7.[4] Unless the given value of the rate of profit is a switch-point, one process will be more expensive than the other. Capitalists will switch to the cheaper process. It is unnecessary to progress with the analysis of this possibility for I have demonstrated that it cannot be sustained. This leaves two possibilities: either all quality-one land and some quality-two land are used or all quality-two land and some quality-one land are used. In the former, quality-two land in marginal while, in the latter, it is quality-one land that is marginal. I now examine these in turn, considering first the case where quality-one land is marginal.

As it is not scarce, quality-one land is free. So, the price equations corresponding to (10.1a)–(10.1c) are:

$$(1+r)(p_1^\alpha a_{11} + p_2^\alpha a_{21}) + w^\alpha l_1 = p_1^\alpha \tag{10.2a}$$

$$(1+r)(p_1^\alpha a_{12} + p_2^\alpha a_{22}) + w^\alpha l_2 = p_2^\alpha \tag{10.2b}$$

$$(1+r)(p_1^\alpha a_{13} + p_2^\alpha a_{23}) + \varrho^\alpha a_{43} + w^\alpha l_3 = p_2^\alpha \tag{10.2c}$$

where the superscript α refers to the fact that quality-one land is free and ϱ^α is the rent per acre on quality-two land.[5] With iron as numeraire, the price of wheat and the real wage can be calculated from (10.2a) and (10.2b), in the same way as for the single-product industries model of Chapter 4. So:

$$p^\alpha = \frac{l_2(1 - (1+r)a_{11}) + (1+r)l_1 a_{12}}{l_1(1 - (1+r)a_{22}) + (1+r)l_2 a_{21}} \equiv \frac{h^\alpha(r)}{g^\alpha(r)} \tag{10.3a}$$

$$w^\alpha = \frac{(1 - (1+r)a_{11})(1 - (1+r)a_{22}) - (1+r)^2 a_{12}a_{21}}{l_1(1 - (1+r)a_{11}) + (1+r)l_2 a_{21}}$$

$$\equiv f^\alpha(r)/g^\alpha(r) \tag{10.3b}$$

The purpose of (10.2c) is to determine ϱ^α, given (10.3a) and (10.3b):

$$\varrho^\alpha = ((1+r)l_1 k(r) + l_2 f^\beta(r) - l_3 f^\alpha(r))/a_{43}g^\alpha(r) \tag{10.3c}$$

where

$$k(r) \equiv a_{12}(1 - (1+r)a_{23}) - a_{13}(1 - (1+r)a_{22}) \tag{10.3d}$$

(10.3c) and (10.3d) are exactly analogous to two expressions defined in Chapter 6: the latter to (6.4), the former to (6.11).

It is clear from (10.2) that extensive rent is determined as a residual. Hence, land in non-basic, at least according to the definition used in single-product industries models.[6] Furthermore, the similarity between (10.3c) and (4.11) of Chapter 4 strongly suggests the interpretation to be placed on the status of extensive rent. Rent resembles profit in being a share of the surplus value but differs from it in not being a constituent of the cost of production. For the price system in (α) is determined solely from (10.2a) and (10.2b), with rent playing an accommodating role in (10.2c). This substantiates the Ricardian argument: 'Corn is not high because a rent is paid, but a rent is paid because corn is high; and it has been justly observed, that no reduction would take place in the price of corn, although landlords should forego the whole of their rent' (Ricardo, 1951, pp. 74–5). So, the marketable commodity price and the real wage are determined from the price equations for the industrial commodity and the agricultural commodity produced on marginal, or no-rent, land.

The maximum rate of profit that can be supported by (α) is given by the smallest positive value of r at which $f^{\alpha}(r) = 0$. The maximum real wage is obtained by putting $r = 0$ in (10.3b). $dw^{\alpha}/dr < 0$ by the familiar results from Chapter 4. In these respects, the properties of technique (α) resemble those of the single-product industries models with only produced means of production. The difference arises obviously with respect to rent. Though I have already discussed the nature of rent, I have not actually determined its sign: is ϱ^{α} always positive or negative or can it assume both signs? Clearly, from (10.2c) or (10.3c), rent in (α) depends on all the technical coefficients and cannot be inferred from knowledge of (10.2a) and (10.2b) alone.

Having derived the properties of technique (α), I now consider technique (β), where all quality-one land is used and quality-two land is marginal. The price equations for (β) are:

$$(1+r)\,(p_1^{\beta}a_{11} + p_2^{\beta}a_{21}) + w^{\beta}l_1 = p_1^{\beta} \tag{10.4a}$$
$$(1+r)\,(p_1^{\beta}a_{12} + p_2^{\beta}a_{22}) + \varrho^{\beta}a_{32} + w^{\beta}l_2 = p_2^{\beta} \tag{10.4b}$$
$$(1+r)\,(p_1^{\beta}a_{13} + p_2^{\beta}a_{23}) + w^{\beta}l_3 = p_2^{\beta} \tag{10.4c}$$

ϱ^{β} is the rent payable on quality-one land. The relative marketable commodity price and the real wage are determined from (10.4a) and (10.4c):

$$p_2^\beta = \frac{l_3(1 - (1+r)a_{11}) + (1+r)l_1a_{13}}{l_1(1 - (1+r)a_{23}) + (1+r)l_3a_{21}} \equiv \frac{h^\beta(r)}{g^\beta(r)} \tag{10.5a}$$

$$w^\beta = \frac{(1 - (1+r)a_{11})(1 - (1+r)a_{23}) - (1+r)^2a_{13}a_{21}}{l_1(1 - (1+r)a_{23}) + (1+r)l_3a_{21}}$$

$$\equiv f^\beta(r)/g^\beta(r) \tag{10.5b}$$

Then, from (10.4b), (10.5a) and (10.5b), I obtain:

$$\varrho^\beta = (-(1+r)l_1k(r) - l_2f^\beta(r) + l_3f^\alpha(r))/a_{32}g^\beta(r) \tag{10.5c}$$

The remarks above about ϱ^α and technique (α) generally apply to ϱ^β and (β) respectively.

Having derived the properties of the individual techniques, I can now attend to the question of choice of technique.

10.3 Choice of Technique in Extensive Rent Models: Part 1 – Two Techniques

In this section, I examine the question of choice of technique for the three-process land model, (10.1). As the same three processes are employed in both techniques, it is a matter of deciding whether quality-one land or quality-two land is marginal. Suppose that technique (α) is initially employed, with quality-one land marginal. Evaluate the second and third processes in (β) at (α)'s prices:

$$s_2(\beta{:}\alpha) \equiv p_2^\alpha - (1+r)(p_1^\alpha a_{12} + p_2^\alpha a_{22}) - w^\alpha l_2$$

$$= 0 \tag{10.6a}$$

$$s_3(\beta{:}\alpha) \equiv p_2^\alpha - (1+r)(p_1^\alpha a_{13} + p_2^\alpha a_{23}) - (1+r)p_4^\alpha a_{43} - w^\alpha l_3$$

$$= -p_4^\alpha a_{43} = -\varrho^\alpha a_{43}/r \tag{10.6b}$$

where $s_i(\beta{:}\alpha)$ is the surplus or loss relative to normal profits of operating process i in (β) at (α)'s prices, $i = 2,3$. In effect, a capitalist in the agricultural sector is evaluating the consequences of switching from first- to second-quality land. The term

$(1+r)p_4^{\alpha}a_{43}$ in (10.6b) refers to the value of land inputs into the third process at the prevailing, i.e. (α)'s, prices. The corresponding value of land outputs, $p_4^{\alpha}a_{43}$, is omitted because land is free if the switch in process is effected: the value of output is just p_2^{α}. If $p_4^{\alpha} > 0$ or $\varrho^{\alpha} > 0$, I conclude from (10.6a) and (10.6b) that losses are made by switching to (β), that is, switching the roles of quality-one and quality-two lands as marginal. On the other hand, $\varrho^{\alpha} < 0$ implies that the switch should be made.

Suppose next that (β) is initially employed. Evaluating the second and third processes in (α) at (β)'s prices, I have using the same arguments as in (10.6):

$$s_2(\alpha{:}\beta) \equiv p_2^{\beta} - (1+r)(p_1^{\beta}a_{12} + p_2^{\beta}a_{22}) - (1+r)p_3^{\beta}a_{32} - w^{\beta}l_2$$
$$= -p_3^{\beta}a_{32} = -\varrho^{\beta}a_{32}/r \qquad (10.7a)$$

$$s_3(\alpha{:}\beta) \equiv p_2^{\beta} - (1+r)(p_1^{\beta}a_{13} + p_2^{\beta}a_{23}) - w^{\beta}l_3$$
$$= 0 \qquad (10.7b)$$

If $\varrho^{\beta} > 0$, there is no reason to switch techniques; on the other hand, if $\varrho^{\beta} < 0$, the capitalist would be justified in switching to quality-one land as marginal.

A stronger conclusion is possible by noting that (10.3c) and (10.5c) imply:

$$\text{sign } \varrho^{\alpha} = (-1)\text{sign } \varrho^{\beta} \qquad (10.8)$$

for values of r feasible for both techniques. So, if (α) is initially employed and $\varrho^{\alpha} < 0$, it follows from the argument in (10.6) that a switch to (β) should be made. From (10.7) and (10.8), I conclude that it will not be profitable to switch back to (α). If rent is non-zero, choice of technique is determinate, in fact unique; if rent is zero, choice of technique is determinate, with both (α) and (β) cost-minimising.

I summarise this discussion as:

Result 19: In the extensive rent model, choice of technique is determinate at each value of r feasible for both (α) and (β), i.e. $0 \leqslant r \leqslant \min(R^{\alpha},R^{\beta})$. Unless $\varrho^{\alpha} = \varrho^{\beta} = 0$, there is a unique cost-minimising technique.

In fact, I have established something stronger, for I have been able to associate the cost-minimising technique with the sign of rent. If (α) is initially employed and $\varrho^{\alpha} > 0$, costs are increased by a switch to (β). If (β) is initially employed, it follows from (10.8) that $\varrho^{\beta} < 0$ and from (10.7) that a switch to (α) reduces costs. So, I have:

> *Corollary 19.1:* Positivity of rent is an indicator of efficiency in choice of technique. Over the range $0 \leqslant r \leqslant \min(R^{\alpha}, R^{\beta})$, rent is positive in one technique if and only if it is negative in the other.

Rent plays a role in the extensive model similar to that of the old machine price in the fixed capital model of sections 9.3–9.6. It is natural to enquire if the real wage also plays the same role in both models. To answer this question, consider, first of all, the expression:

$$\begin{aligned} w^{\alpha} - w^{\beta} &= f^{\alpha}(r)/g^{\alpha}(r) - f^{\beta}(r)/g^{\beta}(r) \\ &= (1+r)a_{21}(-(1+r)l_1k(r) - l_2f^{\beta}(r) \\ &\quad + l_3f^{\alpha}(r))/g^{\alpha}(r)g^{\beta}(r) && (10.9a) \\ &= (1+r)a_{21}\varrho^{\beta}a_{32}/g^{\alpha}(r) && (10.9b) \\ &= -(1+r)a_{21}\varrho^{\alpha}a_{43}/g^{\beta}(r) && (10.9c) \end{aligned}$$

From (10.9b) and (10.9c), I have:

$$\text{sign}\ (w^{\alpha} - w^{\beta}) = \text{sign}\ \varrho^{\beta} = (-1)\text{sign}\ \varrho^{\alpha} \qquad (10.9d)$$

The properties of w^{ι}, $\iota = \alpha, \beta$, are well known, being those of the single-product industries models of Chapters 3–7. Consider Figure 10.1. For $0 \leqslant r < \bar{r}$, $\varrho^{\beta} > 0$ from (10.9d). From *Corollary 19.1*, (β) is the cost-minimising technique. For $\bar{r} < r \leqslant R^{\alpha}$, $\varrho^{\alpha} > 0$ from (10.9d). Over this interval, (α) is the cost-minimising technique. At $\bar{r}$, $w^{\alpha} = w^{\beta}$ and so $\varrho^{\alpha} = \varrho^{\beta} = 0$, implying that both techniques are cost-minimising. A cost-minimising technique does not exist over the interval $R^{\alpha} < r \leqslant R^{\beta}$. To prove this, suppose that (β) is initially employed. $\varrho^{\beta} < 0$ over this interval, in fact over the interval $\bar{r} < r \leqslant R^{\beta}$. So, by the argument in (10.6), (α) is cheaper

Figure 10.1

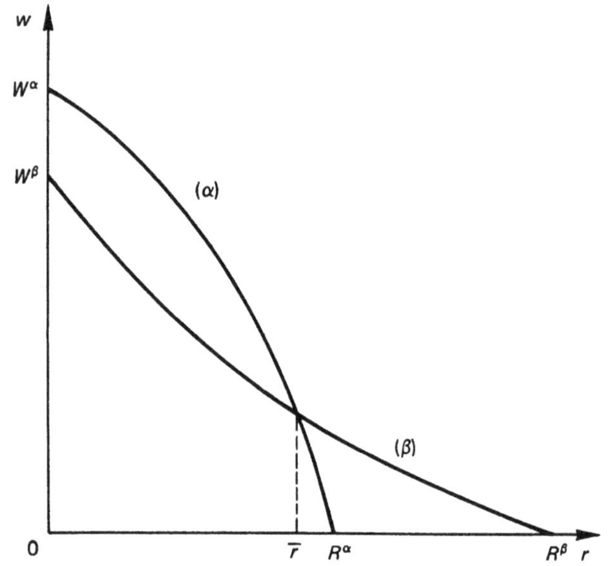

than (β). However, over the interval $R^\alpha < r \leqslant R^\beta$, (α) does not have a positive price system. I conclude that choice of technique can be inferred from the inner envelope of w–r curves. (β) is cost-minimising for $0 \leqslant r < \bar{r}$, (α) for $\bar{r} < r \leqslant R^\alpha$ with both (α) and (β) cost-minimising at $\bar{r}$. Strictly speaking, any value of $r > R^\alpha$ is not feasible for either technique: first, (α) cannot support positive final commodity prices and a non-negative real wage over this interval; second, (β)'s prices are not positive, as $\varrho^\beta < 0$ which implies $p_4^\beta < 0$. So, in the extensive rent model, the feasible range is defined by $0 \leqslant r \leqslant \min(R^\alpha, R^\beta)$, which is to be contrasted with $0 \leqslant r \leqslant \max(R^\alpha, R^\beta)$ for the models of Chapters 3–9 with only produced means of production. I summarise this discussion as:

> *Corollary 19.2:* Choice of technique in the extensive rent model can be determined by reference to the inner envelope of w–r curves.

This contrasts with results on the use of w–r curves for choice of technique in the circulating and fixed capital models of Chapters 3–9. The analysis in this chapter is predicated, it will be recalled, on the assumption that final demand cannot be met by operating only one process in the agricultural sector. If final demand could be met by either process, the usual rule – that the outer envelope of w–r curves indicates choice of technique – would apply: then, with reference to Figure 10.1, (α) would be chosen for $0 \leqslant r < \bar{r}$, (β) for $\bar{r} < r \leqslant R^{\beta}$. The outcome when final demand requires the activation of both processes is rather different: for $0 \leqslant r < \bar{r}$, (β)'s price system rules and quality-two land is marginal; for $\bar{r} < r \leqslant R^{\alpha}$, ($\alpha$)'s price system rules and quality-one land is marginal.

Compare two equilibria in Figure 10.1 with $0 \leqslant r < \bar{r}$: in the first, final demand requires only one process in the agricultural sector while, in the second, it requires both. Thus, in the first, (α) is employed with prices 1, p^{α} and the real wage w^{α}. In the second, (β)'s prices 1, p^{β} and real wage w^{β} rule. Now, from the theory developed in Chapter 6 for single-product industries models, it follows that $p^{\beta} > p^{\alpha}$ and $w^{\beta} < w^{\alpha}$. The resort to less fertile lands (i.e. the extension of the margin) results in an increase in the relative price and a decrease in the real wage. This is a general result which can be extended to the case where the agricultural sector has more than two processes.

The notion of fertility has just been introduced as if it were technical in nature and could be defined independently of income distribution. That this is not so can be easily appreciated from Figure 10.1. Over the interval $0 \leqslant r < \bar{r}$, the order of fertility is (α), (β), indicating that quality-one land should be used first. However, over the interval $\bar{r} < r \leqslant R^{\alpha}$, the order of fertility is reversed (being (β), (α)), implying that quality-two land is used before quality-one land. This reversal contradicts the Ricardian view in chapter II of *The Principles* that the ordering of lands is a technical datum. Note that this contradiction has been achieved without appeal to any of the three phenomena – reswitching, recurrence and capital reversing. It is clear that the Ricardian view can be sustained only if one w–r curve lies completely inside the other (i.e. there are no switch-points between techniques).

The discussion above has served to introduce the concept of the order of fertility. This is defined at a given value of r by the relation between the wage rates of the different techniques. Clearly, this ordering can change with r. In Figure 10.1, there is only one change in the order of fertility, namely at $\bar{r}$. In Figure 10.2a, there are no changes in the order of fertility: quality-two land is always marginal. In Figure 10.2b, there are two changes in the order of

Figure 10.2a

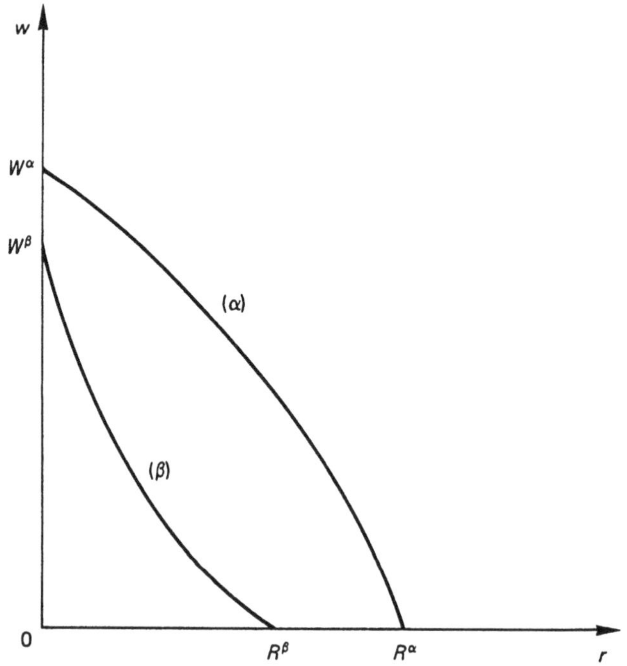

fertility. For low (i.e. $0 \leqslant r < \bar{r}$) and high (i.e. $\bar{\bar{r}} < r \leqslant R^{\beta}$) values of r, quality-two land is marginal; for intermediate values (i.e. $\bar{r} < r < \bar{\bar{r}}$), quality-one land is marginal. In a two-commodity, three-process model, there are at most two switch-points between two single-product industries, circulating capital techniques, as shown in Chapter 6. If the industrial commodity differed between techniques, so that the model resembled that in the Appendix to Chapter 6, there could be at most three switch-points, implying three changes in the order of fertility. The essential point, however, has been captured in Figure 10.2b, not to say Figure 10.1.

10.4 Choice of Technique in Extensive Rent Models: Part 2 – Three or More Techniques

In section 10.3, I demonstrated that for a three-process, two-technique model, the order of fertility depended on income distri-

Figure 10.2b

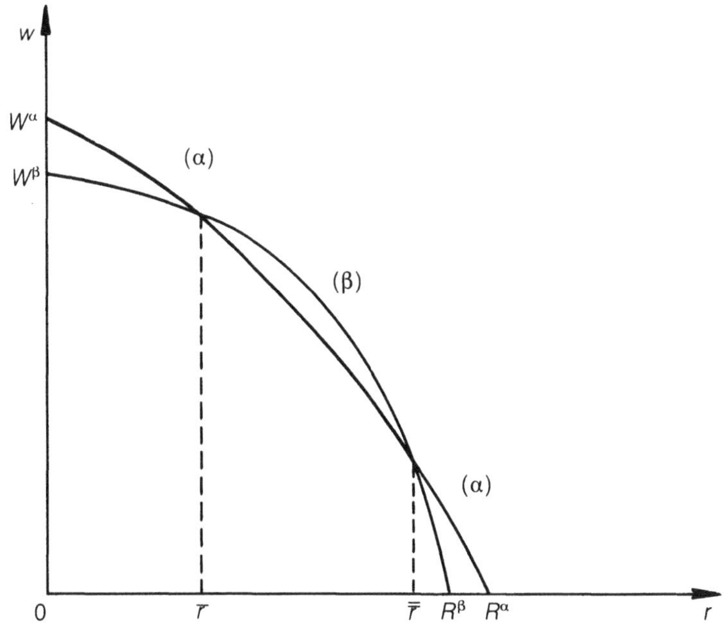

bution. If final demand required the operation of both processes in the agricultural sector, a rent would in general be payable on only one quality of land. With reference to Figure 10.1, it follows that the order of fertility for $0 \leqslant r < \bar{r}$ is (α), (β) with rent paid solely on first-quality land. The ordering of lands by rents corresponds to the ordering of techniques by fertility. This is a general conclusion for the two-technique model, applying not only to the remaining interval in Figure 10.1 but also to Figure 10.2 and the other possibilities that can arise. It is natural to enquire whether it is valid for models with three or more processes in the agricultural sector.

To help fix ideas, consider the following four-process, three-technique model:

Iron

1/2 qr wheat ⊕ 1 labour ⊖ 1 t iron (10.10a)

Wheat

1/2 t iron ⊕ 1 acre quality-one land ⊕ 1/2 labour

⊖ 1 qr wheat ⊕ 1 acre quality-one land (10.10b)

1/8 t iron ⊕ 1 acre quality-two land ⊕ 3 labour

⊖ 1 qr wheat ⊕ 1 acre quality-two land (10.10c)

1/10 t iron ⊕ 1 acre quality-three land ⊕ 1 labour

⊖ 1 qr wheat ⊕ 1 acre quality-three land (10.10d)

Suppose that the level of final demand is such that all three processes in the agricultural sector must be employed. Which quality of land is marginal?

As a preliminary to answering this question, it is necessary to describe the available techniques and state the corresponding price equations. Let (α) be the technique with quality-one land marginal, (β) that with quality-two land marginal and (γ) that with quality-three land marginal. (α)'s price equations are from (10.10):

$$(1+r)p_2^\alpha \cdot 1/2 + w^\alpha \cdot 1 = p_1^\alpha \quad (10.11a)$$

$$(1+r)p_1^\alpha \cdot 1/2 + w^\alpha \cdot 1/2 = p_2^\alpha \quad (10.11b)$$

$$(1+r)p_1^\alpha \cdot 1/8 + \varrho^{\alpha,2} \cdot 1 + w^\alpha \cdot 3 = p_2^\alpha \quad (10.11c)$$

$$(1+r)p_1^\alpha \cdot 1/10 + \varrho^{\alpha,3} \cdot 1 + w^\alpha \cdot 1 = p_2^\alpha \quad (10.11d)$$

where $\varrho^{\alpha,i}$ is the rent per acre of quality-i land, $i = 2,3$, when (α) is the prevailing technique (i.e. quality-one land is marginal). From (10.11a) and (10.11b), with iron as numeraire:

$$w^\alpha = (1 - (1+r)^2/4)/(1 + (1+r)/4) \quad (10.12a)$$

$$p^\alpha = (1 + (1+r)/2)/(1 + (1+r)/4) \quad (10.12b)$$

$\varrho^{\alpha,2}$ and $\varrho^{\alpha,3}$ can then be obtained from (10.11c) and (10.11d) respectively.

If quality-two land is marginal, (10.11) is replaced by:

$$(1+r)p_2^\beta \cdot 1/2 + w^\beta \cdot 1 = p_1^\beta \quad (10.13a)$$

$$(1+r)p_1^\beta \cdot 1/2 + \varrho^{\beta,1} \cdot 1 + w^\beta \cdot 1/2 = p_2^\beta \tag{10.13b}$$

$$(1+r)p_1^\beta \cdot 1/8 + w^\beta \cdot 3 = p_2^\beta \tag{10.13c}$$

$$(1+r)p_1^\beta \cdot 1/10 + \varrho^{\beta,3} \cdot 1 + w^\beta \cdot 1 = p_2^\beta \tag{10.13d}$$

where $\varrho^{\beta,i}$ is the rent per acre of quality-i land; $i = 1,3$, when (β) prevails (i.e. quality-two land is marginal). From (10.13a) and (10.13c):

$$w^\beta = (1 - (1+r)^2/6)/(1 + 3(1+r)/2) \tag{10.14a}$$

$$p^\beta = (3 + (1+r)/8)/(1 + 3(1+r)/2) \tag{10.14b}$$

$\varrho^{\beta,1}$ and $\varrho^{\beta,3}$ can then be calculated from (10.13b) and (10.13d).

Finally, if quality-three land is marginal, the price equations are:

$$(1+r)p_2^\gamma \cdot 1/2 + w^\gamma \cdot 1 = p_1^\gamma \tag{10.15a}$$

$$(1+r)p_1^\gamma \cdot 1/2 + \varrho^{\gamma,1} \cdot 1 + w^\gamma \cdot 1/2 = p_2^\gamma \tag{10.15b}$$

$$(1+r)p_1^\gamma \cdot 1/8 + \varrho^{\gamma,2} \cdot 1 + w^\gamma \cdot 3 = p_2^\gamma \tag{10.15c}$$

$$(1+r)p_1^\gamma \cdot 1/10 + w^\gamma \cdot 1 = p_2^\gamma \tag{10.15d}$$

From (10.15a) and (10.15d), I obtain:

$$w^\gamma = (1 - (1+r)^2/20)/(1 + (1+r)/2) \tag{10.16a}$$

$$p^\gamma = (1 + (1+r)/10)/(1 + (1+r)/2) \tag{10.16b}$$

$\varrho^{\gamma,1}$ and $\varrho^{\gamma,2}$ are calculated from (10.15b) and (10.15c).

Using (10.12a), (10.14a) and (10.16a), I can construct Figure 10.3. The only intersection occurs at $\bar{r} \simeq 0.622$ between w^α and w^β; w^γ lies to the north-east of the other two curves. If only one process in the agricultural sector were required to meet the given final demand, no quality of land could command a rent: hence, (γ) would be cost-minimising by the theory of Chapter 6. Now suppose that the level of final demand requires the activation of two processes in the agricultural sector. Using the theory of section 10.3, quality-one land is marginal for $0 \leqslant r < \bar{r}$ and quality-two land is marginal for $\bar{r} < r \leqslant R^\beta$. The order of fertility is thus (γ),

Figure 10.3

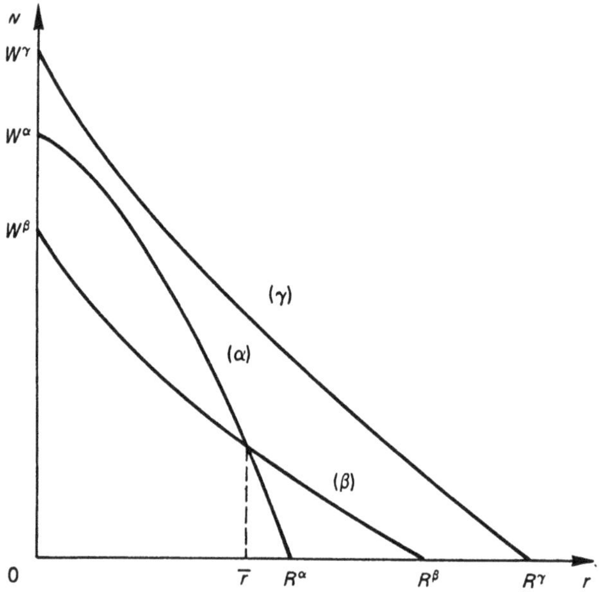

(α) for $0 \leqslant r < \bar{r}$ and (γ), (β) for $\bar{r} < r \leqslant R^\beta$. Quality-three land is the only one to command a rent in this case. Finally, revert to the hypothesis of this section: that three processes must be employed in the agricultural sector. The theory of section 10.3 can be extended: the cost-minimising technique is indicated by the inner envelope of w^α, w^β and w^γ. So, for $0 \leqslant r < \bar{r}$, quality-two land is marginal with rent payable on first- and third-quality lands; for $\bar{r} < r \leqslant R^\alpha$, quality-one land is marginal, with second- and third-quality lands commanding a rent. I now investigate the rents paid, first over $0 \leqslant r < \bar{r}$. From (10.13b) and (10.14):

$$\varrho^{\beta,1} = p^\beta - (1+r)/2 - w^\beta/2$$

$$= \frac{(3 + (1+r)/8)}{(1 + 3(1+r)/2)} - \frac{(1+r)}{2} - \frac{(1 - (1+r)^2/16)}{2(1 + 3(1+r)/2)}$$

$$= (5/2 - 3(1+r)/8 - 23(1+r)^2/32)/(1+3(1+r)/2) \quad (10.17)$$

From (10.13d) and (10.14):

$$\varrho^{\beta,3} = p_2^{\beta} - (1+r)/10 - w^{\beta}$$

$$= (2 + (1+r)/40 - 7(1+r)^2/80)/(1 + 3(1+r)/2)$$

It is a simple matter to show that $\varrho^{\beta,3} > \varrho^{\beta,1}$ for $0 \leqslant r < \bar{r}$. Over this interval, the order of fertility of techniques corresponds to the ordering of lands by rent per acre.

Now consider rents over the interval $\bar{r} < r \leqslant R^{\alpha}$. From (10.11c) and (10.12):

$$\varrho^{\alpha,2} = p^{\alpha} - (1+r)/8 - 3w^{\alpha}$$

$$= (-5/2 + 3(1+r)/8 + 23(1+r)^2/32)/(1 + (1+r)/4) \quad (10.19)$$

From (10.11d) and (10.12):

$$\varrho^{\alpha,3} = p^{\alpha} - (1+r)/10 - w^{\alpha}$$

$$= (-1/2 + 2(1+r)/5 + 9(1+r)^2/40)/(1 + (1+r)/4) \quad (10.20)$$

It can easily be shown that $\varrho^{\alpha,3} > \varrho^{\alpha,2}$ for $\bar{r} < r \leqslant R^{\alpha}$. Over this interval, as over $0 \leqslant r < \bar{r}$, the order of fertility corresponds to the ordering of lands by rent. On the basis of this example, it might be conjectured that the orderings according to fertility and rents are identical. Such a conjecture might be called Ricardian.

> When land of the third quality is taken into cultivation, rent immediately commences on the second, and it is regulated as before, by the difference in their productive powers. At the same time, the rent of the first quality will rise, for that must always be above the rent of the second by the difference between which they yield with a given quantity of capital and labour. (Ricardo, 1951, p. 70)

To see that the Ricardian conjecture cannot be sustained consider the model which is identical to (10.10) except that (10.10d) is replaced by:

1/10 t iron ⊕ 2 acres quality-three land ⊕ 1 labour

⊖ 1 qr wheat ⊕ 2 acres quality-three land (10.21)

Figure 10.3 still describes the configuration of *w–r* curves as only rent per acre on quality-three land is affected – obviously, it is halved. So, for $0 \leqslant r < \bar{r}$, I have $\varrho^{\beta,1}$ as in (10.17) but $\varrho^{\beta,3}$ is now given by:

$$\varrho^{\beta,3} = (1 + (1+r)/80 - 7(1+r)^2/160)/(1 + 3(1+r)/2) \quad (10.22)$$

It can be seen from (10.17) and (10.22) that $\varrho^{\beta,1} > \varrho^{\beta,3}$ for $0 \leqslant r < \tilde{r} \simeq 0.23$ and $\varrho^{\beta,3} > \varrho^{\beta,1}$ for $\tilde{r} < r < \bar{r}$. For $0 \leqslant r < \tilde{r}$, the order of fertility is (γ), (α) but the ordering of lands by rent is first-quality, third-quality. For $\tilde{r} < r < \bar{r}$, the order of fertility is (γ), (α) but the ordering of lands by rent is third-quality, first-quality.

This simple example serves to refute the Ricardian proposition. While it is possible to deduce the order of fertility from the diagram of *w–r* curves, it is not possible to infer the ordering of lands by rent.

This completes the study of the extensive rent model. In sections 10.5 and 10.6, I examine a three-process, intensive rent model.

10.5 Intensive Rent: Description of the Technology

In this section and the next, I assume that land is homogeneous. If land

> is in short supply, this by itself makes it possible for two different processes or methods of cultivation to be used consistently side by side on similar lands determining a uniform rent per acre. While any two methods would in these circumstances be formally consistent, they must satisfy the economic condition of not giving rise to a negative rent. (PCMC, section 87, p. 75)

The other assumptions of sections 10.2 and 10.3 are retained, so that the technology is described by these three processes:

Iron

a_{11} t iron ⊕ a_{21} qr wheat ⊕ l_1 labour ⊖ 1 t iron (10.23a)

Wheat

a_{12} t iron ⊕ a_{22} qr wheat ⊕ a_{32} acres land ⊕ l_2 labour

⊖ 1 qr wheat ⊕ a_{32} acres land (10.23b)

a_{13} t iron ⊕ a_{23} qr wheat ⊕ a_{33} acres land ⊕ l_3 labour

⊖ 1 qr wheat ⊕ a_{33} acres land (10.23c)

Implicit in (10.23) are three techniques of production: (α) consisting of (10.23a) and (10.23b), (β) consisting of (10.23a) and (10.23c) and (γ) consisting of (10.23a)–(10.23c). As in section 10.2, I assume that each technique is productive. In addition, I assume that (α) cannot meet the given final demand but that (β) and (γ) can. This last assumption is essential to ensure that the problem of rent is not vacuous: for, if both (α) and (β) could meet the given final demand, land would not be scarce and rent would not be payable. Choice of technique effectively rests between (β) and (γ). If (β) is employed, not all land is used and so rent is not paid; on the other hand, if (γ) is employed, the intensities of (10.23b) and (10.23c) are such as to take into cultivation all available land so that rent becomes payable. Though it cannot be employed, (α) should not be discarded, as it plays an auxiliary role in the analysis.

Having defined the three techniques, I now derive properties of their price systems. (α)'s price equations are:

$$(1+r)(p_1^\alpha a_{11} + p_2^\alpha a_{21}) + w^\alpha l_1 = p_1^\alpha \tag{10.24a}$$

$$(1+r)(p_1^\alpha a_{12} + p_2^\alpha a_{22}) + w^\alpha l_2 = p_2^\alpha \tag{10.24b}$$

(As (α) is never employed, I can make the convenient assumption that land is a free input.) From (10.24), with iron as numeraire, I obtain:

$$p_2^\alpha = \frac{l_2(1-(1+r)a_{11}) + l_1(1+r)a_{12}}{l_1(1-(1+r)a_{22}) + l_2(1+r)a_{21}} \equiv \frac{h^\alpha(r)}{g^\alpha(r)} \tag{10.25a}$$

$$w^\alpha = \frac{(1-(1+r)a_{11})(1-(1+r)a_{22}) - (1+r)^2 a_{12}a_{21}}{l_1(1-(1+r)a_{22}) + l_2(1+r)a_{21}}$$

$$\equiv \frac{f^\alpha(r)}{g^\alpha(r)} \tag{10.25b}$$

As (α) is a productive, single-product industries, circulating capital technique with only produced means of production, the results from Chapter 4 apply.

Consider next technique (β), where rent is zero by hypothesis. Its price equations are:

$$(1+r)(p_1^\beta a_{11} + p_2^\beta a_{21}) + w^\beta l_1 = p_1^\beta \quad (10.26a)$$

$$(1+r)(p_1^\beta a_{13} + p_2^\beta a_{23}) + w^\beta l_3 = p_2^\beta \quad (10.26b)$$

With iron as numeraire, I obtain:

$$p_2^\beta = \frac{l_3(1 - (1+r)a_{11}) + l_1(1+r)a_{13}}{l_1(1 - (1+r)a_{23}) + l_3(1+r)a_{21}} \equiv \frac{h^\beta(r)}{g^\beta(r)} \quad (10.27a)$$

$$w^\beta = \frac{(1 - (1+r)a_{11})(1 - (1+r)a_{23}) - (1+r)^2 a_{13}a_{21}}{l_1(1 - (1+r)a_{23}) + l_3(1+r)a_{21}}$$

$$\equiv \frac{f^\beta(r)}{g^\beta(r)} \quad (10.27b)$$

the properties of single-product industries techniques from Chapter 4 also apply to (β).

At this stage, it is useful to consider the land requirements in (α) and (β) so that the assumption on final demand can be rationalised. The direct land requirements in the two techniques are given by a_{32} and a_{33}. However, these two coefficients do not indicate the total, or integrated, land requirements to produce a given set of final demands, say F_1 and F_2. To calculate these requirements, refer to sections 3.1 and 3.2. Given final demands F_1 and F_2, the following gross outputs must be produced in technique (α):

$$X_1^\alpha = ((1 - a_{22})F_1 + a_{12}F_2)/((1 - a_{11})(1 - a_{22}) - a_{12}a_{21}) \quad (10.28a)$$

$$X_2^\alpha = ((1 - a_{11})F_2 + a_{21}F_1)/((1 - a_{11})(1 - a_{22}) - a_{12}a_{21}) \quad (10.28b)$$

The total land required to produce F_1 and F_2 when (α) is employed is thus $a_{32}X_2^\alpha$. Analogous expressions to (10.28) can be obtained when (β) is employed: (β)'s land requirement is then $a_{33}X_2^\beta$. If $F_1 = 1$, $F_2 = 0$:

$$X_2^\alpha = a_{21}/((1 - a_{11})(1 - a_{22}) - a_{12}a_{21})$$
$$X_2^\beta = a_{21}/((1 - a_{11})(1 - a_{23}) - a_{13}a_{21}) \qquad (10.29)$$

If $F_1 = 0$, $F_2 = 1$:

$$X_2^\alpha = (1 - a_{11})/((1 - a_{11})(1 - a_{22}) - a_{12}a_{21})$$
$$X_2^\beta = (1 - a_{11})/((1 - a_{11})(1 - a_{23}) - a_{13}a_{21}) \qquad (3.30)$$

The simplest way of justifying the hypothesis that (β) can meet the given final demand but (α) cannot is to assume that (α)'s total land requirement is greater than (β)'s for each set of semi-positive final demands. From (10.28)–(10.30), this implies that:

$$a_{32}/((1 - a_{11})(1 - a_{22}) - a_{12}a_{21}) >$$
$$a_{33}/((1 - a_{11})(1 - a_{23}) - a_{13}a_{21}) \qquad (10.31a)$$

or

$$a_{32}/f^\alpha(0) > a_{33}/f^\beta(0) \qquad (10.31b)$$

By the productiveness assumption, $f^\iota(0) > 0$ for $\iota = \alpha, \beta$; in fact, $f^\iota(r) > 0$ for $0 \leqslant r < R^\iota$. So, from (10.31b):

$$a_{32}f^\beta(0) - a_{33}f^\alpha(0) > 0 \qquad (10.32)$$

Now consider the third technique, where a rent is paid on homogeneous land. The price equations are:[7]

$$(1+r)(p_1^\gamma a_{11} + p_2^\gamma a_{21}) + w^\gamma l_1 = p_1^\gamma \qquad (10.33a)$$

$$(1+r)(p_1^\gamma a_{12} + p_2^\gamma a_{22}) + \varrho^\gamma a_{32} + w^\gamma l_2 = p_2^\gamma \qquad (10.33b)$$

$$(1+r)(p_1^\gamma a_{13} + p_2^\gamma a_{23}) + \varrho^\gamma a_{33} + w^\gamma l_3 = p_2^\gamma \qquad (10.33c)$$

With iron as numeraire, I obtain from (10.33):

$$p_2^\gamma = (a_{32}h^\beta(r) - a_{33}h^\alpha(r)/(a_{32}g^\beta(r) - a_{33}g^\alpha(r)) \tag{10.34a}$$

$$\varrho^\gamma = (-(1+r)l_1k(r) - l_2f^\beta(r) + l_3f^\alpha(r))/(a_{32}g^\beta(r) - a_{33}g^\alpha(r)) \tag{10.34b}$$

$$w^\gamma = (a_{32}f^\beta(r) - a_{33}f^\alpha(r))/(a_{32}g^\beta(r) - a_{33}g^\alpha(r)) \tag{10.34c}$$

where $k(r)$ is defined in (10.3d).

The properties of (α) and (β) are not necessarily transferred to (γ). This can be seen by comparing (10.27a) and (10.27b), on the one hand, with (10.34a) and (10.34c), on the other. In the former, both numerators and the denominator are positive for $0 \leqslant r < R^\beta$, the maximum rate of profit in (β) (obtained as the smallest positive root of $f^\beta(r) = 0$). No such inferences can be drawn from (10.34c), where the numerator is the difference of two quadratics, the denominator the difference of two linear functions. The maximum rate of profit supported by (γ) is not necessarily the smallest positive value of r at which $(a_{32}f^\beta(r) - a_{33}f^\alpha(r)) = 0$; for, there may not be a positive value of r at which this expression is zero. Secondly, even if a maximum rate of profit, R^γ, can be defined, it does not follow that $dw^\gamma/dr < 0$ over the range $0 \leqslant r \leqslant R^\gamma$. In the Exercises, there is a numerical example to illustrate precisely this possibility.

The properties of (γ) can be inferred from those of (α) and (β). Suppose first that (α) and (β) have a switch-point $\bar{r} > 0$, with $p_2^\alpha = p_2^\beta = \bar{p}_2 > 0$, $w^\alpha = w^\beta = \bar{w} > 0$. It is clear from (10.24), (10.26) and (10.33) that, at $\bar{r}$, $p_2^\gamma = \bar{p}_2$, $\varrho^\gamma = 0$, $w^\gamma = \bar{w}$. That is, (γ) shares the switch-point with (α) and (β). Conversely, if (10.33) has solution at r given by $p_2^\gamma > 0$, $\varrho^\gamma = 0$, $w^\gamma > 0$, it follows that $p_2^\alpha = p_2^\beta = p_2^\gamma$, $w^\alpha = w^\beta = w^\gamma$. So, $\bar{r}$ is a switch-point between (α) and (β).

p_2^γ, ϱ^γ and w^γ are continuous functions of r. In a sufficiently small neighbourhood around $\bar{r}$, an assumed switch-point between (α) and (β), p_2^γ and w^γ will be positive; ϱ^γ will be negative for $\bar{r}-e < r < \bar{r}$ and positive for $\bar{r} < r < \bar{r}+e$, or positive for $\bar{r}-e < r < \bar{r}$ and negative for $\bar{r} < r < \bar{r}+e$ (for sufficiently small positive e). Suppose that $\varrho^\gamma > 0$. Then from (10.33a) and (10.33b):

$$(1+\bar{r})(p_1^\gamma a_{11} + p_2^\gamma a_{21}) + w^\gamma l_1 = p_1^\gamma \tag{10.35a}$$

$$(1+\bar{r})(p_1^\gamma a_{12} + p_2^\gamma a_{22}) + w^\gamma l_2 < p_2^\gamma \tag{10.35b}$$

Figure 10.4

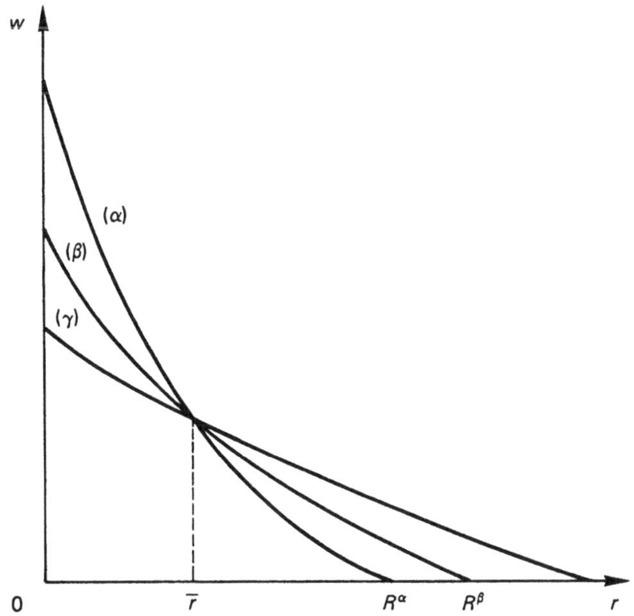

It follows from the theory of Chapter 6 that:

$$w^\gamma < w^\alpha \tag{10.36a}$$

By considering (10.33a) and (10.33c) under the same hypothesis, analogues of (10.35a) and (10.35b) can be obtained, whence:

$$w^\gamma < w^\beta \tag{10.36b}$$

On the other hand, if $\varrho^\gamma < 0$, the inequalities in (10.36a) and (10.36b) are reversed. This provides us with local information on the relationships between the three *w*–*r* curves. Suppose as in Figure 10.4 that $w^\gamma < w^\beta$ for $\bar{r}-e < r < \bar{r}$ and $w^\gamma > w^\beta$ for $\bar{r} < r < \bar{r}+e$. It is a straightforward matter to establish that $\varrho^\gamma > 0$ for $\bar{r}-e < r < \bar{r}$ and $\varrho^\gamma < 0$ for $\bar{r} < r < \bar{r}+e$. Further inferences can be drawn. If there is only one switch-point between (α) and (β), $w^\gamma < w^\beta$ for $0 \leqslant r < \bar{r}$ and $w^\gamma > w^\beta$ for $\bar{r} < r \leqslant R^\beta$. To see this, suppose that $w^\gamma = w^\beta$ at $\tilde{r}$, where $0 < \tilde{r} < \bar{r}$. It follows from the hypothesis, when applied to (10.26) and (10.33), that $\varrho^\gamma = 0$, which in turn

Figure 10.5

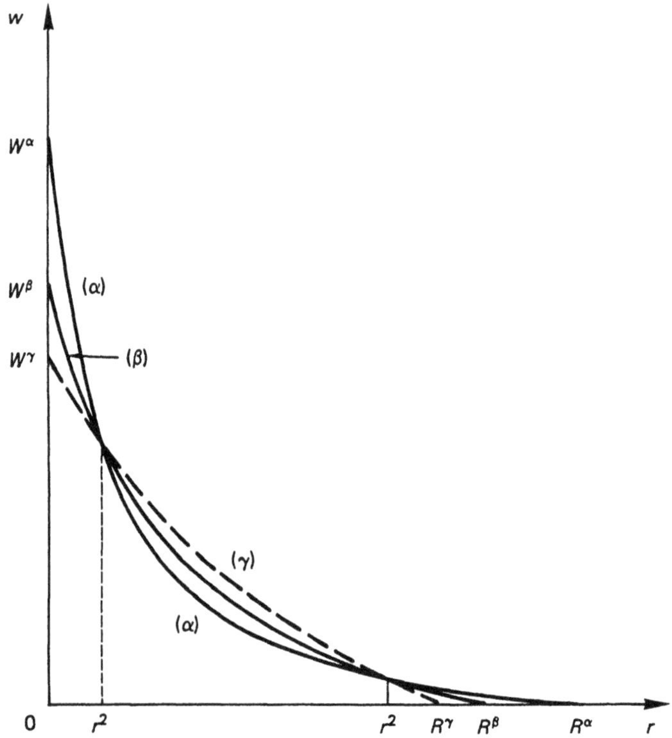

implies that $w^{\alpha} = w^{\beta}$. Hence, $\tilde{r} \neq \bar{r}$ is also a switch-point. This contradicts the fact that $\bar{r}$ is the only switch-point in the case under examination. An exactly similar argument establishes $w^{\gamma} > w^{\beta}$ for $R^{\beta} \geqslant r > \bar{r}$. This discussion deals with the case of only one switch-point between (α) and (β). Consider next the case where (α) and (β) have two switch-points, as in Figure 10.5. The line of argument employed above can be extended to this case so that $\varrho^{\gamma} > 0$ for $0 \leqslant r < r^1$ and $r^2 < r \leqslant R^{\gamma}$, with $\varrho^{\gamma} < 0$ over the intermediate interval. The final case to be considered is when (α) and (β) have no switch-points, as in Figure 10.6. To analyse this, consider (10.26a) from (β)'s price equations, and (10.33a), from (γ)'s price equations, evaluated at $r = 0$:

$$p_1^{\beta}a_{11} + p_2^{\beta}a_{21} + W^{\beta}l_1 = 1 \tag{10.37a}$$

$$p_1^{\gamma}a_{11} + p_2^{\gamma}a_{21} + W^{\gamma}l_1 = 1 \tag{10.37b}$$

Figure 10.6

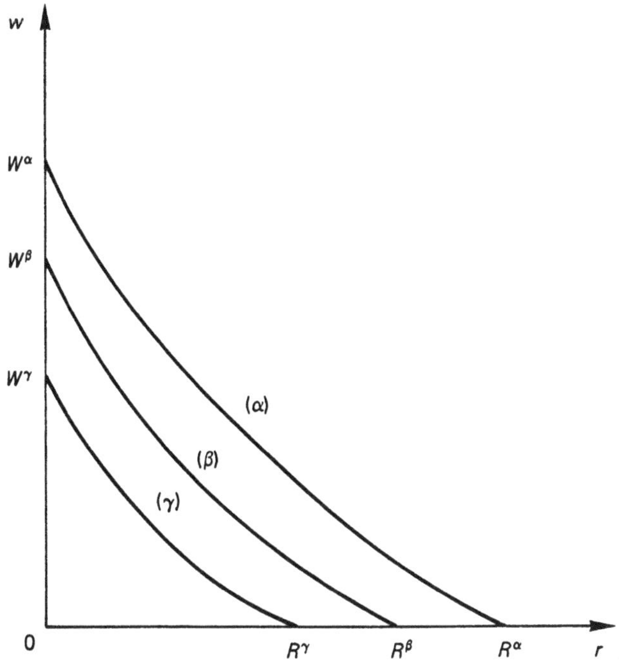

With $W^\beta > W^\gamma$ and $p_1^\beta = p_1^\gamma = 1$, as in Figure 10.6, it follows that $p_2^\gamma > p_2^\beta$ at $r = 0$. $\varrho^\gamma \neq 0$, as there are no switch-points between (α) and (β). Suppose that $\varrho^\gamma < 0$. By the same argument as in (10.35) and (10.36), I obtain:

$$\begin{aligned} w^\gamma &> w^\alpha \\ w^\gamma &> w^\beta \end{aligned} \qquad (10.38)$$

These inequalities are valid for $0 \leqslant r < e$ (where e is a sufficiently small number). (10.38) clearly contradicts the information in Figure 10.6. So, $\varrho^\gamma > 0$. As r increases from 0 to R^γ, ϱ^γ is always positive: for, if $\varrho^\gamma = 0$ at some $\underline{r}$ between 0 and R^γ, w^α and w^β intersect there. With $\varrho^\gamma > 0$ and $w^\gamma \geqslant 0$ for $0 \leqslant r \leqslant R^\gamma$, it follows that $p_2^\gamma > 0$ over the same range. The arrangement in Figure 10.6 is associated with $\varrho^\gamma > 0$.

In Figures 10.4–10.6, I have dealt with the three cases where there is one switch-point, there are two switch-points and there are no switch-points between (α) and (β). Other examples of each case can be analysed in a similar manner. For example, a variant of Figure 10.4 would have $w^{\gamma} > w^{\beta} > w^{\alpha}$ over the interval $0 \leqslant r < \bar{r}$ and $w^{\alpha} > w^{\beta} > w^{\gamma}$ over the interval $\bar{r} < r \leqslant R^{\alpha}$. In such a case, $\varrho^{\gamma} < 0$ for $0 \leqslant r < \bar{r}$ and $\varrho^{\gamma} > 0$ for $\bar{r} < r \leqslant R^{\gamma} < R^{\beta} < R^{\alpha}$. A variant of Figure 10.5 would have $w^{\gamma} > w^{\beta} > w^{\alpha}$ for $0 \leqslant r < r^1$ and $r^2 < r \leqslant R^{\beta}$ and $w^{\alpha} > w^{\beta} > w^{\gamma}$ for $r^1 < r < r^2$: in this case, $\varrho^{\gamma} < 0$ over the lower and upper ranges and $\varrho^{\gamma} > 0$ over the intermediate range. Finally, a variant of Figure 10.6 would have $w^{\gamma} > w^{\beta} > w^{\alpha}$ for $0 \leqslant r \leqslant R$: in such a case, $\varrho^{\gamma} < 0$.

Having derived the properties of the individual techniques, I can now attend to the question of choice of technique.

10.6 Intensive Rent: Choice of Technique

Suppose that (β) is initially employed. (β)'s price system contains an implicit zero rent or land price. Evaluate the first process in the wheat industry at (β)'s prices, i.e.

$$s_2(\gamma{:}\beta) \equiv p_2^{\beta} - (1+r)(p_1^{\beta}a_{12} + p_2^{\beta}a_{22}) - w^{\beta}l_2 \qquad (10.39\text{a})$$

Substituting from (10.27) into (10.39a), I obtain:

$$s_2(\gamma{:}\beta) = (-(1+r)l_1k(r) - l_2f^{\beta}(r) + l_3f^{\alpha}(r))/g^{\beta}(r) \qquad (10.39\text{b})$$

$$= (a_{32}g^{\beta}(r) - a_{33}g^{\alpha}(r))\ \varrho^{\gamma}/g\ (r) \qquad (10.39\text{c})$$

If $s_2(\gamma{:}\beta) > 0$, a capitalist in the agricultural sector can reduce costs by operating both processes. Assume that the switch is made and that (γ)'s prices are established. It is now necessary to evaluate the second process in the wheat industry at (γ)'s prices. If a capitalist switched from using the first process to the second process in the agricultural sector, land would cease to be scarce. So:

$$s_2(\beta{:}\gamma) \equiv p_2^{\gamma} - (1+r)(p_1^{\gamma}a_{13} + p_2^{\gamma}a_{23} + p_3^{\gamma}a_{33}) - w^{\gamma}l_3 \qquad (10.40\text{a})$$

which, from (10.33c), can be rewritten as:

$$s_2(\beta{:}\gamma) = -\rho_3^{\gamma}a_{33} \qquad (10.40\text{b})$$

In (10.40a), land inputs are valued at $\rho_3^{\gamma}a_{33}$ but land outputs are zero.

At this stage, I introduce the assumption:

$$a_{32}g^{\beta}(r) - a_{33}g^{\alpha}(r) > 0 \qquad (10.41)$$

for r in the relevant range. Given (10.32) and (10.34c), this is a natural assumption to make. It follows from (10.39c) and (10.41) that:

$$\text{sign } s_2(\gamma:\beta) = \text{sign } \varrho^{\gamma} \qquad (10.42a)$$

and from (10.40b) that:

$$\text{sign } s_2(\beta:\gamma) = (-1) \text{ sign } \varrho^{\gamma} \qquad (10.42b)$$

(10.42a) and (10.42b) obviously imply that:

$$\text{sign } s_2(\gamma:\beta) = (-1) \text{ sign } s_2(\beta:\gamma) \qquad (10.43)$$

From (10.25b), (10.27b) and (10.41), I obtain after straightforward manipulations:

$$\text{sign } (w^{\alpha} - w^{\beta}) = \text{sign } \varrho^{\gamma} \qquad (10.44)$$

(10.42)–(10.44) are analogous to the equations derived in the extensive rent case. Care needs to be taken with their interpretation, as will become clear later.

Consider Figure 10.4, where $\varrho^{\gamma} > 0$ for $0 \leqslant r < \bar{r}$. Hence, (γ) is the cost-minimising technique over the range $0 \leqslant r < \bar{r}$ by (10.43). The maximum rate of profit that can be supported is R^{β}: over the interval $\bar{r} < r \leqslant R^{\beta}$, ($\beta$) is cost minimising by (10.43), with $\varrho^{\gamma} < 0$. Now, consider Figure 10.6. As $\varrho^{\gamma} > 0$ for $0 \leqslant r \leqslant R^{\gamma}$, ($\gamma$) is cost minimising over this interval. (β) can support a positive price system if $R^{\gamma} < r \leqslant R^{\beta}$, which means that there is at least one feasible technique. However, capitalists in the agricultural sector would find it more profitable to switch from employing just one process to employing both: note that w^{α} lies above w^{β} in this range. This suggests that (γ) is preferred to (β): but (γ) cannot support a positive price system. So, no cost-minimising technique exists over this interval. A similar conclusion applies over the same interval in Figure 10.5. This case is characterised by reswitching:

Figure 10.7

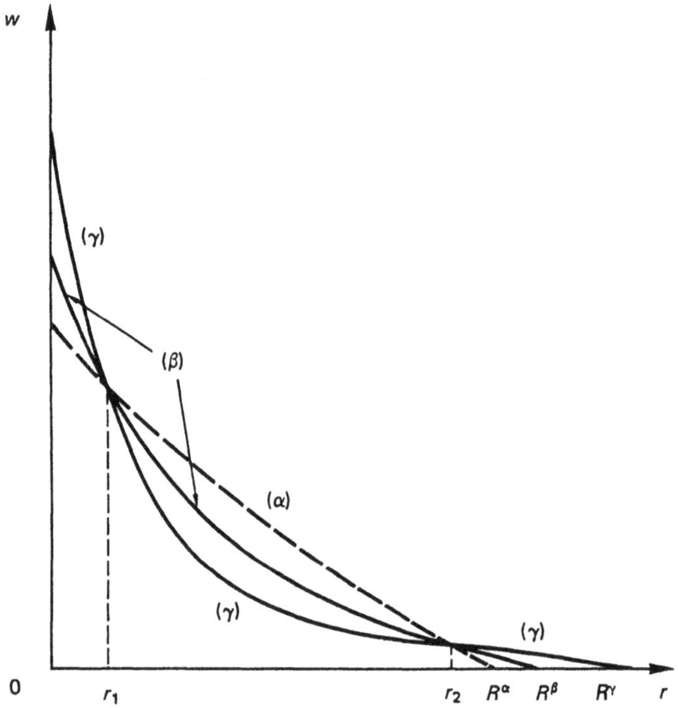

(γ) is cost minimising for $0 \leqslant r < r^1$ and $r^2 < r \leqslant R^\gamma$, with (β) cost minimising over the intermediate interval.

I now summarise the results on choice of technique for the intensive rent model. It will be clear from the above considerations that I need to define the maximum rate of profit that can be supported by (γ) so that I can distinguish between the cases described in Figure 10.4, on the one hand, and Figures 10.5 and 10.6, on the other. In Figure 10.4, $\bar{r}$ is in fact the largest rate of profit that can be supported by (γ): in Figures 10.5 and 10.6, it is R^γ. Non-existence of a cost-minimising technique arises when $R^\gamma < R^\beta < R^\alpha$, as in Figures 10.5 and 10.6. It does not arise in Figure 10.7, where $\varrho^\gamma > 0$ for $r_1 < r < r_2$ and (γ)'s maximum rate of profit is r_2. (β) is cost minimising for $0 \leqslant r < r_1$ and $r_2 < r \leqslant R^\beta$, with (γ) cost minimising over the intermediate interval. So, I have:

Result 20: If $R^\gamma > R^\beta > R^\alpha$, there is a cost-minimising technique at each feasible value of r. If $R^{\gamma} < R^{\beta} < R^{\alpha}$, there is no cost-minimising technique in the interval $R^{\gamma} < r \leqslant R^{\beta}$.

It will be evident from the discussion above that positivity of rent is an indicator that (γ) is the cost-minimising technique. So, I have:

Corollary 20.1: Technique (γ) is cost minimising if and only if $\varrho^{\gamma} > 0$.

I demonstrated in sections 10.2–10.4 that the cost-minimising technique could be inferred from the inner envelope of feasible *w–r* curves. Subject to the qualification raised above and stated in *Result 20*, this can be extended to the intensive rent model. That is:

Corollary 20.2: If $R^{\gamma} > R^{\beta} > R^{\alpha}$, the cost-minimising technique is given by the inner envelope of feasible *w–r* curves. If $R^{\alpha} > R^{\beta} > R^{\gamma}$, the same rule applies for $0 \leqslant r < R^{\gamma}$, but for $R^{\gamma} < r < R^{\beta}$ there is no cost-minimising technique.

10.7 Conclusions

There are two general points to be made at the outset on the analysis of extensive and intensive rent models. First, the choice of technique for a given level of final demand depends on income distribution: as Sraffa observed parenthetically in section 86 with respect to the extensive case: 'Note that the suffixes are arbitrary and do *not* represent the order of fertility, which is not defined independently of the rents; that order, as well as the magnitude of the rents themselves, may vary with the variation of r and w' (PCMC p. 75). The second point is the obverse of the first. I assume that final demand required both qualities of land in sections 10.2 and 10.3, and all qualities of land in section 10.4, to be cultivated. These are not the only assumptions that could be made. For example, I could have assumed that final demand in the three-process model could be met by cultivating either one type or both types of land; similarly, in the four-process model, final demand could be met by using two types of land. In either case, choice of technique at a given income distribution would differ from that which obtained if either both or all three types of land respectively had to be employed. This point is taken up in the Exercises.

There are additional similarities between the analyses of extensive and intensive rent models. For example, positivity of rent is an indicator of efficiency in choice of technique; also, an inner, not the outer, envelope can be used for the purpose of detecting the cost-minimising technique (subject to the point raised above on the level of final demand). However, there are significant differences between the two models which are sufficient to prevent the unqualified statement of conclusions on land models in general: I refer here to the fact that a cost-minimising technique may not exist in an intensive rent model over a feasible range of values of r.

The extensive rent model is similar in a number of ways to the circulating and fixed capital models of Chapters 6 and 9. First, the analysis of price systems in the extensive case is based on the theory established in Chapters 4 and 6: the technique with the marginal land is, in effect, a single-product industries, circulating capital model with only produced means of production. Second, there is a cost-minimising technique at each feasible value of r, as in the circulating and fixed capital models. Third, rent (or the price of land) plays an analogous role to that of the ageing machine price in the fixed capital model: in the former, the technique with positive rent is cost minimising just as in the latter the technique with the positive ageing machine price is cost minimising. Fourth, the w–r frontier is downward sloping, as in the circulating and fixed capital models. Of these four, only the third carries over to the intensive rent model, as a general rule. With respect to first point, it is evident from (10.33) and (10.34) that the theory of Chapters 4 and 6 is not immediately applicable. With respect to the second point, I have shown above that there is not always a cost-minimising technique at each feasible value of r. Nor does the fourth property extend to intensive rent models, as demonstrated by exercise 10. It will be seen in the next chapter that intensive rent models share some of the characteristics of pure joint production systems.

Commentary

In this chapter, I have concentrated on the familiar extensive and intensive rent models of sections 85–88 in chapter XI of PCMC. Other cases, raised in exercises 13 and 14, are discussed by Sraffa in section 89.

Quadrio-Curzio (1980) gives a general account of extensive rent models. D'Agata (1983) provides numerical examples of three-sector intensive rent models in which a cost-minimising technique does not exist for some feasible values of r and there are multiple cost-minimising techniques for other feasible values of r. Woods (1987) discusses a three-process model where the industrial sector has alternative processes but the agricultural sector does not. Bidard and Woods (1987) analyse simple models in which the quality of land is affected by production. Steedman (1982) analyses the wage–rent frontier in a simple model; see also Metcalfe and Steedman (1972). A general analysis of land in linear production models is provided by Salvadori (1986).

The relation between Sraffa's and Ricardo's treatments of land is discussed by Kurz (1976).

Exercises

1. Discuss the Ricardian view that 'A tax on rent would affect rent only; it would fall wholly on landlords' (Ricardo, 1951, p. 173). In particular, assess the effect on commodity prices and the real wage at a given value of r.

2. Consider numerical example given by (10.10a)–(10.10d) in section 10.4.

   (i) Prove that $\varrho^{\beta,3} > \varrho^{\beta,1}$ for $0 \leqslant r < \bar{r}$.

   (ii) Prove that $\varrho^{\alpha,3} > \varrho^{\alpha,2}$ for $\bar{r} < r \leqslant R^{\alpha}$.

3. Consider the numerical example given by (10.10a)–(10.10d) of section 10.4, modified by the process (10.21).

   (i) Derive (10.22).

   (ii) Derive the ordering of lands by rent at each feasible value of r and contrast with the order of fertility.

4. Analyse a four-process, three-technique extensive rent model given by (10.10a)–(10.10c) and:

   1/4 t iron ⊕ 1/4 qr wheat ⊕ 1 acre quality-three land ⊕ 2 labour

   ⊖ 1 qr wheat ⊕ 1 acre quality-three land.

   Derive the ordering of lands by rent and the order of fertility.

5. Analyse a four-process, three-technique extensive rent model given by (10.10a)–(10.10c) and:

   1/3 t iron ⊕ 1/4 qr wheat ⊕ 1 acre quality-three land ⊕ 2 labour

   ⊖ 1 qr wheat ⊕ 1 acre quality-three land.

6. Analyse the following model:

   1/12 t iron ⊕ 1/3 qr wheat ⊕ 1 labour ⊖ 1 t iron

   1/6 t iron ⊕ 1/6 qr wheat ⊕ 1 acre quality-one land ⊕ 1 labour

$\ominus$ 1 qr wheat $\oplus$ 1 acre quality-one land

137/546 t iron $\oplus$ 19/273 qr wheat $\oplus$ 1 acre quality-two land

$\oplus$ 92/91 labour $\ominus$ 1 qr wheat $\oplus$ 1 acre quality-two land

1/8 t iron $\oplus$ 1/24 qr wheat $\oplus$ 1 acre quality-three land $\oplus$ 1 labour $\ominus$

1 qr wheat $\oplus$ 1 acre quality-three land.

Find the ordering of lands by rent and the order of fertility when (i) two qualities of land are employed; and (ii) all three qualities of land are employed.

7. Repeat exercise 6 with the last process replaced by:

   1/8 t iron $\oplus$ 1/2 qr wheat $\oplus$ 1 acre quality-three land $\oplus$ 1 labour

   $\ominus$ 1 qr wheat $\oplus$ 1 acre quality-three land.

8. Derive (10.34).

9. Analyse the following intensive rent model:

   1/4 t iron $\oplus$ 1/4 qr wheat $\oplus$ 1 labour $\ominus$ 1 t iron

   1/4 t iron $\oplus$ 1/6 qr wheat $\oplus$ 3/2 acres land $\oplus$ 1 labour $\ominus$ 1 qr wheat

   $\oplus$ 3/2 acres land

   1/3 t iron $\oplus$ 1/4 qr wheat $\oplus$ 1 acre land $\oplus$ 1/2 labour

   $\ominus$ 1 qr wheat $\oplus$ 1 acre land

10. Analyse the following intensive rent model:

    1/2 t iron $\oplus$ 1/6 qr wheat $\oplus$ 1/30 labour $\ominus$ 1 t iron

    1 t iron $\oplus$ 3/10 acres land $\oplus$ 3/100 labour $\ominus$ 1 qr wheat

    $\oplus$ 3/10 acres land

    3/100 t iron $\oplus$ 3/20 acres land $\oplus$ 9/10 labour $\ominus$ 1 qr wheat

    $\oplus$ 3/20 acres land.

11. Using exercises 20 or 21 of Chapter 6, construct an example satisfying (10.32) which exhibits reswitching.

12. Consider Figure 10.4. Prove that $w^{\gamma} > w^{\beta}$ for $\bar{r} < r \leqslant R^{\beta}$.

13. Consider the effect of introducing a second agricultural commodity. How are the results on choice of technique affected?

14. Suppose that alternative processes are available to produce the industrial commodity, iron. What will be the effect on choice of technique?

15. Discuss the role of (10.39) in the theory of choice of technique.

16. Analyse the extensive rent model of sections 10.2 and 10.3 under the assumption that final demand can be satisfied by cultivating either quality-one land or quality-one and quality-two lands.

17. Analyse the extensive rent model of section 10.4 if final demand requires two qualities of land to be cultivated.

18. Examine the Ricardian view on the ordering of lands (discussed in section 10.3). Can it be justified under the assumption that prices are proportional to embodied labour? (See chapter I of *The Principles*.)

19. Give an account of the role of w–r curves in the theory of choice of technique for land models, paying particular attention to the level of final demand.

20. Does the demand for land vary inversely with rent? (See Steedman, 1982.)

Notes to Chapter 10

1. Alternatively, non-produced means of production are free.
2. There is, thus, a similarity between land and an everlasting machine.
3. It should not be inferred that quality-one land is always 'better' than quality-two land. In any event, this point will be demonstrated below.
4. Where land is either not required or free.
5. 10.2c can alternatively be rewritten as:

   $$(1+r)(p_1^\alpha a_{13} + p_2^\alpha a_{23} + p_4^\alpha a_{43}) + w^\alpha l_3 = p_2^\alpha + p_4^\alpha a_{43} \tag{10i}$$

   p_4^α being the price per acre of quality-two land. By the third assumption of section 10.1, the given acreage is unaffected by the production process so that the value of land, $p_4^\alpha a_{43}$, emerges as a contribution to the value of output. (10*i*) can be rewritten as (10.2c) of the text because the rent per acre of quality-two land is equal to the rate of profit times the price of an acre of quality-two land: the price of an acre of land is the capitalised value of the rent, $p_4^\alpha = \rho^\alpha / r$. Rent is the payment 'to the landlord for the use of the original and indestructible powers of the soil' (Ricardo, 1951, p. 67).
6. I take up this point in Chapter 11 when I define basic commodities for a joint production model.
7. (10.33b) can be rewritten as:

   $$(1+r)(p_1^\gamma a_{12} + p_2^\gamma a_{22} + p_3^\gamma a_{32}) + w^\gamma l_2 = p_2^\gamma + p_3^\gamma a_{32}$$

   which reduces to (10.33b) when it is realised that $\rho^\gamma = r p_3^\gamma$. Similarly for (10.33c).

11
Joint Production

11.1 Introduction

In Chapters 9 and 10, joint production arose in one industry because of the presence of durable means of production, produced or non-produced. In both cases, this was sufficient to require a multiple-product industries framework for the proper analysis of prices of production. In this chapter, I permit intrinsic joint production, of the wool-and-mutton or wheat-and-straw variety, on both industries. Otherwise, the industries share the properties of Chapters 4–7: to be specific, there is only circulating capital and there are no non-produced means of production. It will be seen below that this can create a number of difficulties for the theory developed in Chapters 2–7.

Underlying the analysis of prices in any model is the notion of productiveness. It will be recalled that the necessary and sufficient conditions for productiveness played an important role, not only for the single-product industries models of Chapters 3–7, but also for the fixed capital and land models of Chapters 9 and 10. So, in section 11.2, I deal first of all with the implications of productiveness. In section 11.3, I consider another question that arises on the quantity side of the model from the existence of joint production. For a single-product industries model, where both commodities are basic, a positive final demand for only one good requires both industries to operate a process. On the other hand, in a pure joint production model, where each industry produces a positive net output of both commodities, it is possible that, given a certain set of final demands, only one industry needs to operate a process: this is easily seen when the final demands for the two commodities are proportional to the net outputs from one process. Having dealt in sections 11.2 and 11.3 with questions relating to the quantity side of the model, I concentrate in the rest of this chapter on the existence of prices of production and associated problems in the theory of choice of technique.

11.2 The Quantity System

Let the first and second industries have these processes respectively:

$$X_{11} \text{ t iron} \oplus X_{21} \text{ cwt coal} \oplus L_1 \text{ labour} \ominus Y_{11} \text{ t iron} \oplus Y_{21} \text{ cwt coal} \tag{11.1a}$$

$$X_{12} \text{ t iron} \oplus X_{22} \text{ cwt coal} \oplus L_2 \text{ labour} \ominus Y_{12} \text{ t iron} \oplus Y_{22} \text{ cwt coal} \tag{11.1b}$$

As in earlier chapters, X_{ij} denotes an input of commodity i into industry j's process. As there is joint production, it is necessary to specify both outputs from each process: let Y_{ij} be the output of commodity i from the process of industry j, $i,j = 1,2$. One of Y_{1j} and Y_{2j} can be zero. L_j is the direct labour input into the process of industry j, $j = 1,2$. In the single-product industries case, there was an obvious normalisation for each process: by choosing each gross output to be equal to one, the commodity and labour input flows could be replaced by input–output coefficients. Note that, with joint production, there is no obvious way of normalising the processes in (11.1).

An economy is productive if the gross output of each commodity is greater than the sum of inter-industry requirements. With reference to (11.1), a system is productive if:

Iron

$$Y_{11} + Y_{12} \geqslant X_{11} + X_{12} \tag{11.2a}$$

Coal

$$Y_{21} + Y_{22} \geqslant X_{21} + X_{22} \tag{11.2b}$$

walosi. The three conditions – (3.8a), (3.8b) and (3.11) of Chapter 3 – were derived for a productive single-product industries model.

It might be thought that they have the following analogues for a joint production model:

$$Y_{11} - X_{11} > 0 \quad (11.3a)$$

$$Y_{22} - X_{22} > 0 \quad (11.3b)$$

$$(Y_{11} - X_{11})(Y_{22} - X_{22}) - (Y_{12} - X_{12})(Y_{21} - X_{21}) > 0 \quad (11.3c)$$

Consider now these four numerical examples:

Example 1: $Y_{11} = 6$, $Y_{12} = 3$, $Y_{21} = 5$, $Y_{22} = 8$, $X_{11} = 3$, $X_{12} = 2$, $X_{21} = 4$, $X_{22} = 3$. Clearly, (11.2a) and (11.2b) are satisfied, so that this example is productive. It is easily checked that (11.3) is satisfied. Note that, in this example, $Y_{ij} - X_{ij} > 0$, for all $i \neq j$.

Example 2: $Y_{11} = 5$, $Y_{12} = 2$, $Y_{21} = 3$, $Y_{22} = 7$, $X_{11} = 1$, $X_{12} = 3$, $X_{21} = 5$, $X_{22} = 2$. Conditions (11.2) are again satisfied, as are (11.3). This differs from *Example 1* in that $Y_{ii} - X_{ii} > 0$ for both i and $Y_{ij} - X_{ij} < 0$ for i and $\neq j$, $i,j = 1,2$. This example resembles a single-product industries model as each industry produces a net output of only one commodity, though a positive gross output of both.

Example 3: $Y_{11} = 2$, $Y_{12} = 7$, $Y_{21} = 4$, $Y_{22} = 6$, $X_{11} = 3$, $X_{12} = 2$, $X_{21} = 1$, $X_{22} = 3$. (11.2) is satisfied, as are (11.3b) and (11.3c) but not (11.3a).

Example 4: $Y_{11} = 3$, $Y_{12} = 7$, $Y_{21} = 5$, $Y_{22} = 9$, $X_{11} = 4$, $X_{12} = 3$, $X_{21} = 2$, $X_{22} = 10$. Though (11.2) is satisfied, none of (11.3a)–(11.3c) is.

These numerical examples, particularly 3 and 4, establish that conditions (11.3a)–(11.3c) will in general not play the same role for joint production models as their analogue – (3.8a), (3.8b), (3.8b) and (3.11) of Chapter 3 – do for single-product industries models.

11.3 Final Demand

In section 11.1, I raised the possibility that the components of final demand were proportional to the net outputs from one of the processes. This is illustrated in Figure 11.1, where $Z_j = (Z_{1j}, Z_{2j})$

Figure 11.1

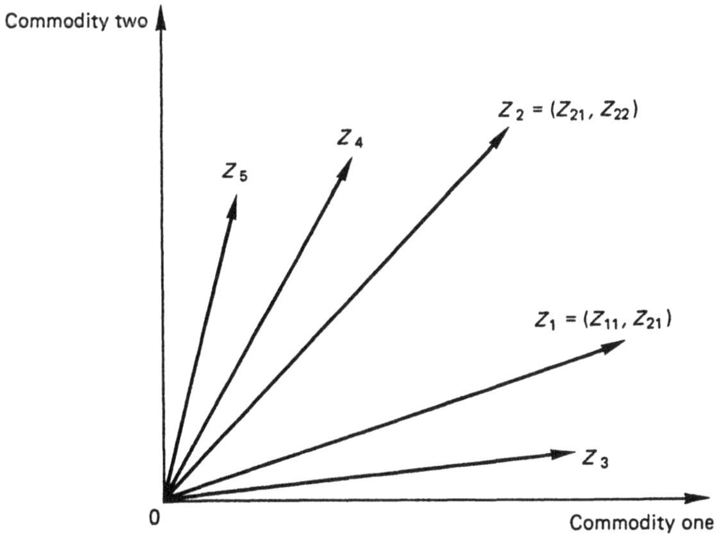

represents the net output from process j, $j = 1,2$. $Z_{ij} \equiv Y_{ij} - X_{ij}$, $i,j = 1,2$. If final demand is proportional to (Z_{11}, Z_{21}), only process 1 needs to be operated. By operating both processes at positive intensities, any set of final demands in the triangle $0Z_1Z_2$ can be generated.

> Take for example the case of two products jointly produced by each of two different methods. The possibility of varying the extent to which one or the other method is employed ensures a certain range of variation in the proportions in which the two goods may be produced in the aggregate. But this range finds its limits in the proportions in which the two goods are produced respectively by each of the two methods, so that the limits are reached as soon as one or the other method is exclusively employed. (PCMC, section 53, p. 47)

If the final demand is given by Z_3 or Z_4 in Figure 11.1, there is a formal solution in which one of the processes is operated at a negative level. Such a solution can be put aside: only one of the processes would be operated, with a quantity of one of the commodities being disposed of.

Sraffa advanced two reasons for equality between numbers of commodities and processes in a technique.

> We shall now suppose two of the commodities to be jointly produced by a single industry . . . The conditions would no longer be sufficient to determine the prices. There would be more prices to be ascertained than there are processes and, therefore, equations to determine them. In these circumstances, there will be room for a second parallel process which will produce the two commodities by a different method and, as we shall suppose at first, in different proportions. Such a parallel process will not only be possible – it will be necessary if the number of processes is to be brought into equality with the number of commodities so that prices may be determined. (ibid., section 50, p. 43)

Two independent production processes are required to determine prices when there are two commodities. This is Sraffa's first reason, on the basis of which he assumes 'that in such cases a second process or industry does in fact exist' (ibid.). Recognising that this assumption may appear unreasonable, Sraffa argued in a footnote as follows:

> Incidentally, considering that the proportions in which the two commodities are produced by any one method will in general be different from those in which they are required for use, the existence of two methods of producing them in different proportions will be necessary for obtaining the required proportion of the two products through an appropriate combination of the two methods. (Footnote 2, p. 43)

A weakness of these arguments is that both final demand (or 'requirements for use') and the technology are given; so if the two processes are described by Z_1 and Z_2 in Figure 11.1 and final demand is given by Z_4, only one process will be operated, or another process, such as Z_5, will be required. But where does Z_5 come from? Stronger arguments, unfortunately beyond the scope of this book, have been advanced by Steedman (1976) and Bidard (1986b) to support equality between numbers of commodities and processes.

11.4 Prices of Production

Taking up the point that two processes of production are in general required for two commodities, Sraffa argued:

> *Any* other method of producing the two commodities will be compatible with the first, subject only to the general requirement of the resulting equations being mutually independent and having at least one system of real solutions: which rules out, for example, proportionality of *both* products and means of production in the two processes. However (and this is the only economic restriction), while the equations may be formally satisfied by negative solutions for the unknowns, only those methods of production are practicable which in the conditions actually prevailing (i.e. at the given wage or at the given rate of profits) do not involve other than positive prices. (PCMC, section 50, p. 44)

The price equations corresponding to (11.1a) and (11.1b) are:

$$(1+r)(p_1X_{11} + p_2X_{21}) + wL_1 = p_1Y_{11} + p_2Y_{21} \quad (11.4a)$$

$$(1+r)(p_1X_{12} + p_2X_{22}) + wL_2 = p_1Y_{12} + p_2Y_{22} \quad (11.4b)$$

as in section 51 of PCMC.

With the first commodity as numeraire, (11.4a) and (11.4b) have formal solution:

$$p_2 = \frac{L_1((1+r)X_{12} - Y_{12}) + L_2(Y_{11} - (1+r)X_{11})}{L_1(Y_{22} - (1+r)X_{22}) + L_2((1+r)X_{21} - Y_{21})} \quad (11.5a)$$

$$w = \frac{((Y_{11} - (1+r)X_{11})(Y_{22}-(1+r)X_{22}) - (Y_{12}-(1+r)X_{12})(Y_{21}-(1+r)X_{21}))}{L_1(Y_{22} - (1+r)X_{22}) + L_2((1+r)X_{21} - Y_{21})} \quad (11.5b)$$

A productive single-product industries model has a positive maximum rate of profit such that its price system is positive and its wage rate is non-negative and decreasing for all values of r between zero and this maximum. Do these properties extend to joint production models? As a preliminary discussion of this question, consider the following numerical examples:

Example 1

1 t iron ⊕ 5 cwt coal ⊕ 1 labour ⊖ 5 t iron ⊕ 3 cwt coal (11.6a)

3 t iron ⊕ 2 cwt coal ⊕ 1 labour ⊖ 2 t iron ⊕ 7 cwt coal (11.6b)

This model is productive. Applying the date to (11.5), I obtain:

$$p_2 = (5+2r)/(7+3r) \qquad (11.7a)$$

$$w = (18 - 24r - 13r^2)/(7+3r) \qquad (11.7b)$$

It is a straightforward matter to establish that $p_2 > 0$, $w > 0$ for $0 \leqslant r < R$ and $p_2 > 0$, $w = 0$ for $r = R = (-24 + \sqrt{1512})/26 \simeq 0.5827$. Also, $dw/dr < 0$ for $0 \leqslant r \leqslant R$. This example resembles the single-product industries models of Chapter 4, both in structure – as $Y_{ii} - (1+r)X_{ii} > 0$ for both i, $Y_{ij} - (1+r)X_{ij} < 0$ *for* $i \neq j$, $i, j = 1,2$ for feasible r – and in properties.

Example 2

3 t iron ⊕ 4 cwt coal ⊕ 1 labour ⊖ 6 t iron ⊕ 5 cwt coal (11.8a)

2 t iron ⊕ 3 cwt coal ⊕ 1 labour ⊖ 3 t iron ⊕ 8 cwt coal (11.8b)

This model is productive. From (11.5) and (11.8), I obtain:

$$p_2 = (2 - r)/(4 + r) \qquad (11.9a)$$

$$w = (r^2 - 18r + 14)/(4 + r) \qquad (11.9b)$$

$p_2 > 0$ for $0 \leqslant r \leqslant R$, $w > 0$ for $0 \leqslant r < R$, $w = 0$ for $r = R = (18 - \sqrt{268})/2 \simeq 0.815$. The single-product industries properties, including $dw/dr < 0$, are also satisfied in this example for $0 \leqslant r \leqslant R$, even though the sign pattern exhibited in *Example 1* is not repeated: in fact, $Y_{ij} - (1+r)X_{ij} > 0$ for all i,j and for all feasible r.

Example 3

5 t iron ⊕ 1 labour ⊖ 6 t iron ⊕ 1 cwt coal (11.10a)

10 cwt coal ⊕ 1 labour ⊖ 3 t iron ⊕ 2 cwt coal (11.10b)

This model is productive. From (11.5) and (11.10), I obtain:

$$p_2 = (-2 - 5r)/(1 - 10r) = (5r + 2)/(10r - 1) \quad (11.11a)$$

$$w_{(1)} = (-1 - 20r + 50r^2)/(1 - 10r) = (-50r^2 + 20r + 1)/(10r - 1) \quad (11.11b)$$

$p_2 > 0$ for $r > 1/10$ and $w_{(1)} > 0$, $dw_{(1)}/dr < 0$ if $1/10 < r < R = (2 + \sqrt{6})/10$. This example illustrates the possibility, which can arise with joint production, that prices and the wage rate are not positive throughout the range $0 \leqslant r \leqslant R$. If the second commodity is chosen as numeraire, I obtain:

$$p_1 = (10r - 1)/(5r + 2) \quad (11.12a)$$

$$w_{(2)} = (-50r^2 + 20r + 1)/(5r + 2) \quad (11.12b)$$

$p_1 > 0$ for $r > 1/10$ and $w_{(2)} > 0$ if $0 \leqslant r < R$.

Straightforward calculations show that $dw_{(2)}/dr > 0$ for $0 \leqslant r < (-4 + \sqrt{30})/10 \simeq 0.148$. That is, for $0.1 < r < 0.148$, the price system is positive and the w–r curve is upward-sloping. The sign of the slope of the w–r curve is thus seen to depend on the choice of numeraire.

Example 3 demonstrates two ways in which the results of Chapter 4 on single-product industries models cannot be extended to pure joint production. First, the price is not necessarily positive throughout the interval $0 \leqslant r \leqslant R$. Second, the w–r curve is not necessarily downward-sloping and, indeed, the sign of its slope can vary. In *Examples 1–3*, the maximum rate of profit, R, is obtained as the smallest value of r at which the numerator of w is zero. This compares with the procedures in Chapters 4 and 9. For the single-product industries, circulating capital model, I have (4.27) of Chapter 4:

$$w = f(r)/g(r)$$

Considerable space was devoted to proving that there exists $R > 0$

such that $f(r) > 0$ for $0 \leqslant r < R$, $f(R) = 0$ and $g(r) > 0$ for $0 \leqslant r \leqslant R$. For the simplest single-product industries, fixed capital model in sections 9.3–9.5, the numerator of the wage is given by (9.16) of Chapter 9; again, considerable space was devoted to proving the existence of a positive value R such that $F(r) > 0$ for $0 \leqslant r < R$, $F(R) = 0$. At this stage, consider the following example due to Manara (1980):

Example 4

$$1 \text{ t iron} \oplus 1.1 \text{ cwt coal} \oplus 3 \text{ labour}$$

$$\ominus 1.09 \text{ t iron} \oplus 1.144 \text{ cwt coal} \tag{11.13a}$$

$$1.1 \text{ t iron} \oplus 1 \text{ cwt coal} \oplus 1 \text{ labour}$$

$$\ominus 1.144 \text{ t iron} \oplus 0.99 \text{ cwt coal} \tag{11.13b}$$

This model is productive. With the first commodity as numeraire:

$$p_2 = (0.042 - 2.3r)/(0.074 + 1.9r) \tag{11.14a}$$

$$w_{(1)} = (0.21r^2 - 0.168r + 0.002836)/(0.074 + 1.9r) \tag{11.14b}$$

For $r > 0.042/2.3 \simeq 0.0183$, $p_2 < 0$. However, the numerator of $w_{(1)}$ does not have any real roots: so $w_{(1)} > 0$ for all $r \geqslant 0$. In this case, the maximum rate of profit of the system is given by the largest value of r at which $p_2 = 0$ and not be the smallest value of r at which the numerator of w is zero. A similar situation can arise in the fixed capital model of Chapter 9 and the intensive rent model of Chapter 10. In both, it may happen that a technique can support a positive real wage for $0 \leqslant r < R$ ($w = 0$ when $r = R$) but not a positive price system over this interval; the ageing machine price may be negative for $\tilde{r} < r \leqslant R$. In such a situation, the maximum rate of profit of the technique in equation is $\tilde{r}$ not R. For further discussion of the problem of defining the maximum rate of profit in a joint production model, see Bidard (1986a).

It can be seen from (11.11a) and (11.12a) that the relative price is negative at $r = 0$. It can be seen from (11.10) that the second process produces a larger net output of each commodity, using the same quantity of labour (2 t iron $\oplus$ 2 cwt coal as against 1 t iron $\oplus$ 1 cwt coal). Hence, the second process is physically more efficient than the first at $r = 0$. It will be shown in the next section that this notion of physical efficiency is relevant to the analysis of the question raised by *Example 3*, namely the existence of positive prices of production.

11.5 Positive Prices

The purpose of this section is to provide a set of necessary and sufficient conditions for a positive price system to exist at a given value of the rate of profit. I observed in section 11.4 that the relative price in (11.11) was negative at $r = 0$ and the second process was physically more efficient than the first: this is an example of a property of the price system being related to a property of the quantity system. As I wish to derive a result on the price system at any value of r, it follows that I must correspondingly extend the notion of physical efficiency. When $r > 0$, the inputs in the price equations are multiplied by $(1+r)$, as in (11.4). If I wish to examine the dual quantity system, each input is multiplied by $(1+ \varrho)$. Thus, the quantity equations corresponding to (11.4) are, given a uniform growth rate ϱ:

$$Y_{11} + Y_{12} = (1+\varrho)(X_{11} + X_{12}) + F_1 \qquad (11.15a)$$

$$Y_{21} + Y_{22} = (1+\varrho)(X_{21} + X_{22}) + F_2 \qquad (11.15b)$$

where F_i is the final demand for commodity i. Let:

$$C_{ij} \equiv C_{ij}(\varrho) \equiv Y_{ij} - (1+\varrho)X_{ij} \quad i,j = 1,2 \qquad (11.16)$$

C_{ij} can be interpreted as the net output of commodity i from process j when there is balanced growth at rate ϱ; that is, the actual stationary state net output plus the increased advances of means of production when there is growth at rate ϱ. Obviously, from (11.16), (11.15) can be rewritten as:

$$C_{11}(\varrho) + C_{12}(\varrho) = F_1 \qquad (11.17a)$$

$$C_{21}(\varrho) + C_{22}(\varrho) = F_2 \qquad (11.17b)$$

Armed with (11.16), I can now describe each production process by a triple, rather than a quintuple as previously. For, at growth rate ϱ, process one can be represented by $\{L_1; C_{11}(\varrho), C_{21}(\varrho)\}$ and process two by $\{L_2; C_{12}(\varrho), C_{22}(\varrho)\}$. Then, given ϱ, the efficiency of the two processes can be compared by examining the respective net outputs and labour inputs. For example, process one is more efficient at ϱ than process two if each net output is at least as great in one, while the labour is at least as great in two. Formalising this notion, I have the following:

Definition 4: One process dominates (or is physically more efficient than) another at growth rate ϱ if there exist two numbers a and b such that:

$$aC_{11}(\varrho) + bC_{12}(\varrho) \geqslant 0 \qquad (11.18a)$$

$$aC_{21}(\varrho) + bC_{22}(\varrho) \geqslant 0 \qquad \text{walosi} \qquad (11.18a)$$

$$-aL_1 - bL_2 \geqslant 0 \qquad (11.18c)$$

Obviously, a and b must be of opposite sign. So, if (11.18) hold with $a > 0$ and $b < 0$, it follows (after scaling, if necessary) that the first process produces at least as much of each commodity as the second process, using at most as much labour; if $a < 0$, $b > 0$, it is the second process that is the more efficient.

As an application of the definition, consider a two-sector, two-process, single-product industries model, as in Chapters 3,4 and 7. Inequalities (11.11) cannot be satisfied because $C_{11}(\varrho)$ and $C_{22}(\varrho)$ are positive, while $C_{12}(\varrho)$ and $C_{21}(\varrho)$ are negative. So, dominance cannot arise in a square single-product industries model.

From this discussion and *Example 3*, both negative prices and dominance by one process of another can occur in multiple- but not single-product industries models. So, it is reasonable to conjecture that the concept of physical efficiency, as defined above, captures an essential difference between the two types of model: sufficiently so as to be able to explain the existence of negative prices under joint production. Consider the co-existence of positive prices of production (at a non-negative rate of profit) with dominance by one process of another; for the sake of simplicity, operate with labour-commanded prices. If the first process dominates the second, say, it follows that, at any set of positive prices, it will obtain the higher rate of profit. However, as I am dealing with prices of production, there is a uniform rate of profit. Consequently, one of the prices must be negative. To conclude, if there is dominance, prices of production cannot be positive. This is the economic explanation of the following:

> *Result 21:* There are positive prices of production at rate of profit r if and only if there is no dominance at growth rate r.

To prove this result formally, I first of all rewrite the price equations (11.4) as:

$$P_1C_{11}(r) + P_2C_{21}(r) - L_1 = 0 \tag{11.19a}$$

$$P_1C_{12}(r) + P_2C_{22}(r) - L_2 = 0 \tag{11.19b}$$

using (11.16) and the definition of labour-commanded prices. In essence, I shall manipulate the inequalities (11.18) and the equations (11.19).

Assume first that (11.19) has a positive solution P_1, P_2. Suppose that (11.18) holds for $\varrho = r$. Multiply (11.19a) by a, (11.19b) by b and add the resulting equations to obtain:

$$a(P_1C_{11}(r) + P_2C_{21}(r) - L_1) + b(P_1C_{12}(r) + P_2C_{22}(r) - L_2) = 0 \tag{11.20a}$$

Next multiply (11.18a) by $P_1 > 0$, (11.18b) by $P_2 > 0$ and add the resulting inequalities to (11.18c) to obtain:

$$a(P_1C_{11}(r) + P_2C_{21}(r) - L_1) + b(P_1C_{12}(r) + P_2C_{22}(r) - L_2) > 0 \tag{11.20b}$$

(11.20b) is plainly inconsistent with (11.20a). Hence, if (11.19) has a positive solution, the inequalities (11.18) cannot be satisfied, which means that there is no dominance at r.

To derive the reverse implication, assume that (11.19) does not have a positive solution. From (11.19), I have:

$$P_1 = (L_1C_{22}(r) - (L_2C_{21}(r))/D \tag{11.21a}$$

$$P_2 = (-L_1C_{12}(r) + (L_2C_{11}(r))/D \tag{11.21b}$$

where

$$D = C_{11}(r)C_{22}(r) - C_{12}(r)C_{21}(r) \tag{11.21c}$$

Suppose that $D > 0$, $P_1 > 0$, $P_2 < 0$. Then from (11.21a) and (11.21b), I have:

$$L_1C_{22}(r) - L_2C_{21}(r) > 0 \tag{11.22a}$$

$$-L_1C_{12}(r) + L_2C_{11}(r) < 0 \tag{11.22b}$$

or after multiplying (11.22b) by -1:

$$L_1C_{22}(r) - L_2C_{21}(r) > 0 \tag{11.23a}$$

$$L_1C_{12}(r) - L_2C_{11}(r) > 0 \tag{11.23b}$$

Now consider the expressions on the left-hand sides of (11.18a) and (11.18b). Associating a with $-L_2$, b with L_1, I have from (11.23a) and (11.23b) respectively:

$$aC_{11}(r) + bC_{12}(r) > 0 \tag{11.24a}$$

$$aC_{21}(r) + bC_{22}(r) > 0 \tag{11.24b}$$

and

$$-aL_1 + bL_2 = 0 \tag{11.24c}$$

by selection of a and b. So, (11.18a)–(11.8c) are satisfied and there is dominance. A similar conclusion obtains if $D > 0$, $P_1 < 0$, $P_2 > 0$. Now suppose that $D > 0$, $P_1 < 0$, $P_2 < 0$. Then from (11.21):

$$(L_1C_{22}(r) - L_2C_{21}(r))/D < 0 \tag{11.25a}$$

$$(-L_1C_{12}(r) + L_2C_{11}(r))/D < 0 \tag{11.25b}$$

As the system is productive at growth rate r:

$$C_{11}(r) + C_{12}(r) > 0 \tag{11.26a}$$

$$C_{21}(r) + C_{22}(r) > 0 \tag{11.26b}$$

Multiplying (11.25a) by (11.26a), (11.25b) by (11.26b) and adding the resulting expressions, I obtain:

$$L_1(C_{11}(r)C_{22}(r) - C_{12}(r)C_{21}(r))/D$$
$$+ L_2(C_{11}(r)C_{22}(r) - C_{12}(r)C_{21}(r))/D < 0$$

or

$$L_1 + L_2 < 0 \qquad (11.27)$$

As $L_1 > 0$, $L_2 > 0$, it follows from (11.27) that $D > 0$, $P_1 < 0$, $P_2 < 0$ cannot hold.

I have so far examined the three possibilities in which the solution of (11.21) is not positive and $D > 0$: the first two lead to dominance and the third cannot occur. Having dealt with the three possibilities when $D > 0$, I now consider those when $D < 0$.

Let $D < 0$, $P_1 > 0$, $P_2 < 0$. Then from (11.21):

$$(L_1C_{22}(r) - L_2C_{21}(r))/D > 0 \qquad (11.28a)$$
$$(-L_1C_{12}(r) + L_2C_{11}(r))/D < 0 \qquad (11.28b)$$

or

$$-L_1C_{22}(r) + L_2C_{21}(r) > 0 \qquad (11.29a)$$
$$-L_1C_{12}(r) + L_2C_{11}(r) > 0 \qquad (11.29b)$$

By the same line of argument as in (11.23) and (11.24), it follows that (11.18a)–(11.18c) are satisfied. Similarly, if $D < 0$, $P_1 < 0$, $P_2 > 0$. Finally, let $D < 0$, $P_1 < 0$, $P_2 < 0$. Then from (11.21):

$$(L_1C_{22}(r) - L_2C_{21}(r))/D < 0 \qquad (11.30a)$$
$$(-L_1C_{12}(r) + L_2C_{11}(r))/D < 0 \qquad (11.30b)$$

The same line of argument as in (11.25)–(11.27) shows that this also leads to a contradiction. So, if the solution to (11.21) is not positive, one of the possibilities cannot occur and the other two lead to dominance.

By combining the arguments when $D > 0$ and $D < 0$, I have shown that, if prices are not positive, one process dominates the other. To conclude: I have proved that, if there are positive prices, there is no dominance and, if prices are not positive, there is dominance. That is, I have established *Result 21*.

This result provides a complete characterisation of positive prices of production. There are positive prices of production at a given rate of profit if and only if, at a growth rate equal to the given rate of profit, one process does not dominate the other. As remarked prior to the statement of *Result 21*, it also applies to single-product industries models. The result has been proved for a two-process model. When fixed capital is treated properly within a two-sector framework, as in Chapter 9, the resulting model has more than two processes. Can *Result 21* be extended to such a model? To do so requires the generalisation of the notion of dominance: from that of one process *vis-à-vis* another to that of one subset of processes *vis-à-vis* the complementary subset of processes. In this way, negative ageing machine prices, which are after all prices of production, can be interpreted in terms of dominance.

11.6 Basic Commodities

The distinction between basic and non-basic commodities can easily be drawn for a single-product industries model with only one technique of production – see section 3.5. As there is a one-to-one correspondence between goods and industries, it is a straigthforward matter to determine whether a particular commodity enters directly or indirectly into the production of all commodities. Complications arise in joint production models because, first, a process can produce more than one output (marketable or not) and, second, a commodity can be produced by more than one process. In either event, it becomes difficult to decide whether a particular commodity enters the production of another commodity: in the first case, it is not obvious *a priori* how a commodity input can be attributed to the separate outputs of the process; a similar comment applies in the second case when, for example, a commodity is produced by two processes, each requiring different commodity inputs. These comments apply not only to the pure joint production models considered earlier in this chapter but also to the fixed capital and land models of Chapters 9 and 10 respectively.

In the single-product industries model of Chapter 3, a commodity is non-basic if and only if the system is decomposable, as illustrated by (3.42) there. The analogue of this pair of price equations for a joint production model occurs when $X_{21} = Y_{21}$ in (11.4) above:

$$(1+r)p_1X_{11} + wL_1 = p_1Y_{11} \tag{11.31a}$$

$$(1+r)(p_1X_{12} + p_2X_{22}) + wL_2 = p_1Y_{12} + p_2Y_{22} \tag{11.31b}$$

Then, if the first commodity is chosen as numeraire, the real wage is determined from (11.31a) and the price of the second commodity from (11.31b). The first commodity can be thought of as basic, the second non-basic.

Suppose next that all inputs and outputs in (11.4) are non-zero and that:

$$X_{21} = dX_{22},\ Y_{21} = dY_{22}, \quad d \text{ constant} \tag{11.32}$$

Subtracting d times (11.4b) from (11.4a), I obtain:

$$(1+r)p_1(X_{11} - dX_{12}) + w(L_1 - dL_2) = p_1(Y_{11} - dY_{12})$$

Collecting this with (11.4b), I have:

$$(1+r)p_1\underline{X}_{11} + w\underline{L}_1 = p_1\underline{Y}_{11} \tag{11.33a}$$

$$(1+r)(p_1X_{12} + p_2X_{22}) + wL_2 = p_1Y_{12} + p_2Y_{22} \tag{11.33b}$$

As (11.33) is formally similar to (11.31), the first commodity is basic, the second non-basic. However, there is one major difference between (11.33), on the one hand, and (11.31) and (11.42) (of Chapter 3), on the other hand. In the latter, the conditions of production in the first industry are independent of those in the second, an invalid conclusion for the former. Thus, the notion of a basic commodity is in general weaker for a joint production model than for a single-product industries model. Roughly speaking, there is both technical and economic decomposability in the single-product industries model while there is usually only economic decomposability in the joint production case.

As further exercises in the use of the notion of a basic commodity, consider the fixed capital and land models of the previous chapters. For purposes of exposition, examine the simplest fixed capital model described in (9.8) of Chapter 9, with price equations (11.9). It might be thought that the old machine is non-basic because, as shown in (11.11), it can be eliminated. However, the elimination of p_3 is not achieved by adding a constant multiple of (11.9c) to (11.9b); it is achieved, in fact, by multiplying the former by $(1+r)$ and adding the resulting equation to the latter. That is, economic decomposability cannot be achieved, at least by trying to eliminate p_3. As it is evident that neither of the other prices can be eliminated, I conclude that all three commodities are basic. Note that, even in an indecomposable single-product industries model, a transformation can be achieved yielding the appearance of decomposability. For the system:

$$p_1 = (1+r)(p_1a_{11} + p_2a_{21}) + wl_1 \qquad (11.34a)$$

$$p_2 = (1+r)(p_1a_{12} + p_2a_{22}) + wl_2 \qquad (11.34b)$$

can be rewritten as:

$$p_1 = (1+r)p_1(a_{11} + (1+r)a_{12}/(1 - (1+r)a_{22}) + w(l_1 + (1+r)l_2/(1 - (1+r)a_{22})) \qquad (11.35a)$$

$$p_2 = (1+r)(p_1a_{12} + p_2a_{22}) + wl_2 \qquad (11.35b)$$

Obviously, I do not infer from (11.35a) that the second commodity is non-basic. Any indecomposable two-sector model can be reduced to (11.35), as part of the solution process. Similarly, in the solution of the fixed capital model, ageing machine prices can be eliminated without implying that the corresponding commodities are non-basic.

This point can be appreciated by considering another example – the intensive rent model of section 10.3. Consider the price equation (10.33) in Chapter 10. Adding $-a_{32}/a_{33}$ times (11.33c) to (11.33b), I obtain:

$$(1+r)\,(p_1^{\gamma}a_{11} + p_2^{\gamma}a_{21}) + w^{\gamma}l_1 = p_1 \qquad (11.36a)$$

$$(1+r)\,p_1^{\gamma}(a_{12} - a_{13}a_{32}/a_{33}) + (1+r)p_2^{\gamma}(a_{22} - a_{23}a_{32}/a_{33})$$

$$+ w^{Y}(l_2 - l_3a_{32}/a_{33}) = p_2^{Y}(1 - a_{32}/a_{33}) \quad (11.36b)$$

With the first commodity as numeraire, p_2^Y and w^Y are determined from (11.36); ϱ^Y can then be obtained from (11.33b) or (11.33c) of Chapter 10. Thus, land is non-basic, as Sraffa argued in section 85. There is economic, not technical, decomposability in the intensive rent model, which resembles the joint production model (11.33) in this respect.

There is an essential difference between, on the one hand, the circulating capital model, (11.34), the fixed capital model of Chapter 9, and the pure joint production model (11.4) where (11.32) is not satisfied, and, on the other hand, the pure joint production model (11.4) where (11.32) is satisfied and the intensive rent model of Chapter 10. In the latter, economic decomposability is achieved by adding a constant multiple of one equation to another; in the former, the multiple applied to an equation depends on r and so is not constant. From the discussion in this section, I advance the following:

> *Definition 5:* In a system where there is an equal number of commodities and processes, a commodity is *non-basic* if its price can be eliminated from a subset of equations by adding a constant multiple of one price equation to at least one other; after the elimination, this subset must have the same number of equations as commodities. A commodity is *basic* if its price cannot be eliminated in this way.

This is essentially the same definition as that provided by Sraffa in section 60 of PCMC.

11.7 Choice of Technique: Part 1

In sections 11.4 and 11.5, I have demonstrated that the theory of prices for a two-process, multiple–product industries model is more complex than the corresponding theory for a single-product industries model. *A fortiori*, it is to be expected that there will be difficulties for a pure joint production model compared with a single-product industries model.

Consider first of all the following technology:

(I): 1 t iron ⊕ 5 cwt coal ⊕ 1 labour ⊖ 5 t iron

⊕ 3 cwt coal (11.37a)

(I): 1 t iron ⊕ 5 cwt coal ⊕ 1 labour ⊝ 5 t iron

⊕ 3 cwt coal (11.37a)

(IIα): 3 t iron ⊕ 2 cwt coal ⊕ 1 labour ⊝ 2 t iron

⊕ 7 cwt coal (11.37b)

(IIβ): 4 t iron ⊕ 3 cwt coal ⊕ 1 labour ⊝ 2 t iron

⊕ 10 cwt coal (11.37c)

where the first industry has only one process, (I), but the second has two, (IIα) and (IIβ), (α) consists of (I) and (IIα), (β) of (I) and (IIϱ), as in Chapter 6. Process (I) produces a net output of 4 t iron and −2 cwt coal, (IIα) a net output of −1 t iron and 5 cwt coal, (IIβ) a net output of −2 t iron and 7 cwt coal. Though each is a multiple-product industry, it does produce a net output of only one commodity, resembling in this respect a single-product industry. Both techniques are productive, as is evident by operating each process at the level of one unit of labour. Any non-negative set of final demands requires both processes to be operated in each technique; that is, a reasonable final demand cannot be met by operating only one process.

Applying the data in (11.37) to (11.5), I have, with the first commodity as numeraire:

Technique (α)

$$p_2^\alpha = (5 + 2r)/(7 + 3r)$$

$$w^\alpha = (18 - 24r - 13r^2)/(7 + 3r);\ dw^\alpha/dr < 0 \qquad (11.38)$$

$$w^\alpha = 18/7;\ R^\alpha = (-24 + \sqrt{1512}/26 \simeq 0.5728$$

Technique (β)

$$p_2^\beta = (6 + 3r)/(9 + 2r)$$

$$w^\beta = (24 - 37r - 17r^2)/(9 + 2r);\ dw^\beta/dr < 0 \qquad (11.39)$$

$$W^\beta = 8/3;\ R^\beta = (-37 + \sqrt{3001})/34 \simeq 0.523$$

It can be seen from (11.38) and (11.39) that both w–r curves are downward-sloping, $W^\beta > W^\alpha$ and $R^\beta < R^\alpha$. Hence, there must be at least one point of intersection between w^α and w^β in the positive quadrant. In the single-product industries model of Chapter 6 and the fixed capital and land model of Chapter 9, I demonstrated that points of intersection between feasible w–r curves were also switch-points between techniques – results that were established as corollaries in the theory of choice of technique by evaluating each technique at the other's prices. To see if this results extends to the pure joint production case, it is necessary to apply the same method of analysis.

Let $s_2(\beta{:}\alpha)$ denote the surplus or loss relative to normal profits when (IIβ) is evaluated at (α)'s prices. From (11.37c) and (11.38), I have:

$$\begin{aligned} s_2(\beta{:}\alpha) &= 2 + 10p_2^\alpha - (1+r)\,(4 + 3p_2^\alpha) - w^\alpha \\ &= (3 - 11\mathrm{r} - 5\mathrm{r}^2)/(7 + 3\mathrm{r}) \qquad (11.40\text{a}) \end{aligned}$$

So:

$$\begin{aligned} s_2(\beta{:}\alpha) &> 0 \text{ for } 0 \leqslant r < \bar{r} = (-11 + \sqrt{181})/10 \simeq 0.245 \\ &= 0 \text{ for } r = \bar{r} \qquad (11.40\text{b}) \\ &< 0 \text{ for } \bar{r} < \mathrm{r} \leqslant R^\alpha \end{aligned}$$

Evaluating (IIα) at (β)'s prices, I obtain from (11.37b) and (11.39):

$$\begin{aligned} s_2(\alpha{:}\beta) &= 2 + 7p_2^\beta - (1+r)\,(3 + 2p_2^\beta) - w^\beta \\ &= (5r^2 + 11r - 3)/(2r + 9) \qquad (11.41\text{a}) \end{aligned}$$

It is clear from (11.40) and (11.41a) that:

$$\begin{aligned} s_2(\alpha{:}\beta) &< 0 \text{ for } 0 \leqslant r < \bar{r} \\ &= 0 \text{ for } r = \bar{r} \qquad (11.41\text{b}) \\ &> 0 \text{ for } \bar{r} < \mathrm{r} \leqslant R^\beta \end{aligned}$$

For $0 \leqslant r < \bar{r}$, (IIβ) reduces costs at (α)'s prices while (IIα) is more expensive than (IIβ) at (β)'s prices. So, over this interval, (β) is the unique cost-minimising technique. For $\bar{r} < r \leqslant R^\alpha$, ($\alpha$) is the unique cost-minimising technique. $\bar{r}$ is a switch-point, both techniques being equally profitable. So, this example resembles the single-product industries and fixed capital models in the sense that choice of technique is determinate at each feasible value of r, i.e. $0 \leqslant r \leqslant R^{\alpha}$, and unique except at a switch-point.

The points of intersection between the w–r curves can be found by equating w^{α} and w^{β} from (11.38) and (11.39). I obtain after straightforward manipulation:

$$25r^3 + 65r^2 + 7r - 6 = 0$$

or

$$(5r^2 + 11r - 3)(5r + 2) = 0 \qquad (11.42)$$

The quadratic factor gives the only point of intersection, $\bar{r}$, in the positive quadrant. So, in this example, the point of intersection between w^{α} and w^{β} is a switch-point; from (11.38) and (11.39), (β) supports the higher real wage for $0 \leqslant r < \bar{r}$, (α) the higher real wage for $\bar{r} < r \leqslant R^{\alpha}$.

The technology described in (11.37) exhibits the same properties as a single-product industries, circulating capital model with regard to choice of technique: first, choice of technique is determinate at each feasible value of r; second, the cost-minimising techniques supports the higher real wage. Thus, the example in (11.37) confirms the theory developed for the simpler single-product industries case. This may come as a surprise, given the content of sections 11.4 and 11.5, and the opening remarks above. To see whether the conclusions drawn from the special case, (11.37), can have any claim to generality, it is necessary either to examine more numerical examples or to provide a general analysis. If a positive result is to be established, the latter course must be adopted. However, if negative results are to be derived, the provision of appropriate numerical examples suffices. (At first, when the outcome is uncertain, the analysis of numerical examples can provide the basis for an educated guess.)

Consider next this technology:

$$\text{(I): } 3 \text{ t iron} \oplus 6 \text{ cwt coal} \oplus 1 \text{ labour} \ominus 6 \text{ t iron} \oplus 5 \text{ cwt coal} \qquad (11.43a)$$

(IIγ): 2 t iron ⊕ 3 cwt coal ⊕ 1 labour ⊖ 3 t iron

⊕ 8 cwt coal (11.43b)

(IIδ): 3 t iron ⊕ 2 cwt coal ⊕ 1 labour ⊖ 5 t iron

⊕ 6 cwt coal (11.43c)

Each process produces a positive net output of both commodities in a stationary state: in this sense, (11.43) differs from (11.37). Yet, (I) produces as net output more of commodity one, iron, while (IIγ) and (IIδ) produce as net output more of the second commodity, coal; in this sense, (11.43) resembles (11.37). Techniques (γ) and (δ), constructed in the obvious way, are both productive. Let final demand be in the proportions of 1 t iron and 1 cwt coal, implying that either (γ) or (δ) and not just one process should be employed. Applying the data in (11.43) to (11.5), I have with the first commodity as numeraire:

Technique (γ)

$$p_2^\gamma = (2 - r)/(4 + r)$$

$$w^\gamma = (14 - 18r + r^2)/(4 + r);\ dw^\gamma/dr < 0 \qquad (11.44)$$

$$W^\gamma = 7/2;\ R^\gamma = 9 - \sqrt{67} \simeq 0.815$$

Technique (δ)

$$p_2^\delta = 1/(3 + 2r)$$

$$w^\delta = (10 - 7r - 6r^2)/(3 + 2r);\ dw^\delta/dr < 0 \qquad (11.45)$$

$$W^\delta = 10/3,\ R^\delta = 5/6$$

Evaluating the alternative processes at the given technique's prices, I have from (11.43) and (11.44):

$$s_2(\delta{:}\gamma) = 5 + 6p_2^\gamma - (1+r)(3 + 2p_2^\gamma) - w^\gamma$$

$$= (2 - 2r^2)/(4 + r) = 2(1 - r^2)/(4 + r) \qquad (11.46a)$$

So:

$$s_2(\delta{:}\gamma) > 0 \text{ for } 0 \leqslant r \leqslant R^\gamma \qquad (11.46b)$$

From (11.43) and (11.45):

$$s_2(\gamma{:}\delta) = 3 + 8p_2^\delta - (1+r)(2 + 3p_2^\delta) - w^\delta$$
$$= (2r^2 - 2)/(3 + 2r) = 2(r^2 - 1)/(4 + r) \qquad (11.47a)$$

So:

$$s_2(\gamma{:}\delta) < 0 \text{ for } 0 \leqslant r \leqslant R^\delta \qquad (11.47b)$$

From (11.46) and (11.47), I conclude that (IIδ) reduces costs at (γ)'s prices, while (IIγ) makes losses at (δ)'s prices. (δ) is the cost-minimising technique for $0 \leqslant r \leqslant R^\delta$.

From (11.44) and (11.45), $W^\gamma > W^\delta$ and $R^\gamma < R^\delta$; hence, there is at least one point of intersection between w^γ and w^δ. Equating (11.44) and (11.45), I obtain as the points of intersection, the solutions of:

$$8r^3 - 2r^2 - 8r + 2 = 0$$

or

$$2(4r - 1)(r^2 - 1) = 0 \qquad (11.48)$$

The only point of intersection in the positive quadrant is $\tilde{r} = 1/4$, which from (11.46) and (11.47) is *not* a switch-point. For $0 \leqslant r < \tilde{r}$, ($\gamma$) supports the higher real wage; for $\tilde{r} < r \leqslant R^\delta$, ($\delta$) supports the higher real wage.

It might be conjectured, on the basis of the results in Chapters 6 and 9, that the cost-minimising technique in a model with only produced means of production supports the higher real wage at a given value of r. Alternatively, it might be conjectured, on the basis of the results in Chapter 10 that the cost-minimising technique in a multiple-product industries model supports the lower real wage. The example, (11.43), effectively refutes both conjectures. The general conclusion to be drawn is that there is no necessary relation between the cost-minimising technique and the technique supporting the higher, or lower, real wage.

In section 96 of PCMC, Sraffa argued that the cost-minimising technique could be identified as that supporting the highest real wage. The numerical example, (11.43), demonstrates Sraffa's arguments to be false in the joint production case. Note that the numerical example satisfies Sraffa's additional assumption introduced in footnote 1, p. 87: 'We assume here (and it is essential for the conclusion) that no commodity's price behaves in the peculiar way described in sections 71–2.' It can easily be seen from (11.44) and (11.45) that there is no such 'peculiar' price behaviour in the example.

11.8 Choice of Technique: Part 2

The two numerical examples in section 11.7 were characterised by the property that choice of technique was determinate at each feasible value of r. Consider now the following example:

$$\text{(I): } 18\text{ t iron} \oplus 5\text{ labour} \ominus 48\text{ t iron} \oplus 10\text{ cwt coal} \qquad (11.49a)$$

$$\text{(II}\varepsilon\text{): } 12\text{ t iron} \oplus 10\text{ labour} \ominus 12\text{ t iron} \oplus 30\text{ cwt coal} \qquad (11.49b)$$

$$\text{(II}\varphi\text{): } 10\text{ cwt coal} \oplus 10\text{ labour} \ominus 12\text{ t iron} \oplus 30\text{ cwt coal} \qquad (11.49c)$$

As in the second example of the previous section, all three processes produce a positive net output of both commodities in a stationary state, with (I) producing more of the first commodity, iron and (IIε) and (IIφ) producing more of the second commodity, coal. Let final demand be in the proportions of 1 t iron to 1 cwt coal, implying that again choice rests between techniques, not processes. Applying the data in (11.49) to (11.5), I have with the first commodity as numeraire:

Technique (ε)

$$p_2^{\varepsilon} = (30 - 12r)/5$$

$$w^{\varepsilon} = (90 - 42r)/5;\ dw^{\varepsilon}/dr < 0 \qquad (11.50)$$

$$W^{\varepsilon} = 18,\ R^{\varepsilon} = 15/7$$

The price system for this technique is well defined for all non-negative r less than or equal to R^{ε}.

Technique (φ)

$$p_2^{\varphi} = (18r - 24)/5r \qquad (11.51a)$$

$$w^{\varphi} = (48 - 18r)(r - 1)/5r \qquad (11.51b)$$

The price system is positive for $4/3 \leqslant r \leqslant 8/3$.

$$dw^{\varphi}/dr = (-90r^2 + 240)/25r^2 \tag{11.51c}$$

so that:

$$\begin{aligned} dw^{\varphi}/dr &> 0 \text{ if } 4/3 \leqslant r < \bar{r} = 2\sqrt{6}/3 \mathrel{\hat{=}} 1.62 \\ &= 0 \text{ if } r = \bar{r} \\ &< 0 \text{ if } \bar{r} \leqslant r \leqslant R^{\varphi} = 8/3 \end{aligned} \tag{11.51d}$$

The maximum real wage occurs when $r = \bar{r}$.

The relevant range of values of r for the question of choice of technique is $4/3 \leqslant r \leqslant 15/7$, as both techniques have positive price systems over this interval. Evaluating (φ) at (ε)'s prices, I have:

$$\begin{aligned} s_2(\varphi{:}\varepsilon) &= 12 + 30p_2^{\varepsilon} - (1+r)p_2^{\varepsilon} - 10w^{\varepsilon} \\ &= 24r^2 - 24r - 48 \\ &= 24(r-2)(r+1) \end{aligned} \tag{11.52a}$$

so that:

$$s_2(\varphi{:}\varepsilon) \gtreqless 0 \text{ as } r \gtreqless 2 \tag{11.52b}$$

in the relevant range. In fact, $s_2(\varphi{:}\varepsilon) < 0$ for $0 \leqslant r < 2$. Evaluating (ε) at (φ)'s prices, I obtain:

$$\begin{aligned} s_2(\varepsilon{:}\varphi) &= 12 + 30p_2^{\varphi} - (1+r)12 - 10w^{\varphi} \\ &= (24r^2 - 24r - 48)/r \\ &= 24(r-2)(r+1)/r \end{aligned} \tag{11.53a}$$

so that:

$$s_2(\varepsilon{:}\varphi) \gtreqless 0 \text{ as } r \gtreqless 2 \tag{11.53b}$$

Regardless of the location of r within the interval $4/3 \leqslant r \leqslant 15/7$, it follows from (11.52b) and (11.53b) that:

$$\text{sign } s_2(\varphi{:}\varepsilon) = \text{sign } s_2(\varepsilon{:}\varphi) \tag{11.54}$$

(In fact, $s_2(\varepsilon{:}\varphi) < 0$ for $r < 4/3$ but (φ)'s price system is negative in this range.)

If (ε) is initially employed for $4/3 \leqslant r < 2$, it follows from (11.52b) that (IIφ) does not reduce costs. As (IIφ) is more expensive than (IIε), there is no reason for the capitalist to switch to (φ). Thus, (ε) is cost minimising over this range. Suppose that (φ) is initially employed over the same range. Then from (11.53b), it follows that (IIε) is more expensive than (IIφ). So, (φ) is also cost minimising over the range $4/3 \leqslant r < 2$. I conclude that, for each value of r greater than or equal to 4/3 but less than 2, choice of technique is determinate but not unique. Now consider the interval $2 < r \leqslant 15/7$. If (ε) is initially employed, it follows from (11.52b) that (IIφ) reduces costs. This justifies a switch to (φ). Suppose that the change of technique is effected and (φ)'s prices are established. Then, from (11.53b), it follows that (IIε) reduces costs at the prevailing prices, implying that there should be a switch back to (ε). Over the interval $2 < r \leqslant 15/7$, each technique is cheaper than the other only at the other's prices. The conclusion is that choice of technique is indeterminate. Contrast this conclusion with that drawn for the interval $4/3 \leqslant r < 2$. Over the lower range, a capitalist would be satisfied with his initial choice of technique, whichever it was. On the other hand, over the upper range, he would be dissatisfied with his choice, whichever it was. At $r = 2$, both techniques are equally profitable, as is evident from (11.52b) and (11.53b): in the terminology of the earlier chapters, this represents a switch-point, as each technique breaks even at the other's prices (in fact, the price systems of (ε) and (φ) are identical at $r = 2$).

This interpretation of $r = 2$ as a switch-point between (ε) and (φ) can be sustained only if one technique is cost minimising for $2-e < r < 2$ and the other is cost minimising for $2 < r < 2+\mathrm{e}$, where e is a small positive number. This is what can happen in the single-product industries models of Chapters 6 and 9 where, as r increases from $\bar{r}-e$ to $\bar{r}+e$, one technique is cost minimising for $r < \bar{r}$, both techniques are equally profitable at $\bar{r}$, and the other technique is cost minimising for $r > \bar{r}$. However, in the joint production example above, both techniques are cost minimising for $r < 2$ and neither is cost minimising for $r > 2$. The familiar transition around a switch-point, characteristic of single-product industries models, does not necessarily extend to pure joint production models. Sraffa's conclusion on choice of technique for

Figure 11.2

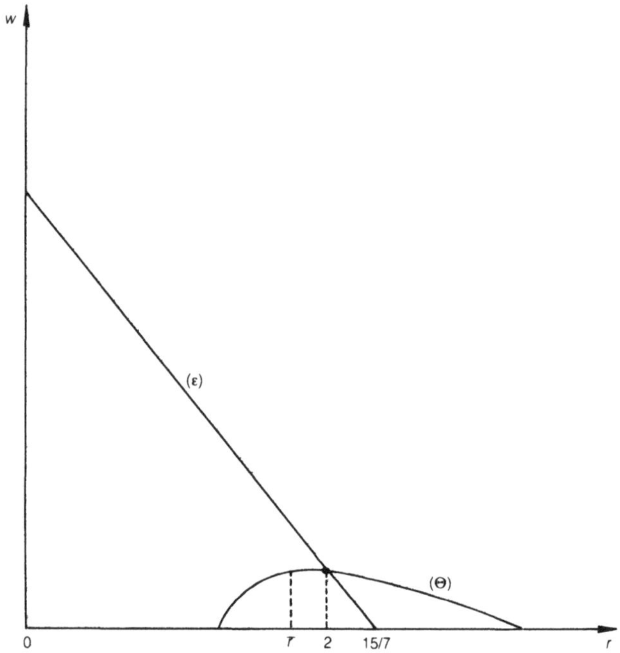

single-product industries models – 'that the *order* of the two methods as to cheapness must be the same in the two systems' (PCMC, section 93, p. 83) – does not apply in multiple-product industries models.

Equating w^{ε} and w^{φ} from (11.50) and (11.51), I have as the points of intersection the solutions of:

$$r^2 - r - 2 = 0 \tag{11.55a}$$

or

$$r = 2, r = -1 \tag{11.55b}$$

This is illustrated in Figure 11.2 overleaf. The conclusion to be drawn from the analysis of w–r curves for this example supports that from the analysis of the second example in section 11.7: namely, the technique supporting the higher real wage is not necessarily cost minimising. In section 11.7, (δ) supports the lower real wage over the interval $0 \leqslant r < 1/4$ but is cost minimising. In this example, the negative conclusion follows trivially because if $r < 2$, both techniques are cost minimising and if $r > 2$, neither is cost minimising.

11.9 Choice of Technique: Part 3 – Okishio's Theorem

In a single-product industries model with only produced means of production – whether capital is circulating or fixed – the introduction of a cost-reducing process results in the adoption of a technique supporting a higher real wage at a given rate of profit: this result is Okishio's Theorem (see *Corollary 11.3*). Consider the second example in section 11.7 for $0 \leqslant r < 1/4$. If (γ) is initially employed, (IIδ) makes super-normal profits at the prevailing prices but (δ) supports a lower real wage than (γ). Trivially, Okishio's Theorem fails for the example in section 11.8 when $2 < r \leqslant 15/7$, where the introduction of a cost-reducing process does not result in the adoption of *any* technique.

As another illustration of the way in which Okishio's Theorem cannot be extended to pure joint production models, consider the following example, where there is joint production in only one industry:

$$\text{(I): } 4 \text{ t iron} \oplus 12 \text{ cwt coal} \oplus 8 \text{ labour} \ominus 8 \text{ t iron} \oplus 16 \text{ cwt coal} \quad (11.56a)$$

$$(\text{II}\psi)\text{: } 2 \text{ cwt coal} \oplus 1 \text{ labour} \ominus 3 \text{ t iron} \quad (11.56b)$$

$$(\text{II}\varkappa)\text{: } 1 \text{ cwt coal} \oplus 1 \text{ labour} \ominus 2 \text{ t iron} \quad (11.56c)$$

Let final demand be in the proportions of 3 t iron to 2 cwt coal. Applying the data in (11.56) to (11.5), I obtain:

$$\begin{aligned} p_2^{\psi} &= 1 \\ w^{\psi} &= 1 - 2r, \quad dw^{\psi}/dr < 0 \\ W^{\psi} &= 1,\ R^{\psi} = 1/2 \end{aligned} \quad (11.57)$$

and

$$p_2^{\varkappa} = (3 + r)/(3 - r)$$

$$w^{\varkappa} = (3 - 6r - r^2)/(3 - r), \quad dw^{\varkappa}/dr < 0 \tag{11.58}$$
$$W^{\varkappa} = 1, R^{\varkappa} = -3 + 2\sqrt{3} \simeq 0.464$$

Evaluating (II$\varkappa$) at (ψ)'s prices, I obtain:

$$s_2(\varkappa:\psi) = r \geqslant 0 \tag{11.59a}$$

and (IIψ) at ($\varkappa$)'s prices:

$$s_2(\psi:\varkappa) = (-r^2 - 5r)/(3 - r) \leqslant 0 \tag{11.59b}$$

For $0 < r \leqslant R^{\varkappa}$, $s_2(\varkappa:\psi) > 0$ and $s_2(\psi:\varkappa) < 0$, implying that ($\varkappa$) is the cost-minimising technique. Yet over this range, ($\varkappa$) supports the lower real wage. From this and the earlier examples, it can be seen that the wage supported by the cost-minimising technique can stand in any relation to that supported by another technique.

11.10 Choice of Technique: Part 4

In this section, I illustrate another possibility that can arise only with joint production. Consider this technology:

$$\text{(I): 10 cwt coal} \oplus \text{10 labour} \ominus \text{10 t iron} \oplus \text{10 cwt coal} \tag{11.60a}$$
$$\text{(II}\lambda\text{): 48 t iron} \oplus \text{10 labour} \ominus \text{48 t iron} \oplus \text{48 cwt coal} \tag{11.60b}$$
$$\text{(II}\eta\text{): 18 t iron} \oplus \text{10 labour} \ominus \text{36 t iron} \oplus \text{36 cwt coal} \tag{11.60c}$$

(I) produces a net output of 10 t iron, (IIλ) a net output of 48 cwt coal, (IIη) a net output of 18 t iron and 36 cwt coal. With final demand in the proportions of 2 t iron to 1 cwt coal, the choice rests between (λ) and (η). Applying the data to (11.5), I have with the first commodity as numeraire:

Technique (λ)

$$\begin{aligned} p_2^{\lambda} &= (5 + 24r)/(24 + 5r) \\ w^{\lambda} &= 24(1 - r^2)/(24 + 5r) \end{aligned} \tag{11.61}$$

Technique (η)

$$p_2^{\eta} = (9r - 4)/(18 + 5r)$$

$$w^{\eta} = 9(2 + r - r^2)/(18 + 5r) \tag{11.62}$$

From (11.61), (λ)'s price system exists for $0 \leqslant r \leqslant 1 = R^{\lambda}$; from (11.62), ($\eta$)'s price system exists for $4/9 \leqslant r \leqslant 2 = R^{\eta}$. Evaluating the alternative processes at the other technique's prices, I have:

$$s_2(\eta{:}\lambda) = (150r^2 + 522r + 372)/(24 + 5r) \tag{11.63a}$$
$$s_2(\lambda{:}\eta) = -(150r^2 + 522r + 372)/(18 + 5r) \tag{11.63b}$$

Clearly, from (11.63), (η) is the cost-minimising technique for $4/9 \leqslant r \leqslant 2$. From (11.63a), $s_2(\eta{:}\lambda) > 0$ even if $0 \leqslant r < 4/9$; though over this interval, (η)'s price system is not positive. The conclusion is that for $0 \leqslant r < 4/9$, (λ) is the only feasible technique (i.e. the only one with positive prices); but it is not cost minimising as (IIη) reduces costs. For $4/9 \leqslant r \leqslant 2$, ($\eta$) is cost minimising. The possibility illustrated here cannot arise in the single-product industries model of Chapter 6, which has a positive price system for $0 \leqslant r \leqslant R$. Under joint production, prices need not be positive over a comparable interval including $r = 0$, as is the case for (η) and as I demonstrated in section 11.5.

The existence of negative prices undoubtedly creates problems in the joint production case for, in section 50 of PCMC, Sraffa excluded those production processes implying such a solution. The rationale for this exclusion is provided in section 70. After observing in section 69 that a price may become negative at a feasible wage rate, Sraffa argues as follows:

> This conclusion is not in itself very startling. All that it implies is that, although in actual fact all prices were positive, a change in the wage might create a situation the logic of which required some of the prices to turn negative; and this being unacceptable, those among the methods of production that give rise to such a result would discarded to make room for others which in the new situation were consistent with positive prices. (p. 59)

The only reason for a change in the process of production is that capitalists have a cheaper alternative. That is, a positive price system comes about, Sraffa appears to argue, through cost minimisation. The example above demonstrates exactly the opposite. Let (η) be initially employed at a rate of profit between 0 and 4/9,

Figure 11.3

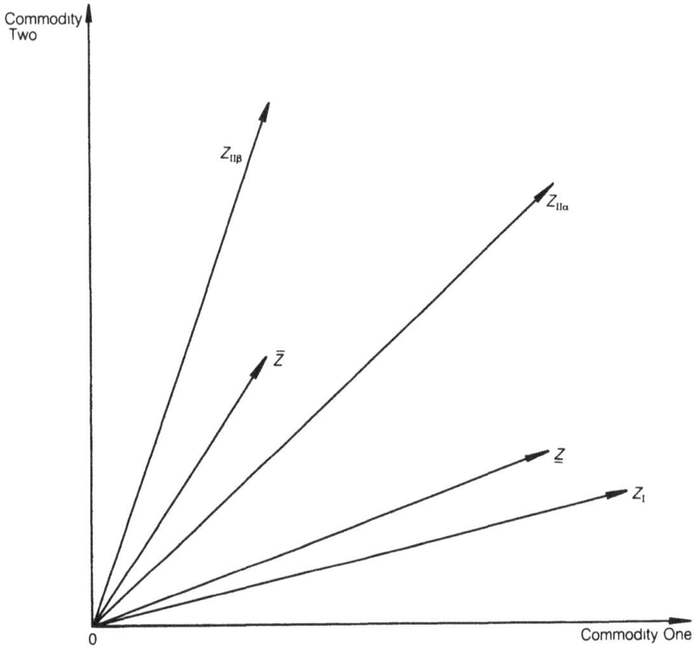

with $p_2^\eta < 0$. Then according to Sraffa's argument, there should be a change in at least one process to effect positive prices. But, from (11.63b), the only alternative, (IIλ), makes losses at (η)'s prices. So, cost minimisation would not bring about the use of (IIλ) if (η) were initially employed. On the other hand, if (λ) were initially employed at the same value of r between 0 and 4/9, the price system would be positive and (IIη) would reduce costs. So, in this case, cost minimisation tends to bring about the selection of that technique which has a negative price.

11.11 Specification of the Technology

The method adopted for the analysis of choice of technique in sections 11.7–11.10 is broadly similar to that in Chapters 7, 9 and 10. For, it is assumed that one industry has only one process available to it, while the other has two. In a single-product industries model with processes (I), (IIα) and (IIβ), it is evident that (IIβ) is the alternative to (IIα) not (I). 'When, however, each process or method produces several commodities and each commodity is produced by several methods, this criterion fails. And the problem arises of how to identify among the pre-existing methods the one to which the new method is an alternative' (PCMC, section 96, p. 86). Why should the new process not be available to both industries?

This problem was avoided in sections 11.7–11.10 by assuming that a second process was available to only one industry: such an assumption is more easily justified for a single-product than for a multiple-product industries model. Closer examination reveals this assumption not to be so arbitrary, for it is based on the level of final demands. To illustrate this point, consider Figure 11.3. Z_I is the net output vector from process (I), similarly for (IIα) and (IIβ). If final demand is given by $O\underline{Z}$, (IIβ) is the alternative to (IIα), not (I); for ((I), (IIα)) and ((I), (IIβ)) can both meet $O\underline{Z}$ by operating their processes at positive levels, while ((IIα), (IIβ)) cannot. Similarly, if final demand is given by $O\bar{Z}$, (IIα) is an alternative to (I) and (IIβ) is a process that will always be employed: in other words, choice rests between ((I), (IIβ)) and ((IIα), (IIβ)). This is to emphasise the point made in section 11.3: in multiple-product industries models, techniques are defined relative to a given final demand.

Sraffa's theory of choice of technique for joint production models, presented in PCMC, section 96, is erroneous. First, he identifies intersections between *w–r* curves as switch-points between techniques: this is not necessarily true, as has been shown above. Second, he argues that the cost-minimising technique is the one supporting the highest real wage; again, from the previous sections, this is not necessarily true.

> Consider the system which at the newly given rate of profits allows of the highest wage; if we regard the wage, instead of the rate of profits, as being given, we shall find that this system will also be the most profitable one since, given *any* of those wages, it will allow the payment of a higher rate of profits than does any other systems. (PCMC, section 96, p. 87)

While it is valid for single-product industries models with only produced means of production, Sraffa's theory of choice of technique is invalid for such multiple-product industries models as those considered in this chapter.

11.12 Conclusion

By considering numerical examples, I have shown in this chapter that the introduction of a cost-reducing process of production can result, inter alia, in:

(a) a lower real wage in the comparison between long-run equilibria (see section 11.9);
(b) a continual switching between two techniques because each is more profitable than the other only at the other's prices (see section 11.8 where $r > 2$);
(c) a negative price for one commodity as a formal solution for long-run equilibrium (see section 11.10).

In addition, I have exhibited these possibilities:

(d) each of two techniques is cheaper than the other only at its own prices (as in section 11.8 with $r < 2$);
(e) points of intersection between w–r curves are not necessarily switch-points between cost-minimising techniques (see the second example in section 11.7).

In each of these ways, joint production models can differ from the single-product industries model of Chapter 6.

In Chapters 6 and 9–11, I have considered models in order of increasing generality. The single-product industries, circulating capital model of Chapter 6 exhibits regularity in the following senses:

(i) a productive technique (ι) has a positive price system and real wage over the interval $0 \leqslant r \leqslant R^{\iota}$;
(ii) the real wage is a decreasing function of r over this interval;
(iii) choice of technique is determinate at each feasible value of r (i.e. $0 \leqslant r \leqslant \max R^{\iota}$) and is in fact unique apart from switch-points;
(iv) the cost-minimising technique supports the highest real wage;
(v) points of intersection of w–r curves are switch-points between techniques.

It was seen in Chapter 9 that a single-product industries, fixed capital technique can support a negative ageing machine price at a feasible value of *r*; and in the land models of Chapter 10, a technique could support a negative land price or rent in its feasible range. This similarity between fixed capital and land models was enhanced by the interpretation that could be placed on negative non-marketable commodity prices: they served as indicators of efficiency in choice of technique. The fixed capital model shared the other properties, (i)–(v), with the circulating capital model while the land models did not. The extensive rent model possesses the property of determinacy in choice of technique, namely (iii), but not (iv). The intensive rent model does not share (ii)–(iv) with the circulating capital model. As demonstrated in this chapter, a joint production model does not necessarily possess properties (i)–(v).

The numerical examples of this chapter provide a basis for the argument that the 'law of the excluded middle' ceases to apply to multiple-product industries models. This law can be said to hold for single-product industries models (with only produced means of production) because a technique is either the cheapest or more expensive than another technique at a given feasible value of *r* (regardless of which technique's prices are actually used in the calculation): there are no other possibilities. By contrast, in a joint production model, it is possible that choice of technique is indeterminate because each of two techniques is cheaper than the other only at the other's prices: this implies non-existence of a cost-minimising technique in a joint production model. Furthermore, it is possible in joint production to have two techniques each more profitable than the other only at its own prices: choice of technique is determinate, as in the single-product industries case, but not unique. Also, in joint production, a cost-reducing technique can have negative prices. It does not follow from these examples that the criterion of cost-minimisation should be abandoned. Such a course of action would be justified only if there was an independent reason for expecting determinacy and uniqueness (combined to give 'regularity') in all cases. Yet the results on determinacy for single-product industries models are themselves based on the cost-minimisation hypothesis. It may be that familiarity with the results from the relatively simpler single-product industries models conditions us to anticipate determinacy in choice of technique for all multiple-product industries models.

In section 1.2, I advanced the view that prices can be interpreted as centres of gravitation. It is possible to make out a case for such an interpretation in single-product industries models, though proper consideration requires specification of a more complex model so that stability can be analysed. The numerical examples discussed in earlier sections, and summarised in (a)–(e), call this interpretation into doubt when there is joint production, even before stability questions are addressed. For, if there is continual switching between two techniques, as in (b), which technique describes the long-run equilibrium or centre of gravitation? Similarly, for (c) and (d).

Commentary

Sraffa discussed pure joint production models in chapters VII–IX of PCMC, considerable space being devoted to the construction of the Standard System. Apparently, Sraffa considered fixed capital and land to be more important than pure joint production – see foonote 1, p. 43 and the first paragraph of section 73. Sraffa treated final demand in joint production in sections 50 and 53 and presented his theory of choice of technique in section 96 of Chapter 12.

In sections 11.4 and 11.5, I have drawn attention to certain difficulties with the notion of prices of production in a multiple-product industries model: see Manara (1980) and Bidard (1986a) for further discussion. Bidard argues in favour of the maximum rate of profit's being defined as in von Neumann models. For an account of the von Neumann model, see Champernowne (1945–6) before von Neumann (1945–6). On the relation between von Neumann and Sraffa, see Steedman (1976), Schefold (1980) and Bidard (1986b), all of which are quite advanced.

Manara (1980) provides a critique of the Standard Commodity in joint production. There are other papers in Pasinetti (1980) and Bidard (1984) dealing with joint production questions. The notion of dominance and its relation to prices of production has been discussed by Filippini and Filippini (1982) among others.

In Woods (1984b), I have discussed Okishio's Theorem in the context of joint production using a slightly different model from that in section 11.9.

The approach to choice of technique adopted here follows Salvadori (1982, 1985) and Bidard (1986c).

Exercises

1. Suppose constant returns to scale obtains for each of the processes in *Examples 1–4*, section 11.2. For each example, find the level at which

each process is operated to meet a final demand of 2 t iron and 3 cwt coal (i.e. obtain formal solutions).

2. Consider Figure 11.1. Prove that, if final demand lies outside the triangle OZ_1Z_2, extended if necessary, it is more profitable to employ a single process than a technique. Illustrate by reference to *Example 1*, section 11.2.

3. Solve the price equations of a two-processes, two-commodity joint production model where $Y_{ii} - X_{ii} > 0$, for both i, $Y_{ij} - X_{ij} < 0$, $i \neq j$.

4. Continuation of 3.
   (a) Contrast the properties of the model in exercise 3 with those of a single-product industries, circulating capital model.
   (b) Show that the model in exercise 3 can be transformed into a vertically integrated single-product industries model. (See Pasinetti, 1973, and Steedman, 1980.)
   (c) Investigate the conditions for relative price invariance in this model.

5. Consider *Example 1* in section 11.4. Check the properties of this technique. What is the effect of changing the numeraire?

6. Analyse the price equations of a two-process model where there is proportionality of both products and means of production in the two processes.

7. Repeat exercise 5 using *Example 2* of section 11.4.

8. Repeat exercise 5 using *Example 3* of section 11.4.

9. Repeat exercise 5 using *Example 4* of section 11.4.

10. Analyse the price system of the following model:

    1 t iron ⊕ 2 qr wheat ⊕ 1 labour ⊖ 2 t iron

    ⊕ 3 qr wheat

    1 t iron ⊕ 1 qr wheat ⊕ 2 labour ⊖ 3 t iron

    ⊕ 3 qr wheat.

11. Analyse the price system of this model:

    1 t iron ⊕ 2 qr wheat ⊕ 1 labour ⊖ 8 t iron

    ⊕ 1 qr wheat

    1 t iron ⊕ 1 qr wheat ⊕ 1/2 labour ⊖ 6 t iron

    Is this model productive?

12. Analyse the following model:

    1 t iron ⊕ 2 qr wheat ⊕ 1 labour ⊖ 8 t iron
    ⊕ 3 qr wheat
    1 t iron ⊕ 1 qr wheat ⊕ 1/3 labour ⊖ 3 t iron
    ⊕ 1 qr wheat.

13. Analyse the following model:

    1 t iron ⊕ 2 qr wheat ⊕ 1 labour ⊖ 21.8 t iron
    ⊕ 11 qr wheat
    1 t iron ⊕ 1 qr wheat ⊕ 1/4 labour ⊖ 7.8 t iron
    ⊕ 4 qr wheat.

14. Analyse the following model:

    5 t iron ⊕ 1 labour ⊖ 8 t iron ⊕ 2 qr wheat
    5 qr wheat ⊕ 1 labour ⊖ 1 t iron ⊕ 9 qr wheat.

(Exercises 10–14 are due to Bidard (1986a).)

15. Analyse this model:

    25 t iron ⊕ 5 labour ⊖ 30 t iron ⊕ 5 qr wheat
    10 qr wheat ⊕ 1 labour ⊖ 3 t iron ⊕ 12 qr wheat.

(Steedman, 1975)

16. Apply the concept of dominance from section 11.5 to *Example 3* of section 11.4.

17. Apply the concept of dominance to *Example 4* of section 11.4.

18. Apply the concept of dominance to exercise 13.

19. Apply the concept of dominance to exercises 8–12.

20. Apply the concept of dominance to *Examples 1–6* of section 9.4 to provide an interpretation of negative ageing machine prices.

21. Can the concept of dominance be applied to rectangular models? (i.e. where the number of commodities is not equal to the number of processes.)

22. Discuss the application of the chain-index method from Chapter 7 to pure joint production models.

23. Analyse the following model:

 2 qr wheat ⊕ 1 labour ⊖ 5 qr wheat

 1 t iron ⊕ 1 labour ⊖ 5 qr wheat ⊕ 1 t iron

 4 labour ⊖ 1 t iron

 i.e. Find the price system of each technique. Determine the ordering of cost-minimising techniques. Construct the aggregate production function, if possible.

24. Repeat exercise 23 for the model consisting of the processes in that question combined with:

 1 qr wheat ⊕ 1 labour ⊖ 3.5 qr wheat.

25. Analyse the following model:

 1 labour ⊖ 2 qr wheat

 1 qr wheat ⊕ 4 labour ⊖ 17 qr wheat

 1 t iron ⊕ 1 labour ⊖ 6 qr wheat ⊕ 1 t iron

 1 labour ⊖ 2 t iron.

 1 t copper ⊕ 1 labour ⊖ 8 qr wheat ⊕ 1 t copper

 2 t copper ⊕ 1 labour ⊖ 3 t copper

26. Analyse the following model:

 2 qr wheat ⊕ 1 labour ⊖ 5 qr wheat

 1 t iron ⊕ 1 labour ⊖ 5 qr wheat ⊕ 1 t iron

 4 labour ⊖ 1 t iron

 14 qr wheat ⊕ 1 labour ⊖ 21 qr wheat

(Exercises 23–26 are due to Bliss (1975). In each of these, at least one of the means of production is in effect everlasting, an amalgam of the treatment of non-produced means of production from Chapter 10 and fixed capital from Chapter 9.)

27. Check techniques (α) and (β) in (11.37)–(11.39).

28. Check techniques (γ) and (δ) in (11.43)–(11.45).

29. Check techniques (ε) and (φ) in (11.49)–(11.51).

30. Check techniques (ψ) and ($\varkappa$) in (11.56)–(11.58).

31. Check techniques (λ) and (η) in (11.60)–(11.62).

32. Analyse the following model:

    18 cwt coal ⊕ 10 labour ⊖ 48 cwt coal ⊕ 10 t iron

    10 t iron ⊕ 10 labour ⊖ 12 cwt coal ⊕ 30 t iron

    12 cwt coal ⊕ 10 labour ⊖ 12 cwt coal ⊕ 30 t iron

    with final demand proportional to 1 t iron, 1 cwt coal.

33. Consider Sraffa's method of constructing alternative techniques in the third paragraph of section 96. Can it be justified?

34. Investigate the question of relative price invariance for a pure joint production model.

35. Consider the numerical examples in sections 11.7–11.10 where choice of technique is either not unique or indeterminate. Are the conclusions altered if the third process is made available only to the first industry, changing final demands if appropriate?

36. Analyse the following model:

    1 qr wheat ⊕ 5 t iron ⊕ 1 labour ⊖ 3.1 qr wheat
    ⊕ 6 t iron

    5 qr wheat ⊕ 1 t iron ⊕ 1 labour ⊖ 6 qr wheat
    ⊕ 3.1 t iron

    1 qr wheat ⊕ 1 t iron ⊕ 1 labour ⊖ 2.1 qr wheat
    ⊕ 2.1 t iron

37. Analyse the following model:

    1 qr wheat ⊕ 5 t iron ⊕ 1 labour ⊖ 1.6 qr wheat
    ⊕ 7 t iron

    The other two processes are the last two from exercise 36.

(Exercises 36 and 37 are due to Bidard, 1986c.)

38. Consider the following model due to Samuelson (1966):

    (α) 1 unit of labour ⊖ 1 new α-machine

    1 new α-machine ⊖ 18 units of output ⊕
    1 1-year-old α-machine

    1 1-year-old α-machine ⊖ 1 2-year-old α-machine

    1 2-year-old α-machine ⊖ 54 units of output

    (β) 1 unit of labour ⊖ 1 new β-machine

1 new β-machine ⊖ 1 1-year-old β-machine

1 1-year-old β-machine ⊖ 63 units of output

(a) Write down the price equations for (α) and (β).
(b) Determine the choice of technique at each feasible value of r.

(Compare exercise 49 in Chapter 9.)

12
Review

12.1 Introduction

In Chapters 2–11, I have concentrated mainly on the exposition and analysis of the theory of value presented in PCMC. In this final chapter, I propose taking a broader view, relating Sraffa's book to his other published work and contrasting Sraffa's, or the neo-Ricardian, approach to the prevailing neo-classical methodology. An overall assessment of Sraffa's output is complicated by the fact that his first major article (Sraffa, 1925) is not generally available in an approved English translation. Rather than rely on an unapproved translation or second-hand accounts, I have decided to put this Italian article aside. In so doing, I am not completely ignoring Sraffa's views on the laws of returns for '(T)he opening pages of this article (i.e. Sraffa, 1926) contain a summary of the conclusions of a paper on "Relazione fra costa e quantita prodotta" published in Vol. II of the Annali di Economia (i.e. Sraffa, 1925)';[1] and there is also Sraffa's related contribution to the 1930 *Economic Journal* Symposium on Increasing Returns and the Representative Firm. In section 12.2, I discuss Sraffa's views on the laws of returns. This provides an appropriate introduction to a general discussion in section 12.3 of Sraffa's contribution to the debate on the theories of value and capital, briefly alluded to in Chapters 6 and 7. In sections 12.4–12.8, I examine some areas of research stimulated by Sraffa's work.

12.2 Sraffa on the Laws of Returns

Sraffa began his 1926 article as follows:

> A striking feature of the present position of economic science is the almost universal agreement at which economists have ar-

> rived regarding the theory of competitive value, which is inspired by the fundamental symmetry between the forces of demand and those of supply, and is based upon the assumption that the essential causes determining the price of particular commodities may be simplified and grouped together so as to be represented by a pair of intersecting curves of collective demand and supply. This state of things is in such marked contrast with the controversies on the theory of value by which political economy was characterised during the past century, that it might almost be thought that from these clashes of thought the spark of an ultimate truth had been struck.[2]

Sraffa's purpose was to dispel any such illusion. His critique was directed at the Marshallian supply curve, based on the laws of increasing and diminishing returns – as he put it, a dark spot disturbing the harmony of the whole theory of value. The foundations of the supply curve 'are actually so weak as to be unable to support the weight imposed upon them'.[3] Sraffa advanced three lines of argument to justify his position.

First, the laws of diminishing and increasing returns were heterogeneous, having different origins and rationales. The natural home for the law of diminishing returns was the theory of income distribution, the law itself originating in the analysis of rent (see chapter II of Ricardo, 1951). By contrast, the law of increasing returns was an aspect of the division of labour within the theory of production (see the early chapters of Smith, 1970). When transferred to the theory of value to constitute the law of non-proportional returns, both had to be modified. For example, the law of diminishing returns was applied to all factors fixed in supply and not just to land; also, some types on increasing returns (such as internal) had to be excluded as they were incompatible with competitive conditions.

Second, granted this heterogeneity, the classification of an industry depended on its defining characteristics. To be specific, the wider the definition of an industry, the greater the likelihood that all firms employing a given factor of production fixed in supply would be encompassed; hence, it would be expected that diminishing returns would play the more important role and the industry could be described in terms of increasing cost. On the other hand, if a narrow definition were adopted, say in terms of a given final commodity produced, increasing returns would be more likely to predominate; in such a case, an industry would employ only a small part of the available supply of each factor of production, with the result that it would experience decreasing costs. The classification of decreasing and increasing cost industries also depended on the time horizon adopted: in the short run, diminishing returns prevailed while, in the longer run, there is a greater probability of increasing returns. These definitional problems by themselves raised serious questions about the validity of constructing an industry supply curve, based on non-proportional costs, to be used in conjunction with an industry demand curve in equilibrium analysis.

Sraffa's third and strongest line of argument related to the nature of the laws of returns themselves. To be useful in determining the equilibrium value of a commodity, the supply curve had to satisfy two conditions: first, it must be independent of the industry demand curve and of the supply curve of every other industry; and, second, it was valid only for small variations in the quantity produced. Consider the case of diminishing returns. If a small number of industries employ the same fixed factor of production, it follows that a more intensive utilisation of the factor by one industry will raise the cost of that factor to all; so, the first condition is not satisfied. Next suppose that many industries employ the fixed factor. A large change in the output of any one industry is required to raise the costs of all: so, the second condition is violated. The conclusion is that either all industries are subject to varying costs or small changes in any industry's output result in proportional changes in cost: if the former, partial equilibrium analysis is invalid[4] and, if the latter, there are constant returns to scale. Similar conclusions can be drawn for the increasing returns case. Internal economies of scale have to be excluded because they are incompatible with competitive conditions. Also, external economies resulting from 'the general progress of industrial environment' have to be ignored, being inconsistent with the conditions of the particular equilibrium of a commodity. This leaves only those scale economies external to the firm but internal to the industry as compatible with competitive conditions. To summarise: first, with respect to diminishing returns, 'very little remains: the imposing structure . . . is available only for the study of that minute class of commodities in the production of which the whole of a factor of production is employed';[5] second, the only type of increasing returns compatible with competition consists of those external to the firm, but internal to the industry, which 'constitute precisely the class which is most seldom to be met with'.[6] Thus, 'supply curves showing decreasing costs are not to be found more frequently than their opposite'.[7] Sraffa's general conclusions on the laws of returns are contained in the final paragraph of the first part of his 1926 article:

> In normal cases, the cost of production of commodities produced competitively – as we are not entitled to take into consideration the causes which may make it rise or fall – must be regarded as constant in respect of small variations in the quantity produced. And so, as a simple way of approaching the problem of competitive value, the old and now obsolete theory which makes it dependent on the cost of production alone appears to hold its ground as the best available.[8]

This is an appropriate juncture to examine the relation between PCMC and his 1926 article. For, as Sraffa stated in the Preface to PCMC, 'the central propositions had taken shape in the late 1920s'.[9] Furthermore, he opened the Preface with a reference to constant returns assumptions.

> Anyone accustomed to thinking in terms of the equilibrium of demand and supply may be inclined, on reading these pages, to suppose that the argument rests on a tacit assumption of constant returns to scale in all industries. If such a supposition is found helpful, there is no harm in the reader's adopting it as a temporary working hypothesis.[10]

In fact, I have made such a supposition, as will be recalled from Chapter 2 onwards: in this respect, I am in the company of Pasinetti (1977a) and Garegnani (1970), among many.

> The temptation to presuppose constant returns is not entirely fanciful. It was experience by the author himself when he started on these studies many years ago – and it led him in 1925 into an attempt to argue that only the case of constant returns

> was generally consistent with the premises of economic theory.[11]

Finally, by way of justifying the comparison between PCMC and the laws of returns article, it was evident to Sraffa that prices of production could have been called costs of production. In section 7 of PCMC, he actually explained why 'the ratios which satisfy the conditions of production have been called "values" or "prices" rather than, as might be thought more appropriate, "costs of production"'.[12] The term 'cost of production' would be adequate for a non-basic commodity, as its price would reflect what had to be paid for means of production, labour and profits to produce it, there being no mutual dependence. However, basic commodities exhibit dependent costs of production, as is clear from chapter II of PCMC and Chapter 3 above.[13]

There is an obvious difference between the objects of analysis in the 1926 article and PCMC. In the former, Sraffa was concerned with 'the study of the equilibrium value of single commodities produced under competitive conditions',[14] that is, with partial equilibrium analysis. In PCMC, he was concerned essentially with the prices of basic commodities in relation to the distributive parameters, what might be called a general equilibrium problem.

The critique of the Marshallian theory of value constituted only the first half of the 1926 article. The second half represented Sraffa's essay at constructing an alternative price theory. He had at least three options. The first was to assume constant returns. As seen above, the temptation to do so was strong – on theoretical grounds at least. For, in the first half of his 1926 article, Sraffa had shown that, if returns to scale were variable, partial equilibrium analysis could not be justified; and if returns to scale were constant, partial equilibrium analysis could be justified but was unnecessary, prices being determined by costs of production. The second option was 'to extend the field of investigation so as to examine the conditions of simultaneous equilibrium in numerous industries'.[15] A foray into general equilibrium analysis was rejected because its 'complexity . . . prevents it from bearing fruit, at least in the present state of our knowledge, which does not permit of even much simpler schemata being applied to the study of real conditions'.[16] The third option, taken by Sraffa, was to abandon the assumption of perfect competition. In the second part of the 1926 article, Sraffa introduced downward-sloping demand curves for the individual firm, thereby initiating the theory of imperfect competition.[17] This theoretical innovation provides implicit support for the argument that Sraffa did not consider constant returns to be empirically more justifiable than increasing or diminishing returns: quite simply, if Sraffa had regarded costs as constant in the real world, an alternative to the standard model of perfect competition would have been unnecessary. However, when attention is transferred to PCMC, it is found that there is no reference to monopolistic competition. The option taken in the 1926 article has been abandoned in PCMC, where it seems that the 'conditions of simultaneous equilibrium in numerous industries' are examined. It has been argued by Harcourt (1972) that 'the passages on monopoly, which gave rise to the "imperfect competition" saga . . . were added to placate an English audience accustomed to the pragmatic judgments about the real world'.[18] PCMC may be more consistent with the original 1925 Italian article in the sense that the former does not contradict the latter's critique of Marshallian theory and, in fact, advances an alternative theory of value. Note that, by adopting an inter-industry framework in PCMC, Sraffa was able to avoid employing any concepts from the theory of imperfect competition.

I have discussed Sraffa's 1926 article at some length. I conclude this section by briefly mentioning Sraffa's contribution to the 1930 *Economic Journal* Symposium on Increasing Returns and the Representative Firm. There, Robertson had attempted to rescue Marshall's notion of the representative firm and to suggest a way by which competitive equilibrium could be reconciled with increasing returns from internal economies. Sraffa was severely critical of this attempt, concluding that Marshall's

> theory cannot be interpreted in a way which makes it logically self-consistent and, at the same time, reconciles it with the facts it sets out to explain. Mr Robertson's remedy is to discard mathematics, and he suggests that my remedy is to discard the facts; perhaps, I ought to have explained that, in the circumstances, I think it is Marshall's theory that should be discarded.[19]

12.3 Sraffa's Contribution to the Theory of Value

Sraffa did not pursue the line of thought initiated in the second half of his 1926 article. Rather, he turned to Ricardo to provide the basis for an alternative theory of value. First, in his Introduction to *The Principles* (1951), he traced the development of Ricardo's thinking, clearly indicating the problems faced in attempts to explain the rate of profit. (Sraffa's Introduction is widely recognised as the major contribution to the rebirth of the surplus approach.) Then, in PCMC, he demonstrated how these problems could be overcome and a satisfactory theory of value established.

I have already referred briefly in section 1.2 to the essentials of the classical approach to the theory of value. Prices of production, or natural prices, define long-run equilibria or long-period positions; they are, as Smith and Ricardo argued, centres of gravitation. If I wished to select just one passage to serve as text for the surplus approach, I could do no better than choose the following from chapter IV of *The Principles*:

> It is this competition which so adjusts the exchangeable value of commodities, that after paying the wages for the labour necessary for their production, and all other expenses required to put the capital employed in its original state of efficiency, the remaining value or overplus will in each trade be in proportion to the value of the capital employed.[20]

Note the role attributed to competition. A similar view was expressed by Marx:

> What competition brings about, first of all in one sphere, is the establishment of a uniform market value and market price out of the various individual values of commodities. But it is only the competition of capitals in different spheres that brings forth the production that equalizes the rate of profit between the spheres. The latter process requires a higher development of the capitalist mode of production than the former.[21]

The establishment of a uniform rate of profit is intimately connected with the development of competition. In the Classical scheme, competition is a characteristic of the whole process of capital accumulation, involving capital mobility and technical change.

The data in the Classical theory of value consists of: first, the size and composition of the national product; second, the conditions of production; and, third, the real wage. Ricardo had argued that the rate of profit was given by the ratio of the value of the surplus product (or overplus) to the value of means of production advanced. In a one-commodity world, the theory of value is not necessary to evaluate this ratio, simply because both numerator and denominator are homogeneous. On the other hand, in a multicommodity world, a theory of value is generally required to reduce the heterogeneous entities to homogeneous quantities (i.e. values). Neither Ricardo nor Marx adequately solved this problem. Taking up the Ricardian text quoted above, it can be seen that, in the surplus approach, prices of production are determined by the conditions of production and the distribution of (the surplus) income, as emphasised in the early chapters of this book. If the surplus value is to be distributed as profits proportional to the value of capital advanced (i.e. as a rate of profit), it is clear that the value of means of production must be known before the surplus can be allocated. Hence, as Sraffa observed in section 6 of PCMC, prices of production and the rate of profit must be determined at the same time. Once the problem is presented in terms of simultaneous determination – as in Sraffa's equations in section 6 of PCMC or as in (3.15) of section 3.3 above – it is evident that the three sets of data for the Classical theory are sufficient to ensure a unique solution for the rate of profit.[22] It is not claimed that Sraffa was the first to present this formalisation,[23] rather that he clarified the analytical method and showed that the rate of profit, not the real wage, could be taken as exogenous without affecting the solution properties. Incidentally, this discussion of the Classical theory of value in relation to output offers an insight into Sraffa's assumption on returns (or rather lack of one) stated in the Preface to PCMC.

> In fact, no assumption (of constant returns to scale) is made. No changes in output and (at any rate in Parts I and II) no changes in the proportions in which different means of production are used by an industry are considered, so that no question arises as to the variation or constancy of returns. The investigation is

> concerned exclusively with such properties of an economic system as do not depend on changes in the scale of production or in the proportions of 'factors'.[24]

Sraffa's position is entirely consistent with that described above: the analysis of value is separable from that of output. Of course, this does not imply that Classical economists deny the influence of prices on outputs and vice versa. Rather, the analysis of prices is undertaken assuming a given level and composition of output; and output is analysed assuming given prices.[25] To be specific, output would be determined in a theory of accumulation and development.

This emphasis on the study of long-run equilibria was also a feature of neo-classical theory: it sufficies here to refer to the work of Jevons (1970), Walras (1954), Wicksell (1934) and Marshall (1920). For example, in chapter V of book V of *The Principles*, Marshall stated the object of his analysis as 'the normal relations of wages, profits, prices, etc, for rather long periods' (p. 315). The characteristic of neo-classical theory was its use of the law of supply and demand[26] in an attempt to provide the basis for explaining the levels of long-run prices (and quantities). Whereas in the Classical approach profits are determined as a residual given the real wage, in the neo-classical approach both income categories are treated symmetrically.[27] Just as the demand for and supply of labour determined the wage rate in neo-classical theory, so the demand for and supply of capital services determined the rate of profit. Now a major problem existed because capital, unlike either labour or land, is a produced means of production and cannot be measured unambiguously in purely physical terms: the amount of capital can be measured only in value terms. The problem was to establish the idea of a market for capital, the quantity of which could be expressed independently of the price of its service (i.e. the rate of profit). If it could, profits could be explained in the same way as wages. To see this, suppose that the demand for capital is a monotonically decreasing function of the rate of profit. Given the quantity of capital supplied, there would be a unique rate of profit. The difficult step in this approach lies in justifying the demand function for capital. Typically, neo-classical economists appealed to substitution in both production and consumption to achieve this. For instance, an increase in the rate of profit in given technical conditions would induce substitution in favour of the cheaper factor, labour. So, for any given quantity of labour employed, a lower quantity of capital would be associated with a higher rate of profit – that is, the demand for capital would be a monotonically decreasing function of the rate of profit. This is the essence of the traditional neo-classical approach to the determination of the normal or long-run rate of profit.

The basic deficiency with this approach is in its treatment of capital, which cannot be measured independently of the rate of profit. As observed above, the value of capital, like that of all produced commodities, depends on the rate of profit, or interest. In his reply to Harrod, Sraffa showed that 'it is not possible to define the quantity of capital in a way that makes (it) independent of the rate of interest'.[28] The reader will have recognised that this point has been discussed at length above. The corollary is straightforward: 'One can only wonder what is the good of a quantity of capital . . . which, since it depends on the rate of interest, cannot be used for its traditional purpose, which is to determine the rate of interest.'[29] A similar view can be found in section 48 of PCMC, where Sraffa considered a two-final-good, maturing-labour inputs model, showing that the relative commodity price at first rises, then falls and finally rises again. To quote at length:

> The reduction to dated labour terms has some bearing on the attempts that have been made to find in the 'period of production' an independent measure of the quantity of capital which could be used, without arguing in a circle, for the determination of prices and of the shares in distribution. But the case just considered seems conclusive in showing the impossibility of aggregating the 'periods' belonging to the several quantities of labour into a single magnitude which could be regarded as representing the quantity of capital. The reversals in the direction of the movement of relative prices, in the face of unchanged methods of production, cannot be reconciled with any notion of capital as a measurable quantity independent of distribution and prices.[30]

Note that this criticism of neo-classical theory has been made without any reference to the three phenomena of Chapters 6 and 7. The introduction of capital reversing, reswitching and recurrence of techniques serves to strengthen the argument. Evidently, the demand for capital is not a monotonically decreasing function of the rate of profit; furthermore, as discussed in Chapter 6, the traditional notion of substitution is called into question.

PCMC is somewhat enigmatically subtitled 'Prelude to a Critique of Economic Theory'. As shown above, it was certainly something more substantial, exposing deficiencies in traditional neo-classical theory concerned with the long run. Furthermore, Sraffa's demonstration of reswitching, together with recurrence and capital reversing (attributable to Champernowne and Cohen), established the general invalidity of aggregate versions of neo-classical theory. Inevitably, the implications of the three phenomena were not immediately recognised, the capital theory debates lasting for the best part of twenty years.[31] However, it is now generally agreed that models employing an aggregate production function satisfying certain properties must be treated with a considerable degree of circumspection, if they cannot be altogether avoided.[32] This comment is particularly applicable to growth theory.

In the discussion above, I have referred to traditional versions of neo-classical theory in which the determination of the long-run equilibrium was central. This position has been abandoned in modern general equilibrium theory[33] in favour of an atemporal or an intertemporal approach, in which emphasis is transferred to the short run (this shift has been chronicled by Milgate (1979) and Garegnani (1976b)). Does Sraffa's critique have any relevance to this modern theory? In so far as Sraffa does not offer any direct comment on the determination of short-run equilibrium, the answer to this question must be no. However, that is to take a restricted view. Acceptance of Sraffa's whole line of argument (i.e. the surplus approach) leads to an examination in the first place of the rationale for this change in emphasis of the object of analysis.[34]

In the modern general equilibrium approach, commodities are defined by their type, physical location and date. Equilibrium is then defined in terms of market-clearing prices, whether for all markets from now onwards (as in the intertemporal model of Debreu (1959), for example), or sequentially (as in the temporary equilibrium model of Hicks (1946)). In either case, there will not generally be a uniform rate of profit in each time period.[35] If a uniform rate of profit were imposed, for example, on the intertemporal model of Debreu, there would in general be no solution: for there is no reason to suppose that the initial endowments of capital goods are appropriate to the structure of demand, which implies that, for those capital stocks in excess supply, the market clearing price would be less than the cost of production. This problem could be overcome by interpreting the capital endowment in value, rather than physical, terms. However, the defects of such an approach are evident, given the arguments of the earlier chapters.[36] What can be said of the short-run equilibrium? Certainly, it cannot be described as a centre of gravitation. Indeed, in a model where profit maximisation is postulated, precisely the opposite is true – the short-run equilibrium is a position from which the economy will definitely diverge.[37] In Classical theory, convergence to natural prices was established through the operation of competition, principally the mobility of capital. Is the neo-classical short-run equilibrium generally described as competitive? If so, how is mobility of capital incorporated? The answer to the first question is yes. An adequate answer to the second question has not yet been found: put simply, how can capital mobility be reconciled with a concept of equilibrium in which there is a non-uniform rate of profit?

The discussion so far has concentrated on the critical aspects arising from Sraffa's work. In concluding this section, I aim to redress the balance by emphasising the constructive aspects of PCMC, even at the expense of belabouring arguments made in earlier chapters.

The first point to be made is that Sraffa provided a consistent explanation of price determination in the tradition of the surplus approach. This is demonstrated most clearly in Part I of PCMC for the single-product industries, circulating capital case and has been discussed in Chapters 2–7 above. There, Sraffa exhibited the dependence of prices of production on both the conditions of production and the distribution of income, using the resulting properties as a basis for his critique of neo-classical theory. Further, he derived the antagonistic relationship between the distributive parameters. To achieve this, he constructed the Standard System, which enabled him to deduce the simple linear equation connecting the rate of profit and the wage rate given in (5.18) of Chapter 5. The virtue of this equation is its simplicity, as Sraffa recognised, its main purpose being to 'give transparency to a system and render visible what was hidden' (PCMC, section 31, p. 23). The idea of an invariable standard of value is undoubtedly appealing, that of a composite commodity with proportional means of production is attractive. Yet, as shown in Chapter 5, despite the problems involved in interpreting the Standard Commodity, Sraffa was well aware of the general distributional relation implicit in any productive technique. Sraffa's explanation of price determination is not restricted to the simplest case analysed in Part I of PCMC. For he treated joint production in general, fixed capital and land in particular, in Part II. The introduction of durable means of production, whether produced or non-produced, creates problems which are analogous, in one sense, to those arising in pure joint production models and, in another sense, to those arising in single-product industries models with alternative techniques. The first problem arises because a given technique may support negative prices at a feasible rate of profit. The second problem arise because in a properly specified model with durable means of production there are implicitly alternative techniques: this is evident in the simplest two-sector model where there is only one durable instrument of production, lasting for at most two periods when employed in one sector; automatically, there are two techniques of production. So, in solving price systems for models with durable means of production, the question of choice of technique arises naturally.

In chapter X of PCMC, Sraffa demonstrated the correct treatment of fixed capital – within the joint production framework. This treatment is not restricted to the case of constant efficiency but can accommodate any pattern of inputs and outputs in the machine-using processes. The price of an ageing machine and hence depreciation charges depend on the distribution of income, as is the case of marketable commodities: this is evident in the analysis of choice of technique when an ageing machine price can be negative over a feasible range of the rate of profit. Contrast this with ad hoc rules of depreciation (e.g. linear or evaporation) which take no account of distributional changes. Aside from the positive aspects of the analysis of the fixed capital model, it is evident that the general methodological point, made in the context of the single-product industries model, is valid: namely, the value of a given stock of physical capital goods cannot be calculated before the rate of profit is known. (This reinforces the point made above that the neo-classical notion of a quantity of capital measured independently of the rate of profit is invalid.) The framework laid down by Sraffa permitted later writers to conclude that the optimal economic lifetime of machinery is not an inversely monotonic function of the rate of profit. Also, the analogues of reswitching and recurrence – namely, the return of the same optimal economic lifetime of machinery over disjoint sets of values of the rate of profit – can be exhibited. These results are injurious to the neo-Austrian versions of neo-classical theory.

Similar general conclusions can be drawn from the analysis of non-produced means of production as from that of fixed capital. For example, in the extensive rent model, the question of choice of technique is disguised as the determination of the marginal land. As in the fixed capital case, choice depends on income distribution; furthermore, the order of fertility is not necessarily identical to the ordering of lands by rent, as Sraffa made clear in section 86 of PCMC. The general point about choice of technique applies also in the case of intensive rent. So, it is possible that, at a certain feasible value of the rate of profit, the given final demand can be met by operating two processes of production while, at a different value of the rate of profit, only one process needs to be used: in the former, land is scarce and a rent is paid while, in the latter, land is not scarce and no rent is paid. This yields an analogous result to that derived in section 6.7 – the demand for land is not necessarily an inverse monotonic function of rent. It also establishes that the notion of scarcity cannot be defined independently of distribution.

12.4 Further Research: Introduction

In considering theoretical developments, it is important to distinguish between the objects and the methods of analysis: for example, the former can refer to theories under investigation, the latter to the means by which the former are examined. It is conceivable that the discovery of new analytical methods can result in theoretical advances because previously unmanageable questions become tractable. Care is therefore necessary in examining new presentations of theory to determine whether there has been a significant development in the object of analysis or the method of analysis, or perhaps both. To illustrate this general discussion, consider recent accounts of microeconomics in terms of duality theory, exemplified by Varian (1984). At first sight, this development, based on the mathematical theory of convex functions, seems to relate to the methods and not the objects of analysis. Undoubtedly, considerable simplification in the presentation of existing neo-classical theory can be achieved by using duality theory. However, it should not be supposed that the results derived by means of this alternative method are immune from the type of criticism raised in earlier sections. Indeed, Gram (1985) and Salvadori and Steedman (1985) demonstrate that the methods of duality theory can equally well be employed for their own purposes by neo-Ricardian as by neo-classical economists.

My main concern in this book has been to provide an account of what Sraffa actually said: in this sense, my stance has been retrospective. It is appropriate in this final chapter to be prospective by briefly discussing some areas of economic theory where the approach inspired by Sraffa has led to a resurgence of interest.

Virtually any neo-classical model employing as an assumption a given endowment of capital is likely to be susceptible to criticism from the Sraffa standpoint. As an illustration, I have chosen to discuss in section 12.5 the critique of standard neo-classical trade theory initiated by Steedman and associates (1979a). They demonstrate not only that familiar theorems are undermined but also that a neo-Ricardian (as distinct from the textbook Ricardian) approach is feasible.

A second area in which the neo-Ricardian approach has yielded new insights is technical change. In section 12.6, I discuss Steedman's account (1983) of the construction of the Harrod measure of technical progress: being directly based on prices of production, it gives due emphasis not only to interdependence between processes but also to the distribution of income and the choice of numeraire. This treatment of technical change is radically different from those usually employed which are based on aggregate production functions.

The third and perhaps the most contentious area chosen for discussion concerns the connection between Sraffa and Keynes. In section 12.7, I briefly summarise the view, advanced by the contributors to Eatwell and Milgate (1983), that neo-classical theory can be replaced by a synthesis of the classical theory of value and the Keynesian theory of output. This topic is contentious partly because the desired synthesis requires a reinterpretation of Keynes' theory in terms of the long run.

12.5 Further Research: International Trade

As a first approach in the theory of international trade, consider a very simple world of two economies, *A* and *B*, both having the same technology to produce the same two commodities. Initially, both economies are closed, with different rates of profit and different relative prices. Once it is permitted, trade will occur under standard, if not entirely realistic, assumptions.[38] With the opening of trade, a uniform world relative price will be established. Does this also imply uniformity of profit and real wage rates? This question can be interpreted as referring to factor–price equalisation. To answer it, consider the relation between the relative price and the rate of profit for an economy with alternative techniques. Suppose that there are these three processes available, one for producing the first commodity, two for the second:

$$(\text{I}) = (0,\ 1/2 : 1) \qquad (\text{II}\alpha) = (1/2,\ 0 : 1/2)$$

$$(\text{II}\beta) = (1/8,\ 0 : 3)$$

With the first commodity as numeraire, I obtain the following:

$$w^{\alpha} = (1 - (1+r)^2)/(5+r) \qquad w^{\beta} = (16 - (1+r)^2)/(40+24r)$$

$$p^{\alpha} = (4+2r)/(5+r) \qquad p^{\beta} = (25+r)/(20+12r)$$

The w–r curves are illustrated in Figure 12.1. It is a straightforward matter to show that:

$$dp^{\alpha}/dr > 0,\ dp^{\beta}/dr < 0;\ \bar{r} \triangleq 0.6223,\ \bar{p} = p(\bar{r}) \triangleq 0.9328.$$

When $r = 0$, $p^{\alpha} = 0.8$. Putting $p^{\beta} = 0.8$, I obtain $\tilde{r} \triangleq 1.0465$. If a relative price is given between 0.8 and 0.9328, there are two corresponding income distributions, one with r lying between 0 and $\bar{r}$ where (α) is employed, the other with r lying between $\bar{r}$ and $\tilde{r}$ where (β) is employed.

Suppose that the technology common to *A* and *B* consists of techniques (α) and (β). With an international relative price lying

Figure 12.1

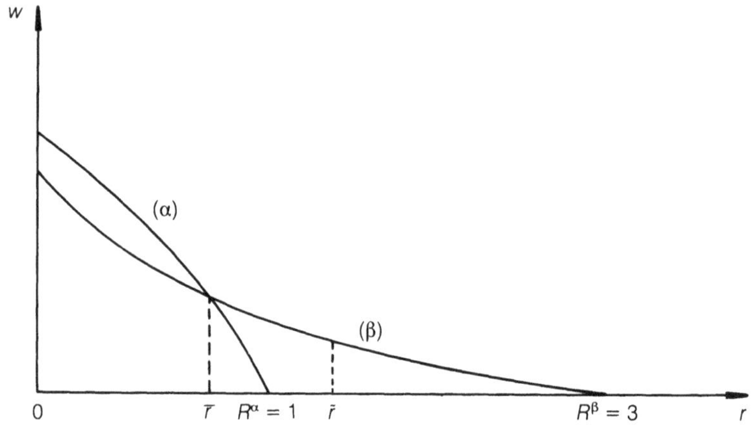

between 0.8 and 0.9328 and both economies producing both commodities, it is possible that different rates of profit would prevail in *A* and *B* and hence different techniques would be in use. In so far as the real wage and the rate of profit can be interpreted as factor prices, this discussion has established that the introduction of trade does not imply factor–price equalisation. Trade effects factor–price equalisation in the two-commodity model above if the relative price is a monotonic function of the rate of profit. Such a condition would be satisfied if, for all feasible techniques, the first sector was more capital intensive than the second or vice versa.[39] Thus, reswitching is consistent with factor–price equalisation while the example above is not. This brief discussion has shown the potential application of capital theory methods, which do not in this instance amount to demonstrating the implications of reswitching or capital reversing, to the theory of international trade.

One of the main results of traditional, or Heckscher–Ohlin–Samuelson, trade theory is that the country with the higher ratio of capital to labour will export the capital-intensive commodity.[40] This result is based on the following assumptions in addition to those mentioned above: each country has a given endowment of factors, identical in quality but different in quantity; there are no factor-intensity reversals in the production of commodities; and consumers have identical homothetic preferences. The factor endowments are usually taken to refer to labour and capital, but is the latter denominated in physical or value terms? Suppose that the capital endowment refers to a set of machines. If traditional trade theory is to concern itself with the analysis of long-run equilibria, such an interpretation of the capital endowment cannot be sustained. For, in a long-run equilibrium, the set of machines is not arbitrarily given but corresponds to the ruling rate of profit. Two alternatives present themselves. First, that traditional theory should concentrate on the short run where the interpretation of capital in physical terms can be justified. Secondly, traditional theory should retain the long-run framework, in which case the capital endowment has to be interpreted in value terms. If the second alternative is adopted, the actual physical composition of the capital stock is variable subject only to the constraint that its value is equal to the endowment. In traditional theory, factor prices are related to endowments. Given that the capital endowment has been interpreted in value terms, the corresponding price is the rate of profit.

The analysis employs the relations exhibited in Figure 12.2: that the relative price is monotonically related to the rate of profit, which in turn is monotonically related to the capital–labour ratio in each industry. Metcalfe and Steedman (1973) have shown that these relations are not generally valid in a world of heterogeneous capital goods (such as would need to be assumed for the application of traditional theory to long-run positions). Using a numerical example taken from Garegnani (1970), they show that the relationships exhibited in Figure 12.3 can hold. While neither capital–labour ratio is now a monotonic function of r, there are no capital-intensity reversals: industry one is always more capital intensive at any value of r. On the other hand, the relative price is not a monotonic function of r. It does not follow that the country with the higher ratio of capital–labour endowments will export the capital-intensive commodity, as may be seen by contrasting Figures 12.2 and 12.3 (overleaf).[41]

Figure 12.2

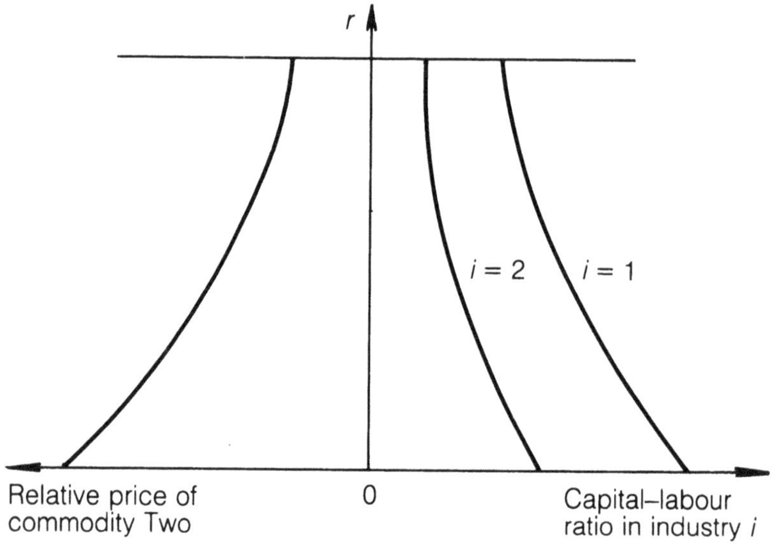

In this section, I have briefly discussed how the theory of prices of production can be used to provide a critique of the traditional approach to international trade theory. It should not be surprising that such a critique can be made given that, in its simplest forms, the Heckscher–Ohlin–Samuelson approach is formulated in terms of endowments of non-produced factors of production, typically land and labour. The substitution of capital, whether in value or physical form, for land is not a trivial matter. Even when intermediate inputs are introduced, production must be allowed to take time so that profits are paid on the value of capital advanced. Once these essential points are taken into account, the deficiencies in the Heckscher–Ohlin–Samuelson approach become apparent and the essentially short-period, exchange-oriented theory cannot survive scrutiny. Though only the critical aspects for trade theory have been discussed here, it is worth mentioning that an alternative neo-Ricardian approach, inspired by Sraffa's PCMC, is available. This alternative, pioneered by Steedman and associates (1979a), treats questions of growth, income distribution and choice of technique within the context of international trade models.

Figure 12.3

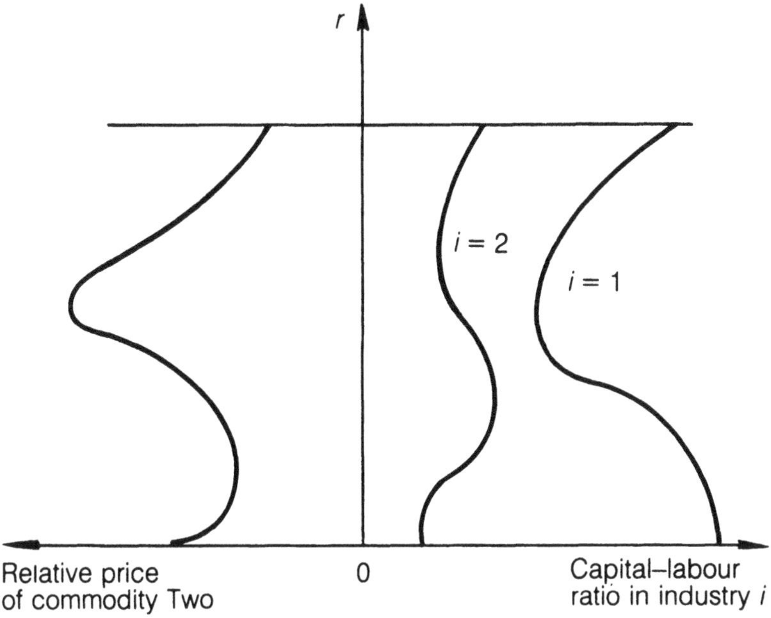

12.6 Further Research: Technical Change

The traditional approach to the measurement of technical change is based on the construction of input and output indices. For example, if, over a given period, the output index rises by b per cent and the input index by c per cent, the rate of technical change can be taken as approximately $(b-c)$ per cent (more exactly as $(100(b-c)/(100+c))$ per cent). Clearly, the rate of technical change is treated as a residual and, in fact, is referred to in the literature as *the* residual, a description indicative of its logical status. The idea underlying this approach is that output growth can be attributed to input growth, on the one hand, and improvements in technical knowledge, on the other. If measures of input and output growth, however approximate,[42] are made, the difference between them can be ascribed to technical change. Though it has, since the early work of Solow (1957),[43] become the standard method of analysis, this growth accounting approach is not the only one available. Indeed, for the purpose of measuring technical change, it is not necessarily the best. Consideration should be

Figure 12.4

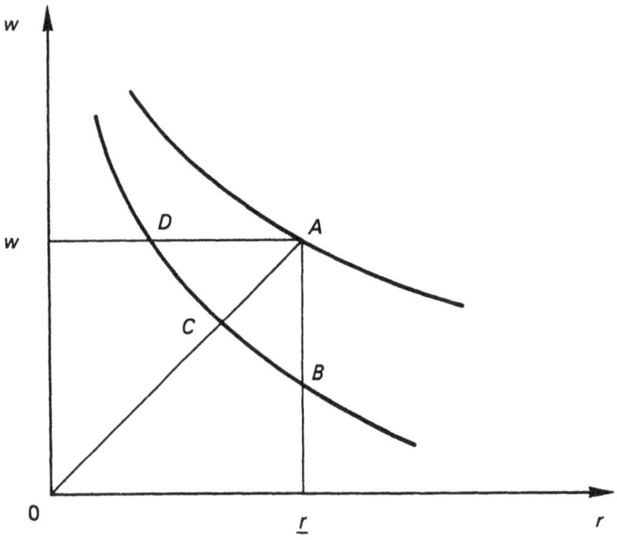

given to the wage rate–rate of profit curve which is, of course, constructed from the technical data underlying the process of production in each sector. If at least one process of production is altered, in other words there is technical change, there will be a shift in the *w–r* curve. Technical change can then be measured by the extent of the shift in the curve, rather than going through the growth accounting exercises.

Some questions immediately arise about this procedure. First, how is the extent of the shift to be measured? In Figure 12.4, the line *DCB* represents part of the initial *w–r* curve, that through *A* part of the *w–r* curve after the technical change. If I assume, following Harrod, that the rate of profit is constant at $\underline{r}$, the extent of the shift is given by the rise in the real wage, $AB/A\underline{r}$. The obverse of this is based on the assumption of a constant real wage: then, according to Solow, the extent of the shift is measured by the rise in the rate of profit, $AD/A\underline{w}$. Finally, under Hicks's assumption of a constant real wage–rate of profit ratio, the extent of the shift is measured along the ray $0A$ by $AC/A0$.[44] Generally speaking, for a given approach (Harrod or Solow or Hicks) and a given change in input–output coefficients, the measure of technical change will vary with income distribution. Under Harrod's assumption, the measure of technical change at $\underline{r}$ will differ from that at any other feasible value of *r*. The inference to be drawn from Figure 12.4 – that there is not a unique way of measuring the shift in the *w–r* curve – is reinforced when it is recalled that a *w–r* curve can be constructed only when a numeraire has been specified. If the standard of value is changed, the *w–r* curve is correspondingly changed. For a given approach (Harrod or Solow or Hicks), the measure of a given technical change will have one value in terms of one numeraire and another value in terms of a second numeraire. This difficulty, if that is what it is, is not peculiar to the theory of technical change measurement. In effect, attention is being drawn to the role of the numeraire, something usually ignored in economic theory.

Having recognised that technical change must be measured in terms of a numeraire, however arbitrarily chosen, it is natural to return to the three approaches illustrated in Figure 12.4. Are they all of equal standing or is there some justification for preferring one to the others? To adopt the Harrod approach is to take the line that 'from a long-run point of view, labour and natural resources are the factors of production in the economy as a whole, while capital goods and the time pattern of production are the means by which the factors are deployed'.[45] This is an appropriate line to take here, as this book has been concerned with long-run analysis involving produced means of production.

In earlier chapters, I dealt with technical change in a stationary framework. For example, in the derivation of Okishio's Theorem (*Corollary 11.3*), where I assumed that a second process of production became available to one sector, the purpose of the analysis was to determine choice of technique. I shall now adopt an approach different in at least two respects. First, I permit technical changes to occur continuously in both sectors. Second, I assume that, at each instant, there is a unique cost-minimising technique. In earlier discussions, I assumed that a sector had a finite number of alternative processes, the problem at hand being the determination of choice of technique. This could be thought of as being achieved fairly quickly through the intervention of an auctioneer (à la Walras) or over a longer time horizon, with the iterative process of section 6.6 occurring at the rate of one process change per sector per year. Now, I take a different view. Instead of an arbitrary finite number of alternative processes being available to a sector in a given time period, I suppose that there are two. A capitalist could continue to operate last year's process; however, as this year's process reduces costs at last year's prices, it would be inefficient to do so. From one period to the next, there is a complete change of technique, that is, a change of both processes. By assuming that only one new process appears in each sector in each year, I can thus avoid the question of choice of technique.

I shall conduct the analysis in terms of the familiar single-product industries, circulating capital model. The price equations are:

$$p_1 = wl_1 + (1+r)(p_1a_{11} + p_2a_{21}) \tag{12.1a}$$

$$p_2 = wl_2 + (1+r)(p_1a_{12} + p_2a_{22}) \tag{12.1b}$$

$$p_1z_1 + p_2z_2 = 1 \tag{12.1c}$$

(12.1c) merely specifies the numeraire. In the Harrod approach, the rate of profit is fixed. Treating technical coefficients as differentiable functions of time, it follows that changes in the technique of production will imply changes in prices and the wage rate. Differentiating (12.1a) – (12.1c) with respect to t, I obtain:

$$\frac{dp_1}{dt} = \frac{dw}{dt}\cdot l_1 + (1+r)\left(\frac{dp_1}{dt}\cdot a_{11} + \frac{dp_2}{dt}\cdot a_{22}\right) + w\frac{dl_1}{dt} + (1+r)\left(p_1\frac{da_{11}}{dt} + p_2\frac{da_{21}}{dt}\right) \tag{12.2a}$$

$$\frac{dp_2}{dt} = \frac{dw}{dt}\cdot l_2 + (1+r)\left(\frac{dp_1}{dt}\cdot a_{12} + \frac{dp_2}{dt}\cdot a_{22}\right) + w\frac{dl_2}{dt} + (1+r)\left(p_1\frac{da_{12}}{dt} + p_2\frac{da_{22}}{dt}\right) \tag{12.2b}$$

$$\frac{dp_1}{dt}\cdot z_1 + \frac{dp_2}{dt}\cdot z_2 = 0 \tag{12.2c}$$

I now rewrite (12.2a) and (12.2b) so that price changes are on one side of the equation and quantity changes are on the other:

$$\frac{dw}{dt} \cdot l_1 - \left(\frac{dp_1}{dt}(1-(1+r)a_{11}) - \frac{dp_2}{dt}(1+r)a_{21}\right)$$

$$= -w \cdot \frac{dl_1}{dt} - (1+r)\left(p_1 \frac{da_{11}}{dt} + p_2 \frac{da_{21}}{dt}\right) \tag{12.3a}$$

$$\frac{dw}{dt} \cdot l_2 - \left(-\frac{dp_1}{dt}(1+r)a_{12} + \frac{dp_2}{dt}(1-(1+r)a_{22})\right)$$

$$= -w\frac{dl_2}{dt} - (1+r)\left(p_1 \frac{da_{12}}{dt} + p_2 \frac{da_{22}}{dt}\right) \tag{12.3b}$$

The right-hand side of (12.3a) is the value of the change in inputs per unit of output of commodity one. Suppose, for the sake of illustration, that all input–output coefficients are reduced: then dl_1/dt and da_{i1}/dt are negative, $i = 1,2$ which implies that the right-hand side of (12.3a) is positive. When divided by p_1, the expression on the right-hand side of (12.3a) is the value of the change in inputs per unit value of output of commodity one: in other words, it is a measure of the rate of technical change, or productivity increase, in industry one. Define:

$$\tau_1 = \left(-w \cdot \frac{dl_1}{dt} - (1+r)\left(p_1 \frac{da_{11}}{dt} + p_2 \frac{da_{21}}{dt}\right)\right)/p_1 \tag{12.4a}$$

Similarly, for the second industry:

$$\tau_2 = \left(-w \cdot \frac{dl_2}{dt} - (1+r)\left(p_1 \frac{da_{12}}{dt} + p_2 \frac{da_{22}}{dt}\right)\right)/p_2 \tag{12.4b}$$

I have mentioned above the case where all input–output coefficients are reduced, where technical change is both labour saving and capital saving. A more realistic example might be one of labour-saving, capital-using technical change, where $dl_j/dt < 0$ and $da_{ij}/dt > 0$, $i,j = 1,2$. The labour-saving, capital-saving case is easy to consider because the new processes are necessarily cost reducing. The labour-saving, capital-using case deserves a little more consideration. For the new processes to be introduced, the bracketed terms in (12.4a) and (12.4b) have to be positive: otherwise, the new processes would not be cost reducing. So, under the two assumptions above, I conclude that there is a positive rate of technical change in an industry if and only if the corresponding technical change is cost reducing. From (12.3a) and (12.4a), I have:

$$p_1\tau_1 = \frac{dw}{dt}\cdot l_1 - \left(\frac{dp_1}{dt}(1 - (1+r)a_{11}) - \frac{dp_2}{dt}(1+r)a_{21}\right) \tag{12.5a}$$

Similarly, from (12.3b) and (12.4b):

$$p_2\tau_2 = \frac{dw}{dt}\cdot l_2 - \left(-\frac{dp_1}{dt}(1+r)a_{12} + \frac{dp_2}{dt}(1 - (1+r)a_{22})\right) \tag{12.5b}$$

The equations for sectoral rates of productivity increase are now given in terms of price and wage changes rather than input changes. Rewrite (12.5a) and (12.5b) as respectively:

$$\frac{dp_1}{dt}(1 - (1+r)a_{11}) - \frac{dp_2}{dt}(1+r)a_{21} = \frac{dw}{dt}\cdot l_1 - p_1\tau_1 \equiv q_1 \tag{12.6a}$$

$$-\frac{dp_1}{dt}(1+r)a_{12} + \frac{dp_2}{dt}(1 - (1+r)a_{22}) = \frac{dw}{dt}\cdot l_2 - p_2\tau_2 \equiv q_2 \tag{12.6b}$$

(12.6a) and (12.6b) resemble the systems of linear equations considered from Chapter 3 onwards. Solving for the price changes, I have:

$$\frac{dp_1}{dt} = (q_1(1 - (1+r)a_{22}) + q_2(1+r)a_{21})/f(r) \tag{12.7a}$$

$$\frac{dp_2}{dt} = (q_1(1+r)a_{12} + q_2(1 - (1+r)a_{11}))/f(r) \tag{12.7b}$$

where:

$$f(r) = (1 - (1+r)a_{11})(1 - (1+r)a_{22}) - (1+r)^2a_{12}a_{21} \tag{12.7c}$$

Substituting from (12.7a) and (12.7b) into (12.2c), I obtain:

$$\frac{dp_1}{dt}.z_1 + \frac{dp_2}{dt}.z_2 = (q_1z_1(1-(1+r)a_{22}) + q_2z_1(1+r)a_{21} + q_1z_2(1+r)a_{12} + q_2z_2(1-(1+r)a_{11})/f(r) = 0 \quad (12.8)$$

On substituting from (12.6) for q_1 and q_2, I then obtain:

$$\frac{dw}{dt}(l_1z_1(1-(1+r)a_{22}) + l_2z_1(1+r)a_{21} + l_1z_2(1+r)a_{12} + l_2z_2(1-(1+r)a_{11})) = p_1\tau_1z_1(1-(1+r)a_{22}) + p_2\tau_2z_1(1+r)a_{21} + p_1\tau_1z_2(1+r)a_{12} + p_2\tau_2z_2(1-(1+r)a_{11} \quad (12.9)$$

Referring to the discussion on Figure 12.1, the Harrod measure of technical change is given by the proportional increase in the real wage at the given rate of profit. So, I define the Harrod measure, H, by:

$$H = \frac{1}{w}.\frac{dw}{dt} = (p_1\tau_1((1-(1+r)a_{22})z_1 + (1+r)a_{12}z_2) + p_2\tau_2((1+r)a_{21}z_1 + (1-(1+r)a_{11})z_2))/ w(l_1((1-(1+r)a_{22})z_1 + (1+r)a_{12}z_2) + l_2((1+r)a_{21}z_1 + (1-(1+r)a_{11})z_2)) \quad (12.10)$$

H thus depends on the rate of productivity increase in each sector (τ_1 and τ_2), the distribution of income (r, w, p_1 and p_2) and the numeraire (z_1 and z_2). Contrast two economies with the same initial technology, income distribution and numeraire but different rates of productivity increase, say τ_1^α and τ_2^α in the first economy and τ_1^β and τ_2^β in the second. The Harrod measure for the first economy, say H^α, will in general differ from that in the second, say H^β. Similarly, contrast two economies with the same corresponding rates of productivity increase and the same numeraire but different income distributions: once again, their Harrod measures will differ. Finally, if they differ only in their numeraires, two economies will have different Harrod measures.

(12.1) is apparently a complicated expression. However, by using the theory developed in Chapter 7, the expression for H can be rewritten, not to say simplified. If I define x_1 and x_2 to be the gross outputs of the two commodities to meet a final demand of z_1 and z_2 and sustain growth at rate r, I have these equations:

$$x_1 = (1+r)(a_{11}x_1 + a_{12}x_2) + z_1 \quad (12.11a)$$

$$x_2 = (1+r)(a_{21}x_1 + a_{22}x_2) + z_2 \quad (12.11b)$$

Solving these equations and substituting in (12.10), I obtain:

$$H = (p_1\tau_1x_1 + p_2\tau_2x_2)/(wl_1x_1 + wl_2x_2) \qquad \text{or} \quad (12.12)$$

$$H = (p_1\tau_1x_1 + p_2\tau_2x_2)/(p_1z_1 + p_2z_2) \quad (12.13)$$

where the denominator in (12.13) is obtained by solving the price equations (12.1a) and (12.1b). (12.12) and (12.13) are weighted averages of τ_1 and τ_2 but the weights do not sum to 1. $p_jx_j > wl_jx_j$ which implies that, if there are produced means of production, the Harrod measure will be larger than both τ_1 and τ_2.

I devote the remainder of this section to the analysis of some special cases. Consider first the case where the direct labour input coefficients decrease at a rate γ and the commodity input–output coefficients are constant:

$$\frac{dl_j}{dt} = -\gamma l_j, \; \frac{da_{ij}}{dt} = 0 \quad i,j = 1,2 \quad (12.14)$$

Using (12.14) in (12.4), I obtain:

$$\tau_j = w\gamma l_j/p_j \qquad \text{or}$$

$$p_j\tau_j = w\gamma l_j \quad j = 1,2 \quad (12.15)$$

Substituting from (12.15) into (12.10) yields:

$$H = \gamma \quad (12.16)$$

Note that this result obtains regardless of income distribution and the choice of numeraire. It may seem obvious that (12.14) implies (12.16) but from (12.12) $\tau_j = \gamma w l_j / p_j < \gamma$, $j = 1,2$. Both sectoral rates of productivity increase are less than γ yet, when account is taken of the interrelations in production, the overall rate of technical change in the Harrod sense is γ.

A variant of (12.14) is given by the following:

$$\frac{dl_j}{dt} = -\gamma_j l_j, \ \frac{da_{ij}}{dt} = 0 \quad i,j = 1,2 \tag{12.17}$$

This differs from (12.14) only in the fact that there are sectoral specific rates of decrease of the labour input coefficients rather than a uniform one. Using (12.17) in (12.4), I obtain:

$$\tau_j = w\gamma_j l_j / p_j$$

or

$$p_j \tau_j = w\gamma_j l_j \quad j = 1,2 \tag{12.18}$$

which, when substituted into (12.10), yields:

$$\begin{aligned} H = {} & (\gamma_1 l_1((1 - (1+r)a_{22})z_1 + (1+r)a_{12}z_2) \\ & + \gamma_2 l_2((1+r)a_{21}z_1 + (1 - (1+r)a_{11})z_2))/ \\ & (l_1((1 - (1+r)a_{22})z_1 + (1+r)a_{12}z_2) \\ & + l_2((1+r)a_{21}z_1 + (1 - (1+r)a_{11})z_2)) \end{aligned} \tag{12.19}$$

or

$$H = (\gamma_1 l_1 x_1 + \gamma_2 l_2 x_2)/(l_1 x_1 + l_2 x_2) \tag{12.20}$$

In this case, H is a weighted average of γ_1 and γ_2 (though it should be recalled from (12.18) that $\tau_j < \gamma_j$).

A third case to consider arises if there are no commodity inputs in either process. Then from (12.10):

$$H = (p_1 \tau_1 z_1 + p_2 \tau_2 z_2)/(wl_1 z_1 + wl_2 z_2) \tag{12.21}$$

$$= (p_1\tau_1z_1 + p_2\tau_2z_2)/(p_1z_1 + p_2z_2)$$

This is a weighted average of τ_1 and τ_2. If:

$$\frac{dl_j}{dt} = -\gamma l_j \quad j = 1,2 \tag{12.22}$$

it follows from (12.4) that:

$$p_j\tau_j = -w\gamma l_j \quad j = 1,2 \tag{12.23}$$

so that from (12.10):

$$H = \gamma \tag{12.24}$$

This is the only case in which the Harrod measure can be equal to the sectoral rates of productivity change.

Consider, finally, the simplest case of labour-saving, capital-saving technical changes where:

$$\frac{dl_j}{dt} = -\gamma l_j, \frac{da_{ij}}{dt} = -\gamma a_{ij} \quad i,j = 1,2 \tag{12.25}$$

Using (12.25) in (12.4), I obtain:

$$p_j\tau_j = \gamma wl_j + (1+r)\gamma(p_1a_{1j} + p_2a_{2j}) \quad j = 1,2$$

$$= \gamma p_j \quad j = 1,2 \tag{12.26}$$

Hence: $\tau_j = \gamma \quad j = 1,2$ (12.27)

At the sectoral level, the rate of productivity increase is γ. Using (12.26) in (12.10), I obtain:

$$H = \gamma(p_1((1-(1+r)a_{22})z_1 + (1+r)a_{12}z_2) + p_2((1+r)a_{21}z_1 + (1-(1+r)a_{11})z_2))/$$
$$w(l_1((1-(1+r)a_{22})z_1 + (1+r)a_{12}z_2) + l_2((1+r)a_{21}z_1 + (1-(1+r)a_{11})z_2))$$

$$= \frac{\gamma(p_1x_1 + p_2x_2)}{w(l_1x_1 + l_2x_2)} \tag{12.28}$$

As $p_j > l_j$, it follows from (12.28) that $H > \gamma$, which is by now an expected result. Technical improvements feed on themselves, so to speak, a point that can be made even more clearly by consideration of two special subcases of (12.25). (12.28) can be simplified in either of two ways: first, by assuming uniform organic composition of capital and, second, by taking the Standard Commodity as numeraire. In either event, (12.28) becomes:

$$H = \gamma(1 + R)/(R - r) \tag{12.29}$$

If R = 30 per cent, r = 10 per cent in (12.29), it follows that:

$$H = 6.5\gamma$$

The Harrod measure of technical change is considerably larger in this example than the uniform rate of sectoral productivity increase. Even if $r = 0$, $H = 4.33\gamma$.

In conclusion, I reiterate two general points made above. The first relates to (12.12): in aggregating productivity increases to obtain the Harrod measure, the weights are the value ratios of sectoral gross outputs to total wages. The second relates to the observation, made frequently above, that H is usually larger than τ_1 and τ_2. Substituting for p_1 and p_2 from (12.1) into (12.12) yields:

$$H = \frac{w(l_1\tau_1x_1 + l_2\tau_2x_2) + (1+r)(p_1(\tau_1a_{11}x_1 + \tau_2a_{12}x_2) + p_2(\tau_1a_{21}x_1 + \tau_2a_{22}x_2))}{w(l_1x_1 + l_2x_2)} \tag{12.30}$$

The first term on the right-hand side of (12.30) is the weighted average of the τ_j's, the weights being the sectoral wage shares; the second term is the value–capital/wage weighted average of the τ_j's, multiplied by $(1+r)$. Only if $a_{ij} = 0$, $i,j = 1,2$, will the Harrod measure be a simple weighted average of the sectoral rates of productivity increase. With produced means of production, H will typically be much larger than τ_1 and τ_2.

12.7 Further Research: Macroeconomics

In Chapters 6 and 7, I discussed some macroeconomic implications of the theory of prices of production: it will be recalled that such central concepts in traditional theory as the aggregate production function and the demand functions for labour and capital (or investment) were called into question. Given that neo-classical macroeconomic theory is unsatisfactory, with what can it be replaced? In this section, I consider a proposed solution.

The starting point for an alternative scheme is the recognition that traditional theory cannot in general determine the long-run equilibrium of the economy: this has been discussed above in the context of price determination. Now, any successful critique of the neo-classical theory of price determination must also be a critique of the neo-classical theory of output, simply because the theory treats prices and quantities as being simultaneously determined. If neo-classical theory is to be rejected, is there an alternative scheme? The contributors to Eatwell and Milgate (1983) suggest an integration of the classical theory of value, exemplified in modern guise by Sraffa's PCMC, with the Keynesian theory of output, suitably modified.

In classical theory, the level and composition of output is taken as given in the determination of prices: questions of value and distribution are analysed separately from those of output. This is not to deny the existence of interrelations between prices and quantities. Rather, separable explanations are sought for price and quantity determination prior to consideration of the interrelations between them. Given this, the development of an alternative to the neo-classical approach requires a theory of output distinct from the theory of value. In Keynes's *General Theory*, the level of output is determined by the level of expenditure, equality being maintained between savings and investment by variations in the level of income: the multiplier process replaces the neo-classical adjustment machanism which is supposed to operate through relative price (i.e. interest rate) variations. The Keynesian theory in terms of the principle of effective demand appears to fit the classical bill because it does not rely on prices and quantities being interdependent; indeed, it is difficult to see how it can coexist with a theory characterised by such joint determination. However, there are at least two questions which must be addressed before the integration of classical and Keynesian theories can be seriously entertained.

Keynes's theory of output determination did not rely solely on the principle of effective demand. His investment function, called the marginal efficiency of capital, is the same as the one employed in traditional theory. By employing such a concept in his theoretical structure, Keynes permitted a connection between income distribution (the rate of interest or profit) and the level of output through the level of investment: hence, changes in the rate of interest could induce changes in the level of investment and then output. Keynes's purpose in the *General Theory* was to demonstrate the possibility of an equilibrium with unemployment of labour. By allowing a functional relation between output and the rate of interest, he opened the way for appropriate changes in the latter to effect a full-employment equilibrium. Having introduced this possibility, Keynes then had to formulate a theory of the rate of interest to prevent this neo-classical adjustment mechanism operating: this explains the presence of the liquidity preference theory. There is an alternative to the approach adopted by Keynes. It is simply to recognise, on the basis of the theory of prices of production, that the marginal efficiency of capital construct cannot be justified and must therefore be jettisoned. The principle of effective demand remains, there now being no potential source of conflict in the determination of output.

Keynes's *General Theory* is usually interpreted as referring to the short run. Is it then possible to effect the desired integration with the classical theory of value, which is essentially long run in nature? In Keynes's short run, 'We take as given the existing skill and quantity of available labour, the existing quality and quantity of available equipment, the existing technique' (p. 245), and so on. Perhaps the usual interpretation of Keynes was reinforced by his assumption (except in chapter 19) of a fixed wage. However, there are grounds for arguing that Keynes's short run is not identical to Marshall's where, for example, firms will not have adjusted capacity and output to satisfy demand. 'This does not mean that we assume these factors to be constant; but merely that, in this place and context, we are not considering or taking into account the effects and consequences of changes in them' (ibid.). Keynes abstracted from population growth, technical change and capital accumulation so that he could concentrate on the permanent forces affecting output and employment. In this respect, his method closely resembles that employed throughout this book. That Keynes was concerned with the long run is clear from chapter 5 of the *General Theory*. 'Although expectation may change so frequently that the actual level of employment has never had time to reach the long-period employment corresponding to the existing state of expectation, nevertheless every state of expectation has its definite corresponding level of long-period employment' (p. 49). Keynes's discussion of the process of transition to a long-period position is exactly analogous to the process of gravitation in classical value theory.

This suggested integration of Keynes and Sraffa to provide a long-period theory of employment is the most contentious of the three areas of research reported here. This may be due to the fact that a novel interpretation is being placed on Keynes's *General Theory*. Concepts still need to be refined, such as the notion of effective demand in the long run. Nevertheless, the purpose of this section, as of the previous two, has been to report on areas of application of Sraffa's approach, not to present a settled body of theory.

12.8 A Lacuna

The rationale for the analysis of prices of production is that provided by the Classical economists – natural prices, characterised by a uniform rate of profit, are centres of gravitation. Yet, apart from brief discussions in sections 1.2 and 12.3, the question of convergence has not been treated in this book. In this final section, I can only give explicit recognition to this lacuna. There are at least two reasons for this state of affairs. The first is that convergence theory is generically difficult. Whether reference is made to neo-classical or neo-Ricardian theory, an accepted account of the stability of equilibrium is lacking (though this is not to say that the same concepts and methods of analysis are employed in neo-classical as in neo-Ricardian theory). The second, though related to the first, is at a more pragmatic level. Such accounts of gravitation as have appeared in the literature require a level of mathematical ability of the reader which is greater than I have assumed in this book. This explains the absence of any formal analysis of gravitation here.

Commentary

Sraffa's 1926 and 1930 articles, together with the Introduction to Ricardo's *Principles* are relevant to sections 12.2 and 12.3, as also is the 1925 article for those who read Italian. There are numerous references in sections 12.4–12.7 that the reader may wish to consult first as part of his own research. To appreciate the points made in section 12.5, it will be necessary to consult the Appendix to Garegnani (1970). Section 12.6 is based on Steedman (1983). Two additional references are worth making. First, with regard to the measurement of technical change, there are papers by Peterson (1979, 1980) which are critical of the conventional approach. Second, there are articles by Nikaido (1983) and Steedman (1984b) discussing aspects of gravitation.

Exercises

1. Derive equation (12.12).
2. Derive equation (12.29) under the assumption of uniform organic composition of capital.
3. Derive equation (12.29) if the Standard Commodity is taken as numeraire. (Use exercise 12 of Chapter 5.)

Notes to Chapter 12

1. Sraffa (1926), p. 535.
2. Ibid.
3. Ibid., p. 536.
4. In this context, note the view expressed by Sraffa in this passage:

> It is well known that such an assumption (i.e. that the two conditions above are satisfied) would not be illegitimate merely because the independence may not be absolutely perfect, as, in fact, it never can be; and a slight degree of interdependence may be overlooked without disadvantage if it applies to quantities of the second order of smalls, as would be the case if the effect (for example of an increase of cost) of a variation in the industry which we propose to isolate were to react partially on the price of the products of other industries, and this latter effect were to influence the demand for the product of the first industry. But, of course, it becomes a very different matter, and the assumption becomes illegitimate, when a variation in the quantity produced by the industry under consideration sets up a force which acts directly, not merely upon its own costs, but also upon the costs of other industries; in such a case, the conditions of the "particular equilibrium" which it was intended to isolate are upset, and it is no

> longer possible, without contradiction, to neglect collateral effects. (ibid., p. 538)

5. Ibid., p. 539.
6. Ibid., p. 540.
7. Ibid.
8. Ibid., pp. 540–1. Also see Sraffa's footnote (4).
9. Sraffa (1960), p. vi.
10. Ibid., p. v.
11. Ibid., p. vi.
12. Ibid., p. 8.
13. See section 7, in particular the third paragraph, where Sraffa explains his reluctance to use the term cost of production on the grounds that it has been linked with the supposition that it stands for a quantity that can be measured independently of the determination of commodity prices.
14. Sraffa (1926), p. 538.
15. Ibid., p. 540.
16. Ibid.
17. See Robinson (1933) and Chamberlain (1933).
18. Harcourt (1972) p. 15.
19. Sraffa (1930), p. 93.
20. Ricardo (1951), p. 91.
21. Marx (1981), p. 281.
22. For more on the Classical theory of ouput, see Garegnani (1970, 1978, 1979, 1984) and Eatwell (1977).
23. Priority can be claimed by Dmitriev (1974).
24. Sraffa (1960), p. v.
25. An illustration of this is provided by Smith's notion of 'effectual demand':

    > The market price of a particular commodity is regulated by the proportion between the quantity which is actually brought to market, and the demand of those who are willing to pay the natural price of the commodity . . . Such people may be called the effectual demanders and their demand the effectual demand. (Smith, 1970, pp. 158–9)

26. The law which, in Classical theory, states that competition enforces gravitation to natural prices, determined by the conditions of production and the distribution of income.
27. Contrast Ricardo's view that 'nothing can affect profits but a rise in wages' (Ricardo, 1951, p. 118) with Malthus's opinion that 'profits (depend) on the demand compared with the supply of capital' (Ricardo, 1952a, p. 77). For Ricardo's position on the influence of supply and demand on prices, see chapter XXX of *The Principles*.
28. Sraffa (1962), p. 478.
29. Ibid., pp. 478–9.

30. Sraffa (1960), section 48, p. 38.
31. These debates originated in the literature with Joan Robinson's 1953 article on the production function and the theory of capital: Gallaway and Shukla (1974) were still trying to prove no-reswitching theorems twenty years later. It is worth remarking that Joan Robinson's main criticism resembled Sraffa's in being methodological rather than relying on the implications of the three phenomena. To her, the neo-classical concept of capital was at fault. Initially, she recognised that the three phenomena could have some role to play in demonstrating this point. However, she later came to regard reswitching (and the other two) as unimportant (see Robinson, 1975).
32. See the various references to Harcourt, who discusses the macroeconomic issues in the capital theory debates at greater length.
33. Called Walrasian theory, though Walras exhibited the same concerns as his fellow neo-classical economists of the late nineteenth century.
34. Recall that, in the Classical scheme, the short run was not the subject of formal analysis.
35. Some authors, such as Bliss (1975), regard this as an advantage of the general equilibrium approach.
36. Garegnani (1976a) has argued forcefully that the neo-classical economists emphasised the short-run equilibrium precisely because they were unable to determine the uniform rate of profit.
37. To take the simplest example, suppose that there is some change in the parameters of the model, be it preferences, production possibilities, the size of ownership of initial endowments.
38. E.g. no transport costs.
39. In other words, all *w–r* curves has the same curvature.
40. Within the confines of a two-country, two-commodity, two-factor world.
41. In Garegnani's model, discussed briefly in the Appendix to Chapter 6, each technique has a specific capital good. The number of capital goods is thus equal to the number of techniques, an equality which does not obtain for the usual multitechnique model employed in this book, where capital goods are common to all techniques. Metcalfe and Steedman base their argument on numerical examples in the Appendix to Garegnani (1970), a feature of which is that there is a continuum of techniques.
42. Evidently, there are two questions to be addressed here. First, can a proper theoretical framework be provided for input and output measurements? If so, the inevitable approximations in calculating input and output growth will be due to inaccuracies in the data. Second, if a proper theoretical framework cannot be provided, what will guide statisticians in their data collection and evaluation of technical change?
43. Solow applied growth accounting in a macroeconomic context, in particular using an aggregate production function. As this latter concept was the subject of discussion in Chapter 7, little needs to be added here. It is, perhaps, of interest to note that Samuelson's article

on the surrogate production function was an attempt to provide Solow with a somewhat belated theoretical framework for his empirical studies.

> What I propose to do here is to show that a new concept, the 'surrogate production function', can provide *some* justification for the validity of the simple J. B. Clark parables which pretend there is a simple thing called 'capital' that can be put into a single production function and along with labour will produce total output.' (Samuelson, 1961–2, p. 193)

44. The assumption of a constant rate of profit or real wage or real wage–rate of profit ratio, as the case may be, is not intended to be a realistic description of the outcome of the technical change. It is made so that a measure can be defined.
45. Robinson (1965, p. 310).

References

Bharadwaj, K. (1970) 'On the Maximum Number of Switches Between Two Production Systems', *Schweizerische Zeitschrift für Volkswirtschafts und Statistik*, vol. 106, pp. 409–29.

Bidard, C. (ed.) (1984) *La Production Jointe* (Paris: Economica).

Bidard, C. (1986a) 'The Maximum Rate of Profits in Joint Production', *Metroeconomica*, vol. 38, pp. 53–66.

Bidard, C. (1986b) 'Is von Neumann Square?', *Zeitschrift für Nationalökonomie*, vol. 46, pp. 407–19.

Bidard, C. (1986c) 'A Sraffian Approach to the Choice of Techniques', unpublished paper.

Bidard, C. and Woods, J. E. (1987) 'Taxes, Lands and Non-basics in Joint Production', forthcoming in *Oxford Economic Papers*.

Bliss, C. J. (1975) *Capital Theory and the Distribution of Income* (Oxford: North-Holland Publishing Co.).

Broome, J. (1977) 'Sraffa's Standard Commodity', *Australian Economic Papers*, vol. 17, pp. 233–6.

Broome, J. (1983) *The Microeconomics of Capitalism* (London: Academic Press).

Bruno, M., Burmeister, E. and Sheshinksi, E. (1966) 'The Nature and Implications of the Switching of Techniques', *Quarterly Journal of Economics*, vol. 80, pp. 526–53.

Burmeister, E. (1968) 'On a Theorem of Sraffa', *Economica*, vol. 35, pp. 83–7.

Burmeister, E. (1980) *Capital Theory and Dynamics*, Cambridge: Cambridge University Press).

Burmeister, E. (1984) 'Sraffa, Labour Theories of Value and the Economics of Real Wage Determination', *Journal of Political Economy*, vol. 92, pp. 508–26.

Chamberlin, E. H. (1933) *The Theory of Monopolistic Competition*, (Cambridge, Mass.: Harvard University Press).

Champernowne, D. G. (1945–6) 'A Note of J. v. Neumann's Article on "A Model of General Economic Equilibrium"', *Review of Economic Studies*, vol. 13, pp. 10–18.

Champernowne, D. G. (1953–4) 'The Production Function and the Theory of Capital: A Comment', *Review of Economic Studies*, vol. 21, pp. 112–35.

D'Agata, A. (1983) 'The Existence and Unicity of Cost-minimising Systems in Intensive Rent Theory', *Metroeconomica*, vol. 35, pp. 147–58.
Debreu, G. (1959) *The Theory of Value* (New Haven, Conn.: Yale University Press).
Dmitriev, V. K. (1974) in *Economic Essays on Value, Competition and Utility* ed. D. M. Nuti (Cambridge: Cambridge University Press).
Eatwell, J. (1975) 'Mr Sraffa's Standard Commodity and the Rate of Exploitation', *Quarterly Journal of Economics*, vol. 89, pp. 543–55.
Eatwell, J. (1977) 'The Irrelevance of Returns to Scale in Sraffa's Analysis', *Journal of Economic Literature*, vol. 15, pp. 61–8.
Eatwell, J. (1987) 'Sraffa', in J. Eatwell, M. Milgate and P. Newman (eds), *The New Palgrave*, vol. 4, pp. 445–52.
Eatwell, J. and Milgate, M. (eds) (1983) *Keynes's Economics and the Theory of Value and Distribution* (London: Duckworth).
Eatwell, J., Milgate, M. and Newman, P. (eds) *The New Palgrave*, 4 vols (London: Macmillan).
Filippini, C. and Filippini, L. (1982) 'Two Theorems of Joint Production', *Economic Journal*, vol. 92, pp. 386–90.
Flaschel, P. (1984) 'The Standard Commodity and the Theory of Income Distribution – A Critical Note', *Australian Economic Papers*, vol. 24, pp. 123–9.
Fujimoto, T. (1983) 'Inventions and Technical Change: A Curiosum', *Manchester School*, vol. 51, pp. 16–20.
Gallaway, L. and Shukla, V. (1974) 'The Neo-classical Production Function', *American Economic Review*, vol. 64, pp. 348–58.
Garegnani, P. (1966) 'Switching of Techniques', *Quarterly Journal of Economics*, vol. 80, pp. 554–67.
Garegnani, P. (1970) 'Heterogeneous Capital, the Production Function and the Theory of Distribution', *Review of Economic Studies*, vol. 37, pp. 407–36.
Garegnani, P. (1976a) 'The Neoclassical Production Function: Comment', *American Economic Review*, vol. 66, pp. 424–7.
Garegnani, P. (1976b) 'On a Change in the Notion of Equilibrium in Recent Work on Value and Distribution', in M. Brown, K. Sato and P. Zarembka (eds), *Essays in Modern Capital Theory* (Oxford: North-Holland Publishing Co.), pp. 25–45.
Garegnani, P. (1978) 'Notes on Consumption, Investment and Effective Demand, I', *Cambridge Journal of Economics*, vol. 2, pp. 335–53. (Reprinted in Eatwell and Milgate, 1983.)
Garegnani, P. (1979) 'Notes on Consumption, Investment and Effective Demand II', *Cambridge Journal of Economics*, vol. 3, pp. 63–82. (Reprinted in Eatwell and Milgate, 1983).
Garegnani, P. (1984) 'Value and Distribution in the Classical Economists and Marx', *Oxford Economic Papers*, vol. 36, pp. 291–325.
Garegnani, P. (1987) 'The Surplus Approach to Value and Distribution', in J. Eatwell, M. Milgate and P. Newman (eds) *The New Palgrave*, vol. 4, pp. 560–74.

Gram, H. (1985) 'Duality and Positive Profits', *Contributions to Political Economy*, vol. 4, pp. 61–77.
Hahn, F. H. (1982) 'The Neo-Ricardians', *Cambridge Journal of Economics*, vol. 6, pp. 353–74.
Harcourt, G. C. (1969) 'Some Cambridge Controversies in the Theory of Capital', *Journal of Economic Literature*, vol. 7, pp. 369–405.
Harcourt, G. C. (1972) *Some Cambridge Controversies in the Theory of Capital* (Cambridge: Cambridge University Press).
Harcourt, G. C. (1975) 'The Cambridge Controversies: The Afterglow', in M. Parkin and A. R. Nobay (eds) *Contemporary Issues in Economics* (London: Longman).
Harcourt, G. C. (1976) 'The Cambridge Controversies: Old Ways and New Horizons – or Dead End', *Oxford Economic Papers*, vol. 28, pp. 25–65.
Harcourt, G. C. (1983) *The Social Science Imperialists* (London: Routledge, Kegal & Paul).
Harcourt, G. C. and Massaro, V. (1964) 'A Note on Mr Sraffa's Subsystems', *Economic Journal*, vol. 74, pp. 712–22.
Harrod, R. F. (1961) Review of PCMC, *Economic Journal*, vol. 71, pp. 783–7.
Hicks, J. R. (1946) *Value and Capital* (Oxford: Oxford University Press).
Jevons, W. S. (1970) *The Theory of Political Economy* (London: Penguin Books).
Kaldor, N. (1984) 'Piero Sraffa', *Cambridge Journal of Economics*, vol. 8, pp. 2–5.
Kaldor, N. (1985) 'Piero Sraffa', *Proceedings of the British Academy*, vol. 71, pp. 615–40.
Keynes, J. M. (1936) *The General Theory of Employment, Interest and Money* (London: Macmillan).
Kurz, H. (1976) 'Rent Theory in a Multisectoral Model' *Oxford Economic Papers*, vol. 37, pp. 18–37.
Kurz, H. (1979) 'Sraffa after Marx', *Australian Economic Papers*, vol. 19, pp. 52–70.
Kurz, H. and Salvadori, N. (1987) 'Burmeister on Sraffa and the Labour Theory of Value: A Comment', *Journal of Political Economy*, vol. 95, pp. 870–81.
Levhari, D. (1965) 'A Nonsubstitution Theorem and the Switching of Techniques', *Quarterly Journal of Economics*, vol. 79, pp. 98–105.
Levine, A. (1974) 'This Age of Leontief . . . and Who? An Interpretation', *Journal of Economic Literature*, vol. 12, pp. 872–81.
Manara, C. F. (1980) 'Sraffa's Model for the Joint Production of Commodities by Means of Commodities', in L. L. Pasinetti (ed.) (1980) pp. 3–18.
Marshall, A. (1920) *The Principles of Economics* (London: Macmillan).
Marx, K. (1981) *Capital*, vol. 3 (London: Penguin Books).
Meek, R. L. (1961) 'Mr Sraffa's Rehabilitation of Classical Economics', *Scottish Journal of Political Economy*, vol. 8, pp. 119–36.

Metcalfe, J. S. and Steedman, I. (1972) 'Reswitching and Primary Input Use', *Economic Journal*, vol. 82, pp. 140–57.
Metcalfe, J. S. and Steedman, I. (1973) 'Heterogeneous Capital and the Heckscher–Ohlin–Samuelson Theory of Trade', in J. M. Parkin (ed.) *Essays in Modern Economics* (London: Longman) and also in Steedman (1979a).
Metzler, L. A. (1950) 'The Rate of Interest and the Marginal Product of Capital', *Journal of Political Economy*, vol. 53, pp. 284–306.
Milgate, M. (1979) 'On the Origin of the Notion of Intertemporal Equilibrium', *Economica*, vol. 46, pp. 1–10.
Morishima, M. (1966) 'Refutation of the Nonswitching Theorem', *Quarterly Journal of Economics*, vol. 80, pp. 520–5.
Neumann, J. von (1945–6) 'A Model of General Economic Equilibrium', *Review of Economic Studies*, vol. 13, pp. 1–9.
Newman, P. (1962) 'Production of Commodities by Means of Commodities', *Schweizerische Zeitschrift für Volkswirtschaft und Statistik*, vol. 98, pp. 58–75.
New Palgrave, The (1987) *see under* J. Eatwell, M. Milgate and P. Newman (eds).
Nikaido, H. (1983) 'Marx on Competition', *Zeitschrift für Nationalökonomie*, vol. 43, pp. 337–62.
Pasinetti, L. L. (1966) 'Changes in the Rate of Profit and Switches of Technique', *Quarterly Journal of Economics*, vol. 80, pp. 503–17.
Pasinetti, L. L. (1969) 'Switches of Technique and the "Rate of Return" in Capital Theory', *Economic Journal*, vol. 79, pp. 508–31.
Pasinetti, L. L. (1973) 'The Notion of Vertical Integration in Economic Analysis', *Metroeconomica*, vol. 25, pp. 1–29.
Pasinetti, L. L. (1977a) *Lectures on the Theory of Production* (London: Macmillan).
Pasinetti, L. L. (1977b) 'On "Nonsubstitution" in Production Models', *Cambridge Journal of Economics*, vol. 1, pp. 389–94.
Pasinetti, L. L. (1979) 'Piero Sraffa' in D. Sills (ed.) *International Encyclopedia of the Social Sciences*, vol. 18: Biographical Supplement (New York: Free Press).
Pasinetti, L. L. (1980) (ed.) *Essays on the Theory of Joint Production* (London: Macmillan).
Peterson, W. (1979) 'Total Factor Productivity in the UK: A Disaggregated Analysis', in K. Patterson and K. Schott (eds) *The Measurement of Capital* (London: Macmillan).
Peterson, W. (1980) 'Capital Goods and Technical Change: Some Theoretical Problems', in T. Puu and S. Wibe (eds) *The Economics of Technical Progress* (London: Macmillan).
Quadrio-Curzio, A. (1980) 'Rent, Income Distribution and Orders of Efficiency and Rentability', in L. L. Pasinetti (ed.) (1980) pp. 218–40.
Quarterly Journal of Economics (1966) Symposium: 'Paradoxes in Capital Theory', vol. 80.
Reder, M. W. (1961) Review of PCMC, *American Economic Review*, vol. 51, pp. 688–95.

Ricardo, D., *The Works and Correspondence*, edited by P. Sraffa (Cambridge: Cambridge University Press)
(1951) *Principles of Political Economy and Taxation* (vol. 1).
(1952a) *Notes on Malthus* (vol. 2).
(1952b) *Pamphlets and Papers, 1815–1823* (vol. 4).

Robinson, J. (1933) *The Economics of Imperfect Competition* (London: Macmillan).

Robinson, J. (1953–4) 'The Production Function and the Theory of Capital', *Review of Economic Studies*, vol. 21, pp. 81–106.

Robinson, J. (1965) *The Accumulation of Capital* (London: Macmillan).

Robinson, J. (1975) 'The Unimportance of Reswitching', *Quarterly Journal of Economics*, vol. 89, pp. 32–9.

Robinson, J. and Naqvi, K. (1967) 'The Badly Behaved Production Function', *Quarterly Journal of Economics*, vol. 81, pp. 579–91.

Roncaglia, A. (1983) 'Piero Sraffa and the Reconstruction of Political Economy', *Banca Nazionale del Lavoro Quarterly Review*, vol. 147, pp. 337–50.

Salanti, M. (1984) 'Prices of Production, Market Prices and the Analysis of Choice of Techniques', *Metroeconomica*, vol. 37, pp. 97–117.

Salvadori, N. (1982) 'Existence of Cost-minimising Systems within the Sraffa Framework', *Zeitschrift für Nationalökonomie*, vol. 42, pp. 281–98.

Salvadori, N. (1985) 'Switching in Methods of Production and Joint Production', *Manchester School*, vol. 53, pp. 156–78.

Salvadori, N. (1986) 'Land and Choice of Techniques within the Sraffa Framework', *Australian Economic Papers*, vol. 26, pp. 94–105.

Salvadori, N. and Steedman, I. (1985) 'Cost Functions and Produced Means of Production: Duality and Capital Theory', *Contributions to Political Economy*, vol. 4, pp. 79–90.

Salvadori, N. and Steedman, I. (1987) 'No Reswitching? No Switching', unpublished paper.

Sato, K. (1976) 'The Neoclassical Production Function: Comment', *American Economic Review*, vol. 66, pp. 428–36.

Samuelson, P. A. (1961–2) 'Parable and Realism in Capital Theory: The "Surrogate Production Function"', *Review of Economic Studies*, vol. 29, pp. 193–206.

Samuelson, P. A. (1966) 'A Summing Up', *Quarterly Journal of Economics*, vol. 80, pp. 568–83.

Schefold, B. (1980) 'Von Neumann and Sraffa: Mathematical Equivalence and Conceptual Difference', *Economic Journal* vol. 90, pp. 140–56.

Schwartz, J. T. (1961) *Lectures on the Mathematical Method in Economics* (New York: Gordon & Breach).

Smith, A. (1970) *The Wealth of Nations*, edited by A. Skinner (London: Penguin Books).

Solow, R. M. (1955–6) 'The Production Function and the Theory of Capital', *Review of Economic Studies*, vol. 23, pp. 101–8.

Solow, R. M. (1957) 'Technical Change and the Aggregate Production

Function', *Review of Economics and Statistics*, vol. 39, pp. 312–20.
Sraffa, P. (1925) 'Sulla Relazione fra Costo e Quantita Prodotta', *Annali di Economia*, vol. II, pp. 277–328.
Sraffa, P. (1926) 'The Laws of Returns Under Competitive Conditions', *Economic Journal*, vol. 36, pp. 535–50.
Sraffa, P. (1930) 'Criticism' and 'Rejoinder', *Economic Journal*, vol. 40, pp. 89–93.
Sraffa, P. (1932) 'Dr Hayek on Money and Capital', *Economic Journal*, vol. 42, pp. 42–53, and 'Rejoinder', pp. 249–51.
Sraffa, P. (1960) *Production of Commodities by Means of Commodities* (Cambridge: Cambridge University Press).
Steedman, I. (1975) 'Positive Profits With Negative Surplus Value', *Economic Journal*, vol. 85, pp. 114–23.
Steedman, I. (1976) 'Positive Profits With Negative Surplus Value: A Reply to Wolfstetter', *Economic Journal*, vol. 86, pp. 873–6.
Steedman, I. (1977) *Marx After Sraffa* (London: New Left Books).
Steedman, I. (ed.) (1979a) *Fundamental Issues in Trade Theory* (London: Macmillan).
Steedman, I. (1979b) 'Fixed Capital and the Surrogate Production Function', in K. Patterson and K. Schott (eds) *The Measurement of Capital* (London: Macmillan).
Steedman, I. (1980) 'Basics, Non-basics and Joint Production', in L. L. Pasinetti (ed.) (1980).
Steedman, I. (1982) 'Joint Production and the Wage–Rent Frontier', *Economic Journal*, vol. 92, pp. 377–85.
Steedman, I. (1983) 'On the Measurement and Aggregation of Productivity Increase', *Metroeconomica*, vol. 35, pp. 223–33.
Steedman, I. (1984a) 'The Empirical Importance of Joint Production', in C. Bidard (ed.) (1984).
Steedman, I. (1984b) 'Natural Prices, Differential Profit Rates and the Classical Competitive Process', *Manchester School*, vol. pp. 123–40.
Steedman, I. (1985a) 'On Input Demand Curves', *Cambridge Journal of Economics*, vol. 9, pp. 165–72.
Steedman, I. (1985b) 'On the Impossibility of Hicks-Neutral Technical Change', *Economic Journal*, vol. 95, pp. 746–58.
Swan, T. W. (1956) 'Economic Growth and Capital Accumulation', *Economic Record*, vol. 32, pp. 334–61.
Varian, H. (1984) *Microeconomic Analysis* (London: W. W. Norton).
Walras, L. (1954) *Elements of Pure Economics* (London: George Allen & Unwin).
Wicksell, K. (1934) *Lectures on Political Economy*, Volume 1 (translated by L. Robbins) (London: Routledge & Kegan Paul).
Woods, J. E. (1979) 'Some More Notes on the Surrogate Production Function', *Metroeconomica*, vol. 31, pp. 211–23.
Woods, J. E. (1980) 'On a Recurring Condition in Capital Theory', *Zeitschrift für Nationalökonomie*, vol. 40, pp. 207–16.
Woods, J. E. (1984a) 'Notes on Sraffa's Fixed Capital Model', *Journal of the Australian Mathematical Society, Series B, Applied Mathematics*, vol. 26, pp. 200–32.

Woods, J. E. (1984b) 'Technical Change, the Rate of Profit and Joint Production', *Economics Letters*, vol 15, pp. 153–6.
Woods, J. E. (1985) 'Exercises in Relative Price Invariance', *Giornale degli Economisti e Annali di Economia*, vol. 44, pp. 135–52.
Woods, J. E. (1987) 'A Note on Rent', *Oxford Economic Papers*, vol. 39, pp. 388–411.
Woods, J. E. (1988) 'On Switching of Techniques in Two-sector Models', *Scottish Journal of Political Economy*, vol. 35, pp. 84–91.
Zarembka, P. (1975) 'Capital Heterogeneity, Aggregation and the Two-sector Model', *Quarterly Journal of Economics*, vol. 89, pp. 103–14.

Author Index

Subject Index

www.ingramcontent.com/pod-product-compliance
Ingram Content Group UK Ltd.
Pitfield, Milton Keynes, MK11 3LW, UK
UKHW020154290926
15471UKWH00005B/873

9 780333 436295